C000256231

SKINS FOR BUILDINGS
The Architect's Materials Sample Book

Copyright © 2004 BIS Publishers, Amsterdam

All rights reserved. No part of this publication may be reproduced or
transmitted in any form or by any means, electronic or mechanical, including
photocopy, recording or any information storage and retrieval system,
without permission in writing from the copyright owner(s).

We have tried to exercise all copyrights within the legal requirements.
Nevertheless, anyone who thinks they can claim certain rights can contact us.

ISBN 90 6369 042 8

SKINS

FOR BUILDINGS
The Architect's Materials Sample Book

Ine ter Borch

David Keuning

Caroline Kruit

Ed Melet

Dr. Kees Peterse

Piet Vollaard

Tom de Vries

Els Zijlstra

BISPUBLISHERS

Contents

Contents

Future Materials

Preface

...the subject of Material is clearly the foundation of architecture, and perhaps one would not go very far wrong if one defined architecture as the art of building suitably with suitable material.

William Morris

Why materials matter

Designing is deciding. Amongst the many decisions taken during the design process, the choice of materials to be used is as crucial as any. It is the point at which an abstract idea takes on concrete form. Naturally, this does not occur in one defining moment, as the design process is not a strictly linear succession of logical decisions. The choice of materials is regularly revised, adjusted or discarded. Nevertheless, every designer is conscious of the importance and inevitability of the moment when an idea is transformed into a material object. However long and for whatever reason it may be delayed, sooner or later a decision has to be made. If the design is to become part of the physical world there is simply no escaping this imperative.

Why this book matters

In view of the importance of the designer's choice of materials, one could be forgiven for assuming that every designer is constantly concerned with remaining abreast of developments in building materials (their characteristics, manner of production, or any other aspects which could affect their use) in order always to be able to make informed choices. However, due to the prevailing generalist tendency – knowing something about everything rather than a great deal about one thing – many designers' knowledge of materials is not always as thorough as it might be. This, in turn, is liable to result in a less-than-optimal choice of materials. And for designers wishing to fill in some of the gaps in their knowledge, a large quantity of manufacturers' and suppliers' catalogues awaits, as well as a dearth of literature from their own field providing a thorough grounding in the topic. This book is an attempt to remedy this situation. In a sense,

it is a substitute for the ideal solution, which would be an immense set of shelves containing specimens and books on all the building materials about which one could possibly want to know. *Skins for Buildings* is a sample book, whose aim is to run the entire gamut of materials, presenting them as physically and objectively as possible, discussing them in a uniform and consistent manner, with attention being paid to the production process, general technical characteristics and peculiarities, and architectural relevance.

Why materials have to make sense

The choice of materials is to a large extent pre-determined by a set of requirements, each important in its own right. These include sustainability, strength, hardness, flammability, waterproofness, heat conductivity and sound absorption. In addition, materials play a huge role in how a building is experienced. Indeed, a material's surface, its skin, is what guides our senses in our perception of walls, floors and roofs and, ultimately, of spaces. Seeing, smelling and 'hearing' these elements not only enables us to register them individually, but also unlocks a virtually limitless range of potential meanings and references which obviously transcend the domain of the purely technical.

Why this book makes sense

Material knowledge is also a prerequisite when it comes to exploiting a material's sensual qualities to the full. However, this knowledge is even more lacking amongst designers than that pertaining to the more technical aspects. For this reason, the present work devotes more attention than is customary to the sensual qualities of materials. Indeed, as far as we know it is the first book of its kind to devote attention not only to the sense of sight but also to those of touch, smell, hearing and taste, expressed in a sensory table. The visual sense is approached in two ways: through photographs of the materials in abstract form at a scale of approx. 1:1, and through photographs of the materials in the context of the structures referenced in the text.

Piet Vollaard   *Els Zijlstra*
Archined   *Materia*

How to use this book

The two hundred building materials covered in the book are arranged in eight chapters, which largely follow the traditional categories for natural materials, beginning with wood and natural stone, moving on to fired and unfired man-made stone, glass and metal, and concluding with plastics. For each family of materials, a large number of 'pure' types are included. Each material family begins with a general introduction in which production methods and general characteristics are discussed. In turn, each material and treatment (and/or additive) has its own short introduction. Each material is presented by means of a full-page photo, accompanied by a short text detailing the material's specific properties and features, one or two photos illustrating its architectural application, and a sensory table.

The sensory table contains information not only about the colour, glossiness, translucency, tactility, texture and hardness of the material in question, but also about less familiar properties such as temperature, odour and acoustic opacity. Although many of these categories might appear to be of a completely subjective nature, most of the values are objectively determined. Each characteristic, with the exception of colour, is subdivided into three values. Only where quantification is not possible, is the given value based on subjective perception.

- **Glossiness** the degree to which a material's surface reflects light.
- **Translucency** degree of diffuse transmission.
- **Texture** the grain and depth of the surface structure as perceived by the human eye and/or skin
- **Firmness** not hardness as such, but the material's surface resilience measured in Shore units.
- **Temperature** tactile temperature, measured in terms of the heat transmission coefficient, such that:
  warm   = 0–0.8 W/m.K
  medium = 0.8–5 W/m.K
  cold   = 5–300 W/m.K
- **Odour** degree to which a material gives off an odour.
- **Acoustic opacity** degree of sound absorption, measured in terms of a material's absorption coefficient.

The aim of presenting as complete a spectrum as possible of available materials served as a guiding principle in determining which materials to include. No material was excluded because it was considered too 'banal' or 'everyday', as a material's nobility ultimately lies in how it is used. An additional criterion for selection was a material's ability to be used as a 'skin': as a recognizable and usable surface for a façade, interior wall or floor. Finally, only those materials were included which are actually available at the present time, and whose use is not restricted by financial or legal considerations. It should be noted, though, that all these criteria were applied with a healthy dose of common sense, with the notion, 'every rule is made to be broken' being invoked every now and then. The work concludes with a brief survey of the future potential of materials that are either not yet available or only to be had at great monetary or technological expense.

This book is primarily intended for architectural use in the Western European context. In some cases, though, the form and availability of a given material are determined by local conditions. Thus, each region has its own varieties of brick and stone, while what is a standard treatment in some countries is sometimes virtually unknown in others. Despite our best efforts to maintain an international orientation, the book's country of origin – the Netherlands – will at times be evident in our choice of materials, their descriptions or the products referenced.

Each chapter was written by an author specialized in that particular field. Within the pre-determined format, each author had a degree of freedom regarding the treatment and documentation of his/her topic. Thus, whilst the differences between the chapters are in part determined by their topics, they also reflect the individual approaches of the different authors. In the wood chapter, for example, not all wood varieties are suitable for large façade surfaces and some are no longer used in external applications because of limited durability. In addition, the number of available wood and stone varieties is so vast as to render completeness impossible. In such cases, the level of availability and application were taken into account when selecting varieties for inclusion.

The greatest degree of local variation is probably to be found in connection with fired man-made stone, as names, dimensions, building regulations and production methods can vary widely, sometimes even between two adjacent areas. Nevertheless, in choosing materials for this group an effort was made to concentrate on the most widely used varieties.

One chapter that might be considered somewhat out of place in a survey of 'pure' materials, is that concerning unfired man-made stone, better known as concrete. However, it was felt that excluding such an ubiquitous material as concrete would have been even less appropriate since it would undermine the aim of relative completeness. It should also be noted in connection with concrete that it, too, is subject to local variations in use and production methods. With plastics, as with wood and stone, the huge number of available products resulted in preference being given to the most widely used and available materials.

In an effort to make the book more accessible to different nationalities, translations of the material names, additives and treatments have been included in German, French, Spanish, Italian and Dutch (in this order). Indexes for each of these languages will be found at the back of the book.

We would like to take this opportunity to thank all those who have contributed to the realization of *Skins for Buildings*: authors and editors, translators and photographers, the lithographer and the designers, and last, but not least, the printer. We would also like to thank all architects, photographers and suppliers who have so willingly and enthusiastically provided visual material and information for this book.

BIS Publishers
Amsterdam 2004

Wood

Holz | Bois | Madera | Legno | Hout

History

'Wood' is a collective name for an extremely versatile organic material derived from a large group of botanical species. The characteristics of wood, including its appearance, its workability, strength, durability and its resistance to all kinds of external influences, are determined by the type of wood, the effects of soil and climate and also of forest management, which is to say measures affecting growth, including trimming, thinning, fertilizing and harvesting methods. For humans, wood has always been an important aid in making survival possible, or at least more agreeable. You can use wood to build a fire to warm yourself and to prepare food, to fashion a weapon to defend yourself, to make a boat to move to a new location, or to build a house to live in, protected against the outside world.

Until fairly recently, wood was an almost inexhaustible natural resource for building materials that can be worked into usable dimensions with relatively simple means. A machete or hatchet may be sufficient to peel a trunk, cut it to the desired length and to divide it into round or angular sections. The long history of wood means that

Project British School, The Hague (1997)

Architect Dirk Jan Postel, Kraaijvanger . Urbis

Photographer Jeroen van Amelsvoort

highly advanced working methods and a wide range of application possibilities have been developed for its use, so that in all its forms, from trunk to fibre, it is employed by numerous industries as a basic material for widely diverse products. This diversity in the forms in which wood is found is also reflected in building construction, from the raw, unworked trunk, as in MVRDV architects' Holland Pavilion at Expo 2000 in Hanover, to the wood fibre in cardboard tubes used by Shigeru Ban in the Japanese pavilion at the same exhibition.

What is Wood?

Wood is a vegetable tissue built up of tiny cells with cross-sections of a few hundredths of a millimetre and a length that may extend to several millimetres. The cell walls are composed primarily of cellulose and hemicellulose, which demonstrate good tensile strength, and lignin, which is good at absorbing compressive forces. Lignin, which is also referred to as wood matter, is present in all 'woody' plants. In many kinds of wood, there is a visible difference between the light-coloured sapwood in the outer area of the tree stem and the darker heartwood in the centre of the stem. Sapwood is responsible for the transportation of water and nutrients. Depending on the age and type of tree, wood tissue gradually loses its transport function, starting at the centre of the stem. During this process, the cell structure changes, giving the tree its strength and also producing a natural durability in the heart of the tree. Trees with heartwood usually grow older than trees composed solely of sapwood.

Woods are divided into two major groups, coniferous and non-coniferous, or deciduous. Because these two groups are usually referred to as softwoods and hardwoods (despite the fact that some coniferous woods are harder than many types of deciduous wood), the distinction between softwoods and hardwoods will also be made in this chapter. There are literally thousands of species of trees, only a small proportion of which are classified and marketed as building material. Only a limited number of these have either natural or added properties that make them suitable for the exterior of buildings.

Softwoods

Softwoods are woods from coniferous or cone-bearing trees and are relatively simple in structure. The growth rings are built up of a light-coloured section formed in the spring and consequently called springwood or earlywood, that is composed of relatively thin-walled cells. In the darker portion of the growth ring, formed in the summer and called summerwood or latewood, the cell walls are thicker and contain less air, making them appear darker. These elongated cells, known as tracheids or fibres, occur only in coniferous woods. Rays are also present, running perpendicular to the growth rings. They are made up of ribbon-like cells and provide for the horizontal transport of fluids. Some coniferous woods also have longitudinal parenchyma cells for the storage and distribution of reserve nutrients. A number of coniferous woods also have so-called resin ducts, or canals, running in a lengthwise direction. These long and very fine conduits have no cell wall and are located between the parenchyma cells. Resin canals may sometimes also be found running horizontally between the rays. The softwoods most commonly found in building façades are Oregon pine, redwood and Western Red Cedar.

Hardwoods

Hardwoods derive from broad-leafed trees and are more complex in structure than softwoods. In hardwoods, the dual function of the softwood tracheids is split between smaller wood or zylem fibres, which serve as supporting tissue, and wood vessels, which transport fluids. Wood fibres have a thick wall and make up the bulk of the wood. The walls of vertically stacked wood cells are often missing, creating continuous canals, called vessels. In the growth rings of a number of hardwoods, the vessels in the earlywood are larger and those in the latewood smaller. This is called ring porosity and is particularly common in oak, ash, chestnut and robinia, giving flat-sawn wood (cut on the tangential surface of the trunk) a distinct flame figure. Ring porosity is rare in tropical woods. In some species, such as cherry, walnut, cedar and teak, the transition between earlywood and latewood is gradual. These are the semi-porous or diffuse-porous woods. In maple, beech, poplar and birch, there is only slight gradation in the size of the vessels across the growth rings. These are the non-porous woods. Chemical substances and deposits in the cell walls can affect the colour and other properties of the wood. For example, ebony owes its pitch-black colour to black substances in the wood fibres, while silica deposits in the rays of basralocus make it resistant to shipworm. Vessel-clogging parenchyma pouches in American white oak impede the flow of fluids, making it impossible to saturate the wood with preservatives. The presence of resins can make would difficult to glue.

Composites and Additives

Wood can be used in solid form, but can also be processed into sheet materials, in which veneers, shavings, chips or fibres are glued under pressure into flat sheets of relatively large dimensions. In plywood, several layers of veneer are stacked with the grain directions of alternate sheets at right angles, and glued together; the wood chosen for the outermost layer determines its final appearance. The quality of the veneer, the type of wood used, the binder, the thickness of the veneer and the number of layers, as well as any treatment ultimately applied to the surface, all help determine whether a given plywood is suitable for outdoor applications.

Depending on the composition and processing, sheet materials made of wood fibres, shavings or chips, in which wood particles are pressed together with additional substances to form flat sheets, can in certain circumstances be used in exterior applications. These wood-based composite materials exhibit little or no resemblance to wood. Finishing techniques such as milling and perforating can impart interesting surface structures to composite sheet material. Three-dimensional elements can be produced by extruding or mould pressing an emulsion of wood fibres mixed with additives. Another well-known composite is linoleum, in which ground cork (the bark of the cork oak) is mixed with linseed oil and chalk and hot-pressed into a thin sheet. Linoleum is used mainly as a floor covering.

Wood-like Materials

Along with wood, there are various other wood-like organic products that are used in construction. Familiar examples include cork, bamboo, cane, thatch and willow canes, but grass and coconut are also a possibility. These products can be applied in façades and roofs in their natural form, but they can also be processed, with or without the addition of other materials, into composites suitable for exterior applications, such as sheeting or panelling. Moreover, products such as paper or cardboard, produced from the fibres of wood or woody plants, can also be made suitable for exterior use by the application of a waterproof coating or film.

Wood in Architecture

The enormous variation in species and manifestations make wood one of the most frequently used materials in building construction.

Project Gewild Wonen building expo, Almere (2001)
Architect Min2 bouw-kunst
Photographer Min2 bouw-kunst

Not only its surface appearance, but also its structural and transmission properties offer architects great design freedom and expressive potential. The decision to use wood is often a decision in favour of craftsmanship, durability and environmentally aware building. Architecture in which wood plays a dominant role does not belong to one specific style. It ranges from traditional or trend-following architecture to avant-garde and ultra-modern, and every style in between. Wood does not submit to the limitations imposed by any single design style, and every known style has examples in which wood is an emphatic presence. The defining factors for the architecture are the choice of wood, how it is finished, the detailing and the degree to which the architectural volume is constructed of wood, possibly in combination with other materials. The function the wood serves also contributes to the expressiveness of the visual design. For example, visually definitive wooden elements may also have a structural, a decorative or a cladding function, and a combination of functions is not uncommon.

For the most part, in as far as it is used for building exteriors, wood serves a protective purpose, whereby protection against climatological conditions is paramount. A very frequent means by which wood is used in façades (or in sloping roofs) is in the form of horizontal, vertical and sometimes diagonally mounted wooden planks, either flat or profiled. Familiar mounting techniques include weatherboarding (clapboarding in Northern America), board and batten, tongue and groove and bevel and channel siding. Both roofs and façades can be clad with overlapping shingles. Flat sheets in which the external appearance of wood remains a visual presence, mostly processed laminate or plywood, make it possible to clad larger areas in one go. In addition to the attractiveness of the natural pattern or 'figure' in the wood, the arrangement of the sheet material is itself an important expressive tool.

The treatments to which wood products are subjected can bring about remarkable transformations, resulting in a complete metamorphosis in the appearance of the façade. The application of colour in the form of paint is of course the most common example, but cutting perforations, grooves or other shapes into the wood can also give wood products – and the façade in which they are used – a completely different and sometimes striking appearance. In addition to semi-finished products made from wood or wood-like materials, these organic materials can also be employed in a more or less untreated form that serves to emphasize their organic origins. Tree trunks, debarked or intact, as well as thatch, straw, bamboo and sedum coverings are contemporary examples that are not infrequently intended as a political statement of sorts.

In order to prevent moisture, bacteria or insect damage to wood surfaces, it is important that sufficient attention be paid to detailing. This applies regardless of how wood is used in the exterior, but is especially true for claddings that form a closed surface. Connections, whether between wooden elements or with adjacent materials, and any ventilation installations behind the wood constructions, must be of good quality in order to preserve the properties of the wood in question. Even for woods that require no protective treatment because their durability increases as they turn grey – Western Red Cedar is a familiar example – careful use and detailing is essential to prevent the surface from being marred by uneven greying or even algae and ultimately fungal growth.

Environment

The increasing popularity of wood during the last century meant that the speed with which wood was being harvested far outpaced the speed with which it grew back. Many forests were indiscriminately exploited on a large scale in order to harvest valuable species of

Project Retirement dwellings, Eelde (2000)
Architect Onix
Photographer SAPh, Rob de Jong

wood. At the same time, the increase in human population meant increased pressure to clear forests for agriculture. The combination of these factors led to severe deforestation, particularly in tropical and subtropical regions. A natural source of basic materials is consequently in danger of disappearing, but even more important is the negative effect that this would have on the global environment. Growing trees absorb carbon monoxide and produce oxygen in a cycle that is of fundamental importance for sustaining human and animal life. Mature forests, it should be noted, are CO_2/O_2 balanced, because the amount of oxygen consumed as wood decomposes as a result of fungus and fire, is equal to that generated or used in the growth of wood. An important advance in this context is the development of systems for sustainable forest management, coupled with a certification system for the continuous maintenance of forests on a worldwide level. This was one of the results of the establishment in 1993 of the Forest Stewardship Council (FSC). The aim of this international association, which includes owners of forested lands as well as timber companies, is to improve forestry management around the world. The norms established by the FSC for good, sustainable forest management apply to both tropical and non-tropical forests and relate to the environment, social conditions and economic factors. There are now over 60 different FSC forest systems in place in over 149 countries.

One of the most important principles of the FSC is that forest management should be directed at maintaining the ecological functions and integrity of the forested region, by safeguarding biodiversity, water and soil quality and unique and vulnerable ecosystems and landscapes. Since the system must also be economically viable, forests of relatively fast-growing trees are planted to supply the required amount of commercial timber. These plantations are intended to complement natural forests, not replace them. Their prime function is to reduce the pressure on natural forests, encouraging their recovery and protection. One way of giving fast-growing species the quality associated with tropical hardwoods, is to treat their wood with preservatives. This can be done either by coating the surface with a paint or varnish or by chemical impregnation in which an active, usually toxic substance penetrates deep into the wood. The most frequently used substances are creosote oil and preservative salts; other substances like bifluorides and borax are used on a much smaller scale.

Future

An alternative to chemical preservation is to effect a modification of a wood's properties (durability, strength) without resorting to environmentally hazardous substances. One such treatment entails heating in water under pressure, drying and heating in a dry condition, which produces wood with class 1 or class 2 durability, comparable to tropical hardwood. The rapid development of more eco-friendly methods of preservation means that wood species that were previously unsuited or only marginally suited to outdoor applications can now be considered. Furthermore, environmental awareness stimulates the recycling of wood and wood products for use in new products and applications. For example, the use of paper and cardboard in construction, notably in Japan, appears to offer an unexpectedly wide range of possibilities for architectural expression. Inspired by worldwide developments, both producers and designers are finding that there is still plenty of scope for the development of new applications.

Softwoods

Weichholz | Bois Résineux | Maderas blandas | Legno dolce | Naaldhout

Softwoods are distinguished from hardwoods by the composition and structure of the wood. They are generally softer than hardwoods, although there are exceptions. Softwoods are from coniferous or cone-bearing trees, although the needles of some species, such as the Chili pine, look more like scales or leaves. With the exception of the larch, coniferous trees stay green in winter, shedding about a third of their needles. Softwood trees in general have a longer clear stem than European hardwood trees, whose stem also narrows in diameter more rapidly as it grows taller. As a result, long timbers from European woods are usually from softwood species. Even longer clear stems occur in some tropical hardwood species.

The composition and structure of softwood are relatively simple. The annual build-up of stem wood consists of earlywood and latewood, with connecting cells running perpendicular to these growth rings. Earlywood, produced in the spring, is light-coloured and comprised of thin-walled cells. Latewood or summerwood makes up the darker portion of the growth rings. The cell walls of latewood are thicker and contain less air, making them look darker. These elongated cells,

Project Stanwell Park House, Australia (1997)
Architect Lahz Nimmo Architects
Photographer Brett Boardman Photography

called tracheids or fibres, are characteristic of softwoods. The relative density of latewood and earlywood varies greatly, depending on the conditions of growth. On tangential or flat-sawn boards, the alternation of light and dark-coloured wood produces the flame figure characteristic of softwood.

The transport of fluids from one cell to another is regulated by wall pits, or small openings or recesses in the fibre wall. In softwoods, where these openings are referred to as 'bordered pits', a flexible thickening in the heart of the pit may lead to the closing off of the opening. Thus, bordered pits not only provide unimpeded water transport, but also function like a valve. The withdrawal of water from the cell cavity via the wall pits leads to a build-up of capillary forces such that the thickened pit membrane (torus) is drawn towards the pit opening, hermetically sealing the cell wall and preventing air from entering the nutrient-filled cells. If the water columns, which stretch from the roots to the crown of the tree, were to be interrupted the tree would die. However, this same life-enhancing mechanism occurs as wood dries, when it not only interferes with the drying process, but it also inhibits impregnation. Spruce, for example, is for this reason difficult to treat with preservatives.

Running perpendicular to the growth rings are ribbon-like cells called rays which are responsible for the horizontal transport of fluids. The rays in softwoods are so small that they cannot be distinguished with the naked eye. In addition to the two cell types already mentioned, some softwood species have other types of cells. For example, parenchyma cells run lengthwise and provide for the storage and distribution of reserve nutrients. In a number of softwood species, so-called resin canals are also found in between the parenchyma cells. These long, very fine conduits or ducts have no cell walls. Resin canals may sometimes also be found on the horizontal surface between the rays. Woods with a high resin content are more resistant to attack by fungi and insects. On the other hand, resin can adversely affect the adhesion and durability of varnishes or paint coats.

Softwood Species

Most industrially used softwood species come from Europe and North America, with a few from South America. In total, 10 to 15 species supply the major portion of the market. Softwoods are generally not very durable. One notable exception is Western Red Cedar, whose durability is comparable to that of such hardwood species as bangkirai, karri and sapupira. It is followed, in order of decreasing durability, by Douglas fir and Oregon pine, pitch pine, larch, Scots pine or European redwood, fir, hemlock, spruce or whitewood and parana pine. A number of softwoods (pitch pine, fir, hemlock and parana pine) will not be discussed in this book because they are either insufficiently durable or are no longer commercially available in significant quantities.

Applications

Softwoods are a popular building material for both interior and exterior applications. The wood is easy to work, available in large quantities and has sufficient strength for a variety of structural applications. In façade construction, softwoods are used as cladding. They are also employed for structural elements such as laminated ('glulam') beams and timber frame construction. The softwoods most

Project Private House Wageningen (2000)
Architect Liong Lie, 123 DV
Photographer Brakkee & Scagliola

commonly used for façade claddings are larch, Oregon pine and European redwood or Scots pine, but above all spruce and Western Red Cedar. Generally, façade claddings are an assemblage of continuous, sometimes wholly or partially overlapping boards, with all kinds of different mouldings, which can be applied horizontally, vertically or diagonally. Non-corroding metal is generally advised for fixings because many of the substances present in the wood can react with 'ordinary' metals, resulting in blue or black streaks in the wood.

All untreated woods will eventually turn grey when exposed to the outside air. Some species do this in an attractive, uniform fashion. This is especially true of Western Red Cedar, where natural greying produces a soft, silvery sheen. However, overly wet conditions or inappropriate detailing may cause this to be marred by algae growth or unsightly staining. If softwoods are impregnated beforehand with preservatives, façade surfaces can be left unfinished, allowing the natural greying of the wood to remain visible, although in most cases surface cracks are liable to occur.

Surface treatments can be used to give the wood a colour, to protect it against greying or to stabilize it and so prevent it from working. To prevent the wood from working after it is in place, some form of all-round treatment is recommended. The systems used vary from opaque paint products, which hide both the structure and the colour of the wood, to transparent products, which allow the structure of the wood to remain visible and which – depending on whether pigments are added – may or may not colour the wood.

It is mostly softwoods that are used in the various composite products in which veneers, wood wool, chips, shavings and fibres are processed with glues and/or other binders to create the new products. Composites with plastics are also available.

Project Playhouse, Groningen (2003)
Architect Onix
Photographer SAPh, Rob de Jong

Douglas | Oregon Pine

Douglas-Tanne / Oregon-Pinie | Sapin de Douglas / Pin d'Oregon | Abeto Douglas / Pino de Oregón |
Abete Douglas / Pino dell'Oregon | Amerikaans grenen

Project ROB | Nisa building, Lelystad (1998)
Architect KCAP Architects and Planners
Photographer KCAP Architects and Planners

Project Il Palazzo, Alkmaar (2002)
Architect Min2 bouw-kunst
Photographer Min2 bouw-kunst

A native of North America, *Pseudotsuga menziesii* is also grown in Europe, New Zealand and Australia. Depending on where it is grown, it is referred to as Douglas fir or Oregon pine. In the Netherlands, the latter term is usually a brand name for imported Douglas fir wood. In exceptional circumstances, the tree, which normally reaches 40 to 60 metres in height, can grow to a maximum of 90 metres, with a clear, straight trunk of more than 20 metres. Older examples in particular produce a straight-grained, knot-free wood with an attractive, slightly orange, yellow-brown colour. In young trees, the colour is more reddish. The contrast in colour between earlywood and latewood in the growth rings produces a clear, striped figure in quarter-sawn or radial sawn wood and a flame figure in flat-sawn wood. Douglas fir is resin-bearing, which can result in greasy stripes or patches on planed wood.

Technical Aspects

Douglas fir is available in large sizes. Its favourable strength properties make suitable for construction purposes. The modulus of elasticity in defect-free wood can reach 13500 N/mm^2. Although Douglas fir is amongst the more durable softwoods, it almost always needs to be surface protected. Resin must be removed by degreasing before either solvent- or water-based paints will adhere to the wood.

Applications

Douglas fir is marketed as square-edged timber and rectangular beams, but above all in the form of plywood. Although mainly used in interiors, given a protective surface, transparent or otherwise, it can also be used on the outside of buildings where it appears mainly in frames and as structural timber and to a lesser degree as façade cladding.

Colour	**orange-like**, **yellowish brown**
Glossiness	glossy, satin, **matt**
Translucence (%)	**0** – 20 – 40 – 60 – 80 – 100
Texture	sharp, **medium**, dull
Hardness	hard, **soft**, depressible
Temperature	**warm**, medium, cool
Odour	strong, **moderate**, none
Acoustic opacity	good, **moderate**, poor

European Redwood | Scots Pine

Europäisches Redwood-Holz / Schottische Pinie | Séquoia Européen / Pin d'Ecosse | Secuoya europea / Pino escocés |
Pino silvestre / Pino scozzese | Europees grenen

Project Den Daalder, Boxtel (2002)
Architect Min2 bouw-kunst
Photographer Min2 bouw-kunst

Project Nieuw Terbregge, Rotterdam (2003)
Architect Ineke Hulshof
Photographer Willem van Det

European redwood comes from the long-needled, white or Scots pine, a conifer that grows to an average of 30 metres and is found all across Europe, as well as in northern Asia. The wide growth range means that the tree grows under very different climatological conditions, resulting in wide variations in the structure of the wood. As in most coniferous woods, the sapwood in European redwood is extremely white, contrasting sharply with the much darker heartwood. The heartwood is initially light brown, becoming a yellowish to reddish brown over the course of time. The presence of reaction wood sometimes produces a darkening that is visible in the sapwood, but is not noticeable in the heartwood. A resinous wood, it has a straight grain and fine texture and produces a striped figure in quarter-sawn wood and a flame pattern in flat-sawn wood. European redwood smells pleasantly of resin or terpentine.

Technical Aspects

The mechanical properties of the sapwood in European redwood are virtually the same as those of the heartwood. For outdoor applications, the wood should be treated with a preservative. Although the heartwood has the same limited natural durability as spruce, its higher resin content makes it better resistant to fungi and insects. When sapwood is treated with a preservative, there is no longer any differentiation from the heartwood. The relatively high resin content, which sometimes produces dark, sticky patches, makes it necessary to degrease the wood before applying a surface finish.

Applications

Redwood is used in a great many different sectors, depending on the quality of the wood. These range from the packaging industry for low-quality wood to furniture making for the better wood. In building construction, it is used mainly for structural members and for interior frames and joinery. For exterior use it must be treated with preservatives.

Colour	**yellowish to reddish brown**
Glossiness	glossy, satin, **matt**
Translucence (%)	**0** – 20 – 40 – 60 – 80 – 100
Texture	sharp, **medium**, dull
Hardness	hard, **soft**, depressible
Temperature	**warm**, medium, cool
Odour	**strong**, moderate, none
Acoustic opacity	good, **moderate**, poor

Larch

Lärche | Mélèze | Alerce | Larice | Lariks

Project Gewild Wonen, building expo, Almere (2001)
Architect FARO Architecten
Photographer SAPh, Rob de Jong

The larch tree is a deciduous conifer, shedding its needles in winter-time. Vitruvius first made mention of the larch (the Romans named it *larix*, after the alpine town of Larignum) when he spoke of a wood that was fairly resistant to woodworm, but which could also with-stand fire and became hard as stone when pounded into the ground. The larch is a member of the Pinaceae or pine family and is found across a wide region, including Japan, Russia, Siberia, various parts of Europe, and in both western and eastern North America. Relatively heavy for a coniferous wood, the larch has a straight grain and fine texture. The larch tree rapidly produces heartwood with colour variations from light yellow-brown to a reddish brown. The sapwood is a dirty white. Larch has clearly visible growth rings with light-coloured earlywood and dark latewood, producing an attractive flame figure on flat-sawn wood and clearly defined stripes on quarter-sawn wood.

Technical Aspects

Although larch is considered one of the most durable of the soft-woods, a protective surface treatment is recommended, certainly in the case of external applications if only to prevent discoloration due to ultraviolet light. Larch is a hard wood (according to Janka, varying from 2600 to 3900 N/mm^2).

Applications

Larch, which is available as roundwood, sawn timber and planks, is often finished with a transparent coating so as not to obscure the attractive pattern. Its wide range of applications, warm colour and pleasing figure make it an exceptionally appealing and popular wood, at home in both simple and high-end architecture. As larch continues to shrink and swell over time, it is wise to take this rather nervous behaviour into account in the detailing.

Project Delftechpark Office, Delft (2002)
Architect Marcel van der Schalk Architects
Photographer Willem van Det

Colour	**yellowish brown to reddish brown**
Glossiness	glossy, satin, **matt**
Translucence (%)	**0** – 20 – 40 – 60 – 80 – 100
Texture	sharp, **medium**, dull
Hardness	hard, **soft**, depressible
Temperature	**warm**, medium, cool
Odour	strong, **moderate**, none
Acoustic opacity	good, **moderate**, poor

Spruce | Whitewood

Fichte / Weißholz | Epicéa / Bois Blanc | Picea / Tilo | Abete / Abete bianco | Vuren

Project Nesvera House, Usti nad Labem, Czech Republic (2000)
Architect Jan Jehlik Architectural Office
Photographer Jan Brodsky

Several coniferous species found across large areas of the world, including Canada, the United States, Europe and Northern Asia, have so many characteristics in common that they are generally traded worldwide under the same name. They belong to the Pinaceae family. The trees that produce European whitewood, however, have different names in different countries (*fijnspar* in Holland and *gran* in Sweden, for example), which can lead to confusion. The height of the trees varies from 20 to 60 metres. The average length of the cylindrical, branch-free trunk is 20 metres, with a bole diameter from 60 to 120 cm. There is little difference in colour between heartwood and sapwood, but there is a marked colour difference between the lighter earlywood and the darker latewood. The almost white freshly cut wood turns yellowish brown after sustained exposure to light and air. This straight-grained, fine textured wood contains a relatively high amount of resin that is often concentrated in resin pockets and that is released when the wood is sawn. The wood can be fine or coarse-grained, depending on where it is grown.

Technical Aspects

Spruce or whitewood is not durable and is vulnerable to blue stain. When there is a diagonal direction to the grain, rapidly dried wood will warp quickly and is liable to contain numerous loose knots.

Applications

For a number of applications, spruce is treated with preservatives to extend its limited natural durability. It is primarily used for structural purposes, in window and door frames, and both interior and exterior panelling. It is often used in chipboard and plywood.

Project De Burcht, Bergen (1998)
Architect Min2 bouw-kunst
Photographer Elly Valkering

Colour	white to yellowish brown
Glossiness	glossy, satin, **matt**
Translucence (%)	**0** – 20 – 40 – 60 – 80 – 100
Texture	sharp, **medium**, dull
Hardness	hard, **soft**, depressible
Temperature	**warm**, medium, cool
Odour	strong, **moderate**, none
Acoustic opacity	good, **moderate**, poor

Western Red Cedar

Rotzeder | Cèdre rouge de l'ouest | Cedro colorado occidental | Cedro rosso canadese | Western Red Cedar

Project RIAGG, Leiden (1999)
Architect Team4 Architects
Photographer SAPh, Rob de Jong

Project Batavia Building, Amsterdam (2000)
Architect Frits van Dongen, de Architekten Cie.
Photographer johnlewismarshall.com

Western Red Cedar (*Thuja plicata*) is a North American conifer with exceptional qualities. Its main growing areas are the rainforests of British Columbia in western Canada, where trees can grow to 75 metres in height and be more than 1000 years old. The northwestern United States are another important source. The wood has a characteristic cedar smell and a bitter taste.

Technical Aspects

The wood produced by these forest giants is light, soft (1470 N Janka hardness rating), has a straight grain and fine texture. Flatsawn wood frequently has an attractive flame figure. Its range of warm colours, from yellow-brown (like Oregon pine) to pinkish (like Californian redwood), and from salmon-coloured to chocolatey brown, make it a much-loved wood. Darker wood is usually from the heart of the stem. Characteristic of Western Red Cedar is its high natural durability, probably due to the presence of ß-thujaplicine, which means that it can be used with no protective treatment, even for exterior applications. Rain may, however, cause the chemicals to bleed, producing stains on underlying brickwork. In favourable circumstances, Western Red Cedar quickly assumes an attractive, even, silvery colour. Because it is not strong, structural applications are rare. Window and door frames need to be more heavily built than is usually the case.

Applications

For exterior applications, Western Red Cedar is primarily processed as square edge timber in a variety of types and sizes suitable for façade cladding. In the form of hand-split shakes or machine-made shingles, it can be used for covering both roofs and façades. Stainless steel or aluminium fixings are recommended, as the wood's natural preservatives will not only corrode iron or brass fixings but also cause blueblack discoloration in the wood. On north-facing surfaces in damp and dark environments, the much-admired, attractive greying of the wood will be seriously marred by stains and algae.

Colour	**light yellowish brown to salmon or chocolate**
Glossiness	glossy, **satin**, **matt**
Translucence (%)	**0** – 20 – 40 – 60 – 80 – 100
Texture	sharp, **medium**, dull
Hardness	hard, **soft**, **depressible**
Temperature	**warm**, medium, cool
Odour	**strong**, **moderate**, none
Acoustic opacity	good, **moderate**, poor

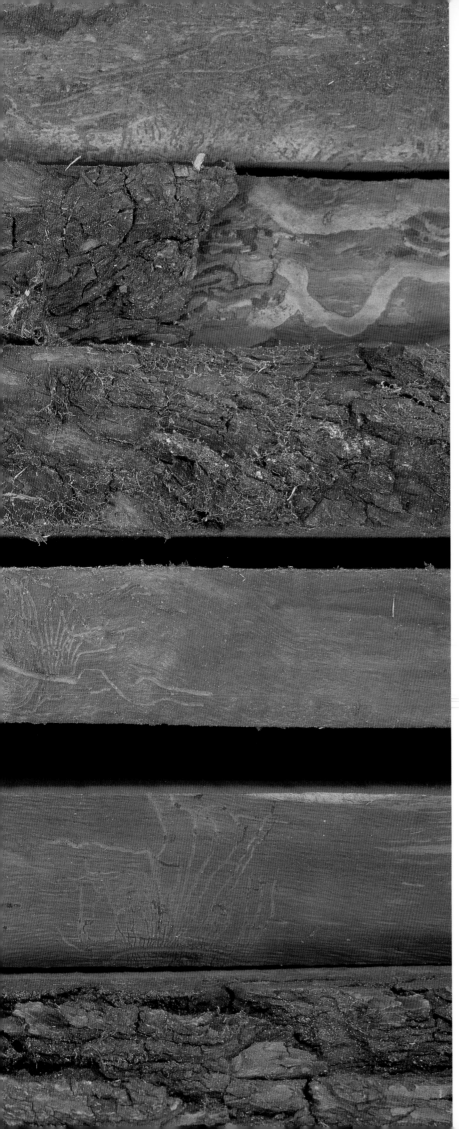

Hardwoods

Hartholz | Bois Feuillus | Maderas duras | Legno duro | Loofhout

Hardwoods come from broad-leafed trees, which may be either ever-green or deciduous, and have a more complex structure than soft-woods. Softwoods are characterized by tracheids, long, thin-walled, tubular cells that transport nutrients and provide mechanical support. In hardwoods, that dual function is divided between wood fibres and wood vessels. Wood fibres, which usually form the main bulk of hardwoods, are similar to softwood tracheids, but are shorter, with a thicker wall. Water is transported by the wood vessels, which are comprised of vertically arranged cells whose adjoining walls have dis-appeared, resulting in continuous canals. On cross-cut surfaces, the vessels appear as pores, on longitudinally-cut surfaces, as small grooves. Wood in which the wood vessels are larger in earlywood than in latewood and the transition is fairly abrupt, is referred to as ring-porous. Examples are oak, ash and robinia. Ring porosity is less frequent in tropical hardwoods because of the even build-up of wood throughout the year. On flat-sawn surfaces, ring porosity pro-duces a characteristic flame pattern. In some hardwoods, such as walnut, teak and cedar, there is a difference between the large ves-sels in the earlywood and the smaller vessels in the latewood, but the transition is more gradual. These are known as semi-porous. Finally, there are diffuse-porous woods, such as maple, beech, birch and poplar, in which wood vessels of differing sizes are evenly distributed across the growth rings.

The rays, which are responsible for the horizontal transport of fluids, are far more varied in hardwoods than in softwoods. In European white oak, for example, they can reach 75 millimetres in height, pro-ducing a characteristic silver grain figure in quarter-sawn wood. Although shorter, the rays in beech also result in a distinctive appear-ance on the tangential surface.

Composition

The wood vessels in the heartwood of many types of hardwood con-tain substances or exhibit deposits on the cell walls which give the wood its specific characteristics (including colour) and make identifi-cation of wood type easier. It is such substances that turn ebony black and make basralocus resistant to shipworm. The natural dura-bility of the wood is also often the result of cell-wall deposits that contain substances with fungicidal or insecticidal properties. As hard-wood sapwood turns to heartwood, the vessels are sometimes invad-ed by balloon-like extrusions from the parenchyma known as tyloses, which sometimes completely close off the vessels. The heartwood of American white oak, for example, becomes waterproof as a result of these ingrowths (important for wine barrels and shipbuilding), but is equally unable to absorb preservatives, unlike the American red oak which is unaffected by tyloses. Only a few hardwood trees contain resin and resin ducts. These are an abnormal phenomenon resulting, for instance, from distress or bruising.

Finally, a characteristic distinguishing feature of hardwoods is the presence of a layered structure, produced because the various wood elements are arranged in more or less wavy, horizontal layers. This layered structure presents as very fine perpendicular stripes on the tangential (flat-sawn) surface. Sometimes this is very clear, as in bas-ralocus and American mahogany, sometimes less so, or, as in African mahogany and wengé, barely evident at all.

Project Sandal wood private house, Istanbul (2000)
Architect GAD Architecture
Photographer GAD Architecture

Hardwood Species

Colonization introduced the Western world to an enormous variety of tropical woods, mainly hardwoods. Of the 50,000 known tropical woods, 5000 proved to be commercially useful. The former colonial powers, especially England, France and the Netherlands, carried out a great deal of scientific work on the properties of these 'new' woods. In their countries of origin, tropical woods were especially widely used in shipbuilding, whereas European imports of tropical woods were chiefly employed in building homes. After the Second World War, rapid construction led to a steadily decreasing supply of softwoods and increased the demand for tropical woods. Naturally durable woods, such as basralocus and azobé, were extensively used in harbours and waterways.

Along with the traditional methods of preserving wood with tar and oil products (such as creosote), metal-based methods were developed during this period. A number of factors contributed to the increased use of what had hitherto been less frequently used woods. Following a period of hasty and often poor quality construction, standards were tightened. The question of durability acquired a dominant role, the more so because the increasingly well-insulated homes (the result of more energy-efficient building construction) suffered from condensation and moisture build-up due to design and construction defects. Durable woods had, and often still have the (unintended) effect of accommodating such design flaws.

The aggressive logging of tropical forests during the second half of the 20th century also generated such serious environmental consequences that regulated wood production was necessary in order to keep up with the pace of wood consumption. Along with wood from sustainably managed production forests, environmentally friendly methods of wood preservation are now making it possible to use types of hardwoods that had previously not been considered for commercial (architectural) applications. Bintagor, from the Solomon Islands, is an example. The supply is limited, so it is thus far not very widely used.

Applications

The great diversity of available hardwoods entails a similarly wide range of applications. In general, commercial hardwoods are more durable than the available softwoods. Untreated hardwood is also more common than untreated softwood. Furthermore, the structure and colour of hardwoods, such as is visible on the surface, are generally more highly valued than those of softwoods, so that hardwoods are more often used in 'visible' applications, notably in the interior for panelling and furniture. Like softwoods, hardwoods can be used for a variety of structural applications and are employed in façades for the construction of window and door frames and in continuous surfaces of non-overlapping, partially overlapping and completely overlapping boards laid horizontally, vertically or diagonally, complete with all manner of different mouldings. The less durable woods can be impregnated beforehand with a preservative or be given a surface coating which may also impart a colour to the wood and so prevent it from greying. These systems vary from opaque paint products, which completely obliterate both the structure and the colour of the wood, to transparent products that leave the structure and colour of the wood visible and – depending on whether pigment is added – colour the wood to a greater or lesser degree.

Because of their sometimes very special visual characteristics, hardwoods are frequently used in composites in which the veneers of the selected hardwood play a dominant role. In general, the scarcer a wood is, the more highly valued (and more expensive) it will be. Costly hardwoods such as walnut and mahogany will consequently be found primarily in the interior, in panelling, cabinetry and furniture.

Project Recycled Australian redgum, Casuarina Beach House, Australia (2002)
Architect Lahz Nimmo Architects
Photographer Brett Boardman Photography

Azobé

Azobé | Azobé | Azobe | Azobé | Azobé

Project Bell bridge, Zijpe (1997)
Architect Joke Zaal
Photographer John Ruis, Prinsen Waterbouw

Azobé, or ekki, grows in tropical West Africa. The tree grows to an average height of 40 metres, with a clean trunk of 25 to 30 metres. Thanks to its exceptional properties, azobé is used primarily in situations where heavy or demanding conditions apply. Azobé is a so-called sinker, which is to say that the wood, either wet or dry, is heavier than water. The heartwood is reddish brown. Under the influence of light it turns dark red to deep brown, sometimes with a violet sheen. The sapwood is about 2 cm thick and is usually light red to greyish-yellow, contrasting clearly with the heartwood. There is an orange-brown zone between the sapwood and heartwood. This transitional wood has the same characteristics as the heartwood. The texture of azobé is fairly coarse and its grain usually but not always regular. The wood frequently exhibits an interlocked grain, producing a figure of alternating light and dark bands on the radial cut.

Technical Aspects

Azobé is very strong and hard. It has exceptionally good natural durability, making preservative treatment or a protective coating unnecessary. Since the wood greys with the passage of time, a non-filming coating should be applied if the original wood colour is to be maintained. Azobé is generally supplied in large dimensions, free of defects. To prevent cracks from forming during drying, crosscut ends are often coated with a wax emulsion. The wood's high shrinkage rate must be taken into account in the detailing of structures. Azobé's extreme hardness, combined with strong movement, make it inappropriate for gluing.

Applications

Because azobé is very durable and can absorb heavy loads, it is a popular choice for bridges, jetties, sluice gates and the like. It is also very suitable for decking, sheet piling and fencing. Since it is highly susceptible to cracking in overly thin dimensions – and also because it cannot be glued – its use in façade panelling is not advised.

Project Hof van Hoytema, Amsterdam (2003)
Architect Heren 5
Photographer Kees Hummel

Colour	reddish brown to dark-red or deep-brown
Glossiness	glossy, satin, **matt**
Translucence (%)	**0** – 20 – 40 – 60 – 80 – 100
Texture	sharp, **medium**, dull
Hardness	hard, **soft**, depressible
Temperature	**warm**, medium, cool
Odour	strong, **moderate**, none
Acoustic opacity	good, **moderate**, poor

Bankirai

Bangkirai | Bangkirai | Bangkirai | Bangkirai

Project Visual Art Centre, Groningen (2001)
Architect Onix
Photographer SAPh, Rob de Jong

Project Marks and Kampstra bar, Maastricht (1996)
Architect Bruls and Co.
Photographer Arjen Schmitz

Bangkirai is the general name given to a group of heavy woods found primarily in Malaysia. These members of the *Shorea* species, to which many merantis also belong, have widely differing properties, in particular with respect to volumetric mass and the associated natural durability. The heavier woods (averaging 930 kg/m^3) are called bangkirai, a term initially applied to an Indonesian wood with similar properties which is no longer available. Depending on the type and the location where they are found, trees in the *Shorea* group (including bangkirai) are 35 to 40 metres high, with a clear trunk 20 to 25 metres in length. Fresh-cut heartwood is yellow to greyish brown, but exposure to daylight quickly changes it to brown and eventually dark brown. The structure of the wood is even and fine, with a strong interlocked grain, producing striped quarter-cut surfaces. Small, whitish stripes running lengthwise are produced by resin canals.

Technical Aspects

Bangkirai is very durable, very hard and strong. Even with slow and careful drying the wood exhibits considerable shrinkage, resulting in surface cracks and end splitting. Bangkirai often contains a water-soluble gum that can stain adjacent surfaces, a problem that can (at least temporarily) be avoided by thoroughly rinsing the planks with water. However, it may still begin to bleed again after years of exposure to wind and weather.

Applications

The strength and durability of bangkirai makes it ideally suited to outdoor applications in a range of road and water works, such as (plank) bridges, jetties, decking and sheet piling. Gates, fencing and outdoor furniture are also made of bangkirai. Its resistance to acids and other chemicals makes it suited to industrial use. Bangkirai's susceptibility to cracking makes it is less appropriate for finer applications, such as wall claddings.

Colour	**brown to deep-brown**
Glossiness	glossy, satin, **matt**
Translucence (%)	**0** – 20 – 40 – 60 – 80 – 100
Texture	sharp, **medium**, dull
Hardness	hard, **soft**, depressible
Temperature	**warm**, medium, cool
Odour	strong, **moderate**, none
Acoustic opacity	good, **moderate**, poor

Beech

Buche | Hêtre | Haya | Faggio | Beuken

Project Teylers Museum, Haarlem (1996)
Architect Hubert Jan Henket
Photographer Philip Driessen

Project Renovation office, Muiden (1998)
Architect Gert-Jan Hendriks, de Architectengroep
Photographer Luuk Kramer

By the time they are felled, beech trees are 80 to 100 years old and on average 45 metres high, with a 9-metre-long clear trunk. They grow primarily in Europe, notably the central highlands of France, the Carpathians and Bosnia, as well as in the hardwood forests of eastern North America. There is little distinction between sapwood and heartwood. Fresh-cut heartwood is white to light brown, turning yellowish-brown on exposure to air and light. Steamed beech is pink to light red. Beech has characteristic stripes on offset quarter-sawn surfaces. They are from one to four millimetres long, and are the bisected rays in the wood. Flat-sawn surfaces have a subtle flame figure. The wood is fine and even-textured, with a grain that is usually straight, but sometimes wavy.

Technical Aspects

Beech readily absorbs moisture and consequently has low natural durability. It is a hard, strong, splinter-free wood that is easy to glue, bend and finish. Wood from southern climates has a milder structure and is therefore often easier to work. The wood is susceptible to burning when worked with blunt tools or when screws are driven without pre-drilled holes. While drying, differences in tangential and radial shrinkage can cause warping and checking. Beech responds well to steaming, which causes it to change colour and become more elastic, making it easy to bend and peel. Steaming also reduces internal tensions in the wood, reducing the likelihood of checking and warping. Impregnating beech with preservatives or subjecting it to 300 atmospheres of pressure at 115 °C increases the volumetric mass and improves its mechanical properties.

Applications

Because of its limited durability, beech is most commonly used indoors. Furniture, toys and household goods are products that are frequently made of this hard, splinter-free wood (bent and/or laminated). In addition to the use of solid beech in staircases and floors, panelling with a beech veneer is often used to finish doors, walls and ceilings, both indoors and outdoors. Layers of beech veneer bonded with synthetic resin under high pressure (marketed as Lignostone, among others) can be used structurally in columns and joists.

Colour	**whitish to light brown, steamed pink to reddish**
Glossiness	glossy, satin, **matt**
Translucence (%)	**0** – 20 – 40 – 60 – 80 – 100
Texture	sharp, **medium**, dull
Hardness	hard, **soft**, depressible
Temperature	**warm**, medium, cool
Odour	strong, **moderate**, none
Acoustic opacity	good, **moderate**, poor

Iroko

Iroko | Iroko | Iroko | Iroko | Iroko

Project Tripolis office building, Amsterdam (1994)
Architect Aldo van Eyck
Photographer Kees Hummel

Iroko is a tropical African hardwood from a tree averaging 50 metres in height. Some varieties are also known by the name of kambala. The wood has a moderately coarse texture and an irregular grain, sometimes straight, but often interlocked or wavy. This yellowish-brown wood, which quickly turns golden brown when exposed to light, can contain hard deposits of calcium carbonate that impede its workability. It can cause serious discoloration when it comes in contact with other woods. Iroko contains chlorophorin, an allergic sensitizer that cause severe respiratory irritation and dermatitis in those who work with it. The chemical components of iroko can delay hardening in any freshly poured cement with which it comes into contact.

Technical Aspects

Iroko is a strong, stable and durable wood. The heavier it is, the darker the colour and the more durable the wood. These characteristics vary significantly and depend on where the tree is grown. Cross-grained timber may crack and warp during drying. Iroko's workability is comparable to that of oak. Stainless steel is recommended for fixings, as contact with iron will generate a grey to black discoloration.

Applications

Strong, durable and stable, iroko is widely used, both indoors and outdoors, in floors, staircases and furniture, as well as in frames, doors and façade panelling. It is also made into veneers. Iroko can be used without any surface treatment. Paints and varnishes dry slowly due to the chemical substances in the wood. Pre-treatment with a thinner can reduce this problem in some paint systems.

Colour	**yellowish brown to gold- or dark-brown**
Glossiness	glossy, satin, **matt**
Translucence (%)	**0** – 20 – 40 – 60 – 80 – 100
Texture	sharp, **medium**, dull
Hardness	hard, **soft**, depressible
Temperature	**warm**, medium, cool
Odour	strong, **moderate**, none
Acoustic opacity	good, **moderate**, poor

Karri

Karri | Karri | Karri | Karri | Karri

Project Apenheul zoo, Apeldoorn (1971)
Architect Sjef Füss
Photographer Centrum Hout | johnlewismarshall.com

Karri is an Australian wood and closely related to another Australian wood, Jarrah. Karri has a straight, tall trunk and can grow to extraordinary heights. Specimens measuring 100 metres have been cited. The trees have a smooth bark and a small crown. The heartwood is reddish brown. The texture is moderately coarse and the interlocked grain produces a striped figure. Series of axial resin ducts are sometimes found in the wood, running parallel to the growth rings.

Technical Aspects

Karri dries slowly and may exhibit serious splitting. It also has a tendency to warp. Fibres may be pulled out of the wood during tooling. Karri is very durable and strong and freshly cut wood is extremely heavy (1150 kg/m^3). Karri can be distinguished from jarrah by burning a small piece of wood. Its ash is white, whereas jarrah ash is black.

Applications

The excellent natural durability of karri means that no surface treatment or preservative is needed for exterior applications. Karri is used outdoors in bridges, piers and the like. In Australia, it is used for a wide variety of purposes, including structural timber. Indoors, it is often found in flooring, including parquet.

Colour	**reddish brown**
Glossiness	glossy, satin, **matt**
Translucence (%)	**0** – 20 – 40 – 60 – 80 – 100
Texture	sharp, **medium**, dull
Hardness	hard, **soft**, depressible
Temperature	**warm**, medium, cool
Odour	strong, **moderate**, none
Acoustic opacity	good, **moderate**, poor

Mahogany

Mahagoni | Acajou | Caoba | Mogano | Mahonie

Project BSI Bomenservice, Baarn (1998)
Architect MIII Architects
Photographer Centrum Hout | johnlewismarshall.com

Project City Building, Rotterdam (1995)
Architect Bosch Architects
Photographer Willem van Det

The mahoganies include three botanically distinct species of wood, but they have so much in common in terms of structure, applications and colour, that they can all be included under the general name of mahogany. Mahogany is valued above all for its colour, combined with attractive variations in the figure of the grain.

Swietenia mahogany is found in Central and South America and the Caribbean. It has also been planted in Africa and Asia. Growing up to 30 metres high, the tree has a relatively long clear trunk. The heartwood is salmon-coloured, pink, red to reddish-brown, developing over time into a deep red to brown, with an exceptional golden-tinted lustre. The sapwood is white to yellow. The generally straight grain shows a variety of figures with names such as dappled, watered and mottled.

Sapeli mahogany grows in central Africa and has a pinkish red heartwood that later turns deep brown. On radial surfaces the clearly visible interlocked grain produces the characteristic regularly striped surface. As with Swietenia mahogany, irregularities in the direction of the grain can give the wood and attractive appearance. In contrast to other mahoganies, Sapeli has a definite cedar-like scent.

Sipo mahogany comes from West Africa and has a reddish-brown heartwood, sometimes with an almost violet tint. Exposure to sunlight can cause naturally finished wood to lose its red tint and turn golden brown.

Technical Aspects

Mahoganies are sturdy, tough, moderately strong and relatively soft woods with average durability (Sapeli is the least durable). It dries only moderately but shows little tendency to split or warp. In damp conditions it will cause corrosion and black discoloration in iron.

Applications

Swietenia mahogany is primarily used indoors for floors, staircases and panelling, but it is also used in furniture and yacht building. Outdoors it can also be used for frames.

Colour	**reddish brown to gold-brown or deep-brown**
Glossiness	glossy, **satin**, **matt**
Translucence (%)	**0** – 20 – 40 – 60 – 80 – 100
Texture	sharp, **medium**, dull
Hardness	hard, **soft**, depressible
Temperature	**warm**, medium, cool
Odour	**strong**, moderate, none
Acoustic opacity	good, **moderate**, poor

Maple

Ahorn | Erable | Arce | Acero | Esdoorn

Project Danish pavilion, Hanover Expo (2000)
Architect BYSTED A/S
Photographer Søren Nielsen

Maple is found in Europe, Western Asia and the eastern United States and Canada. The tree height and the length of clear trunk depend on the region where the tree is grown and can vary widely. On average, maples grow to between 20 and 25 metres high. The white colour of both sapwood and heartwood is an important characteristic trait. Special varnishes and bleaching agents are used to prevent discolouring. The wood usually has a fairly even structure. In general maple has a straight grain, but occasionally it presents a regular wavy pattern that is highly prized for furniture and musical instruments. American maple also sometimes develops a mottled figure, known as bird's-eye maple. A rather sharp definition of the growth rings can result in a finely striped figure in quarter-cut wood and a subtle flame figure on flat-sawn surfaces. The small silver-grain markings on quarter-sawn wood and a silky sheen are distinguishing features of maple wood.

Technical Aspects

Maple is only moderately durable, but is hard and dense, with a fine texture. The wood is very easy to bend and dries slowly, with some risk of discoloration. In order to prevent the latter, the temperature for kiln drying should be below 50 °C.

Applications

Maple's very light colour makes it a highly valued wood in veneers and plywood used in the production of furniture and other articles where light wood is desired, chess and draught pieces being familiar examples. The attractive dappled, bird's-eye, flowered and wavy figures found in maple wood are shown to best effect when processed as panelling for cabinetry. With the exception of the heartwood of American hard maple, maple takes readily to impregnation and surface treatments. Because of its limited resistance to exposure, maple is seldom used for exterior applications.

Colour	**white-yellow**
Glossiness	glossy, **satin**, matt
Translucence (%)	**0** – 20 – 40 – 60 – 80 – 100
Texture	sharp, **medium**, dull
Hardness	hard, **soft**, depressible
Temperature	**warm**, medium, cool
Odour	strong, **moderate**, none
Acoustic opacity	good, **moderate**, poor

Meranti

Meranti | Meranti | Meranti | Meranti | Meranti

Project BSI Bomenservice, Baarn (1998)
Architect MIII Architects
Photographer Centrum Hout | johnlewismarshall.com

Project Archipel, Almere (2001)
Architect Loof & Van Stigt Architects
Photographer Willem van Det

Meranti grows in South-East Asia. Apart from white and yellow meranti, the best-known variety is a dark red meranti from trees that grow to 30 or 40 metres with clean trunks up to 30 metres long. The colour difference between the heartwood and the sapwood is clearly visible. The sapwood is 2 to 6 centimetres wide and a grey, pinkish brown. After drying, meranti heartwood is a dark, reddish-brown. The wood has a very regular structure with little figure. Fine, whitish lines on lengthwise surfaces are caused by resin channels with a light-coloured, solid content. Small bore holes are often found in the heartwood, caused by certain green wood borers that only attack standing or freshly sawn wood. A PHND (pinholes no defect) label indicates that the boring insects have been destroyed and that the pinholes do not indicate defective wood. A period of great popularity, during which large quantities of meranti were consumed, was followed by a period of steep decline in quality, due mainly to unrestrained felling and the planting of fast-growing varieties. Since then, legislation, controlled forest management and restrictions on harvesting have brought the quality of meranti back up to the desired high standards.

Technical Aspects

Meranti dries reasonably fast, with little distortion. Its durability is average to moderate, depending on the density and moisture content.

Applications

Meranti is one of the most versatile of woods and is used in many applications. It is suitable for both indoor and outdoor carpentry in panelling, windows, doors, frames, staircases and trusses. Because the wood lends itself to peeling, it is also often used in veneer and plywood. As meranti plywood weathers quickly on exposure to ultra violet radiation, it is less suitable for outdoor use.

Colour	**reddish brown**
Glossiness	glossy, satin, **matt**
Translucence (%)	**0** – 20 – 40 – 60 – 80 – 100
Texture	sharp, **medium**, dull
Hardness	hard, **soft**, depressible
Temperature	**warm**, medium, cool
Odour	strong, **moderate**, none
Acoustic opacity	good, **moderate**, poor

Merbau

Merbau | Merbau | Merbau | Merbau | Merbau

Project MoMu, Antwerp (2000)
Architect Marie-José Van Hee
Photographer Willem van Det

Project De Vrolike Eik, Amsterdam (1997)
Architect M3H Architects
Photographer Kees Hummel

Merbau is a South-East Asian wood from a tree some 30 to 50 metres in height, with a clear trunk up to 25 metres long. The heartwood has very varied colours, ranging from yellow, orange and red to greyish brown. Once exposed to light, it quickly darkens to nearly black. The economically less interesting pale yellow sapwood is relatively wide in young trees. For this reason, it is mainly older trees with a diameter of at least 60 centimetres that are felled. The even structure of the wood does not have a particularly expressive figure, but depending on the direction in which the wood is sawn, attractive flame figures or vague stripes may become visible. The characteristic faint yellow stripes on the surface are caused by the filling present in the wood vessels. The vessels also contain a gum-like substance that is visible as dark brown stripes or spots. This substance is soluble in water and can lead to staining in untreated wood used outdoors – the so-called merbau bleeding. The surface of planed wood has an attractive gloss and feels slightly greasy to the touch.

Technical Aspects

Merbau is very durable, strong and hard, and has an even structure. It dries slowly, without checking or distortion. Nor does the wood work much once it has dried. It contains substances that protect iron fixings from corrosion but attack aluminium.

Applications

Given its many excellent properties, merbau is suitable for many purposes, both indoors and outdoors. It is used in construction work (including water-related structures), floors, stairs, windows, doors, frames and roofing. Merbau timber intended for exterior use is usually treated immediately after production with a protective coating, such as a varnish, stain or paint, to prevent the wood from bleeding. Stains on untreated wood can be removed with an ammonia solution.

Colour	**brownish grey to dark reddish brown**
Glossiness	glossy, **satin**, **matt**
Translucence (%)	**0** – 20 – 40 – 60 – 80 – 100
Texture	**sharp**, **medium**, dull
Hardness	hard, **soft**, depressible
Temperature	**warm**, medium, cool
Odour	strong, **moderate**, none
Acoustic opacity	good, **moderate**, poor

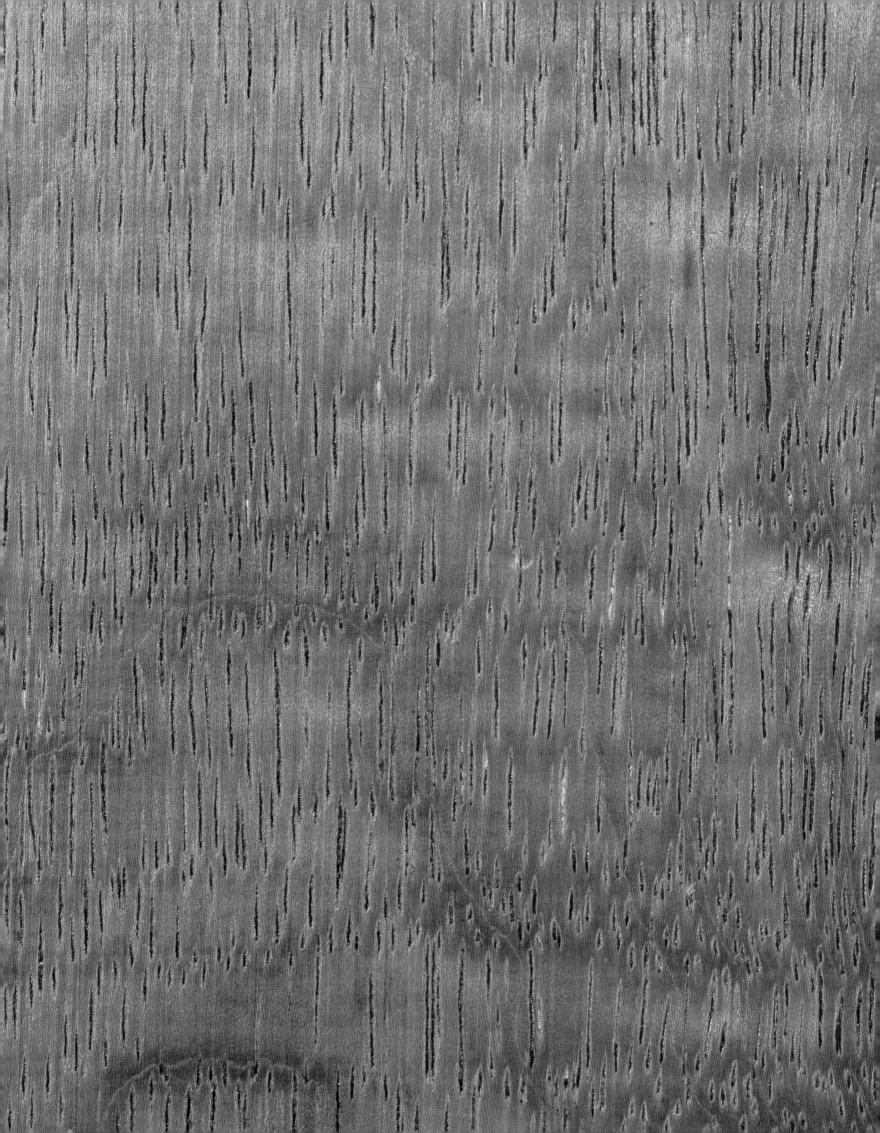

Oak

Eiche | Chêne | Roble | Quercia | Eiken

Project Eine-Welt-Kirche, Schneverdingen (2000)
Architect Lothar Tabery
Photographer Lothar Tabery

Project Music School, Groningen (1999)
Architect Onix
Photographer SAPh, Rob de Jong

Oaks are relatively fast-growing hardwood trees that in favourable conditions can grow to 40 metres tall. The wood has several very recognizable distinguishing features. On the cross-cut, the rays and ring porosity are clearly visible. On quarter-cut wood, the broad rays produce oak's characteristic silver-grain figure. On the flat-sawn surface, ring porosity creates a flame figure. Oak heartwood is usually yellowish in colour and darkens attractively with exposure to light. The less durable sapwood is lighter in colour. The properties of oak vary with the species, of which there many. Familiar examples include European white oak and American white and red oaks, named after the continents where they originally grew. The vessels in red oak contain no tyloses, making it more open to water and less durable than other species, and consequently less suitable for exterior use.

Technical Aspects

Depending on the species, oak dries fairly slowly with a tendency to splitting, deformation and discoloration. The finer species native to Europe are in general firmer, stronger, heavier and harder than the coarser American varieties. European varieties are also more durable and with the appropriate surface treatment can be used in outdoor conditions. Oak contains tannin, causing rapid corrosion in metals. To avoid the resulting blue-black discoloration in the wood, stainless steel fixings are recommended.

Applications

Oak is found in virtually all industries. It is used for floors and structural timber, but also in furniture, shipbuilding, toys and wine casks (tannin-bearing varieties only). Quarter-cut oak has the least tendency to work and is consequently preferred for frames, doors and floors. Oak is available as square edged and unedged timber, sawn timber and veneer.

Colour	yellow to yellowish brown and brown
Glossiness	glossy, satin, **matt**
Translucence (%)	**0** – 20 – 40 – 60 – 80 – 100
Texture	sharp, **medium**, dull
Hardness	hard, **soft**, depressible
Temperature	**warm**, medium, cool
Odour	strong, **moderate**, none
Acoustic opacity	good, **moderate**, poor

Robinia

Robinie | Robinia | Robinia | Robinia | Robinia

Project Private housing, Borneo Sporenburg, Amsterdam (2000)
Architect Ruimtelab
Photographer Kees Hummel

Project Visitor's centre Landschap Noord-Holland, Landsmeer (2003)
Architect Kees Hoope
Photographer Kees Hoope

Robinia (named after the brothers Jean and Vespasien Robin, French botanists who first planted the tree in Europe) originates from North America. After its introduction into Europe around 1600, other parts of the world followed suit. Because the fast-growing, 25 to 30 metre tree has a tendency to grow crooked and also has a short clear trunk, robinia wood is only available in short lengths. The heartwood has a yellow to brownish grey colour that takes on an attractive golden brown sheen when exposed to sunlight, before eventually turning grey. Robinia sapwood is light in colour and 1 to 2 centimetres thick. The ring-porous wood is usually straight-grained, with a moderately fine texture.

Technical Aspects

Robinia is very durable, very dense, difficult to split and rather hard, with a notable difference between the soft earlywood and the hard latewood. Drying is slow and must be done with care, as the wood is inclined to warp. Once dry, it is fairly stable. Finger jointing and/or lamination are accepted methods of producing longer lengths of robinia wood. Stainless steel fixings are recommended if robinia is used outdoors, as the high tannin content produces blue-black stains when it comes into contact with iron. Contact with copper and brass produces a light brown discoloration.

Applications

Robinia absorbs water rather slowly and quickly releases it again. This property makes robinia very suitable for façade construction. It is a popular material for road and waterway construction (sheet piling, bridges and decking). It is usually laminated for use as structural members, as well as for door and window frames. Its appearance makes it an attractive material for floors, furniture and toys.

Colour	**yellowish to brownish green**
Glossiness	glossy, **satin**, matt
Translucence (%)	**0** – 20 – 40 – 60 – 80 – 100
Texture	sharp, **medium**, dull
Hardness	hard, **soft**, depressible
Temperature	**warm**, medium, cool
Odour	strong, **moderate**, none
Acoustic opacity	good, **moderate**, poor

Sapupira

Sapupira | Sapupira | Sapupira | Sapupira | Sapupira

Project Thermo Staete, Bodegraven (1999)
Architect Klaas de Wit
Photographer Edifico

Project Malburgen-West, Arnhem (2000)
Architect Marco Henssen and Frank Hemeltjen, M3H Architects
Photographer Michel Claus

The sapupira tree grows in South America's Amazon region and may reach a height of 45 metres, with a clear trunk of about 15 metres. The heartwood is yellow or orange brown to dark brown. Exposed to light, the wood turns light brown. The yellowish-white sapwood is 3 to 10 centimetres thick and stands out slightly from the heartwood. The colour variation between the light parenchymal tissue and darker fibre tissue is characteristic of sapupira. This also applies to the dark gum marks, which are seen by some as extremely decorative. In general, the wood has a coarse texture and a straight grain, but an interlocking or wavy grain is also frequently seen.

Technical Aspects

Dried slowly, sapupira shows little warping. Rapid drying may, however, result in surface checks and warping. When green, this durable wood is very heavy, at about 1200 kg per cubic metre.

Applications

Sapupira is suitable for treatment with solvent-based paints. Water-based systems do not adhere as well and a brown discharge of chemical substances may occur. If the solid content of the paint is too low, the darker patches in the wood may assume a pasty appearance. Sapupira offers a wide variety of application possibilities including frames, doors, stair treads, outdoor and interior woodwork. Its durability also makes it suitable for marine decking, bridges, benches and elements for road and waterway construction. Sapupira can be used in façade joinery.

Colour	**yellowish white and dark brown**
Glossiness	glossy, satin, **matt**
Translucence (%)	**0** – 20 – 40 – 60 – 80 – 100
Texture	**sharp**, **medium**, dull
Hardness	hard, **soft**, depressible
Temperature	warm, **medium**, cool
Odour	strong, **moderate**, none
Acoustic opacity	good, **moderate**, poor

Teak

Teak | Teck | Teca | Teak | Teak

Project Isala College, Silvolde (1996)
Architect Mecanoo
Photographer Christian Richters

Project Centrum Hout, Almere (1992)
Architect Jan Plas Loenen
Photographer Centrum Hout | johnlewismarshall.com

Teak, which grows in Indonesia, Thailand, Myanmar and India, retains a hint of romance thanks partly to the elephants who still haul trunks out of forests where the trees grow alone or in groups. It is one of the few tropical trees to shed its leaves in the dry season. The tallest examples, from Myanmar, grow 45 metres high, with a clear trunk of 27 metres. Teak was one of the first trees to be cultivated and has been grown on Indonesian plantations since 1800. A characteristic of teak production is the practice of ringing, or cutting into the heartwood around the trunk a few years before the tree is felled, in order to initiate a natural drying process. Teak wood is golden to chocolate brown, sometimes with black veins. Unusually for a tropical wood, it is semi ring-porous with recognizable growth rings. The grain is coarse to fairly coarse, sometimes with a slightly interlocking grain. The wood has a greasy feel and smells like leather. So-called plantation teak from South or Central America has the same technical properties as Asian teak, but markedly less figure and a lighter colour.

Technical Aspects

Teak is very durable, has good strength for relatively low weight and exhibits little movement. It shows remarkable resistance to extreme temperature fluctuations and has a low shrinkage rating. It is resistant to chemicals and does not react to iron. The wood dries slowly and the attractive coloration is liable to darken and become dull when kiln dried.

Applications

Teak can be used untreated in which case it will turn grey, or can be treated with (transparent) varnish after having been degreased. Teak oil prevents greying and imparts a lustre to the wood. An expensive wood, teak is used mainly in situations that do justice to its appearance. Along with familiar applications in shipbuilding and the furniture industry, teak is also used in interiors (floors, stairs, panelling) and exteriors (windows, doors, frames, joinery).

Colour	**gold-brown to chocolate with black lines**
Glossiness	glossy, **satin**, matt
Translucence (%)	**0** – 20 – 40 – 60 – 80 – 100
Texture	sharp, **medium**, dull
Hardness	hard, **soft**, depressible
Temperature	**warm**, medium, cool
Odour	strong, **moderate**, none
Acoustic opacity	good, **moderate**, poor

Vitex

Vitex | Vitex | Vítex | Vitex | Vitex

Project Wilhelminahof, Rotterdam (1997)
Architect West8 urban design & landscape architecture
Photographer Jeroen Musch

A tree of variable height, the vitex grows to a maximum of 45 metres, with a grooved and irregularly shaped clear trunk of 10 to 15 metres. Vitex grows in tropical Asia, particularly Indonesia, Papua New Guinea and the Solomon Islands. The heartwood colour varies enormously, from light yellow, through yellowish brown, greenish or pinkish grey to reddish brown and brown. The 4 to 8 cm wide sapwood is yellowish and barely distinguishable from the heartwood. The wood has an even, fine to coarse texture, with a straight to interlocked or wavy grain. The surface has little gloss. Vitex woodchips will turn water yellow to yellow green.

Technical Aspects

Vitex is durable, heavy, hard and strong. It dries readily and shows little tendency to warp, but if dried too quickly, it will develop surface checks that in turn disrupt the balance in the moisture content. When boiled in water, vitex takes on a greenish to brownish yellow colour and some varieties of vitex are in fact the source of a yellow dye.

Applications

Vitex takes well to a finishing with solvent-based paints but water-based systems do not work as well. Vitex wood is used for durable constructions, waterway structures and joinery such as façade claddings. It is also used in furniture and flooring.

Colour	**from pale yellow to brown**
Glossiness	glossy, satin, **matt**
Translucence (%)	**0** – 20 – 40 – 60 – 80 – 100
Texture	sharp, **medium**, dull
Hardness	hard, **soft**, depressible
Temperature	**warm**, medium, cool
Odour	strong, **moderate**, none
Acoustic opacity	good, **moderate**, poor

Walnut

Walnuss | Noyer | Avellano | Noce | Noten

Project Koopmanshuis, PONs Automobielhandel, Leusden (2002)
Designers Arno Twigt, Jim Smith and Linda Vogt, QuA Associates
Photographer Hans Fonk

Walnut comes from trees that reach a maximum of 30 metres and have a clear trunk no longer than 6 metres. The walnut grows in Europe and Asia, eastern North America, and in Central and South America. The grain is straight, sometimes curly or wavy. The characteristic black figure in the grey to dark brown wood is caused by the walnut's wavy annual rings. Veneer made from the burls found on some walnut trees is sold as root walnut and is very valuable.

Technical Aspects

Walnut is in general strong, tough, dense and moderately durable. Drying must be done slowly and carefully in order to avoid cracking or warping. Straight-grained walnut bends well. In humid conditions, if walnut comes into contact with iron, it causes bluish-black discolorations. The light colour of the sapwood, which is susceptible to insect damage, turns dark when dried quickly and is consequently often mixed with the darker heartwood.

Applications

Its limited dimensions and availability make walnut a relatively expensive wood. Walnut is used primarily in the furniture industry, for turning and for making sculptures and carvings. Walnut is also processed as veneer, plywood or other sheet material for use as (expensive) panelling.

Colour	**grey to dark-brown with black lines**
Glossiness	glossy, **satin**, matt
Translucence (%)	**0** – 20 – 40 – 60 – 80 – 100
Texture	sharp, **medium**, dull
Hardness	hard, **soft**, depressible
Temperature	**warm**, medium, cool
Odour	strong, **moderate**, none
Acoustic opacity	good, **moderate**, poor

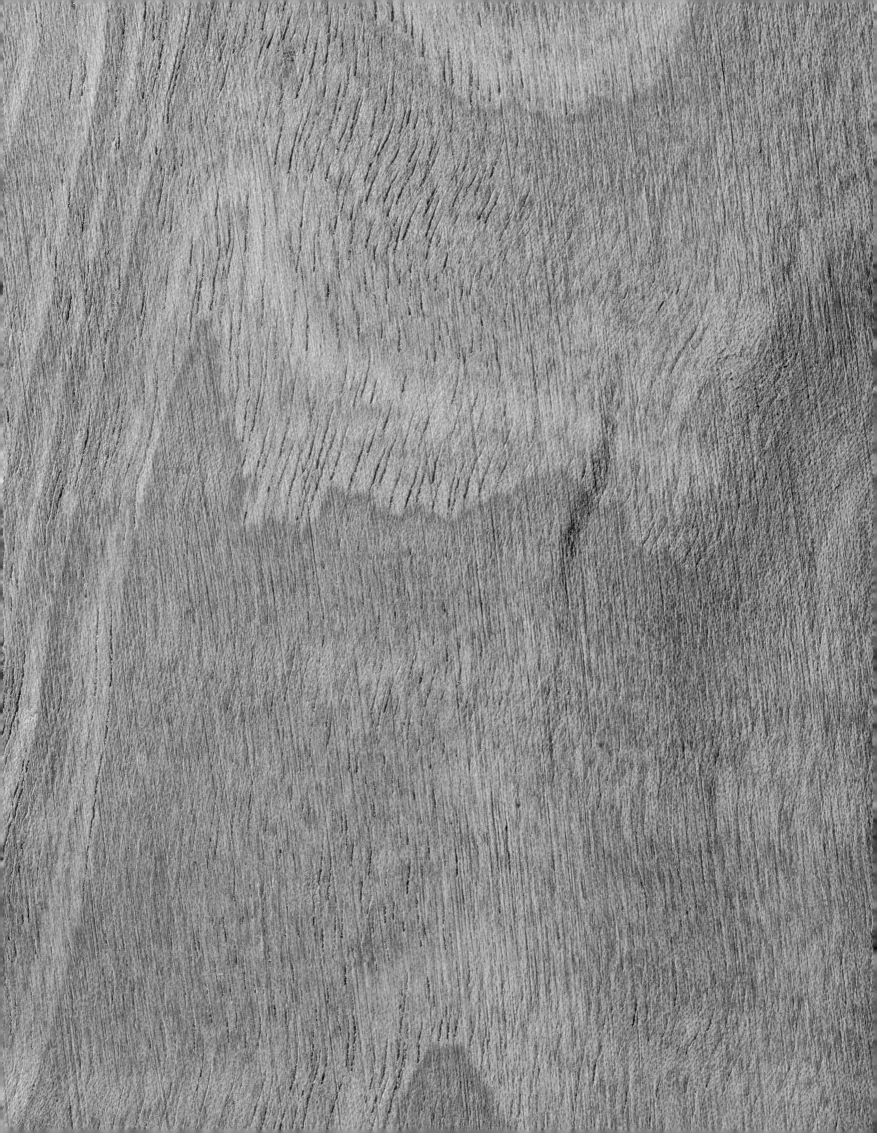

Other Woody Materials

Andere holzartige Materialien | Autres matériaux ligneux | Otros materiales leñosos | Altri materiali legnosi | Andere houtproducten

Wood and agricultural crops belong to the so-called renewable materials, unlike such non-renewable materials as (petrochemical) plastics and quarried or mined materials like minerals and metals. From an environmental standpoint, there is growing interest in the use of renewable materials in building construction. Renewable materials are those materials that become available again within a foreseeable period, either through natural growth or controlled cultivation. Because both agricultural crops and wood can be regrown interminably, they contribute to a durable and sustainable supply of raw materials for human society. They are neutral in terms of carbon dioxide emissions and make a positive contribution to the international goal of reducing greenhouse gases. Moreover, with the world's supply of oil expected to run out during the course of this century, resulting in a dramatic rise in the cost of extraction and thus also in the market price of energy and oil-based raw materials, renewable materials are in many instances logical alternatives.

Renewable Materials

Wood is of course the best-known renewable building material. Examples of renewable materials other than wood, are the woody products referred to in this chapter, including bamboo, cane, willow rods, sedum, grass, coconut and cork, as well as paper and cardboard. Stimulated by worldwide concern for the environment, and with the help of modern techniques, many producers have developed completely new applications for these renewable materials. These often involve techniques and applications that are in fact centuries old but which have been abandoned over the course of time. For example, the use of willow rods and straw bales as a support for mud walls is once again the subject of interest. Similarly, another woody material, bamboo, is no longer exploited solely for its stem, but is now also being processed into laminates with countless application possibilities. Timber-frame construction and renewable building materials form an ideal combination in which the positive properties of both can be used to the full.

Although many of these renewable materials when used as building materials have a considerably shorter lifespan than conventional building materials (unless their natural durability is extended by preservative treatment) there are several situations where this could well be seen as an advantage. Buildings often have a physical lifespan well in excess of their economic viability. Demolition and renovation often take place far too soon, so that the building cycle becomes an unnecessarily large contributor to the production of waste. The need for 'dematerialization' in order to prevent the exhaustion of natural resources (such as fossil fuels, metals and the non-renewable building materials), and the need to use materials with a low environmental impact, consequently continue to grow. A renewable material like cardboard may offer a solution. Cardboard, which is composed of wood fibre-based and recyclable paper, has a relatively short lifespan as a building material. The material is highly suitable for reuse, while building systems based on cardboard are also easy to adapt to the widely varying and often temporary needs of clients. Famous examples of building projects that take advantage of these qualities are to be found in Japan, where exorbitant land prices mean that buildings in the major cities are often demolished within ten years in order to make way for a new use of the space. But examples of the use of

Project XX Office, Delft (1998)
Architect J.M. Post, XX Architects
Photographer Herman van Doorn

Project Moss and sedum roof, De Hoep, Castricum (2003)
Architect Min2 bouw-kunst
Photographer Min2 bouw-kunst

less durable but renewable materials in semi-permanent building construction can be found in other countries, too. In the Netherlands, for example, the estimated useful life of the offices of XX Architects in Delft determined the choice of materials (which included cardboard).

Living Materials

Of quite a different order are the renewable materials included here among the woody products, which fall into the category of living and green products of nature such as grass, sedum and other types of vegetation. These products, whose biological origins are in a way similar to those of wood, are used in building construction while they are still growing. A higher form of renewability is hardly conceivable. Although primarily employed on flat or sloping roofs, new techniques have now made it possible to use them on vertical surfaces. The main reasons for using living flora as cladding are its potential as camouflage and its image as an environmentally friendly material. During plant growth, carbon dioxide is absorbed from the atmosphere, thereby contributing to the reduction of greenhouse gases. Thus, a green roof can compensate both physically and visually for a grassy meadow that has disappeared to make way for building construction. Since it is well nigh impossible to assign structural or transmission values to green claddings, they should not be seen as a substitute for other building materials. On the other hand, their camouflaging potential may be of great importance to the quality of the experience of the built environment. For observers looking down on it, a green roof can be seen as a continuation of the landscape. Moreover, an accessible and trafficable green roof may, thanks to the dual use of land, make an economic contribution to the project. In heavily built-up areas or places where brick and mortar would be totally out of place, green façades can provide 'air', or avoid an undesirable disturbance of the visual landscape.

Future

Given the ever-growing interest in renewable materials and the need to employ them as a replacement for materials that involve the use of non-renewable resources, the development of countless new products can be expected in the future. Not only the production of the raw materials themselves, but also the production of building materials that incorporate renewable raw materials, are still in their infancy. Management and control of the production fields and forests play a large role in the drawing up of (worldwide) quality criteria. In many cases, further research will be needed to provide workable measurement results that will make it possible to assign structural and transmission values to these materials.

Bamboo

Bambus | Bambou | Bambú | Bambù | Bamboe

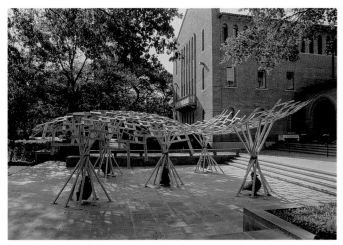

Project Bamboo grid shell, Rice University Art Gallery, Houston (2002)
Architect Shigeru Ban
Photographer Grant Suzuki

Project Bamboo staircase, Pearce, London (2001)
Designer Plyboo®
Photographer Plyboo®

Bamboo is a building material that has many traditional applications in Asia, Africa and Central and South America. There are more than 500 species of this tree-like member of the grass family. A principal characteristic of the fast-growing bamboo plant is its woody stem which, unlike wood, is hollow with joints at regular distances. A new shoot of the Giant Bamboo is full-grown in five to ten years and is as big as a tree, with strength properties comparable to those of a 300-year-old oak. This makes bamboo an interesting renewable material and, with careful plantation management, an inexhaustible source of high-grade building materials. The larger species are particularly suitable for the production of industrial bamboo.

Technical Aspects

Well-prepared bamboo has a long lifespan, judging from a 3000-year-old cane bridge in China. In terms of weight, the tensile strength of industrial bamboo fibres ranks with that of steel. Bamboo is moreover hard (harder than oak) and flexible, making it suitable as a building material in areas prone to earthquakes. It also has a great natural resistance to fire. Untreated bamboo turns grey when exposed to the elements.

In the last ten years, new processing techniques and knowledge of modern adhesives have enormously increased bamboo's range of constructional applications. Strips sawn from the hollow stem are pared and planed to the right thickness. They are then placed, either immediately or after treatment, in a drying kiln where the white colour changes to a shade of caramel, after which they are pressure glued into planks or sheets in which the distinctive bamboo joints are still visible. Thicker panels for furniture are made by bonding together several sheets laid crosswise to one another.

Applications

Bamboo is used both indoors and outdoors. Externally, the untreated bamboo stems can do duty as bearing or semi-bearing structural elements or as decoration. Overlapping halves can be used for roof coverings. Bamboo shingles make a decorative cladding for both roofs and walls. Composite and glued bamboo products are applied exclusively in the interior in floors and panels. A clear varnish or wax is the finish usually prescribed for bamboo products. Since the improvement in quality afforded by current protective methods still leaves a lot to be desired, composite and glued bamboo products are unsuitable for permanent outdoor applications.

Colour	**yellowish brown or caramel**
Glossiness	glossy, satin, **matt**
Translucence (%)	**0** – 20 – 40 – 60 – 80 – 100
Texture	sharp, **medium**, dull
Hardness	**hard**, soft, depressible
Temperature	warm, **medium**, cool
Odour	strong, **moderate**, none
Acoustic opacity	good, **moderate**, poor

Sedum, Green Façades and Green Roofs

Sedum, Grünfassaden und Gründächer | Sedum, façades et toitures vertes | Fachadas y tejados ecológicos con capa vegetal (de sedum) | Sedum, facciate e tetti verdi | Sedum en grasdaken en -gevels

Project Groundscraper, Istanbul (1997)
Architect GAD Architecture
Photographer GAD Architecture

Project Dutch Pavilion, IGA Rostock (2003)
Architect Atelier Kempe Thill
Photographer Ulrich Schwarz

Cladding flat and sloping roofs and façades with living vegetation adds aesthetic qualities but also contributes to an ecologically enhanced environment. The growth can consist of succulents (sedums or stonecrops), herbs, moss, grass or some combination of these. Bushes and trees can also be used on garden roofs. The choice of the type of 'green' roof often depends on the bearing capacity of the roof structure. The weight to be carried is in turn determined by the required thickness of the substrate. Three centimetres is sufficient in the case of sedum and herb roofs. For grass roofs the substrate should be at least 8 cm thick for a flat roof and 15 cm for a slope. The required thickness for so-called garden roofs depends on what is to be planted. The substrate for steeply raked green roofs or vertical green façades has to meet special requirements. A new development is to contain the substrate in baskets that are either self-supporting or attached to a stable rear wall. For vertical surfaces planters are also used; depending on the type of plants, they may be arranged in several rows one above in order to ensure complete coverage of the surface.

Technical Aspects

A planted surface always retains moisture resulting in poor drying. For this reason, a 'warm roof' construction is recommended in which the insulation is applied on the exterior of the roof structure for a more favourable vapour pressure. The thermally insulating properties of substrates and vegetation are limited. On the other hand, a green roof can achieve a considerable degree of sound insulation. It is advisable to have a double-layer, fully adhesive roof covering system on a thick underlay. Every planted surface must include a drainage layer. The upkeep of 'green' buildings requires special attention and techniques.

Applications

Besides the great visual appeal, cladding buildings with living flora can also have an ecological impact. 'Green' buildings can become part of the surroundings by hiding the brickwork structure underneath. Flat green roofs camouflage the building when seen from nearby taller buildings; green sloping roofs and façades camouflage it at ground level.

Colour	**green**
Glossiness	glossy, satin, **matt**
Translucence (%)	**0** – **20** – **40** – 60 – 80 – 100
Texture	**sharp**, medium, dull
Hardness	hard, soft, **depressible**
Temperature	warm, **medium**, cool
Odour	**strong**, **moderate**, none
Acoustic opacity	good, **moderate**, poor

Cardboard

Karton | Carton | Cartón | Cartone | Karton

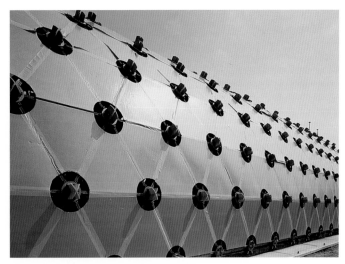

Project Temporary theatre, Apeldoorn (1992)
Architect Hans Ruijssenaars, de Architectengroep
Photographer Jan Derwig

Project Japanese Pavilion, Hanover Expo (2000)
Architect Shigeru Ban
Photographer Hiroyuki Hirai

Cardboard can be classified as a woody product as it is made from recycled or pristine paper pulp usually with a softwood basis. Cardboard can be solid or built up of several layers as in corrugated cardboard. Gluing several layers of cardboard together creates a strong multi-purpose material. Broadly speaking, cardboard appears in two forms: wound or in flat sheets. It comes in bendable and non-bendable forms and can be applied in partition walls as a solid sheet or as a composite board with a core of cardboard honeycomb or some such lightweight material. Cardboard is best known and most used as a cheap lightweight packaging material that can be infinitely recycled. By impregnating it and/or giving it a damp- and fireproof finish it can be used in internal and external building construction. The preservation costs are quite steep in comparison with the price of the material itself, which is why cardboard is mainly used for makeshift structures like pavilions and temporary housing.

Technical Aspects

In the construction world cardboard is a relative newcomer whose physical properties have scarcely been specified as yet. Although it has been used as a loadbearing material in a number of projects, cardboard as a building material is still in an experimental stage. Meanwhile the cardboard industry has latched on to its new potential applications and developed variants compatible with the designs architects are making today. One example is double-curved corrugated cardboard sheets.

Applications

Famous applications of cardboard in architecture can be found in the work of the Japanese architect Shigeru Ban. His designs include a building for Expo 2000 in Hanover and temporary accommodation for people who had lost their homes in the Kobe earthquake of 1995. The main supporting structure consists of cardboard tubes wrapped in plastic foil. Other designers have followed Shigeru Ban in his endeavour with projects that incorporate sheets or laminae of cardboard as façade cladding and roofing panels. In the interior, cardboard is used for furniture and lightweight partitions.

Colour	**yellowish brown**
Glossiness	glossy, satin, **matt**
Translucence (%)	**0** – 20 – 40 – 60 – 80 – 100
Texture	sharp, medium, **dull**
Hardness	hard, **soft**, depressible
Temperature	warm, **medium**, cool
Odour	strong, **moderate**, none
Acoustic opacity	good, **moderate**, poor

Coconut Fibre

Kokosfaser | Fibre de noix de coco | Fibra de coco | Fibra di cocco | Kokos

Project ZaZa Restaurant, Amsterdam (2003)
Designer Plyboo®
Photographer Jeroen van Amelsvoort

Project Private house, Amsterdam (2003)
Designer Plyboo ®
Photographer Plyboo ®

Coconut fibre or coir comes from the hard husk of the fruit of the coconut palm, a tree found throughout the tropics. The tough, light to dark brown fibres are 10 to 20 cm long. A relatively hardy material, coconut fibre can be used in places where other plant fibres would be more prone to decay. Ground coconut shell can be compressed into sheet material with excellent strength properties. No chemical additives are required since the shell's high level of lignin acts as a natural adhesive.

Technical Aspects

The good soundproofing capacity of coconut fibre sheets makes the product particularly suitable for damping low-frequency vibrations. Coconut fibres are impervious to electrostatic charge and not susceptible to fungal or insect attack. Coconut fibre products can be made extra fire-retardant by impregnation, for instance with one of the borates. Coir mats are shock-absorbent and let the air through. Hot-pressed sheets of ground coconut shell are exceedingly stiff and strong and have a relatively high density comparable to those made from phenol-bonded high pressure laminates. The sheets are resistant to moisture and attack by insects and micro-organisms.

Applications

For industrial applications, coconut fibre is manufactured into elastic fibre mats and sheets using a bonding agent such as latex. Traditionally, coconut fibres have been mainly used in mats and floor coverings, but these days they are also often used as geotextiles in civil engineering works (e.g. on sites with a high noise level), and as a substrate in horticulture for fusing the aerial roots of certain plants and grasses. Processed into mats, the fibres, held in stable frames if necessary, form a bed for 'green' screens, façades and roofs. Coconut matting can be used out of doors for dispersing rainwater, stabilizing the soil and regulating the soil temperature. Moreover, the structure of the underlying soil is improved and enriched by this biodegradable fungus-free product. High-density coir boards, with or without a coating, can be deployed as a wood substitute for cladding panels or, in smaller units, as roof shingles.

Colour	**light to dark-brown**
Glossiness	glossy, satin, **matt**
Translucence (%)	**0** – 20 – 40 – 60 – 80 – 100
Texture	sharp, medium, **dull**
Hardness	hard, **soft**, depressible
Temperature	warm, **medium**, cool
Odour	**strong**, moderate, none
Acoustic opacity	**good**, moderate, poor

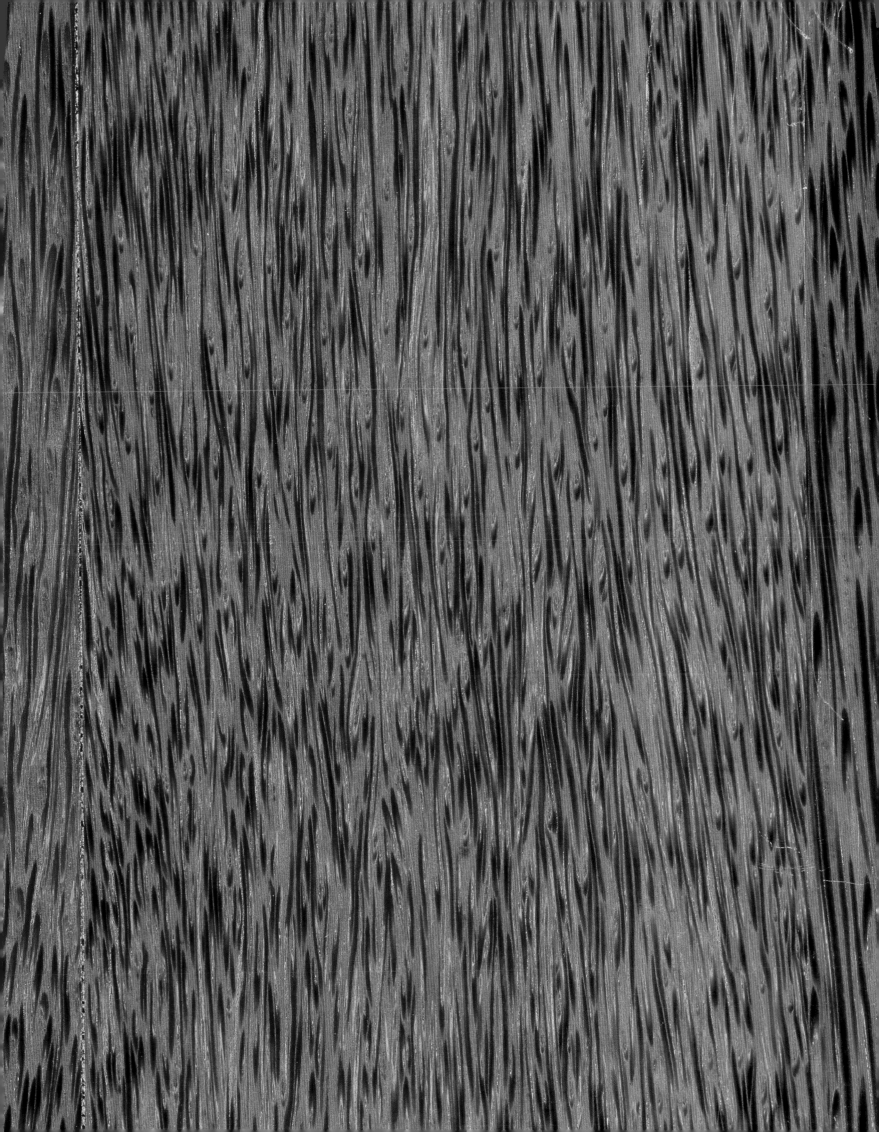

Cork

Kork | Liège | Corcho | Sughero | Kurk

Project Portuguese Pavilion, Hanover Expo (2000)
Architect Alvaro Siza
Photographer Herman van Doorn

Cork is obtained from the bark of the cork oak. There are 2.2 million hectares of cork groves worldwide, half of which are in Portugal. The cork oak can live for 200 years and is stripped of its bark every six to ten years. Seventy per cent of the cork is granulated for use in a whole range of products. The first harvest of virgin bark is mainly used for making bottle-stoppers. Granulated cork is steam-expanded in an autoclave into large blocks from which sheets of various thicknesses are then sawn. The resin present in cork, known as suberine, acts as a natural adhesive in this process. Expanded cork can be cut into more decorative shapes.

Technical Aspects

The bark of the cork oak protects it against heat, dessication and insects. Cork is elastic and has low thermal conductivity. The sheet material needs no added chemicals such as glue or fire retardants, being naturally fire resistant and water repellent. It is also resistant to biodegradation. Its low compressibility means that it can be walked on.

Applications

The special properties of expanded cork makes it eminently suitable for both thermal insulation and soundproofing in the construction industry. When used as flooring, it is protected against wear with a coating of varnish and is obtainable in a wide range of colour designs. Expanded cork can also be used for cladding panels. A celebrated example is the Portuguese Pavilion at Expo 2000 in Hanover, a design by Alvaro Siza in which the façade was clad with 10 cm thick cork panels laid in a half-brick bond.

Colour	**brown**
Glossiness	glossy, satin, **matt**
Translucence (%)	**0** – 20 – 40 – 60 – 80 – 100
Texture	sharp, **medium**, dull
Hardness	hard, soft, **depressible**
Temperature	**warm**, medium, cool
Odour	strong, **moderate**, none
Acoustic opacity	**good**, moderate, poor

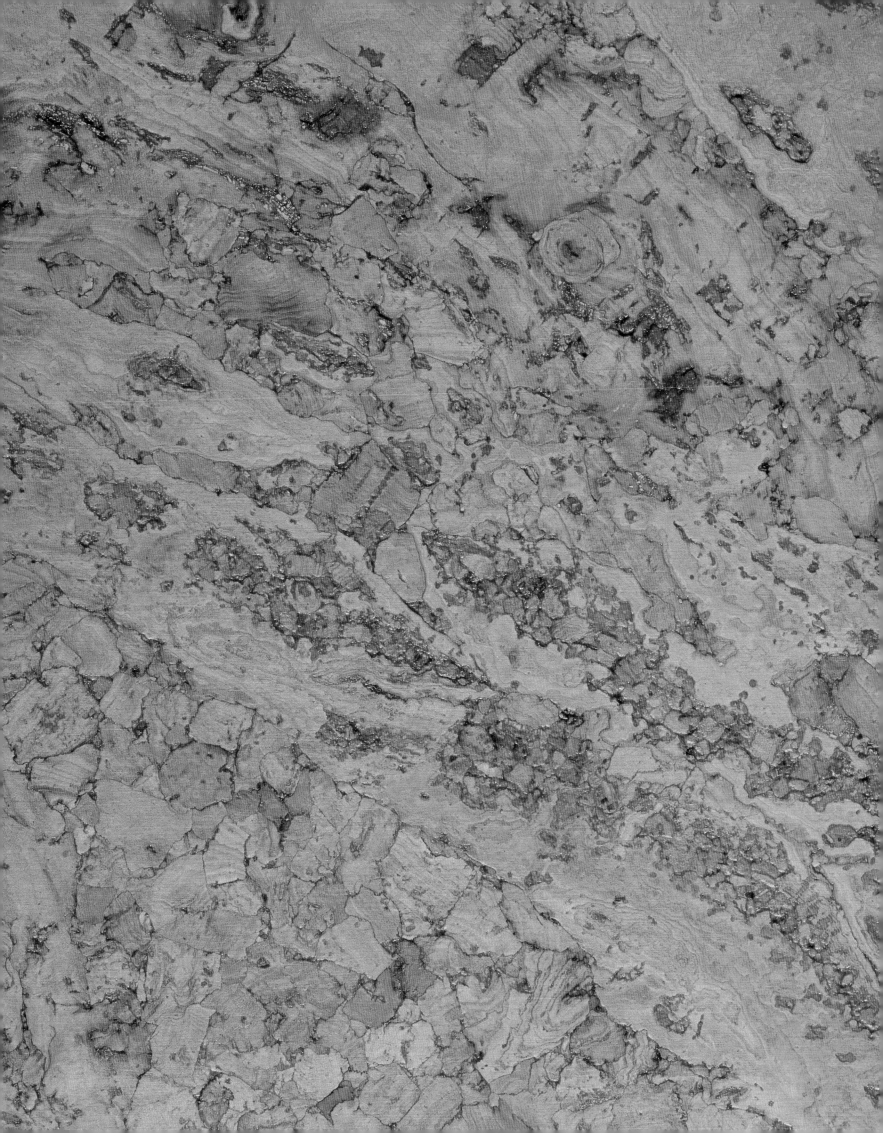

Paper

Papier | Papier | Papel | Carta | Papier

Project Japanese Pavilion, Hanover Expo (2000)
Architect Shigeru Ban
Photographer Hiroyuki Hirai

Paper is the product of a pulping process involving cellulose-rich plants. The most common raw material is softwood, although other fibrous plants such as papyrus, hemp and flax are also suitable. The cellulose fibres are extracted from plant materials by removing lignin and other vegetable components. Paper is made by draining the fibre pulp on a screen. As the pulp dries the fibres mesh together firmly into an unbroken layer which loses its cohesion again on becoming damp. This means that paper can be recycled several times.

Technical Aspects

A wide diversity of paper products can be obtained with different strength properties, moisture resistance, surface structure, gloss, colour and so forth, depending on the type of fibrous material, the production process and the additives used. Paper is naturally water-absorbent and combustible, so appropriate measures need to be taken when using it in building construction.

Applications

Because paper responds well to pressure, it is a cheap and quick means of decorating internal walls. In wood fibre composites such as medium and high density fibreboard (MDF and HDF), oriented strand board (OSB), chipboard and plywood, the finishes are usually laminated with a melamine-impregnated layer of paper as decoration. Making paper damp-proof allows it to be used in more water-based applications. Milk and fruit juice cartons immediately come to mind. A world-famous example of its architectural application is in the roof of the Japanese Pavilion at Expo 2000 in Hanover. Architect Shigeru Ban used impregnated paper as a wind- and rainproof cladding for the structure of cardboard tubes. These days recycled paper is also used as thermal and acoustic insulation in cavity or partition walls, and as a seamless, sprayable finishing layer on internal walls.

Colour	**variable**
Glossiness	glossy, satin, **matt**
Translucence (%)	**0 – 20 – 40** – 60 – 80 – 100
Texture	sharp, medium, **dull**
Hardness	hard, soft, **depressible**
Temperature	warm, **medium**, cool
Odour	strong, **moderate**, none
Acoustic opacity	good, moderate, **poor**

Reed and Cane

Schilf- und Zuckerrohr | Roseaux et Canne | Junco y caña | Giunchi e canne | Riet

Project Private house, Gorssel (2003)
Architect Maas Architects
Photographer Joost Kreuger, Riet ABC bv

Project Info centre, Almere (2001)
Architect de Architectengroep
Photographer Kees Hummel

Reed is a perennial grass type found in water or on boggy ground along the edge of marshes, lakes, streams, et cetera. Depending on the type of site, it can attain a height of four metres. Reed often grows across large surfaces or in shallow floating mats. Bundled reed is suitable for thatching roofs. This thatching reed has a yellowish, fresh colour and strong, thick-walled stems with a white base.

Technical Aspects

Thatching reed has to be tough as well as hard; the straight sections of 1.6 to 2 metres are used. Reed is cut in the winter after the first frost, so that the leaves can be easily removed. Though fine and slender reed has greater visual appeal, the coarser variety is more durable. A diameter of 5 to 8 mm 'breathes' better and is less likely to close up so that it lasts longer. Reed has a lifespan of at least 25 years, but 40 years or longer is not exceptional. After the reed has been bundled, the thatchers lay it on the roof in parallel rows. Reed weighs around 130 kg/m³ when highly packed. A square metre of thatched roof 30 cm thick weights 40 kg. Reed used as vertical cladding is only moderately insulating. Means used to prevent thatch fires include chemical fire retardants and clay fireproof granules.

Applications

Thatching reed is used on both the roof and sides of houses, usually out of aesthetic considerations. A reed cladding requires constant maintenance. In a so-called open structure, the bundled reed is attached to battens with wire. These days, in the interests of both construction and comfort, thatched roofs usually have a continuous underlay of plywood, oriented strand board or some other sheet material with the bundles of reed fixed to it with screws.

Colour	**yellowish green-brown**
Glossiness	glossy, satin, **matt**
Translucence (%)	**0** – **20** – 40 – 60 – 80 – 100
Texture	**sharp**, medium, dull
Hardness	hard, soft, **depressible**
Temperature	**warm**, medium, cool
Odour	strong, **moderate**, none
Acoustic opacity	good, **moderate**, poor

Willow Rods

Weidenruten | Osier | Varas de arce | Vimini | Wilgentenen

Project Garden Au Prieur Notre Dame d'Oran (1995)
Architect Sonia Lesot | Patrice Taravella
Photographer Jan Derwig

Project Willow art in 'Bol van Utrecht', Utrecht (1996)
Architect Manette Zeelenberg
Photographer Manette Zeelenberg, www.haik.nl

Willow rods are the wiry shoots of small willow trees or osiers and measure from one to two metres. A bed of these shoots gives the best yield after five years and continues to produce for a further twenty years or so. The 8-9 mm thick rods are cut during the winter months (November to March) after the willows have shed their leaves, and can be put to use immediately. If the rods have dried out, they will require several hours of soaking to regain their flexibility. The rods, which are available in different thicknesses, are sold in bundles usually for wickerwork and basketry.

Technical Aspects

Willow rods are tough and flexible. Not all are suitable for basketry and wickerwork, notably those with side shoots of their own. Willow contains salicylic acid which acts as an analgesic (aspirin is a derivative of salicylic acid).

Applications

Willow rods are often used for fences, for repairing or protecting river banks, for controlling humid environments and for improving the bearing capacity of soft soil. Wickerwork screens are effective as acoustic baffles along motorways. A familiar use of willow rods in rural building construction is as a lattice support for traditional lime plaster walls and as a bearing framework in half-timbered façades, a function it shares with straw bales. These days willow is a visible decorative element in façades and elsewhere. The bark of willow shoots was once used for tanning hides. It is less well-known that willow is used as a biomass crop for renewable fuel.

Colour	**brown**
Glossiness	glossy, satin, **matt**
Translucence (%)	**0 – 20** – 40 – 60 – 80 – 100
Texture	**sharp**, medium, dull
Hardness	hard, soft, **depressible**
Temperature	**warm**, medium, cool
Odour	strong, **moderate**, none
Acoustic opacity	good, **moderate**, poor

Composites

Holzverbundwerkstoffe | Composites de bois | Amalgamas de madera |
Compositi del legno | Samenstellingen van hout

History

Because wood is relatively easy to work and generally responds well
to adhesives, this natural product is suitable for the fabrication of
many by-products that involve bonding wood to wood or to other
types of materials. This can result in either finished or semi-finished
products, the latter being called composite materials here. The excellent bonding properties of wood have long been known. The ancient
Chinese and Egyptians were already using glues based on natural
materials, such as animal bones or vegetable starch, to join wood
and to produce composites. Plywood, in which layers of veneers are
glued together with the direction of the grain alternating, has been
around for over two thousand years. In the last two centuries, during
the industrial revolution, but also as the result of the Second World
War, enormous technical developments took place not only in fabrication techniques but also in the development of adhesives based on
plastics, whereby the range of available composite materials has
expanded enormously. The same period also saw an explosive development in the production of plastics. These 'new' materials, in combination with wood and woody products, have led to still more products with characteristics that affect not only appearance but also
technical properties, such as durability. Many composites owe their
existence to the reuse or exhaustive use of existing wood products:
offcuts and recycled wood often make up the major part of such
products. Conversely, other composites are produced from carefully
selected or even specially produced wood elements.

Variants

Products in which wood in some or other form is combined with
another type of material to produce a composite are extremely varied. They can be categorized according to the ratio of wood to non-
wood components, which is not to say that products in which wood
is the predominant component necessarily look like wood products.
For example, laminated chipboard does not resemble wood at all,
whereas other products in which the percentage of wood is minimal,
such as plastic sheet material topped with a thin wood veneer, have
the appearance of solid wood. These are all examples of products
with a layered structure. Composites may also have other structures,
such as those in which the component materials are individually visible in the surface.

Also included under wood composites are those products consisting
exclusively of wood elements bonded together by means of glues or
adhesives. Here, too, there are a great many variants which are categorized according to the size of the component wood elements.
They include products such as linoleum, which is composed mainly of
wood fibres ground into wood meal, where the original form of the
wood is no longer recognizable. On the other hand, there are composites in which the major components are planks or strips of wood.
They turn up in products where the required size is simply not
obtainable with the chosen type of wood. Laminated beams and
trusses and laminated wood for window and door frames are familiar
examples of this type of composite. A relative newcomer is engineered timber, a composite built up of planks glued together to form
a solid, thick slab of wood from which entire, self-supporting wall
and roof structures can be built.

Project Housing Group, Almere (2001)
Architect UN Studio
Photographer Christian Richters

In between the extremely small wood meal particles and the big planks of laminated timber is a range of wood components varying in size from wood fibre and wood wool to woodchips and shavings. Fibreboard, such as MDF (Medium Density Fibreboard), particle board and wood wool slabs, as well as OSB (Oriented Strand Board), are examples of this kind of composite. These products, which are pressed into sheet form with the help of binders, often form the base or support for yet other composite materials. A distinction is drawn between platen pressing and extrusion pressing. In platen pressing the fibres or chips are generally randomly oriented. The mixture of wood chip and resin is rolled out into mats and subjected to a pressure of 2 to 3 N/mm² and a temperature of 120 to 200 °C between the plates of a platen press. Extrusion pressing is a continuous process in which a rammer presses the emulsion through the heated steel die into a continuous flat sheet. By changing the shape of the die, other forms can be made. Because the fibres or chips are mainly at right angles to the board face, these products are generally weaker than the products of platen pressing. The binding agent is usually urea formaldehyde (UF) or, for moisture-resistant products, phenol formaldehyde (PF) or a mix-condensate of melamine, urea and formaldehyde (MUF).

Plywoods are a special type of composite, in that the component parts are layers of veneer glued crosswise to one another to form stiff boards.

Properties

The properties of the various composite products in which wood plays a major role are very diverse and are determined chiefly by the dimensions of the wood elements involved, the binders used and the ratio of wood to other components. Generally speaking, when the wood elements are small, the quality of the binder or of the other constituents is decisive. For example, it is thanks to the binder and high-pressure bonding techniques that the small wood fibres in MDF produce relatively strong sheet material. On the other hand, it is the very fine wood meal in linoleum that gives this composite its excellent thermal insulating properties. Veneers are always used as part of a composite – sometimes invisibly, as the middle layer in three-ply, in which case the technical qualities of the type of wood used matter most, sometimes visibly, as a face veneer on multiply or some other base, in which case the visual qualities carry most weight. The durability of the composite depends on a variety of factors. If the composite consists exclusively of wooden planks glued together, then the durability of the product is determined by the durability of the type of wood used. If the composite is primarily determined by materials other than wood, or by the binder, then the type of wood is of little or no importance.

Applications

The durability of wood-based composites – for the most part produced in sheet form – usually determines whether the product is employed indoors or outdoors. The great advantage of flat sheet composites is not only that they are generally easy to work with, but also that large areas can be clad with a single sheet. Further finishing, usually in the form of a coat of paint, depends on the quality of the exposed top layer. In addition, other mechanical surface treatments, such as perforation or mouldings, can enhance the appearance of composite sheeting. When treated with a protective opaque or transparent coating, non-durable composites can also be used for outdoor applications. This applies particularly to plywoods, but also to products in which only the top layer consists of veneer. Composites made exclusively of wood planks or strips can be used in accordance with the properties of the type of wood used. The relatively large dimensions obtainable in such products extend their application possibilities.

Project German Pavilion, Hanover Expo (2000)
Architect Florian Nagler
Photographer Bruynzeel

Linoleum

Linoleum | Linoléum | Linóleo | Linoleum | Linoleum

Project Harlekino forte flooring (2003)
Architect Alessandro Mendini
Photographer Forbo Flooring

Project Proust sotto flooring (2003)
Architect Alessandro Mendini
Photographer Forbo Flooring

Linoleum is a smooth floor covering consisting of oxidized linseed oil and rosins mixed with fillers such as wood meal, limestone and pigments, the whole hot-pressed (calendered) onto a jute fabric or polyester glass fibre backing. The linoleum is coloured by adding different pigments. For patterned (marbled) linoleum, different coloured linoleum granulates are mixed together homogeneously.

Cork linoleum is a variation that uses cork granules instead of wood meal. This creates a linoleum with a comfortable feel and pleasantly warm underfoot. Another variation is corkment which also uses cork granules but with no added pigments. This material is used as an underlay for floor coverings with the aim of increasing foot warmth and comfort. As a rule, linoleum is applied in sheets but it is also obtainable as tiles.

Technical Aspects

Linoleum has both thermally and acoustically insulating properties. The material is elastic, antistatic and has a smooth surface. Linoleum is glued to a smooth surface without a seal between adjoining sheets or tiles. In a moist environment the seams can be milled (c. 3 mm) and then sealed with a welding wire.

Applications

Linoleum is generally used indoors as a flooring finish. Bulletin Board is a variation that can applied as a wall finish or for notice boards. When used as a ceiling finish, the linoleum is affixed to the panels before these are put in place. Another variation is so-called furniture linoleum. Here the jute backing is replaced with a layer of paper, making the material suitable for furniture surfaces. There are no known outdoor applications.

Colour	**variable**
Glossiness	glossy, satin, **matt**
Translucence (%)	**0** – 20 – 40 – 60 – 80 – 100
Texture	sharp, **medium**, dull
Hardness	hard, soft, **depressible**
Temperature	**warm**, medium, cool
Odour	strong, **moderate**, none
Acoustic opacity	good, **moderate**, poor

Cement-bonded Particle Board

Zementgebundene Platten | Panneau de Particule liant ciment | Tablero de cemento aglomerado de virutas de madera mineralizadas |
Pannello di particelle legate con cemento | Cementgebonden houtspaanplaten

Project Fokke & Wubbolts Communications, Amsterdam (2000)
Architect Machiel Spaan, M3H Architects
Photographer Kees Hummel

Wood particle and fibre boards can be divided into resin-bonded and mineral-bonded boards. The first group, which includes chipboard and medium density fibreboard (MDF), uses colourless synthetic resins so that the colour of the wood shows through. Mineral-bonded boards generally adopt the colour of the binding agent used, for instance cement, gypsum or anhydrite. Cement-bonded particle boards are made by compressing wood particles and a cement binder at a high pressure and temperature into homogeneous panels. Recently, the characteristically grey board has become available in colours that are uniform throughout. These black, yellow or red varieties are only obtainable in a sanded model where the wood fibres are visible in the surface.

Technical Aspects

Cement-bonded particle board has a high fire resistance and, owing to its great weight, a high airborne sound insulation value and a high resistance to mechanical loads.

Applications

The material can be used as external cladding or as sheathing in timber frame construction. For a natural look, it can also be applied in a wholly untreated form. Untreated boards are not always of equal thickness and may require sealing with a joint compound whose thickness depends on the temperature and relative humidity of the space. If these are constant, the boards can be mounted with a tongued and grooved joint or pressed together unmediated. If the board is chosen solely because of its technical properties, it can be finished in water-based acrylic emulsion or mineral paint. Plastering and tiling are other possible finishes for seamlessly mounted boards.

Colour	**grey or variable**
Glossiness	glossy, satin, **matt**
Translucence (%)	**0** – 20 – 40 – 60 – 80 – 100
Texture	sharp, medium, **dull**
Hardness	**hard**, soft, depressible
Temperature	warm, **medium**, cool
Odour	strong, **moderate**, none
Acoustic opacity	good, moderate, **poor**

Woodwool Slabs

Holzfaserplatten | Panneaux légers en laine de bois agglomérée | Losetas de viruta fina | Pannelli in lana di legno | Houtwol platen

Project Rooswijk, Zaanstad (1995)
Architect Min2 bouw-kunst
Photographer Ger van der Vlugt

Woodwool slabs are made by compressing long strands of wood fibres derived mainly from preserved softwoods (although broad-leaved trees such as poplar and lime are also used) mixed with a bonding agent, generally cement or caustic calcined magnesite. Woodwool slabs were first developed in the early years of the 20th century. Most are made in Europe and America. The traditional, smooth and homogeneous woodwool slabs have now been joined by many variants, most notably the following. Reinforced slabs are strengthened with laths of hardwood or preserved wood. Composition slabs may include a layer of insulating material such as mineral wool, polystyrene or phenol formaldehyde foam. Woodwool slabs are also available with a decorative finish, colour-sprayed or with a moulded edging. Slabs used for constructional purposes have a higher compression and thus a greater density.

Technical Aspects

Woodwool slabs are obtainable in varying thicknesses and dimensions. The thickness and structure determine the bending strength and compressibility. Cladding structures with woodwool slabs can increase their fire resistance. A key property of woodwool slabs is their soundproofing and sound-absorbing capacity owing to their open structure. They can also be successfully applied in sprung soundproofing floors.

Applications

Woodwool slabs are often used as fire-retarding, soundproofing or thermally insulating cladding on walls and ceilings. In their sound-absorbing capacity they can also be used freestanding or free-hanging in which case they are left unpainted so that they retain their open structure. The slabs are fixed to the underlay with staples, rivets, glue or special cramps, depending on the application. When applied in external walls as thermal insulation, the slabs often have a mineral plaster finish.

Colour	**yellowish brown or variable**
Glossiness	glossy, satin, **matt**
Translucence (%)	**0** – 20 – 40 – 60 – 80 – 100
Texture	**sharp**, medium, dull
Hardness	hard, **soft**, depressible
Temperature	**warm**, medium, cool
Odour	strong, **moderate**, none
Acoustic opacity	**good**, moderate, poor

Laminates

Schichtstoffplatten | Bois strié | Laminados | Laminati | Laminaten

Project Heidecke building, Altenweddingen (1997)
Architect Heidecke bv
Photographer Bruynzeel

Project Gewild Wonen building expo, Almere (2001)
Architect Min2 bouw-kunst
Photographer Sjaak Henselmans

Laminated timber can assume a number of forms. The term laminate refers to products in which several layers of material are glued together. A sheet laminate composed entirely of wood is described under 'Plywood'. Laminates of planks or battens result in thicker but narrower products which are used in relatively small dimensions for window and door frames and in larger dimensions for massive beams capable of achieving extremely large spans.

Laminates that include layers of other materials besides wood have opened the way to new and often durable applications. Variants include sheet laminates in which only the top layer is of wood (veneer) while the underlying layers are of one or another synthetic material, for instance reconstituted polycarbonate or sheets of melamine paper.

The inverse version, where the core is of wood or a wood composite (such as chipboard or MDF) and the top layer is a sheet of paper saturated in a synthetic resin, also constitutes a laminate. Known as melamine sheet, the appearance of this much less durable variety depends on the decorative paper used.

Technical Aspects

The technical properties of laminated sheet material vary tremendously. The laminate thickness, the quality of both the core and the glue are the key determining factors. As the top layer usually has a synthetic resin finish, the surface is able to withstand moisture. The stiffness and durability of the whole is largely determined by the quality of the core. An extremely durable version has a core of compressed layers of paper saturated in synthetic resin and a top layer of veneer with a resin finish. Such boards are suitable for external use in façades.

Woods that occur only in small, defect-free dimensions can be laminated together to produce larger elements. Large to extremely large timber spans can be achieved using glued laminated beams (also known as 'glulam').

Applications

Depending on the durability of the core, sheet laminates are used to cover large surface areas without joints. The so-called melamine sheets are only applied internally. Variants with cores of resin impregnated paper are used for visible façade woodwork and are selected on the basis of the face veneers. There are as yet no known external applications for laminates with a polycarbonate core.

Colour	**woody**
Glossiness	glossy, satin, **matt**
Translucence (%)	**0** – 20 – 40 – 60 – 80 – 100
Texture	sharp, **medium**, dull
Hardness	hard, **soft**, depressible
Temperature	**warm**, medium, cool
Odour	strong, **moderate**, none
Acoustic opacity	good, **moderate**, poor

Plywood

Sperrholz | Contreplaqué | Contrachapado | Compensato | Triplex

Project Zen Patio, High School Utrecht (1995)
Architect Mecanoo
Photographer Bruynzeel

Plywood is probably the best-known and commonest form of laminated wood. It consists of several layers or 'plies' of veneer (usually an odd number) bonded together with the grain of adjoining plies at right angles to each other. The commonest form is three-ply with a balanced construction of three layers. This strong sheet material was made back in ancient Egypt but large-scale production did not get under way until the beginning of the 20th century. Initially, plywood was made from alder and birch, but improved production techniques made possible the use softwoods and tropical woods, which also allowed it to be made in much larger sheets. As a rule, individual plywoods take their name from the wood type used for the face veneer.

Technical Aspects

The technical properties of a material made up entirely of wood veneers vary widely. The critical factors are the laminate thickness, the wood types used and the quality of the adhesive. Another essential aspect is the amount of defect-free wood involved. Plywood is strong in both directions owing to the layers being stacked at right angles.

Applications

Thanks to its dimensions, strength and good workability, plywood enjoys a very wide range of applications. Besides being used for constructional purposes, plywood is also suitable for covering large surfaces – both indoors and out – in a single span, with the top layer usually being painted or given a transparent stain. When left in view, plywood is selected according to the face veneer. The cross-cut edges need careful finishing to prevent the plies from delaminating in a moist environment. Given a finishing coat of transparent synthetic resin, plywood can stand up to the dampest conditions, although it remains susceptible to mechanical damage.

Project Camperdown House, Australia (1994)
Architect Lahz Nimmo Architects
Photographer Brett Boardman Photography

Colour	**woody**
Glossiness	glossy, satin, **matt**
Translucence (%)	**0** – 20 – 40 – 60 – 80 – 100
Texture	sharp, **medium**, dull
Hardness	hard, **soft**, depressible
Temperature	**warm**, medium, cool
Odour	strong, **moderate**, none
Acoustic opacity	good, **moderate**, poor

Bruynzeel Garant ® Regina Mahogany transparant laquered plywood façade panels. Quality guaranteed by Bruynzeel Multipanel Int, Zaandam, Netherlands

Timber Composites

Holzverbundwerkstoffe | Composites de Bois | Aglomerados de maderas | Compositi di legname | Geprefabriceerde houtproducten

Project Parasite, Las Palmas, Rotterdam (2001)
Architect Korteknie Stuhlmacher Architects
Photographer Anne Bousema

Project No19, mobile studio, Leidsche Rijn, Utrecht (2003)
Architect Korteknie Stuhlmacher Architects i.c.w. BikvanderPol
Photographer Christian Kahl

These products include beams assembled from stacked and bonded battens and planks. This technique enables relatively small sections of defect-free wood, generally from softwoods, to be combined into larger units for window and door frames, for example. It is also used for assembling large joists, columns and trusses for use in large-scale timber structures.

A relatively new product consists of thick, solid bonded softwood panels which are produced industrially as wall, floor or roof elements. These are usually composed of three to thirteen layers of laminated pine bonded with the direction of the grain at right angles using melamine formaldehyde or resorcinol formaldehyde. A forerunner of these all-solid boards was a version with gaps between the timber core strips. As its fire-retardant qualities left much to be desired and the core gaps made an ideal home for mice, the centre-to-centre distance was reduced at little extra cost into a solid core.

Technical Aspects
Timber composites can attain spans of more than 50 metres, depending on their design. These multifunctional and solid boards are at once loadbearing, dividing and insulating. The system lends itself well to producing made-to-measure sections. Boards up to 4.8 metres wide and 14.8 metres long can be produced with a fire resistance rating of 30 to 90 minutes, depending on the thickness.

Applications
Timber composites are used in beam format for numerous uses including door and window frames and structural members (columns, joists, trusses). The monolithic boards mean that the work can be done quickly and so the system is mainly applied in fast-track domestic construction. However, their special properties also enable large spans, sculptural forms and even corner-spanning window openings. With no need for intermediate supports such as columns and lintels, the design freedom is that much greater. Depending on the use the board is to serve, it can be finished with a variety of materials; a higher grade board for exposed work is available on request. There is even a curved variety of board, made using vacuum suction, for constructing curved roofs and even domes.

Colour	**woody**
Glossiness	glossy, satin, **matt**
Translucence (%)	**0** – 20 – 40 – 60 – 80 – 100
Texture	sharp, **medium**, dull
Hardness	hard, **soft**, depressible
Temperature	**warm**, medium, cool
Odour	strong, **moderate**, none
Acoustic opacity	good, **moderate**, poor

Wood
Treatments and Finishes
Bearbeitung und Beschichtung | Traitements et Finitions | Tratamientos y acabados | Trattamenti e finiture | Bewerkingen en afwerkingen

History
Since ancient times, treatments applied to the surface of wood (and other materials, such as stone and metal) have had a primarily decorative function. By using a hard, sharp implement to inscribe figures and patterns in the surface, meanings and messages could be recorded and preserved for posterity. Decorative elements applied in this way also served to increase the status of their surroundings. The labour-intensive woodworking techniques used in the past still adorn countless priceless and highly revered objects made with wood. These include not only utilitarian objects and furniture, but all kinds of structures, both indoors and out. Although certain societies have excelled in perfecting such handcrafted finishing techniques, they represent a universal, artistic, but above all emblematic activity that is found all around the world. Woodworking and finishing techniques are by no means restricted to the surface of the wood, but are often applied right through, giving them even greater visual strength. Wood finishes in buildings are found primarily in elements that are assigned an additional function. In interior spaces, these include space dividers, doors and panelling. On the exterior, they include window shutters, door panels and roof trimmings.

Along with mechanical tooling of wood, whereby portions of the wood are removed, there are also treatments that add something. The most obvious example is the application of a coat of paint which not only makes the material more attractive but also serves to protect it. Although it has a more limited lifespan, paint can be used to impart the same meanings to wood as mechanical tooling. A technique that has been all but forgotten is that of painting a relatively inexpensive wood to create the illusion of a more expensive type of wood or even a costly natural stone.

Functional Motives
The gradual trend towards functionality during the 20th century resulted in the virtual extinction of many of the finishing techniques mentioned above. On the other hand, technical quality requirements and environmental considerations cast a number of finishes in a different light. For example, augmentation and perforation of a surface

Project Sterappelhof, Zoetermeer (2002)
Architect Bear Architects
Photographer Willem van Det

can result in considerably improved acoustic properties. Corrugated, perforated and faceted wall and ceiling surfaces have become quite common in spaces that must meet high acoustic demands. Although finishing wood with paint has never gone away, practical requirements with respect to the durability of timber structures and building elements have resulted in new paint systems and preservative treatments aimed at extending product life. These are often surface treatments – included here under finishes – that offer new expressive possibilities for products made of wood.

Emotions

Following a period in which severe, no-nonsense architecture prevailed, there now seems to be renewed interest in decorative elements. The functionally motivated enhancement of the material's technical properties resulted in sophisticated new finishing processes that are now being deployed in the realization of countless new

Project Platowood floor in De Hoep, Castricum (2003)
Architect Min2 bouw-kunst
Photographer Min2 bouw-kunst

(decorative) forms. Computer-controlled machines for moulding, perforating, punching and bending produce some quite stunning results, while digital technology makes it possible to execute a unique design directly and with great precision. In more and more designs, the severe, flat planes of cubist architecture are being replaced by sloping and double curved planes embellished by richly moulded, sinuous, curled, even crumpled surfaces. Whereas the finishes applied in the past usually had a direct or indirect meaning, this is not always so apparent in contemporary architecture. The choice of a more or less embellished surface seems to be determined mainly by sensory criteria, such as softness, tactility, warmth and the like, and perhaps also by a desire to distance ourselves from the once so admired simplicity inspired by 'form follows function'.

The Role of Wood

Ornament, decoration and emotion have long been closely associated with the material wood, and with the revival of interest in organic architecture, there is once again scope for these phenomena. One practical obstacle – high labour costs – is being tackled in the timber industry by the introduction of automated systems to perform

the time-consuming work previously carried out by craftsmen. This they do much faster, more accurately and more economically, although for a perfect final result there is still room for a finishing touch by the expert human hand. The choice of materials, too, displays a development in line with new marketplace demands. The use of a relatively unknown African wood, fuma, in the manufacture of moulded plywood, and the production of moulded units by extruding or press moulding an emulsion of wood fibres are just two examples of this new market-sensitive trend. They will undoubtedly be joined by many more in the near future.

Coating, Preserving and Modifying

Beschichtung, Konservierung und Vergütung | Enrobage, Conservation et Modification | Revestimiento, preservación y modificación | Rivestimento, preservazione e trasformazione | Coaten, verduurzamen en modificeren

Project Renovation Sloterparkbad, Amsterdam (2000)
Architect Roy Gelders
Photographer Bruynzeel

Project Sveaparken, Schiedam (2003)
Architect Wolbrand van der Vis
Photographer Willem van Det

There are various ways of protecting wood against fungi and insects and so prolonging its lifespan. Coating is done with varnish, paint and the like, primarily to protect the outer layer but often also for cosmetic purposes. Coatings may be either opaque or transparent depending on how much pigment they contain. The main determinant of the product's properties is the binder. It might be an alkyd resin, possibly with a modifying agent, or have an acrylate base. Besides these environmentally harmful and unhealthy solvent-based paints there are also water-soluble and water-based paints with a binder of acrylic resin dispersed in water. Traditional oil paints using natural binders are rarely used anymore.

Another traditional, life-prolonging method with a deeper action involves coating, immersing or impregnating the wood by vacuum-pressure, with an agent consisting of a solvent and an active, toxic ingredient. Substances commonly used in the past, such as the poisonous creosote oil, CCA, bifluorides and borax, have all but disappeared. Bifluorides and boron are highly mobile and prone to leaching. There is a large group of organic wood preservatives under development that are often less environmentally hazardous and have no effect on the appearance of the wood.

Wood can be made more durable through modification, a process that involves no toxic biocides. A distinction can be made between the already widely available thermally modified wood, in which the woody matter is converted, and the newer chemically modified wood, in which agents are added to the wood with a view to modifying specific properties. It is now possible, within reasonable limits, to alter every property of a wood: 'tailor-made' wood has become a reality.

Rapid advances in methods of wood preservation mean that woods previously unsuited for use out of doors are now eligible for that purpose.

Applications

Methods like coating and preserving can, when added pigments are used, change the colour of a wood completely. Even the surface structure will disappear beneath several coats of paint. A judicious use of preservation methods can greatly affect the impact of wood on the architecture.

Colour	**variable or woody**
Glossiness	**glossy, satin, matt**
Translucence (%)	**0 – 20 – 40 – 60 – 80 – 100**
Texture	sharp, **medium, dull**
Hardness	**hard**, soft, depressible
Temperature	warm, **medium**, cool
Odour	**strong, moderate, none**
Acoustic opacity	good, **moderate**, poor

Veneering

Furnieren | Placage | Barniz o chapeado | Impiallacciatura | Fineren

Project De Vesting, Someren (1998)
Architect Sjaak 't Hoen
Photographer Bruynzeel

Project Bank Insinger de Beaufort, Amsterdam (2000)
Architect Hans Ruijssenaars, de Architectengroep
Photographer Jan Derwig

Veneering, whereby a thin layer of a more attractively grained wood is laid over a plainer type, was already being practised in ancient Egypt. After a thousand-year intermission the technique was perfected from 1500 onwards, mainly in Italy and France. The woods used for veneers are subject to the vagaries of fashion. Whereas the darker varieties (mahogany, ebony, walnut) used to be popular, these days people tend to prefer lighter woods such as pear, cherry and maple. There are two types of veneer: sliced veneer, cut from the half or quarter log one layer at a time, and rotary-cut veneer, whereby the rotating whole log is stripped by a fixed knife. Rotary-cut veneers are mainly used for plywood. In the first-named method the way the block is sliced is decisive for the pattern of the grain. Besides the standard properties of the wood, the presence of interlocked grain, ring porosity, early and latewood, silver figures, knots, natural deviations in the trunk and burrs are key determinants of the veneer's appearance. The backing is usually exceedingly flat plywood, chipboard or MDF.

A relatively new variant is produced by stacking layers of painted or unpainted veneers into a block and then cutting new veneer from it, a technique that can produce some extraordinary effects. A more durable version of this 'constructed veneer' can be achieved by bonding the veneers with melamine paper.

Technical Aspects
Rotary-cut veneers vary in thickness from 0.6 to 4 mm. Sliced veneer is usually around 0.55 mm, but thickness ranging from 0.1 to 6 mm are also possible.

Applications
Rotary-cut veneers are used to make plywood and as a counter or backing veneer in panels. High-grade rotary-cut veneer is used decoratively in parquet flooring. Sliced veneer is used mostly in the furniture industry, in kitchen interiors, cupboards and tables but also for doors, wall and ceiling panels and the top layer of parquet. Durable variants (in combination with synthetic materials) can also serve as external wall claddings. In inlaid work (intarsia), different types of veneers can be combined to create motifs and patterns. Paper-thin veneers can be bonded to all kinds of shapes, including curves, using vacuum techniques. When varnishing a veneer with an open structure it may be necessary to fill the pores first.

Colour	**woody**
Glossiness	glossy, **satin**, **matt**
Translucence (%)	**0** – 20 – 40 – 60 – 80 – 100
Texture	sharp, **medium**, **dull**
Hardness	hard, **soft**, depressible
Temperature	**warm**, medium, cool
Odour	strong, **moderate**, none
Acoustic opacity	good, **moderate**, poor

Milling

Fräsen | Fraisage | Fresado | Fresatura | Frezen

Project De Gevulde Gracht, Dordrecht (2003)
Architect Kees Rijnboutt, de Architectengroep
Photographer Kees Hummel

Milling is a mechanical technique for shaping the surface of wood and other materials using rapidly rotating cutters. Usually the basic material is a fibreboard such as MDF or veneered sheet material. Computer-aided milling machines, programmed by Computerized Numerical Control (CNC), can perform three-dimensional cutting directly from CAD drawings, opening up virtually limitless possibilities. The simplest milling process produces a linear groove that may then be further elaborated. A more complex milling operation might entail working the whole surface to produce irregular undulations. Milling need not necessarily be confined to surfaces. Wood products can be milled in full depth to produce patterns that vary from tendril-like curls to a tautly designed rhythm. Milling always increases the surface area, to sound-absorbent as well as visual effect. Milled surfaces are in fact often chosen for acoustic reasons.

Technical Aspects

Milling is pre-eminently intended for sheet material, although it may also be applied to solid wood. In principle, any type of sheet can be used, though types with an extremely fine structure such as MDF give the best results. The acoustic effects depend on the quantity and nature of the cuts. Sheets that are milled linearly can be bent under certain conditions.

Applications

Milled wood products are generally in sheet-form and are used indoors in walls and ceilings for sound insulation. Applied to smaller pieces of real wood, milling offers a wealth of variation in mouldings, plinths and other woodwork. Where milling is designed to have a visual effect, it can be used decoratively (always depending on the durability of the material involved) both indoors in furniture or wall and ceiling panels and outdoors in cladding material.

Colour	**woody**
Glossiness	glossy, satin, **matt**
Translucence (%)	**0** – 20 – 40 – 60 – 80 – 100
Texture	**sharp**, medium, dull
Hardness	**hard**, soft, depressible
Temperature	**warm**, medium, cool
Odour	strong, **moderate**, none
Acoustic opacity	**good**, **moderate**, poor

Perforating and Punching

Perforieren und Stanzen | Perçage et Poinçonnage | Perforar y horadar | Perforazione e punzonatura | Perforeren en stansen

Project Ministry of OCW, The Hague (2003)
Architect Trude Hooykaas
Photographer Jan Derwig

Project De Hoep, Castricum (2003)
Architect Min2 bouw-kunst
Photographer Sjaak Henselmans

When wood-based sheet material is perforated or punched, it generally produces a pattern of sorts. The material most often used is fibreboard such as MDF or a veneered board. The holes, which may be full-depth or confined to the surface, can assume many some of which may leave an all-round edge of smooth, unworked board. Though mostly done for acoustic reasons, the decorative aspect of perforating and punching is not unimportant.

Technical Aspects

Perforating and punching are techniques ideally suited to sheet materials. Although in principle applicable to every type of board, those with an extremely fine structure such as MDF give the best results. The acoustic performance depends on the number and nature of the holes.

Applications

Perforated wood products generally come in sheet form and, like milled wood, are used indoors in walls and ceilings for sound absorption. In such cases an additional dark material, for instance canvas, is usually placed behind the panelling to prevent views through. Again, the visual impact of perforated or punched wood, whether indoors in furniture or as wall and ceiling panels, or outdoors as cladding, largely depends on the durability of the material used.

Colour	**woody**
Glossiness	glossy, satin, **matt**
Translucence (%)	0 – **20** – **40** – **60** – **80** – 100
Texture	**sharp**, medium, dull
Hardness	hard, **soft**, depressible
Temperature	**warm**, medium, cool
Odour	strong, moderate, **none**
Acoustic opacity	**good**, moderate, poor

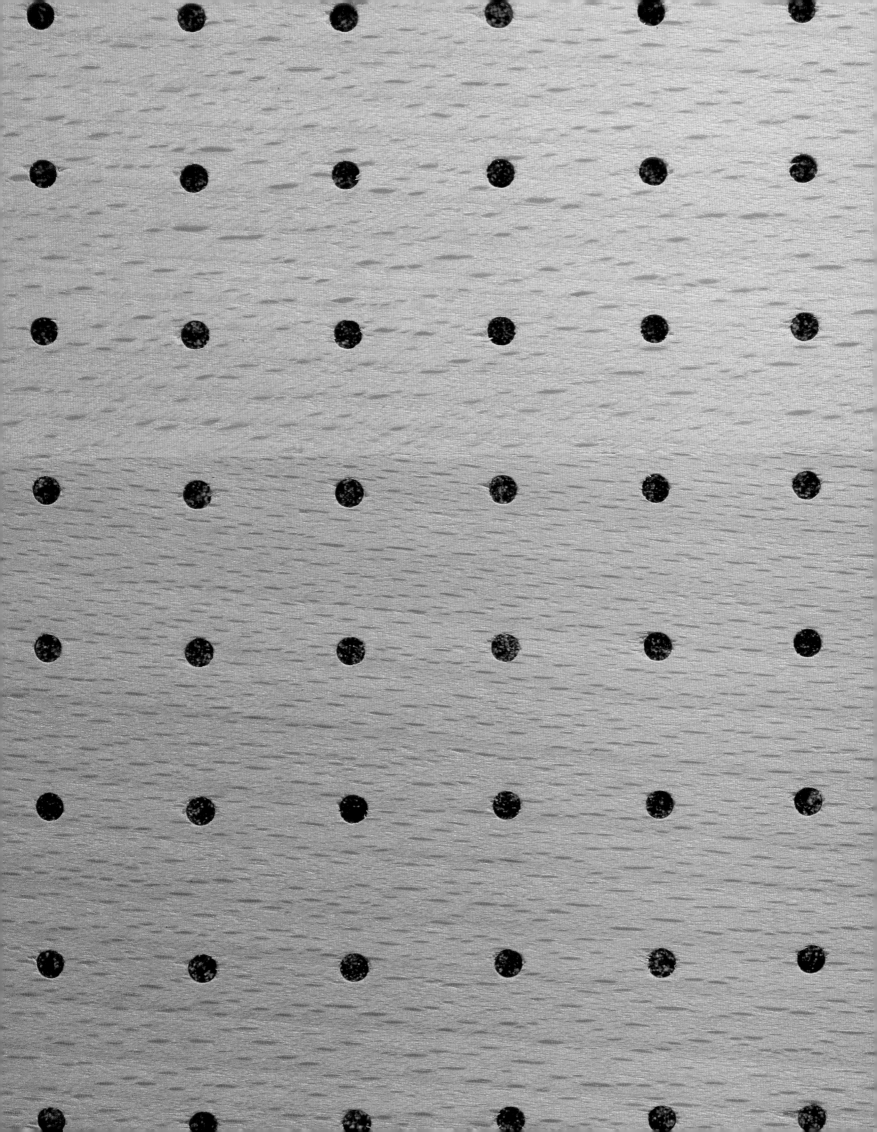

Bending

Biegen | Flexion | Curvatura | Curvatura | Buigen

Project Bent Western Red Cedar in the Zakmes, Hilversum (1997)

Architect Min2 bouw-kunst

Photographer johnlewismarshall.com

The most suitable wood-based material for making convex and concave shapes is plywood made up of two, three or more layers of veneer.

Flexible two-ply consists of two extremely thin layers of veneer (each 0.6 mm thick) bonded together with their grains parallel using a melamine-based adhesive which fuses with the two layers during the compression process. Just about any wood can be chosen for the face veneer. The material can be used as wallpaper where it can almost turn a 90-degree corner.

Flexible three-ply is intended as a decorative finish for curved shapes. Its flexibility comes from the extreme thinness of the board combined with the elastic melamine-based adhesive. In the main, flexible three-ply consists of two gaboon (okoumé) veneers bonded with grain directions at right angles and a high-grade face veneer. Flexible three-ply has a bending radius of 40 mm.

Flexible multi-ply can be up to 20 mm thick and usually consists of veneers from the poplar or silk cotton tree, both of which have good bending properties, bonded to a stabilizing core of a sturdier wood such as Japanese maple or okoumé. For the sake of appearance, flexible multi-ply is usually finished with a extremely thin veneer or synthetic sheet. Flexible multi-ply has a bending radius of 60 mm.

Curved products can be made from other flat sheet composites besides the flexible plywoods described above. The close succession of grooves cut into one side of MDF boards immediately come to mind.

Technical Aspects

The silk cotton tree (*Ceiba pentandra*, also known as fuma) is an African wood with an exceptionally low density, an open structure and long fibres as well as an average hardness and high bending strength, higher than say ash or oak. The same obtains for the fast-growing poplar. Bending always takes the direction of the fibre and follows the length or breadth of the board depending on how the face veneers are aligned.

Applications

Flexible multi-ply can be screwed, nailed or stapled to a framework consisting of rails, strips of multi-ply or both. It can be finished with a coat of paint or a decorative sheet material. In the case of painting or spraying, the open surface structure of the outer veneer must be covered with a dense layer of thin plastic sheeting or an ultra-thin layer (0.8 to 1.5 mm) of flexible three-ply.

Colour	**woody**
Glossiness	glossy, **satin**, **matt**
Translucence (%)	**0** – 20 – 40 – 60 – 80 – 100
Texture	sharp, **medium**, dull
Hardness	hard, **soft**, depressible
Temperature	warm, **medium**, cool
Odour	strong, **moderate**, none
Acoustic opacity	good, **moderate**, poor

Natural Stone

Naturstein | Roche Naturelle | Piedra natural | Pietre naturali | Natuursteen

Few building materials come in so many variants as natural stone. At present, architects can choose from some 8000 different varieties, and although many traditional European varieties are becoming more expensive and consequently less likely to be used for ordinary buildings, the total number of natural stone types seems set to increase in the coming years, given the clock-like regularity with which 'new' varieties appear on the market. Countries like South Africa, India and China in particular are becoming increasingly important suppliers: the quantity of stone available is enormous, the quality high and the labour costs low. For a long time these countries, like those in South America, were uninteresting because they were unable to deliver dimension stone. In recent years, however, their market share has increased because they have acquired sophisticated sawing machines and are able to sell directly to national dealers instead of via stone processing plants in Italy. Sea transport costs have also plunged dramatically.

The introduction of these 'exotic' varieties is a definite enrichment of the natural stone palette. Each variety of natural stone has its own specific characteristics, depending on which metal salt, sediment or plant happened to be present during formation. Chance plays a major role in the formation of stone. Traditional European varieties like Bianco Carrara marble remain unequalled, although the recently introduced South African slate, with its many different shades of colour, does tend to put its drab, blue-grey European relatives in the shade. Nonetheless, these new varieties have still to prove themselves in the northern European climate.

The Role of Natural Stone

Of those 8000 or so varieties of natural stone, by no means all are suitable for use in façades or for a specific type of finishing such as polishing, tooling or flaming. Decisions about where and how best to use a particular stone depend on its 'genetic make-up', in other words, its origins. Roughly speaking, natural stone types can be divided into three main groups: igneous, sedimentary and metamorphic.

The primary component of igneous rocks, of which granite is undoubtedly the best-known, is silicon dioxide. This substance makes igneous rock hard and resistant to polluted environments and is also responsible for the fact that, when used in a façade, polished granite retains its lustre for thousands of years. Granite is so hard, however that polishing it is a labour-intensive and expensive process.

Next there are the sedimentary rocks, formed in rivers and seas. There are two kinds of sedimentary rock, clastic rock (petrified deposits of clay or lime) and precipitated rock (petrified precipitation of lime from lime-saturated water).

Finally, there are metamorphic or 'changed-form' rocks. These are formed when movements in the earth's crust expose already formed igneous or sedimentary rock to extreme pressures and/or temperatures, causing them to undergo a change of form or metamorphosis. Limestone becomes marble, clay turns into slate, sandstone into quartzite and even granite can be transformed into gneiss. Limestone and marble, with some 800 variants, are the building industry's most important stones. They consist in large part of

calcium carbonate: an attractive, neutral, but also fragile basis. Acid rain and air pollution react with the calcium carbonate, causing unsightly damage to the stone's surface. Polishing limestone and marble exposed to the outdoor air is pointless as the lustre lasts for only about three years. Another disadvantage of these stones is their poor frost resistance, and while impregnation offers some protection, it also eventually entails additional maintenance.

In any case, such a treatment seems to be at odds with the image we have of stone. Is stone not the most durable of all building materials? After all, most historical monuments are of stone and most of them have been remarkably successfully in withstanding the passage of time. Stone's seemingly timeless quality, as well as its temperamental character, have fascinated humanity since ancient times. Ever since the early Egyptian pharaohs used granite for their first pyramid, deploying whole armies of slaves and craftsmen in the process, natural stone has been the obvious choice for all architectural expressions of might and indestructibility. The palaces of the Persian kings, the great buildings of ancient Greece and Rome, the cathedrals and castles of the Middle Ages are all inconceivable in any other material. Towards the end of the 19th century, significant improvements to

Description Grey granite in Etang Sannes, Creuse (Hc. 1500)
Photographer Jan Derwig

the saws used to cut stone, and the introduction of new, strong building materials that were easier to test for flaws than stone, inevitably led to a change in the role of stone. Whereas up to that time, heavy, massive blocks of stone had served both as a structural and a finishing material, conveying an expression of impregnable strength, it was now possible to use other materials for the structure and to face it with a curtain of thin stone slabs. This division of function inevitably made the use of stone less problematical. As such, it was a logical step in the development of construction technology. Stone is obviously capable of absorbing immense compressive forces: in Gothic cathedrals, for example, the stones absorb only a twentieth of the forces they are theoretically capable of bearing. However, stone has three major disadvantages. Firstly, most natural stone, including granite, is poor at withstanding sudden shocks. Secondly, it can absorb great compressive forces, but virtually no tensile forces. Even more problematical is the fact that, as a product of nature, it is always subject to imperfections somewhere within it that could render the stone much weaker than expected. The risks implicit in these drawbacks can all be eliminated through the use of structural frames made of reinforced concrete or steel, materials which have the added advantage of being considerably cheaper than solid natural stone.

For a long time after this, architects accepted the structurally subordinate role of natural stone and regarded it as a finishing material. In 1992, however, the Spanish architects Martorell, Bohigas and Mackay decided to give stone a very prominent role in their Pavilion of the Future at that year's World's Fair in Seville. Here was a paradox: one of the oldest building materials was to provide the visual identity of a building housing an exhibition of future technologies. In fact, the combination was less paradoxical than it appears. Engineering ingenuity and computer-processed stone were in fact indispensable to the realization of the structure's sculptural elements. The building's enormous arches of Rosa Porriño granite owed their stability to the strength of the stone and the geometry of the construction and to an ingenious steel construction. The architects and the structural designer, Peter Rice, demonstrated with this project that natural stone is indeed a building material of the future, at least when combined with contemporary technology.

Renzo Piano achieved a comparable structural tour de force by choosing Trani stone for the arches of his colossal Padre Pio Church in San Giovanni Rotondo. Here, too, natural stone is combined with a steel auxiliary construction which transfers the forces from the roof to the arches and distributes the load evenly. Gilles Peraudin opted for the other, almost archaic method in a number of small buildings, including two wineries. He employed limestone blocks for both columns and beams. The short spans in these buildings virtually eliminate the danger of collapse due to irregularities in the stone. In the Netherlands, a huge granite boulder just missed out being used in a similar manner in Theehuis de Posbank in Rhenen. This beautiful restaurant by architect Bjarne Mastenbroek stands on top of a lateral moraine and Mastenbroek had originally wanted to visualize these natural forces by placing the restaurant on the boulder. In theory this was possible, but it meant testing the stone's strength and it was this that proved impossible: it entailed exerting such immense forces on the stone that, if it had broken, the test laboratory itself could have

been destroyed as a result. Instead the boulder was hollowed out and a steel column was driven through its heart.

These problems highlight a major problem: extensive testing of a stone's structural qualities is time-consuming and expensive. One alternative to this is to set much lower values for a construction, but this makes the structure heavy, massive and thus also expensive. Another alternative is to devise ingenious hybrid constructions in which natural stone is used together with steel. This, too, places great demands both on the skills of the structural engineer and on the budget. All this helps to explain why solid stone structures remained isolated incidents in the twentieth century.

Natural Stone Rediscovered

Following its change of role – from heavy, solid support to relatively inexpensive façade facing – natural stone was plunged into an identity crisis. It continues to be seen as strong, reliable, solid and expensive. Architects are consequently torn between a method of detailing

Project Pink Alsation limestone, Tingueley Museum, Basel (1996)
Architect Mario Botta
Photographer Thomas Dix

that would accentuate these 'natural' (but no longer accurate) associations and one that would negate them by revealing the stone's true thinness.

German architect Joseph Paul Kleihues chose the latter option in his Museum of Pre- and Early History in Frankfurt (1989). By exposing the bronze suspension, Kleihues makes it quite clear that the stone used is thin and relies on the construction behind it for its stability. Richard Meier played a subtle game with traditional associations and detailing in the J. Paul Getty Center in Los Angeles (1997). He used large blocks of travertine whose size is perceptible in many places, yet he also had the frames protrude from the stone.

The difficulty of attaining uniform detailing is demonstrated by Michael Graves's Humana Building in Louisville, Kentucky (1985). Graves was clearly in two minds: by employing a system of fake joints and infill blocks for the sills and at the corners, he created the impression of solid stone blocks. If one looks at the reveals, however, it is obvious that thin slabs have been used. There are always a number of places like this where it is extremely difficult, if not impossible, to disguise the thinness of the slabs, even though the latest assembly systems make possible an all but invisible suspension.

In today's most widely used suspension system, the stone slabs are suspended from four steel dowels inserted into holes in the sides or at the top and bottom edges of the stone slabs. The fastening is such that it allows the slabs to expand and contract by moving along the anchors. Another way of allowing for movement is to employ two loadbearing anchors and two flexible spacers which are able to deform as the stone expands and contracts. There is also a 'blind' variant in which conical holes are milled into the back of the slab. The plugs that fit into these holes expand to fill the hole, thereby forming an integral part of the stone. This particular system provides for a suspension free of compressive forces suitable for hanging thin slabs (a granite slab need be only 20 mm thick instead of the usual 30 mm).

Attaching the anchors to the back of the slabs does not mean that they can be laid without joints, which would reinforce the illusion of a solid stone wall. Allowance must be made for sawing tolerances of several millimetres. In addition, all stone expands, some types a lot (tuff: 1 mm/m/100 °C), others, significantly less (sandstone: 0.2 mm/m/100 °C). Some types of marble may, if the cycle of expansion and contraction is repeated often enough, even undergo permanent expansion in which the stone's crystalline structure is damaged and, with it, its elasticity. If insufficient allowance is made for expansion in a natural stone façade, the thin slabs will bulge or crack. Famous examples of this effect are Arne Jacobson's Aarhus Town Hall and Alvar Aalto's Finlandia Hall in Helsinki. Joints 5 mm wide are the minimum in a façade with rear anchoring; a standard joint is 8 mm wide.

Thus, whatever the mounting method used, joints are inevitable. They can, however, be camouflaged. In his Town Hall at Alphen aan de Rijn, Erick van Egeraat did not use stone slabs but slightly thicker strips that were laid one on top of the other as it were. The visible sides of the stone were rough-hewn, which makes the joint less noticeable and contributes to an impression of a wall of solid stone blocks. In this way, van Egeraat achieved a visual solution for a detailing problem that has plagued architects ever since thin slabs were introduced.

The research into the architectural significance of natural stone carried out by Erick van Egeraat and Bjarne Mastenbroek, as well as by other leading architects like Peter Zumthor, Renzo Piano, Sir Norman Foster, Gilles Perraudin, Rem Koolhaas, Meindert von Gerkan and Herzog & De Meuron, is symptomatic of the material's revival. Natural stone's return as a high-profile façade material, and, to a lesser degree, building material, is striking. For a long time stone was out of favour (except as a floor covering); the age-old association of natural stone with power and strength was probably considered less in keeping with the spirit of modernism than the new 'industrial'

materials. The fact that so many star architects have started to use natural stone again in their prestigious buildings automatically means that the role of stone in buildings will be investigated and that architects will once again make play with the meanings conveyed by stone and the detailing of stone. This can only lead to a further widening and deepening of natural stone's significance for architecture, and in the end this will undoubtedly prove to be far more important than the number of stone types available.

Igneous Rock

Tiefengestein | Roche Ignée | Rocas volcánicas | Rocce ignee | Stollinggesteente

Igneous rock used to be referred to as primordial rock on the assumption that, because it was formed deep beneath the earth's surface, it was also the oldest rock: a logical assumption, perhaps, but nonetheless incorrect. There are many stone types which are considerably older than some igneous rocks. In fact, igneous rock is still in the process of being formed at this very moment, although total production time runs into millions of years! Another misconception is that igneous rock is necessarily harder than other types. In point of fact, some sedimentary types are extremely hard and some igneous rocks are relatively soft.

Origin and Properties

The properties of igneous rock are directly related to the place where it is formed, deep below the earth's surface. The extremely high temperatures prevailing there allow magma to solidify slowly, providing optimal conditions for crystal growth. The result is a completely crystalline structure and striking uniformity among stone from the same location. Whereas nearly every slab of sedimentary stone is different, owing to the chance presence during formation of one or another metal oxide, crystal or organic life, igneous rock obtained from the same quarry exhibits hardly any differences in colour, structure or quality.

The most important and best-known igneous rock is undoubtedly granite, which accounts for no less than 92% of all igneous rock. Granite is composed primarily of three minerals: quartz, mica and feldspar. Quartz, which gives the stone its hardness, strength and durability, is usually transparent, but sometimes brown or grey. Mica – often black biotite – provides contrast. Too high a content of this mineral, however, makes for flakiness. Feldspar, which is what gives granite its colour, is the most important constituent for the overall appearance. Feldspar consists of crystals of many shapes and sizes and a colour palette ranging from red, yellow and brown to blue and green. Some granites consist almost entirely of feldspar and are often bright red in colour. Although granite contains other minerals, only these three are visible to the naked eye.

By no means all igneous rock is suitable for use as a building material. Too high an iron content, for example, can render a given stone unusable, as oxidising iron salts can cause unsightly rust-coloured spots to appear. More seriously, this process may adversely affect the quality of a stone if the oxidising iron causes pressure in the crystal structure in the stone, resulting in flaking. Other chemical processes during formation can also affect these granites in such a way as to make them unusable. For example, the feldspar component may be converted into kaolinite, a white mineral that diminishes the stone's strength. Finally, a stone may be rendered unusable by the presence of wider veins of quartz or feldspar.

The granite types that end up on the market, however, are always of an impeccable quality. The stone has a very dense structure that makes it virtually impenetrable to water. Like all igneous rock, it is also frost resistant. Its compressive strength varies somewhat; the 'weakest' varieties have a compressive strength of $1.2 \; 10^5 \; kN/m^2$, whilst the strongest ones can withstand compressive forces up to $2.0 \; 10^5 \; kN/m^2$. As with most other stone types, its shock resistance

Description Sanaa, Yemen
Photographer Jan Derwig

Genuine Granite

Because the term *granite* is not just the name of a stone, but also an indication of quality, many stones that are not in fact granite are nonetheless marketed as such. 'Black granite', for example, is a misnomer for what is typically dyke rock. Another stone often passed off as granite is syenite, an igneous rock containing hornblende instead of mica. In such cases (and this applies equally to quartzite and gneiss) nomenclature is not all that important since a particular stone is often selected for its appearance. Besides, all these stones are of a similar high quality to genuine granite. The same cannot be said of limestone, which is also sold as granite: the durability of most limestone varieties is nothing like that of granite. Selling them as granite entails a potential risk to safety.

Project Granite interior Musée d'Orsay, Paris (1987)
Architect Gae Aulenti
Photographer Jan Derwig

is significantly lower. This – together with that fact that a stone is always liable to contain some invisible defect that could significantly diminish its strength – makes granite a not entirely reliable building material. In addition, granite's low shock resistance affects its fire resistance. Uneven expansion causes cracks which become even wider during fire extinguishing.

Granite owes its durability to its hardness. Wear is minimal and only occurs after many years of use. However, this advantage must be weighed against a disadvantage. Although granite is theoretically suited to all types of finishing, its very hardness makes this difficult. Bush-hammering, which best does justice to the roughness of the stone's crystals, is fairly unproblematical and is indeed the most popular finish. Comparable results are achieved by flaming (whereby the surface is heated, causing the outermost layer to crack) which also brings out the rugged character of the stone. In contrast, finer finishes, such as tooling and boasting, are almost impossible and, given the coarse crystal structure, fairly pointless. Although granite's hardness makes grinding and polishing arduous it is frequently done and it must be said that once granite has been given a gloss it will retain it for many years to come.

Black Granite

Schwarzer Granit | Granit noire | Granito negro | Granito nero | Zwart graniet

Project CBS Building, New York (1965)
Architect Eero Saarinen
Photographer El Poder de la Palabra © epdlp.com

Project Jakob-Kaiser-Haus, Berlin (2002)
Architect Pi de Bruijn, de Architekten Cie.
Photographer Linus Lintner

Natural stone has traditionally been used to express power and strength. The same applies to skyscrapers. An example of what happens when the two are combined is Eero Saarinen's CBS Building in New York. The external construction of the 149.5 metre high tower is clad with a black Canadian granite. No wonder that it quickly acquired the nickname 'the Black Rock'.

Technical Aspects

Granite is igneous rock, the oldest and hardest kind of stone. Its compressive strength varies according to type, ranging from 120 to 220 N/mm². However, like almost all natural stone, its resistance to shock is low.

Officially, granite is classified as magmatic rock, created as a result of the solidification of magma, and is characterized by the even distribution of its mineral particles. It does not feature large structures, but does produce relatively coarse crystals. Unofficially, however, volcanic and metamorphic rock types are sometimes also classified as granite. 'Black granite', for example, is often actually gabbro, basalt or diorite. In the end, it is mineral composition that determines a stone's type.

In addition to black granite, there are also white, yellow, green, blue and red variants. The stone's nuances are best appreciated when it is polished. Once polished, it retains its lustre indefinitely. However, due to its hardness, polishing is a difficult and therefore expensive finish. A cheaper, and consequently popular, alternative is bush hammering, which has the added advantage of complementing the rugged character of granite.

Applications

All granite types are hard, frost-resistant, impervious to acids and extremely hardwearing. As such, the stone is suitable for use in all parts of a building.

Colour	**grey**, **white**, **green**, **blue**, **red**
Glossiness	**glossy**, **satin**, **matt**
Translucence (%)	**0** – 20 – 40 – 60 – 80 – 100
Texture	sharp, **medium**, **dull**
Hardness	**hard**, soft, depressible
Temperature	warm, **medium**, cool
Odour	strong, moderate, **none**
Acoustic opacity	good, moderate, **poor**

Gray-Shulman

Gray-Shulman | Gray-Shulman | Shulman Gris | Granito Gray-Shulman | Grijze Sholman

Project Bibliotheca Alexandrina, Alexandria, Egypt (2002)
Architect Snøhetta
Photographer Gerald Zugmann

Since about 4000 BC, all monumental buildings in Egypt have been made from granite, thus making it the obvious choice for the façade cladding of the new Alexandria Library. It, too, was built using granite from the Aswan District. However, whereas the ancient Egyptians preferred the pink variant (e.g. for the famous obelisks of Cleopatra), the Oslo-based firm of Snøhetta chose Gray-Shulman granite for their immense library. Given that the slabs are 15cm thick, cost was obviously no object.

Technical Aspects

Granite is a light-coloured igneous rock which solidifies deep beneath the earth's surface. Owing to the depth at which this takes place, the process unfolds extremely slowly, giving the crystals every opportunity to 'grow'. Indeed, they are often visible to the naked eye. The stone has a large quartz component, but an even larger proportion of orthoclase feldspar. It is the feldspars that largely determine the colour of granite which can be white, red, blue, green, pink or yellow among others. Quartz, which accounts for 20 to 50 per cent of granite, is what makes it so strong. Despite its high compressive strength, the stone's crystalline structure makes it highly susceptible to sudden shocks.

Applications

One of the hardest of stone types, granite is used in situations where load and/or weathering are greatest: stairs, balconies, thresholds. Its structure allows for a range of treatments from polishing, flaming and grinding to bush hammering. Chiselling is more difficult due to the stone's hardness and the relative coarseness of the crystals. That the signs and letters from every known alphabet engraved on the huge granite façade of the Alexandria Library (to a design by Norwegian artist Jorunn Sannes) were chiselled out by hand is eloquent testimony to the prestige of the project.

Colour	**grey**
Glossiness	**glossy**, **satin**, **matt**
Translucence (%)	**0** – 20 – 40 – 60 – 80 – 100
Texture	sharp, **medium**, **dull**
Hardness	**hard**, soft, depressible
Temperature	warm, **medium**, cool
Odour	strong, moderate, **none**
Acoustic opacity	good, moderate, **poor**

Natural Stone – Igneous Rock

Migmatite – Multicolour Red

Multicolour Red – Migmatit | Rouge multi couleur – Migmatite | Rojo multicolor – Migmatita | Rosso multicolore – Migmatite |
Multicolour Red – Migmatiet

Project Office building, Leeuwarden (1997)

Architect Jorna Natuursteen

Photographer Sake de Jong, Jorna Natuursteen

Some natural stone types are a little too eye-catching to find their way into 'high architecture', where preference is typically given to less extravert varieties. Multicolour Red is a migmatite and a good example of an expressive natural stone. As such, it is especially popular in office buildings and hotel lobbies where a chic message is desired.

Technical Aspects

Most natural stones, however colourful, have a static appearance. Granite's slow solidification process gives its crystals the opportunity to grow evenly, so that they are clearly visible. Sedimentary rock often has a more irregular surface due to the fossils and decomposed plant remnants it contains. In the case of migmatite, however, the patterns appear to be part of the primordial mass itself. The magma flow – in effect, the stone's genesis – has been captured in the stone. Migmatite, which is formed when new liquid rock penetrates existing rock, is a composite of metamorphic rocks (in fact, two gneiss types). So although migmatite is in part a metamorphosis of granite, it is impossible to confuse it with granite as its texture is completely different. In other respects, however, migmatite is virtually identical to granite. It has a high compressive strength (150-250 N/mm^2), excellent frost resistance and colour-fastness and polished surfaces retain their lustre for many, many years. Generally, Multicolour Red is a reddish orange, but other colours also occur, including bright red and black. It originates from India and a similar stone is found in Brazil.

Applications

Migmatite has thus a very distinctive appearance. The excellent properties of Multicolour Red and other migmatites make them extremely versatile. They can be used both indoors (walls, floors, counters) and outdoors without any problem. They can even be used in places where the stone is subject to heavy loading, such as stairs and window sills. As with all stone, highly polished surfaces do not stand up well to a lot of traffic.

Colour	**black**, **grey**, **white**, **yellow**, **red**
Glossiness	**glossy**, **satin**, **matt**
Translucence (%)	**0** – 20 – 40 – 60 – 80 – 100
Texture	sharp, **medium**, **dull**
Hardness	**hard**, soft, depressible
Temperature	warm, **medium**, cool
Odour	strong, moderate, **none**
Acoustic opacity	good, moderate, **poor**

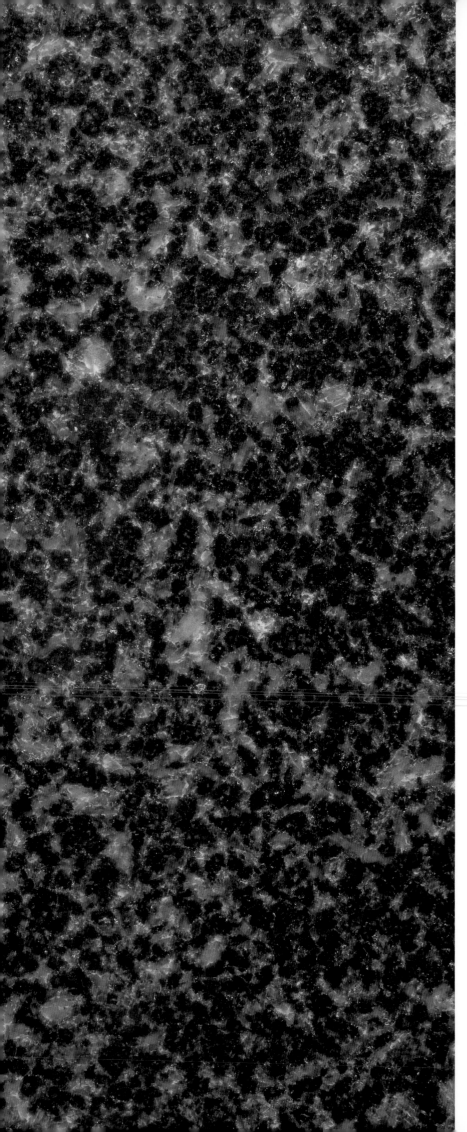

Dyke Rock and Extrusive Rock

Ganggestein und Ergussgestein | Roche de Filon et Roche Extrusive |
Piedra de escollera y roca eruptiva | Pegmatite e rocce effusive |
Gang- en uitvloeiïnggesteente

The magma at the earth's core is perpetually restless and under enormous pressure. It will take any opportunity it finds to spew through cracks in the strata. The further the magma is able to penetrate the earth's 40 to 50 km thick crust, the lower the temperature of the stratum where it ultimately stops and the faster it will solidify. This has certain consequences for the crystals in the stone. Rock that forms in the cracks of the earth's crust is called *dyke rock*. Volcanic eruptions bring the magma all the way to the earth's surface where it solidifies too quickly for crystal formation. Rock formed in this way is called *extrusive rock*.

Origin and Properties

It is only logical that dyke rock should contain smaller crystals than igneous rocks like granite which solidify very slowly owing to the extremely high temperature prevailing in the strata where this occurs. Such conditions encourage the growth of large crystals. When the prevailing temperature is lower, however, solidification will obviously proceed more rapidly and yield smaller crystals. In fact, dyke rock often contains larger crystals as well, but these were formed at an earlier stage and carried along by the magma. Generally speaking, dyke rock is formed in two phases.

Project Van Gogh Museum, Amsterdam (1998)
Architect Kisho Kurokawa
Photographer Kees Hummel

Project Office building, Aruba (2003)
Architect Project Planners & Designers NV
Photographer Dekker Natuursteen

It is not always easy to distinguish between granite and dyke rock. This is especially true of porphyry, the best-known form of dyke rock. Hence categories like granite-porphyry, which includes the red deer brown used by Kisho Kurokawa for his extension to Amsterdam's Van Gogh Museum. Apart from the grey-red colouring of this variant, porphyry can also be light yellow, brown or black depending on the crystals it contains. Its properties are similar to those of granite (very hard, high compressive strength, good weather resistance) and occasionally even superior. Unlike granite, some types of porphyry are impact resistant. These excellent characteristics make it eminently suitable for use in road construction.

Dolerite or diabase is easier to differentiate from igneous rock types. It comes in shades of green only and has a very fine crystal structure. Its compressive strength ranges from 18 to 27 10^5 kN/m^2. Like granite and porphyry, dolerite is suitable for polishing although the gloss is much less durable than that of granite: polished dolerite façade cladding becomes dull after some 20 years, and after 50 years it will begin to discolour. Other treatments, such as bush-hammering or grinding are also possible. Dolerite's characteristic colouring, light-green spots on a dark background, is best revealed by grinding. One drawback of this stone (and of all other dyke rock types) is that large slabs are rare.

The best-known extrusive rocks are basalt and basalt lava. In its natural surroundings basalt can make for fascinating effects. Basalt that solidifies while still in the mouth of the crater shrinks as it cools, eventually forming angular columns that can reach 15 metres or more. Such formations are known as columnar basalt. Table formations and boulders also occur.

Dyke and Extrusive Rock as Façade Materials
Basalt is useful for the construction industry, but not as a conventional façade cladding. Swiss architects Herzog & De Meuron used basalt boulders for a California winery, but they were placed in reinforcement nets and consequently function more as a semi-open screen than a traditional façade. Basalt is unsuitable for façade slabs as its glasslike structure makes it far too hard and brittle to be worked. Its

brittleness is especially frustrating since it has a fairly high compressive strength of 5.5 10^5 kN/m^2. It is therefore used primarily in pulverized form to make rock wool. Blocks of basalt are used as wave breakers.

Oddly enough, basalt lava makes good façade slabs. The main difference between it and basalt is that during its formation gas was able to escape from the molten mass. As a result, most types of basalt lava are porous but nevertheless have good frost resistance. Zählava differs from normal basalt lavas in that its structure is so dense as to render it suitable for polishing. Seekanter, though also less porous than normal basalt lava, cannot be polished.

It remains curious that stones that are broadly speaking composed of the same minerals should have such different characteristics. Like granite, the varieties of extrusive rock discussed here are all basically composed of feldspar, mica and quartz, yet because of the relative speed with which they solidified, their structure could scarcely be more different from that of granite. Qualitatively, they are clearly inferior to igneous stone types.

Basalt

Basalt | Basalte | Basalto | Basalto | Basalt

Description Ajanta Temple, Aurangabad (late 5th century)
Photographer Thomas Dix

Project Hallgrimurs Church, Reykjavik (1986)
Architect Gudjon Samuelsson
Photographer James Davis | Alamy

Herzog & De Meuron have given basalt an architectonic connotation. For a winery in California's Napa Valley, the Swiss architects were looking for a material that would help regulate the interior climate naturally, enabling them to dispense with the traditional American air-conditioning. Blocks of basalt placed between steel reinforcement nets absorb the sun's heat during the day and release it again at night. A byproduct of this solution is the wonderfully tempered daylight that enters the halls through the gaps between the basalt blocks.

Technical Aspects

Basalt is an extrusive rock. Owing to rapid solidification during its formation, it has a glass-like structure and properties. Basalt is extremely hard, with an E-modulus of 1×10^8 kN/m^2, but it is also quite brittle. Blocks of basalt have sharp edges, just like glass. It is usually quarried from polygonal pillars formed during the cooling and shrinking of the lava. It is also found in the form of 'pillows' and as irregular lumps. Although normally a deep grey or bluish black, other colours also occur, such as the yellow-brown Maoi found on Easter Island. Basalt sometimes contains large minerals, among which green olivine.

Applications

Basalt is not a building material as such. Despite its extreme hardness and brittleness it lends itself to polishing and bush-hammering. It is also pulverized on a large scale for use in the asphalt and cement industries. Rock wool insulation is also made from basalt. Since Herzog & De Meuron's innovative use of the material in the United States, many other architects have designed façades and partitions made from stone-filled steel mesh, albeit not always using basalt.

Colour	variable
Glossiness	glossy, satin, **matt**
Translucence (%)	**0** – 20 – 40 – 60 – 80 – 100
Texture	**sharp**, medium, dull
Hardness	**hard**, soft, depressible
Temperature	warm, **medium**, cool
Odour	strong, moderate, **none**
Acoustic opacity	good, moderate, **poor**

Basalt Lava

Basaltlava | Lave Basaltique | Lava basáltica | Basalto lavico| Basaltlava

Project Museum of Modern Art, Vienna (1990)

Architect Ortner & Ortner

Photographer Rupert Steiner

When the Romans built Trier's Porta Nigra at the end of the 2nd century AD, they chose basalt lava. The dark, almost black colour was intended to enhance the imposing character of the 36-metre-high structure. Actually, the building only really lives up to its name when viewed from a distance. Closer to, the stone reveals exquisite colour nuances.

Technical Aspects

Basalt lava is an extrusive rock and always has a somewhat porous appearance. Its surface is strewn with tiny cavities, remnants of the gas bubbles that were present during the stone's formation. The porosity has no effect on the stone's frost resistance, however, as the openings are confined to the surface and water has no chance of penetrating deep into the rock. Niedermendig basalt lava, for example, exhibits no weathering effects even after several hundred years. With an E-modulus between 150 and 250 N/mm^2, basalt lava is often referred to as 'tough' and in the past it was difficult to work. Today, though, it can be worked in a variety of ways. In principle it can even to some extent be polished, albeit while sacrificing the stone's true character. The colour is typically dark grey with blue, green and brown hues. There is also a red variant, whose colour results from the presence of free iron.

Applications

Due to its excellent weather resistance, basalt lava is an ideal cladding for façades. Proof that it is possible to create highly varied façades with this stone was provided by Ortner & Ortner in the Museum of Modern Art in Vienna, for which they used basalt lava from several different Eifel quarries. To make their façade even more interesting, they varied the widths of the joints beyond the minimum 1 cm required to accommodate the width of the anchor strip and to compensate for the stone's expansion. Aside from cladding for façades, basalt lava can also be used for steps and thresholds. Thanks to the numerous surface cavities, the stone is not slippery when wet. Glazed basalt tiles are also available nowadays.

Colour	**grey blue**
Glossiness	glossy, **satin**, **matt**
Translucence (%)	**0** – 20 – 40 – 60 – 80 – 100
Texture	sharp, **medium**, **dull**
Hardness	**hard**, soft, depressible
Temperature	warm, **medium**, cool
Odour	strong, moderate, **none**
Acoustic opacity	good, moderate, **poor**

Sedimentary Stone

Sedimentgestein | Roche Sédimentaire | Rocas sedimentarias |
Rocce sedimentarie | Sedimentair gesteente

In view of the huge number of different varieties of sedimentary rock, this is undoubtedly the most important stone type. Of the 1,500 available varieties of natural stone, over 800 are sedimentary. Within this group, limestone and its metamorphic form, marble, account for the greatest number of varieties. Sedimentary stone varieties undoubtedly owe their popularity to their neutral background (the granites by comparison are generally very, sometimes overly, vibrant), relative softness – which makes them easy to work and suitable for virtually all finishes – and relative inexpensiveness.

Origin and Properties

Limestone is formed in a manner completely different from granite. Whilst these igneous rocks have silicon dioxide as their mineral basis, making them extremely hard and durable, limestone's basic ingredient is the much more fragile calcium carbonate. Two separate

Project Jura Grau in staircase of Arena, Hilversum (1998)
Architect Min2 bouw-kunst
Photographer Elly Valkering

processes can lead to the formation of limestone, a biological and a chemical process. The biological process typically involves molluscs and other shellfish, which use the calcium carbonate they find in water to make shells or exoskeletons. When these creatures die, their bodies decay and their calcium-based shells are deposited as sediment, which in turn is pulverized by the effects of erosion. Over many thousands of years, such calcium deposits are piled upon one another, layer by layer. Increasing pressure from above gradually compresses the layers of calcium into stone. In some limestone varieties, such as Trosselfels or shell limestone, the calcium is deposited on coral or on shells, which remain clearly recognizable in the stone. Occasionally partially intact shells or other fossils are incorporated in the stone. Whereas in most limestone varieties the action of pulverization, sedimentation and compression renders the component shells and exoskeletons unrecognizable, this is not the case in blue limestone which has a markedly different structure from that of most other limestone varieties. Although the bodies of the crinoids or sea lilies responsible for the stone's calcium decay, their skeletons are converted into calcite which remains visible in the stone. The crystals in the calcite are in turn bound together to form stone.

The chemical formation process is more straightforward and is based on the evaporation of water containing calcium. Through increasing pressure, what begins as sludge is slowly but surely transformed into a solid crystalline structure.

Pure limestone is in principal white. However, in most cases it contains traces of various metal salts which impart colour or 'colour clouds' to the stone. In addition, because the process of sedimentation and the transformation of calcium sludge into limestone proceeds so very slowly, all manner of 'contaminants' (such as plant stems) end up in the limestone layers where they can have quite a significant impact on the stone's structure and colour. As the plant matter decays, gas is released from the calcium sludge, leaving behind cavities and cloudlike patterns in the stone. Travertine is the best-known stone type exhibiting of this effect. As long as the stone

Project Wine store, Vauvert (1999)
Architect Gilles Perraudin
Photographer Serge Demailly

is not used in block form and is not fresh from the quarry, the cavities will not affect the stone's frost resistance, as the width and depth of the cavities allows freezing water to expand. However, if the cavities have been filled during formation with calcite, this can cause problems when the stone is worked. More troublesome than such cavities are patches of 'dead stone', or incompletely petrified parts, which can seriously undermine a stone's cohesion.

Sedimentary Stone as a Façade Material

Limestone can be problematical when used in façades because the calcium dioxide it contains not only makes it beautiful, but generally quite vulnerable, as well. This is certainly the case in the acid environments typical of most industrialized countries where rain containing carbon dioxide converts the limestone into soluble salt. After the façade dries, this salt is converted once more into a 'lime crust' that can substantially detract from the stone's beauty, especially if the stone in question is strongly coloured. In addition, polishing is quite pointless for many varieties as they will soon lose their lustre again in the outside air.

These are all problems of a primarily aesthetic nature. A more serious technical problem is the fact that 80% of limestone varieties with a denser structure are not frost resistant. For example, the Trani stone used by Renzo Piano for his magnificent Padre Pio Church at San Giovanni Rotondo in Italy could not be used in countries with a cold, damp climate. As the water that has penetrated the stone freezes, it expands, causing micro-cracks and gradually enabling the water to penetrate deeper and deeper into the stone. If this continues for long enough the cracks can become as deep as the façade slab itself, leading to potentially dangerous situations.

A problem of a different nature is that of stone expansion. Frequent changes in temperature can give rise to internal pressure. This is not a problem with thick façade slabs but nowadays façade slabs are getting ever thinner because new fixing techniques are being developed that make this possible and also of course because they are cheaper. In these thinner slabs, repeated expansion and shrinkage can cause the stone to bulge and even to break.

These problems do not hold for all varieties of limestone (some, like Comblanchien, have good frost resistance) and limestone can in any case be protected from weathering by means of impregnation. Nevertheless, these negative characteristics have led to limestone and marble no longer being very widely used as façade cladding in countries with an acid environment, especially if there is also a risk of frost. And that is a pity for they are beautiful stones.

Blue Limestone

Blaukalkstein | Calcaire bleu | Caliza azul | Calcare blu | Hardsteen

Project Bonnefanten Museum, Maastricht (1991)
Architect Aldo Rossi
Photographer Jan Derwig

Project Santen House, Borneo (2000)
Architect Rapp & Rapp
Photographer Kim Zwarts

Despite its strong Belgian associations, blue limestone occurs in other countries as well. Nevertheless, it rankles somewhat that Aldo Rossi should have chosen the Irish variant for his prestigious Bonnefanten Museum in Maastricht rather than stone from nearby Henegouwen. One reason for his choice is that the Irish variant weathers slightly better over time. Otherwise, the differences between the two types are quite minimal, the most noticeable one being that when sawn the Belgian variant gives off a sulphur smell that is largely absent with the Irish variant.

Technical Aspects

Belgian blue limestone is still sometimes referred to as Belgian granite. However, despite its high compressive strength (112 to 156 N/mm^2), it is completely unrelated to granite. Granite is igneous rock while blue limestone is a sedimentary rock. Its bluish-grey colour is due to its coal content; the more intense the colour, the costlier it is. Lighter ringlets are visible against the stone's dark background. Seams in the form of sinuous black lines may also be present. These form a bituminous partition between two layers and can lead to fracturing. The stone may also exhibit white veins and white calcite spots. The stone's hardness makes it well-suited for polishing, but the lustre does stand up well to outdoor weathering.

Applications

Blue limestone is suitable for both indoor and outdoor use. In polished form it may be used as an internal wall cladding, but not as flooring because of the high maintenance required. Once wear has occurred, the stone is liable to become slippery when wet, making it unsuitable for front steps or stair treads. The stone can be pitched, bush-hammered, boasted and drove. Cutting away the surface creates a special effect, as the stone's interior is lighter in colour than the deep grey, polished surface.

Colour	**grey**, **blue**, **black**
Glossiness	**glossy**, **satin**, **matt**
Translucence (%)	**0** – 20 – 40 – 60 – 80 – 100
Texture	sharp, **medium**, **dull**
Hardness	**hard**, soft, depressible
Temperature	warm, **medium**, cool
Odour	strong, moderate, **none**
Acoustic opacity	good, moderate, **poor**

Saint Maximin

Saint Maximin | Saint Maximin | Saint Maximin | Saint Maximin | Saint Maximin

Project American Center, Paris (1994)
Architect Frank O. Gehry
Photographer Kees Hummel

The American Center in Paris was the first building in which Frank O. Gehry used 'curved' natural stone. It was a surprising choice given his predilection for geometrically challenging forms but he chose it because he regards Paris as 'the city of limestone'. The fragility of present-day limestone slabs in comparison with the sturdy blocks of the past was highlighted by this building: many of the Saint Maximin limestone slabs in the façade's lowest course were badly damaged by vandals shortly after the building's inauguration.

Technical Aspects

The Saint Maximin stone used in the American Center is a limestone. Limestone consists of calcium carbonate and is formed by chemical or biological processes. In its pure form, limestone is white. The presence of any metal salts will give it a yellow, black, green, red or brownish colour. Limestone exists in a wide variety of types; even pieces from one and the same quarry can vary in hardness, colour and structure. Limestone is liable to various defects. Its cavities and cracks may be filled with vitreous crystalline lime (white veining). Although this does not in itself make the stone weaker, if the filling is incompletely petrified and contains earthy particles, the stone may lack cohesion.

Applications

Not all types of limestone can be used in places with damp climates and polluted air, as they are not resistant to the effects of acid rain and water containing carbon dioxide. In addition, most types are not frost resistant. Many types of limestone are, however, suitable for dressing. Even polishing is possible, although the stone's lustre disappears rapidly outdoors. All limestone and, consequently all marble types, are prone to lime bloom or efflorescence, which leaves a greyish white film on façades. Efflorescence can be mitigated by impregnating the stone with a hydrophobic material. This bonds to the inside of the stone's pores and makes the surface water repellent. This treatment offers no protection against an aggressive environment, however.

Colour	**beige, pink**
Glossiness	glossy, **satin, matt**
Translucence (%)	0 – **20** – 40 – 60 – 80 – 100
Texture	sharp, **medium, dull**
Hardness	**hard**, soft, depressible
Temperature	warm, **medium**, cool
Odour	strong, moderate, **none**
Acoustic opacity	good, moderate, **poor**

Comblanchien

Comblanchien | Comblanchien | Comblanchien | Comblanchien | Comblanchien

Project Louvre Pyramid, Paris (1989)
Architect I.M. Pei
Photographer Kees Hummel

Project Lyon-Satolas Station, Lyon (1994)
Architect Santiago Calatrava
Photographer © Ralph Richter | Architekturphoto

The Grand Staircase of the Paris Opéra is one of the world's most renowned staircases. Ever since the building's opening, Parisian high society has used it as a place to parade their extravagant attire. The Opéra was built of Comblanchien, a stone that continues to be used in prestigious projects, albeit less and less often as a façade cladding. It was used to pave the floors of Santiago Calatrava's TGV station at Lyons as well as those of I.M. Pei 's Louvre pyramid.

Technical Aspects

Comblanchien is often erroneously classified as marble. In fact, it is a French limestone, found near the village of the same name in the Côte d'Or region. It is one of the hardest limestones, having a compressive strength of 260 N/mm^2, and is formed through oolitic sedimentation. Ooliths are tiny grains of calcium containing mineral or organic dust particles in their centres. As with all limestones, the colour of the stone is determined by impurities present during formation. Comblanchien owes its brown-beige colour and red veins to an extremely small quantity of iron ore. In all other respects, the stone is quite neutral. Glass veins may occasionally occur but they do not affect its quality. Small grey concavities are also sometimes present. Comblanchien is frost resistant, but is vulnerable to acids.

Applications

In places with a damp climate and polluted air, Comblanchien has ceased to be a popular choice for façade cladding. However, historical examples, like the Paris Opéra and the Palace of Justice in Brussels, are proof that when regularly washed by rain the stone can remain beautiful for long periods of time. Façades not washed by rain are soiled by air pollution.

In addition to being used as a wall or façade cladding, the stone can also be used for floors, stairs and pedestals (New York's Statue of Liberty stands on a Comblanchien plinth). The stone can be polished, ground, honed and flamed. When the stone is flamed, the fossilized shells turn into white spots.

Colour	**beige, pink**
Glossiness	glossy, **satin, matt**
Translucence (%)	0 – **20** – 40 – 60 – 80 – 100
Texture	sharp, **medium, dull**
Hardness	**hard**, soft, depressible
Temperature	warm, **medium, cool**
Odour	strong, moderate, **none**
Acoustic opacity	good, moderate, **poor**

Travertine

Travertin | Travertin | Mármol travertino | Travertino | Travertin

Project Kunsthal, Rotterdam (1992)
Architect Rem Koolhaas, OMA
Photographer Kees Hummel

A stone with mythical connotations, travertine is also one of the few natural stones used by leading architects from ancient times to the present day. The Coliseum in Rome (80 AD) consists primarily of travertine blocks; for the columns in front of St. Peter's in Rome (1667), Bernini had 276 twenty-metre-high columns cut out of the quarries of Campidoglio; Mies van der Rohe's German Pavilion at Barcelona (1929) and Farnsworth House (1950) both have floors of travertine; and for their Kunsthal (Rotterdam, 1992), Rem Koolhaas' OMA employed one travertine façade as counterpoint to the concrete façade and aluminium façade cladding.

Technical Aspects

Travertine is a type of limestone formed by sedimentation in flowing calcareous water or by acidic water containing CO_2 flowing over limestone and causing the calcium carbonate in the stone to dissolve. Once the rate of flow has subsided, the CO_2 escapes and the carbonate precipitates. The slower the process, the more compact the structure of the resulting travertine and the better the quality of the stone. The holes in the stone are the result of washed-away clay or the decomposition of plant stalks trapped in the sediment. The lowest layers of the travertine usually have smaller holes, a more even structure and colour gradation and are generally more highly rated. Building slabs cut at right angles to the bands exhibit the typical laminated structure of travertine. Slabs cut parallel to the bands display a swirling pattern. The best-known travertine comes from Italy and is bright to pale yellowish in colour. There are also white, brown and red travertines.

Applications

Despite its holes, travertine is a fine façade cladding. Its frost resistance is excellent if used in slab rather than block form. Its hardwearing qualities make it a suitable flooring material. To prevent dirt accumulating in the holes, these can be filled with a synthetic resin or cement.

Project Zwitserleven Building, Amsterdam (1993)
Architect Pi de Bruijn, de Architekten Cie.
Photographer Brakkee & Scagliola

Colour	**beige, white, yellow, red, brown**
Glossiness	glossy, **satin**, **matt**
Translucence (%)	0 – **20** – 40 – 60 – 80 – 100
Texture	**sharp**, **medium**, dull
Hardness	**hard**, soft, depressible
Temperature	warm, **medium**, cool
Odour	strong, moderate, **none**
Acoustic opacity	good, moderate, **poor**

Trani

Trani | Trani | Trani | Pietra di Trani | Trani

Project Padre Pio Pilgrimage Church, San Giovanni Rotonda (1991)
Architect Renzo Piano Workshop
Photographer Gaudenti Sergio | Corbis Kipa | TCS

Natural stone's ability to withstand pressure virtually unaided has obvious structural implications. While natural stone makes excellent columns, beams are more problematical. In his design for the Padre Pio church in San Giovanni Rotondo, Renzo Piano circumvented the problem in a manner as brilliant as it is ancient, by placing blocks of Trani stone in an arch. The church, which, with its 6000 m² floor area, is Italy's largest after St. Peter's in Rome, has arches of up to 50 x 16 metres. These are not completely natural arches, though, as a steel construction embedded in the stone ensures that sufficient pressure is exerted on the stone elements to avoid tensile stress.

Technical Aspects

With a compressive strength of 185 N/mm², Trani stone is not especially strong, and the fact that it was nevertheless suitable for the gigantic Padre Pio church speaks for the effectiveness of the construction principle employed there. This Italian limestone is 95% calcium. It also contains minerals such as dolomite and quartz. It owes its cream colour to a small quantity of limonite. There are also variants with reddish arabesques (Trani filetto rosso) and a yellower one (gialetto). The limonite can also give the stone's polished surface an extremely fine, net-like structure. Besides the smooth varieties, there are others, such as Trani cocciolato with a higher component of fossils (e.g., mussels and ooliths). Trani's high water permeability means that it is not frost resistant.

Applications

Trani stone can only be used in the way Piano employed it in frost-free areas; in colder climates its use is restricted to indoors. It can be used in block form and in the form of façade panels. As with almost all other limestones, this Italian type is also highly suitable for polishing, although outdoors it rapidly loses its lustre as a result of patination.

Colour	**beige**
Glossiness	glossy, **satin**, **matt**
Translucence (%)	0 – **20** – 40 – 60 – 80 – 100
Texture	sharp, **medium**, **dull**
Hardness	**hard**, soft, depressible
Temperature	warm, **medium**, cool
Odour	strong, moderate, **none**
Acoustic opacity	good, moderate, **poor**

Boulders

Rollsteine | Rochers | Rocas | Massi | Keien

Project Den Daalder, Boxtel (2002)
Architect Min2 bouw-kunst
Photographer Min2 bouw-kunst

Project City Hall Barbarasteeg, Delft (1990)
Architect Mecanoo
Photographer Kees Hummel

Boulders are an ancient building material. In regions where usable boulders were readily available, they were stacked to form simple walls. Although all such walls were built in much the same way and consequently look quite similar, each wall reflects something very specific about its location. The actual boulders used determine to a large extent the 'personality' of the resulting structure. Significantly, this type of wall has always been used by great architects, right down to the present day. Amongst others, Le Corbusier, Frank Lloyd Wright, Eduard Bru, Renzo Piano and Sverre Fehn have created magnificent buildings with walls made of boulders.

Technical Aspects

Boulders are usually of a high quality. They have led a turbulent life – swept along by rivers, pushed ahead of the ice caps. Had they not been hard, they would have been reduced to gravel. A boulder may consist of any of the harder stone types. Sverre Fehn and Eduard Bru both used granite boulders; in Germany, sandstone boulders predominate. But there are boulders of gneiss, quartzite, porphyry, limestone and virtually all other stone types. As a result, a boulder's shape, colour, strength and other properties can vary widely. However, because of their genesis, all boulders have rounded corners. Colours include black, blue, grey, red, yellow, green and white. They are usually resistant to frost and have a high compressive strength.

Applications

Boulders are actually only suitable for the walls of moderately high buildings. They can be simply stacked one upon the another or cemented together with mortar. In contrast to walls made of large blocks, the strength of a wall made of boulders is largely determined by the strength of the connection between the stones.

Colour	**grey**, **brown**, **black**
Glossiness	glossy, **satin**, **matt**
Translucence (%)	**0** – 20 – 40 – 60 – 80 – 100
Texture	sharp, **medium**, **dull**
Hardness	**hard**, soft, depressible
Temperature	warm, **medium**, cool
Odour	strong, moderate, **none**
Acoustic opacity	good, moderate, **poor**

Other Sedimentary Stones

Sonstiges Sedimentgestein | Autres roches sédimentaires | Otras piedras sedimentarias | Altre rocce sedimentarie | Overige sedimentaire gesteenten

The difference between the sedimentary stones dealt with in this section and the limestones, lies in the origin of their smallest particles. Limestone is composed of calcium which, having been deposited as sediment, is slowly transformed by biological or chemical processes and under ever-increasing pressure, into stone. The two most important sedimentary stones discussed here – sandstone and tuff stone – have a much stronger source material as their basis: sandstone derives from igneous rock and tuff stone can be regarded as a by-product of volcanic activity.

Origin and Properties

Sandstone, as its name suggests, has its origins in the sedimentation of sand. Sand is nothing more than fine particles of igneous rock worn away by rain. Rivers carry the sand particles away and deposit them as soon as the current's velocity diminishes. Through the increasing pressure of the upper layers and the presence of binding agents such as clay, calcium or silicic acid, the grains are joined to form a relatively hard stone with its own specific properties.

Tuff stone forms after volcanic ash has settled in water containing carbon dioxide. The closer the stone occurs to the volcanic crater, the more pieces of hard igneous rock – granite or basalt lava – it will contain. Such stone, also known as core stone, is of much better quality than stone found further away from the crater which contains

Project La Saline Royale, Arc et Senans (1778)
Architect Claude Nicolas Ledoux
Photographer Jan Derwig

Project Italian sandstone in Oysseus, Schoorl (1998)
Architect Min2 bouw-kunst
Photographer Min2 bouw-kunst

a higher proportion of ash that renders is much less usable. Tuff stone that is not good enough to be used as a façade material or flooring can be pulverized to make trass (an additive in hydraulic mortar). Owing to the special conditions necessary for its formation, tuff stone is relatively rare. Sandstone and limestone, by contrast, are extremely plentiful.

Tuff stone has the greatest range of colours of all sedimentary stone, blue being the only colour in which it does not occur. Sandstone is particularly well-represented in the light hues (white, cream, yellow) and red (due to the presence of iron oxide during formation). Green (due to glauconite) and brown are less common, whilst black, grey and blue sandstone are extremely rare.

Although all three are sedimentary in origin, the properties of limestone, sandstone and tuff stone differ considerably owing to the different circumstances of their formation. Limestone is the most vulnerable of the three; most limestones are not frost resistant, whereas 80% of all sandstones and tuff stones are well able to withstand frosty weather. This is particularly surprising in the case of tuff stone which is quite soft and more than moderately porous. Its protective mechanism works in essentially the same manner as that of travertine: although the cavities in the stone allow the water to penetrate quite deeply, these same cavities absorb the pressure exerted by the expanding frozen water and prevent it from cracking the stone. Limestone has also proven vulnerable to acid environments.

Sandstone, too, is a naturally vulnerable stone, but is able to protect itself: the silicic acid in the quarry water forms a protective coating on the surface of the stone after evaporation. Cleaning a sandstone façade consequently defeats its own purpose since it results in the removal of this coating. Without it the stone will be more vulnerable to soiling and, worse still, to damage. Sandstone's rough, grainy surface (which also makes grinding or polishing pointless) does mean that dirt adheres more easily to façade slabs of this stone than to slabs of smoother stone, such as limestone. Even if its protective layer is intact, sandstone is still vulnerable to damage in an acid environment. Although the grains of sand themselves are not affected

by these aggressive substances, the binding agents are less resistant and this can result in a sandy surface. Sandstone can, however, be protected against such effects, for example by treating it with silicon ester. Gravel sandstones are somewhat harder than normal sandstone and thus better able to withstand the effects of an increasingly acid environment. They are also fire resistant but their coarser appearance may not be to everyone's taste.

Sandstone and Tuff as Façade Materials

The effects of the environment and certainly of time on sandstone are clearly visible in old buildings. Sandstone was once used extensively and with much decoration in such structures, not least because of its plentifulness and the fact that many sandstone varieties are quite soft, and thus easy to work. Over the years, though, the mouldings of many plinths and cornices have been worn away by erosion. Until recently, the restoration of such buildings in the Netherlands was very difficult because the Sandstone Decree of 1951 prohibited the working and finishing of sandstone. This legislation was prompted by the fact that the working of sandstone releases fine particles which can cause the deadly stonecutter's disease. The Decree made it necessary to replace damaged sandstone by other, visually similar, natural stone such as basalt lava or tuff stone. The decree has since been modified to the extent that sandstone elements in listed buildings may now be replaced with sandstone. Sandstone façades for new buildings continue to be out of the question in the Netherlands. Even this is quite surprising, as in other countries, especially Germany, sandstone is used extensively in construction. It goes without saying that stoneworkers in those EU countries where sandstone is extracted and worked, are well-protected against stonecutter's disease. Of course, there are alternatives to sandstone. Tuff stone resembles it in many respects, as does basalt lava when viewed from a distance. The fact remains, however, that sandstone's characteristic grainy structure and consequently rough surface is virtually impossible to imitate. Façades like those of Michael Wilson's British Embassy in Berlin (2000) testify to the architectural beauty of a stone which the Netherlands must unfortunately do without.

Project Slambor House, Decin, Czech Republic (2001)
Architect Jan Jehlik Architectural Office
Photographer Jan Jehlik

Sandstone

Sandstein | Grès | Arenisca | Arenaria | Zandsteen

Project Royal Palace, Amsterdam (1665)
Architect Jacob van Kampen
Photographer Kees Hummel

Project New British Embassy, Berlin (2000)
Architect Michael Wilford
Photographer © Andreas Secci | Architekturphoto

Nowhere are traditions – including the use of natural stone – more jealously guarded than in Berlin. Accordingly, the star architects entrusted with revitalizing the city following the fall of the Wall were presented with a detailed list of design do's and don'ts. The British architect Michael Wilford complied somewhat tongue in cheek. He duly clad the new British embassy with sandstone as stipulated, but detailed the façade in such a way that it looks like a kind of screen. To add insult to injury, protruding from this natural stone façade are huge, brightly coloured cubes that are completely at odds with Berlin tradition.

Technical Aspects

Sandstone is one of the most widely occurring types of stone. It consists primarily of quartz particles, but can also contain feldspar and other minerals. Under great pressure from the strata above them, and with loam or lime as binding agent, these particles are compressed into stone. The granular composition remains evident regardless of the type of finishing (e.g. polishing, flaming or grinding). Although most types are frost resistant, sandstone is quite a fragile stone. It does, however, have an inbuilt self-protective mechanism in the form of the silicic acid contained in the quarry water. After the water has been released and evaporated, the acid forms a hard protective layer on the stone's surface. For this reason, cleaning sandstone is not recommended, as it results in the removal of this layer. German Schönbrunner sandstone is one of the most richly coloured types, with bright yellow, beige, pink and green colour clouds.

Applications

Sandstone was used for the façade of the seventeenth-century palace on Dam Square in Amsterdam. Since 1951, however, the use of sandstone in construction has been prohibited in the Netherlands because the particles released when it is worked can cause stonecutter's disease. An exception is made for restoration projects when there is no comparable substitute stone, but permission must first be sought from the Health and Safety Inspectorate. Such restrictions are virtually unknown in other European countries. Although banned from construction, sandstone is often used for flagstones in Dutch gardens.

Colour	**black, grey, white, yellow, red**
Glossiness	glossy, satin, **matt**
Translucence (%)	**0** – 20 – 40 – 60 – 80 – 100
Texture	**sharp, medium,** dull
Hardness	**hard,** soft, depressible
Temperature	warm, **medium,** cool
Odour	strong, moderate, **none**
Acoustic opacity	good, moderate, **poor**

Shell Limestone

Muschelkalkstein | Calcaire conchylien | Cobertura caliza | Calcare con conchiglie | Muschelkalksteen

Project Congress Centre, Weimar (1999)
Architect Von Gerkan, Marg und Partners
Photographer H.Chr. Schink | PUNCTUM

As only the 'core' stone from a shell limestone quarry can be guaranteed to meet the highest requirements, slab dimensions are usually limited to a maximum of 2000 x 1000 mm. The fact that slabs measuring 2590 x 1360 mm were used for the conference centre in Weimar is indicative of the scale of this project. The centre was designed by Von Gerkan, Marg und Partner and the stone comes from Kelheim. In common with many other former high-tech architects who once embraced glass, steel and concrete, Von Gerkan are increasingly opting for natural materials.

Technical Aspects

Shell limestone contains a high proportion of corals, small marine animal skeletons and shells trapped in the precipitation of lime mud. Apart from these shell fossils, the stone's appearance is also determined by fossilized plants and the holes left by decomposed plant matter. Shell limestone is 96% lime. It may also contain iron oxide and, very occasionally, quartz; these 'impurities' give the stone special accents. Shell limestone is primarily found in Germany (south of Würzburg) and Switzerland. Despite the relatively small area where it is found, differences between quarries can be surprisingly great. The stone's colour varies from brown-grey and reddish all the way to blue. The blue variant is the hardest and is suitable for polishing. The best stone is obtained from a quarry's densest bed and is called core stone. Core stone cannot be polished; it can, however, be fine honed to a very smooth finish. Although the quality of core stone is generally high, it sometimes contains quite big loam-filled cavities.

Applications

Shell limestone has only been exploited on a large scale for building since the early 20th century. Core stone is suitable for internal walls and ornamentation and as a façade cladding, although the slabs must be at least 4 cm thick. Under normal circumstances, stone on the rain-affected sides of a building exhibits little or no discolouration. The types Goldbank, Blaubank and Edelblau cannot be used as façade cladding.

Colour	**brown grey, bluish grey**
Glossiness	glossy, satin, **matt**
Translucence (%)	**0** – 20 – 40 – 60 – 80 – 100
Texture	sharp, **medium, dull**
Hardness	**hard**, soft, depressible
Temperature	warm, **medium**, cool
Odour	strong, moderate, **none**
Acoustic opacity	good, moderate, **poor**

Danube Limestone

Donaukalkstein | Calcaire danubien | Caliza del Danubio | Calcare del Danubio | Trosselfels

Project San Giovanni Battista Church, Mogno (1996)
Architect Mario Botta
Photographer Christian Richters

There are many reasons for using natural stone. The Gerling Insurance Group, for example, wanted to use Danube limestone for its new premises because its existing building was clad with it, and because the proven durability of this material had become linked in their minds to the image of dependability they desired for their company. Foster & Partners used Danube limestone to clad the head elevations of the three towers, which, in addition to office space, also contain apartments. The remaining elevations are of glass and steel.

Technical Aspects

Danube limestone is related to shell limestone but whereas the lime in shell limestone binds together a number of different shell types, in Danube limestone the lime formed a deposit on a coral reef. The stone's basic material makes it much stronger than most shell limestones. Its compressive strength is 167 N/mm^2, its bending strength 10.2 N/mm^2. It is frost resistant and, in principle, also hard enough to be polished. However, when used outside it does not retain its lustre for very long. Lime efflorescence has little or no negative effect on the stone's character, as its own cream colour is very close to that of lime. Besides its colour, its vibrant surface is also an important feature.

Applications

Danube limestone is found primarily in the vicinity of Regensburg, Germany. After the architects had settled on this material, they discovered that the quarry had been closed for some time. As with shell limestone, only the core stone is of good quality and once this has been worked out further quarrying becomes uneconomic. However, the quarry was reopened specially for this building. Since polished Danube limestone soon becomes dull, the stone for the Gerling complex was ground to a mat finish. The insurer's logo was engraved in the stone. Polished Danube limestone can be used as a wall covering and as flooring although in the latter case it is liable to lose its shine through wear.

Colour	**brown grey**
Glossiness	glossy, satin, **matt**
Translucence (%)	**0** – 20 – 40 – 60 – 80 – 100
Texture	sharp, **medium, dull**
Hardness	**hard**, soft, depressible
Temperature	warm, **medium**, cool
Odour	strong, moderate, **none**
Acoustic opacity	good, moderate, **poor**

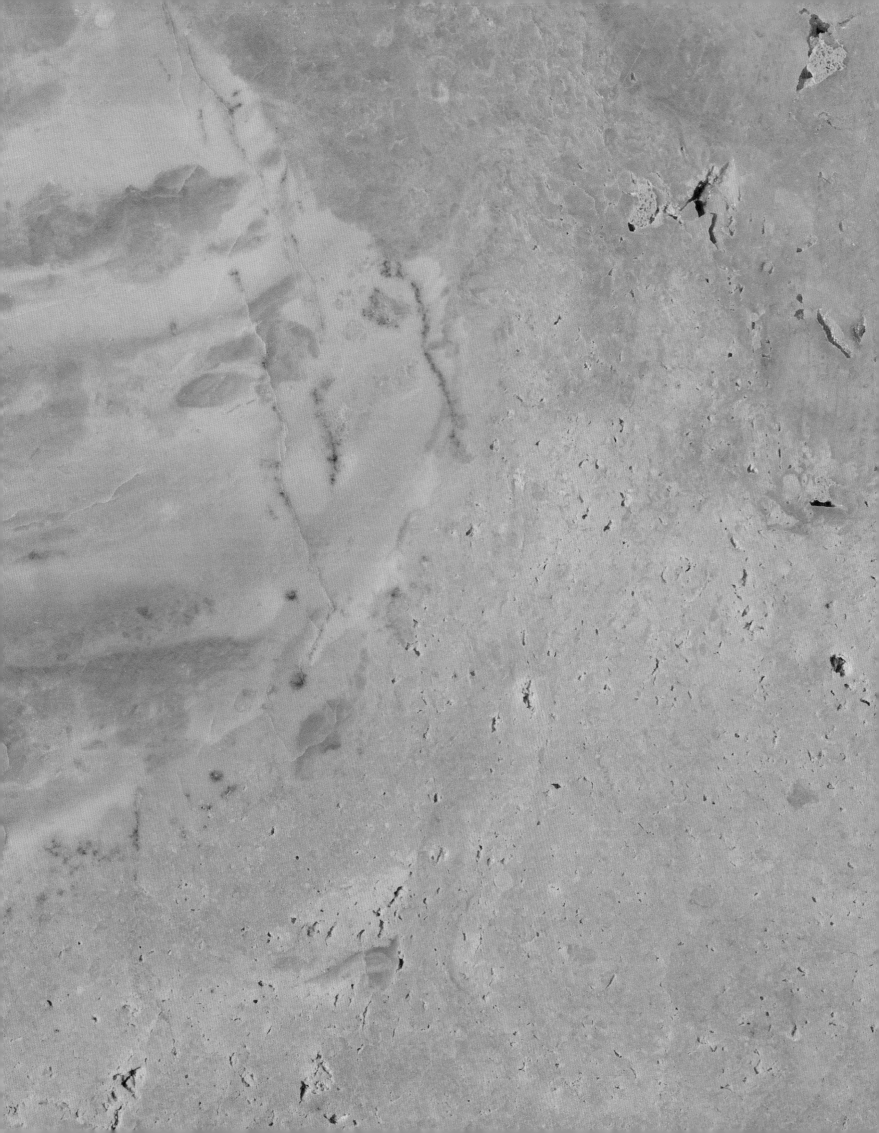

Tuff

Tuffstein | Tuf | Tufo o toba | Tufo | Tufsteen

Project Kölner Dom, Cologne (c. 1842)
Architect Vincenz Statz
Photographer © Ralph Richter | Architekturphoto

In a house in Latium, Italy, tuff has been employed in a manner harking back to ancient times. The outer walls are made of heavy, 25 cm-thick blocks which absorb the heat in the summer, keeping the interior cool. The material's relative softness made it possible to cut the blocks with a high degree of precision. Like most other natural stone types, tuff was already in use in ancient times. The famous Lion Gate of Mycenae is made of tuff, as is Cologne Cathedral.

Technical Aspects

Tuff is relatively soft and, like basalt lava, visibly porous. Like basalt lava it is formed in the wake of a volcanic eruption. Tuff is formed when volcanic ash precipitates in groundwater containing carbon dioxide. The further the stone is found from the volcano from which it came, the more open its structure. Despite its porous surface, most types of tuff are reasonably durable and frost resistant. There are several types of tuff with a surprisingly wide range of colours, much wider than basalt lava with which tuff has so much in common. It is available in black, white, yellow, green, red and blue variants. Not all types are suitable for façade cladding. One of the best is Ettringer tuff, which has a dense structure and a compressive strength of approximately 40 N/mm^2. The Ettringer variant can be recognized by its white spots.

Applications

Tuff has a wide range of possible applications, both in new construction and the restoration of monuments. As the house in Latium demonstrates, tuff can be used both in block and slab form. Depending on their dimensions, slabs range in thickness from 60 to 80 mm. Tuff can be boasted and tooled, but not polished. It is too soft to be used for stair treads or as flooring.

Colour	**black**, grey, **white**, **crème**, **yellow**, **red**, **brown**, **green**
Glossiness	glossy, satin, **matt**
Translucence (%)	**0** – 20 – 40 – 60 – 80 – 100
Texture	sharp, **medium, dull**
Hardness	**hard**, soft, depressible
Temperature	warm, **medium**, cool
Odour	strong, moderate, **none**
Acoustic opacity	good, moderate, **poor**

Metamorphic or Changed-form Stone

Metamorphes Gestein oder Umwandlungsgestein | Roche métamorphique |
Roca metamórfica o alterada | Pietre metamorfiche | Metamorfe gesteenten

Stone that results when nature decides to repeat the baking process
is called metamorphic. The process of mountain range formation and
other upheavals in geological strata, subject stone that has already
been formed to immensely high temperatures and pressures once
again, thereby altering its properties. In most instances, this leads to
an enhancement of the stone's intrinsic qualities.

Origin and Properties

There are two basic metamorphic processes. In the one, a stone's
structure is altered by the heat generated by certain geological
events such as the different strata shifting in relation to one another
or, somewhat less earth-shattering, a volcanic eruption. In the other
type of metamorphosis, change is brought about by pressure, for

Project The Collective Garden, Hoofddorp (2002)
Architect Heren 5
Photographer Kees Hummel

example when stone is squeezed by the folding of the earth's crust.
A prominent feature of most metamorphic stone is the stratification
resulting from the shrinkage which occurs during the cooling process.
This often makes it relatively easy to split extremely hard stone and
thus to produce slabs from it. However, the layers are typically irregular, and obtaining flat slabs of large dimensions is consequently a
difficult and often costly undertaking.

The best known and most widely used metamorphic stone is
undoubtedly marble, yet it is often not looked upon as a metamorphic stone and many material books even classify it among the limestones. This is because the properties of 'true marble' are not always
markedly superior to those of the limestone from which it was metamorphosed. For example, genuine marble, which has a crystalline
structure, soils more rapidly than 'ordinary' limestone; when it
expands through exposure to sunlight, it can be more problematical
than limestone, as its crystals all expand in one particular direction,
such that slabs made of them are more prone to bulging than slabs
of other limestone types. In addition, limestone has more vibrant
colours, as well as a wider range of hues than marble. This often leads
to ornamental limestone varieties being used in place of genuine
marble. Nevertheless, since the brand name 'marble' sells better than
'limestone', ornamental limestones are often marketed as marble.
Azul Macaubas bears a superficial resemblance to marble. It has the

like all stone, serpentino is liable to contain hidden flaws so its actual rating is a much lower 10 N/mm². Another property of serpentin is its excellent fire resistance. Whilst fire transforms limestone into unslaked lime and creates cracks in granite that break open during fire extinguishing, serpentino withstands fire quite well.

Other metamorphic varieties include dolomite marble (a metamorphic form of dolomite), granulite (from paragneiss, itself a metamorphic form of sedimentary rock), orthogneiss (from granite) and migmatite. The last is something of an odd man out in the world of metamorphic rock, since it is only partly a metamorphic form of granite. Its non-metamorphic component consists of solidified

Project Tropenpunt Mauritskade, Amsterdam (2002)
Architect Erick van Egeraat Associated Architects
Photographer Christian Richters

Project City hall Alphen aan de Rijn (2002)
Architect Erick van Egeraat Associated Architects
Photographer Tjerk van Duinen | Beisterveld Natuursteen

same fine crystalline structure with even more stunning colours and micas. In fact, Azul Macaubas is a much better quality stone than marble. It is also a good deal more expensive, not only because of its qualities, but also because it is found only in Brazil. Its properties are similar to those of granite. Azul Macaubas is in fact a quarzite, a metamorphic form of sandstone that is so hard that it can be used to cut glass – steel cannot scratch it. However, this hardness makes it difficult to work, while its stratification makes slabs with large dimensions extremely rare.

Slate, too, is clearly superior to its unusably soft sedimentary parents, clay and shale. Slate is a result of the high temperatures generated whilst the earth's crust was being folded to form new mountain ranges; these temperatures yielded extremely hard and heavy stone. In addition to slate's great hardness, another important characteristic is its stratification, which makes it possible to split off wafer-thin slices. In addition, it is extremely watertight. These properties make it especially well-suited as a roof covering. Nowadays it is also increasingly being used as a façade cladding.

One remarkable metamorphic stone is serpentin, which is related to asbestos and occurs near it. Serpentin's most prominent feature is its fibrous structure. Its maximum bending strength is an impressive 6 x 104 kN/m². Theoretically it should make good structural beams, but

magma. As a result, the stone contains very (in some cases overly) vibrant flow patterns. Migmatite is a clear demonstration of the fact that metamorphic rock embraces a wide spectrum of different stones.

In contrast to sedimentary or igneous rock, metamorphic rocks are united not by their composition but by the transformation process they have undergone. Even though their properties are in many cases better than those of their parent stone, they are still more clearly related to it than to their fellow metamorphic stones.

Metamorphic Stone as a Façade Material

If these totally different stones have anything in common, it is perhaps their versatility. Because they have undergone an additional process that has generally resulted in improved properties, they are suitable for just about any application and can consequently be used both in façades and on floors.

Quartzite

Quarzit | Quartzite | Cuarcita | Quarzite | Kwartsiet

Project Thermal Baths, Vals (1996)
Architect Peter Zumthor
Photographer © Ralph Richter | Architekturphoto

Swiss architect Peter Zumthor wanted the thermal baths at Vals in Switzerland to look as if they had been hewn out of the quartzite-bearing mountain behind them. The baths' thick walls resemble massive quartzite slabs placed one upon the other. In reality, both the inner and outer leaves are made up of slabs of varying thicknesses and the cavity between the two walls is filled with reinforced concrete. Despite their immense hardness, these quartzite slabs had to be made with extreme precision; the permissible tolerance for a length of 320 cm was a mere 1 mm.

Technical Aspects

Quartzite is metamorphosed sandstone. High pressures and high temperatures over a very long period weld the grains of sand into dense, fine-grained crystalline rock. The 'welding' between the quartz grain and the cementing agent (silica) is so strong that fractures go through the quartz rather than, as in sandstone, through the cementing agent. That quartzite nevertheless lends itself well to working is due to the laminated structure that forms during the cooling process. The thickness of the layers varies from 10 to 40 mm. As with slate, this lamination makes it difficult to obtain large slabs, which are consequently very expensive. Quartzite comes in a variety of colours, including a greyish yellow, various green hues, brown and nearly black. Its quartz crystals give it a sparkling surface. Norwegian Alta quartzite, which contains high levels of mica, has a mother of pearl appearance. This type can be sanded or polished, but the laminations make this a difficult process since the stone must first be ground until it is all the same thickness.

Applications

Quartzite's extreme hardness, its durability and the roughness of its cleft surface make it an ideal stone for floor tiles or stair treads. It is now also used quite often as a façade cladding. Most types are weather and acid resistant. However, some types, like Oppdal and Vasto, may fade a little over time.

Project Library Dortmund (1999)
Architect Mario Botta
Photographer © Ralph Richter | Architekturphoto

Colour	**grey, white, crème, yellow, red, brown, green, blue**
Glossiness	**glossy, satin, matt**
Translucence (%)	**0** – 20 – 40 – 60 – 80 – 100
Texture	sharp, **medium, dull**
Hardness	**hard**, soft, depressible
Temperature	warm, **medium**, cool
Odour	strong, moderate, **none**
Acoustic opacity	good, moderate, **poor**

Azul Macaubas Bahia

Azul do Macaubas Bahia | Azul Macabaus Bahia | Macaubo Bahía Azul | Azul Macaubus Bahia | Azul Macaubas Bahia

Project Nord/LB Landesbank, Magdenburg (2002)

Architect Bolles + Wilson

Photographer Christian Richters

The new Nord/LB Landesbank in Magdeburg stands between Germany's oldest gothic cathedral and the city's baroque town hall, reason enough for its architect, Peter Wilson, to opt for a fairly intro-verted volume. The façade needed to be imposing but at the same time it was required to minimize the bank's presence and give it a time-worn aura in keeping with the 800-year-old cathedral. This all helps to explain Wilson's choice of Azul Macaubas, a very rare, and consequently, very expensive stone – it is some fifteen times as expensive as 'mere' granite, the price being partly determined by the patterns on the slabs.

Technical Aspects

Azul Macaubas is found only in the Brazilian state of Bahia. The stone is classified as a quartzite. It is a very unusual one since it does not occur in beds, like most types of natural stone, but in spherical formations. This makes extraction, and more especially prospecting, difficult. However, the search is well worth the effort as the stone is characterized by unrivalled variety: no two slabs of Azul Macaubas are the same. Owing to the presence of the mineral dumortierite, blue predominates, but the colour palette ranges from pink through blue to grey. Black flecks may also occur. Like most quartzites, Azul Macaubas is colourfast, frost resistant and unaffected by acid envir-onments.

Applications

Generally speaking, the fixing of quartzite slabs is no simple matter. Because the stone is composed of thin layers, boring holes in the sides of the slabs for mounting purposes may cause the slab to split. However, Azul Macaubas is an exceptionally homogeneous type and can be fixed using anchors. In Magdeburg it was decided for safety's sake to use a concealed suspension whereby the pins were attached to the backs of the 20 mm-thick slabs and the slabs suspended from the steel structure by the pins. Once polished, Azul Macaubas retains its lustre for a long period of time. It can also be ground.

Colour	**blue, white, pink, black**
Glossiness	**glossy, satin, matt**
Translucence (%)	**0** – 20 – 40 – 60 – 80 – 100
Texture	sharp, **medium**, **dull**
Hardness	**hard**, soft, depressible
Temperature	warm, **medium**, cool
Odour	strong, moderate, **none**
Acoustic opacity	good, moderate, **poor**

Gneiss

Gneis | Gneiss | Gneiss | Gneiss | Gneis

Project City Hall, Ternberg (1997)
Architect Riepl Riepl Architects
Photographer Josef Pausch

Project Church Mogno, Tessin (1995)
Architect Mario Botta
Photographer Robert Stadler

The most striking thing about Aldo Rossi's Quartier Schützenstraße in Berlin is the extremely cheerful use of colour, as though here, where the Wall once divided the city in two, its bright colours are intended to wipe away the past. Each house in the ensemble sports a different colour and different materials. Rossi combined a grey-green Italian paragneiss with bright green window frames and placed this wall opposite an orange façade. Actually, gneiss is quite often deployed as a contrast material by architects. In his famous church in Mogno, Mario Botto alternated dark grey bands of gneiss with white marble; in Ternberg, Peter Riepl placed a dark grey cube clad with Brazilian gneiss beside the bright white town hall.

Technical Aspects

Gneiss, which is a metamorphic form of granite, contains the same base materials and exhibits many of the same characteristics as its mother stone. Gneiss is formed at great depths, giving it a dense structure and high compressive strength of 15×10^4 kN/m². Like granite, gneiss contains coarse-grained minerals. Its mica deposits, for example, are visible to the naked eye and distributed in parallel sheets. Owing to the enormous pressure, gneiss is often laminated; despite its hardness to is easy to work. In Europe, the stone occurs on the southern side of the Alps in Switzerland, Italy and Austria. Europe also imports gneiss from other parts of the world, like Juparana from Brazil. Whereas the latter is yellowy-brown with white veins and clouds, the European varieties have primarily green and grey hues. In addition to clouds, gneiss may also exhibit a striped or speckled surface, depending on the direction of sawing. Sawing the stone parallel to the layers is more likely to produce clouds.

Applications

Although virtually all types of gneiss absorb water more readily than granite, resulting in a darker appearance, the stone is frost resistant. This makes it well-suited for use in façades, in either block or slab form. Gneiss takes well to polishing and many types retain their lustre for long to extremely long periods of time. It can also be sanded, bush-hammered, honed, sand-blasted and flamed.

Colour	**black, grey, white, yellow, red, brown, green, blue**
Glossiness	**glossy, satin, matt**
Translucence (%)	**0** – 20 – 40 – 60 – 80 – 100
Texture	**sharp, medium, dull**
Hardness	**hard**, soft, depressible
Temperature	warm, **medium**, cool
Odour	strong, moderate, **none**
Acoustic opacity	good, moderate, **poor**

Natural Stone – Metamorphic or Changed-form Stone

Slate

Schiefer | Ardoise | Pizarra | Ardesia | Leisteen

Project State Authority Offices for Brandenburg and Mecklenburg-Vorpommern (2001)
Architect Von Gerkan, Marg und Partners
Photographer Christian Kahl

Project Helicon building, The Hague (2000)
Architect Soeters Van Eldonck Ponec Architects
Photographer Jeroen van Amelsvoort

Slate is very easy to split due to its laminated structure. The only disadvantage of this structure is that it makes large slabs difficult to obtain. The enormous 1 x 1 metre slabs of Norwegian slate (Pillarguri) used in Sjoerd Soeters' Helicon Building in The Hague are indeed an exception to the rule.

Technical Aspects

Slate is a metamorphic rock. Particles of loam loosened by flowing water settle as soon as the water's speed diminishes sufficiently. Increasing pressure in turn leads to the formation of claystone. The tectonic forces and high temperatures associated with mountain formation metamorphose the clay into slate. In Pillarguri stone, a so-called mica slate, this natural 'baking process' has produced a very hard and dense stone that is completely impermeable to water. In addition to mica, the stone contains feldspar and quartz.

The colour palette, especially since the introduction of South African and Indian slates, is extremely wide, ranging from purple/blue and green to yellow/red. In general, the European varieties are more evenly coloured, while the African and Indian ones are more variegated.

Applications

Whereas slate roofs have been laid in more or less the same manner for centuries, slate façade cladding permits greater freedom in the mode of attachment. Although its laminated structure must of course be taken into account, the number of fixing methods is now quite large. It can be done in a relatively traditional manner, whereby the top of the slate tile is fastened with nails and the lower edge rests on a small hook, but the slate can also be attached to the background structure using mortar (as in Erick van Egeraat's town hall in Alphen aan de Rijn) or mounted on cramp irons (Soeters' Helicon Building) or a steel frame (Arata Isozaki's Museum of Mankind at La Coruña). Besides being used as façade cladding, Norwegian slates in particular make excellent floor coverings because of their resistance to wear.

Colour	**grey blue**, **purple**, **green**, **brown**
Glossiness	glossy, satin, **matt**
Translucence (%)	**0** – 20 – 40 – 60 – 80 – 100
Texture	sharp, medium, **dull**
Hardness	**hard**, soft, depressible
Temperature	warm, **medium**, cool
Odour	strong, moderate, **none**
Acoustic opacity	good, moderate, **poor**

Serpentine

Serpentin | Serpentine | Serpentina | Serpentino | Serpentino

Project Musikgymnasium Schloss Belvedere, Weimar (1996)
Architect Thomas van den Valentyn
Photographer Rainer Mader

Serpentine has a fibrous structure, giving it the extremely high bending strength. This would make it attractive as a structural material, were it not for the high risk involved in using natural stone for load-bearing members. This is why no structures have as yet been made using serpentine. However, splendid staircases have been built with serpentine treads fixed on one side only. Serpentine is also frequently used as reinforcement in stone structures, with the serpentine being glued to the stone.

Technical Aspects

Serpentine is a chlorite slate that owes its green colour to its chloride content. Like slate and quartzite, it is a highly laminated stone type, but unlike them it has a fibrous structure which gives it a formidable bending strength of $6 \cdot 10^4$ kN/m². Its compressive is about $2 \cdot 10^5$ kN/m². Serpentine, in the narrow sense, is found between Lexxo (Italy) and St. Moritz, whereas chlorite slates as a group occur much more widely. The best-known Italian serpentine is the speckled Serpentino Victoria which is harder and somewhat paler in colour than other types. In addition to the green variant, serpentine also occurs in black, yellow, red and brown. Only 20 per cent of all types are frost resistant and thus suitable for façades in colder climates. Although its dense structure lends itself to polishing, façade cladding made of the stone loses its lustre and discolours slightly after only 5 to 10 years. In addition to polished serpentine there is also a rough or split version, known as spaccato, in which the slabs are split along natural cleavage lines. Serpentine has excellent fire-resistance.

Applications

Although it should in theory be possible to employ serpentine in a construction where it is subjected to bending loads, in practice it is never used structurally in building parts because of the ever-present risk of hidden inconsistencies that might adversely affect the bending strength. However, the stone's superior bending strength does mean that larger slabs can be used than would be possible with other materials. In addition to stair treads and façade cladding, serpentine can also be used as a flooring.

Colour	**black, yellow, red, brown, green**
Glossiness	glossy, **satin, matt**
Translucence (%)	**0** – 20 – 40 – 60 – 80 – 100
Texture	sharp, **medium, dull**
Hardness	**hard,** soft, depressible
Temperature	warm, **medium,** cool
Odour	strong, moderate, **none**
Acoustic opacity	good, moderate, **poor**

Natural Stone – Metamorphic or Changed-form Stone

Greek Marble

Griechischer Marmor | Marbre grec | Mármol griego | Marmo greco | Grieks marmer

Project Baha'i House of Worship, New Delhi (1986)
Architect Fariburz Sahba
Photographer Thomas Dix

Project St. Pius Church, Meggen (1996)
Architect Franz Füeg
Photographer Robert Stadler

Franz Füeg had originally wanted to use onyx for his Church of St. Pius in Meggen, in imitation of his great exemplar, Mies van de Rohe. When it became clear that the stone could not be supplied in time, he switched to Greek marble quarried at Mt. Pentelikon, from where, some 2500 years ago, the Greeks obtained the marble for the Parthenon. Füeg used thin, 28 mm thick slabs in a steel construction, thereby allowing opalescent light to enter the church through the stone. Even thinner slabs (20 mm) were used for the top course, so that the light entering from above is brighter, appropriately enough for a church.

Technical Aspects

Pure marble is white and results from the metamorphosis of calcareous rock. Its veins and swirls of colour are due to the presence of chemical impurities and metal salts in the original limestone. The same phenomenon accounts for the rare black, yellow, green and reddish variants. The compressive strength of marble varies from 80 to 180 N/mm². Most marble types have good frost resistance. Polishing helps reveal the full beauty of their colours.

Applications

Marble suffers the same disadvantage as most limestone types. When the stone is used outside, the lime effloresces and the colours of the more veined marble types gradually disappear beneath a whitish haze (patination). However, on the whiter types, such as this Greek type or Italian Carrara marble, the lime bloom may be barely noticeable. A greater technical problem is marble's vulnerability to sunlight, acid rain and industrial pollution. Hydrophobic impregnation of the surface is possible but it does not halt the process of patination, merely retards it by making it more difficult for rain to penetrate the stone.

Colour	**white veined**
Glossiness	glossy, **satin**, **matt**
Translucence (%)	0 – 20 – **40** – 60 – 80 – 100
Texture	sharp, **medium**, **dull**
Hardness	**hard**, soft, depressible
Temperature	warm, **medium**, cool
Odour	strong, moderate, **none**
Acoustic opacity	good, moderate, **poor**

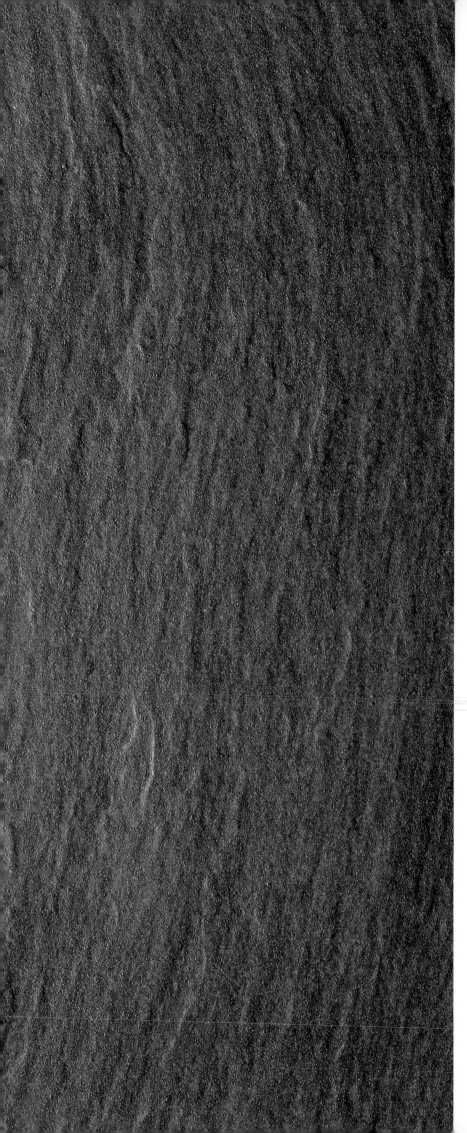

Natural Stone
Additives

Zuschlagstoffe für Naturstein | Additifs | Aditivos para piedra natural |
Additivi alla pietra naturale | Toevoegingen natuursteen

Natural stone granules are a fairly ordinary construction material in countries with good natural stone deposits. There, huge quantities of natural stone rubble, such as limestone (Belgium), porphyry, quartzite (Central Europe) and granite (Norway) are available to be turned into aggregates for concrete. This contrasts with countries like the Netherlands, where natural stone is relatively scarce and consequently more costly, but where gravel is in generous supply. (River gravel, which consists primarily of quartz, is also a natural stone – sedimentary rock, to be precise – but is generally not classified as such.) It is a material's availability and thus its cost, which determines how exclusive or conventional its use will be.

The quality of concrete depends to a large extent on the strength of its aggregates. Given the same quality of cement, the addition of

Project Continental Hotel, Lignano (2002)
Architect Oscar Rizzatto
Photorapher Ariostea

granite aggregate and river gravel will yield the strongest concrete (cube compressive strength after 28 days: 38.7 N/mm^2) and the addition of quartzite the weakest (cube compressive strength after 28 days: 33.3 N/mm^2). As well as strength, other considerations may also play a role in the selection of an aggregate. One of these is shape: flat stones are obviously not suitable, whilst an angular aggregate will result in a looser packing, with cavities that will in turn need to be filled with a fine aggregate such as sand. The amount of water required also varies from one aggregate to another, depending on the size and shape of the granules. Some natural stone types, such as limestone, may contain rubble dust and this, too, necessitates a larger quantity of water which in turn makes the concrete more expensive.

Accordingly, not all natural stone types are suitable for use as aggregates. Important factors to be borne in mind when selecting a stone aggregate are the strength, resistance to wear and, in some cases (e.g. limestone), the thermal properties of the stone in broken form. Each prospective aggregate must therefore be tested individually in order to ascertain the precise consequences of its use. For example,

Project Residential building, Milano (2002)
Architect Giovanni Mistretta
Photographer Ariostea

when crushed natural stone is used as either coarse or fine aggregates anything from 10 to 50 litres of water extra per cubic metre of concrete may be required.

If the concrete is to be exposed, the type of aggregate employed will of course help determine the concrete's appearance. It makes quite a lot of difference whether dark Norwegian granite, pink Scottish granite, grey porphyry or greenish quartzite is added to the concrete. To ensure that the aggregate will be visible on the surface, it is however necessary to wash the concrete to remove the outer layer of cement paste. The tiny sparkling particles in the marble aggregate Herman Haan used for a villa in the Dutch town of Malden, for example, give an extra dimension to the precast concrete wall.

If employed solely as an aggregate, the amount of natural stone ultimately visible will be a matter of chance. There is, however, a way of ensuring that the outer skin of a concrete wall is made up entirely of natural stone granules. First the bottom of the mould is covered with a 2 cm-thick layer of natural stone granules; then concrete to which an aggregate has already been added is poured on top. If wished,

the finished element can be polished. Although stone aggregate used in this way does not really affect the concrete's strength, it does improve its durability and, thus, that of the wall. First and foremost, the stone helps to cover the reinforcement. For this reason, the stone used must neither be too porous nor have a composition which accelerates so-called concrete cancer.

The properties of the stone used will also affect how the wall stands the test of time. Coloured marble varieties, in particular, are not well suited for this application: they are vulnerable to aggressively acid environments, have low frost resistance and are subject to lime efflorescence which detracts from their appearance. In contrast, quartzite, gneiss and granite are ideal for finishing concrete.

In fact, this method has long been used for making simple mosaics. As far back as 1600 BC, the Chaldeans pushed pieces of granite, marble and other natural stones into the mortar used for the palace at Uruk. Until Alexander the Great, mosaics were primarily an Asiatic art, but in the wake of his conquests, mosaics were used in many Greek and Roman buildings. The mosaics in Byzantine buildings represent a high point of the art. The Byzantines not only decorated the walls of their palaces and basilicas with mosaics, but their floors and ceilings as well. The Moors, finally, introduced precast mosaic floor elements: pieces of stone, glass and occasionally precious stones were bound together with plaster in the workshop, and these very fragile mosaic tiles were then transported to the palaces. In composite tiles, the present-day version of these Moorish tiles, the natural stone component is bound hydraulically or with synthetic resin. When used for walls, they are 10 to 20 mm thick and quite delicate. A more robust tile is achieved by applying the mixture of natural stone granules, which may consist of any non-foliated type, and binding agent to a concrete base. Once compressed, polished and honed, such tiles are very hardwearing and are a popular choice for supermarket floors.

More seamless, and consequently smoother and more hygienic, are the traditional terrazzo floors so long out of fashion but now making a comeback. Their properties are basically excellent and possibly better than those of many massive stone floors. Terrazzo floors, which consist of stone granules rolled in a cement layer, are hardwearing, retain their gloss and have an extremely dense structure that renders them completely watertight. In addition, the product is malleable and can be used to cover any shape. In the 1920s, decorative street furniture was clad with a layer of terrazzo, which was then known as 'granito'. This name was eventually dropped and replaced by 'terrazzo' because 'granito' sounded too much like 'granite', and if there is anything this product does not resemble, it is granite, or any other natural stone for that matter. This is also the greatest drawback of this floor and wall covering: despite all efforts to imitate the richness of genuine natural stone it is, and remains, fake.

High-tech Stone

Hightech-Stein | Pierres high-tech | Piedra high-tech | Pietra sintetica | High-tech steen

Project Malossi commercial & office building, Calderara di Remo (2003)
Architect Alessandro Franceschini
Photographer Ariostea

Project Londras Hotel, Milano Marittimos (2001)
Photographer Ariostea

The ecological advantages and disadvantages of stone is a much-discussed topic. Whilst most stone varieties are extremely durable, their extraction leaves gaping holes in the landscape. Such damage is sometimes camouflaged by turning quarries into tourist attractions or by flooding them with water. In addition, the most intensively used European natural stone varieties have inevitably become scarcer. Synthetic stone – itself not particularly environmentally friendly due to its production process – could, however, make an important contribution to improving the situation. Its manufacturer refers to his range of products as high-tech marble and not without justification, as they bear an amazing resemblance to natural stone, whilst their properties are similar to those of glazed tiles, and thus superior to those of many limestones.

Technical Aspects

In essence, the process of making high-tech marble mimics the natural process: calcium particles are compressed under great pressure and temperatures. The resulting stone can be given a wide range of colour nuances, from a yellowish white ground with red veins to a black ground with white veins. Aside from the broad colour palette, the stone's technical properties are also impressive. Whilst marble and other limestone types can no longer be used in acid, damp environments, these man-made stones not only stand up to acid rain, but are also frost-resistant.

Applications

Up to now, high-tech marble has for the most part been used as a flooring. However, its properties are so outstanding that it can also be used in façades where the ready availability of a wide selection of fitting pieces makes it much easier to create the illusion of massive blocks than with 'ordinary' natural stone slabs, as it eliminates the laborious process of shaping the fitting pieces. High-tech marble can be both honed and polished. To increase its slip resistance, it can also be given the texture of rough-hewn stone.

Colour	**variable**
Glossiness	**glossy**, **satin**, **matt**
Translucence (%)	**0** – 20 – 40 – 60 – 80 – 100
Texture	sharp, **medium**, **dull**
Hardness	**hard**, soft, depressible
Temperature	warm, **medium**, cool
Odour	strong, moderate, **none**
Acoustic opacity	good, moderate, **poor**

Stone-glass Laminate

Schichtstoff aus Stein und Glas | Pierre/verre feuilleté | Laminado piedra-vidrio | Vetro laminato ricoperto di marmo | Steinglass

Project Christ Pavilion, Hanover Expo (2000)
Architect Von Gerkan, Marg and Partners
Photographer © Ralph Richter | Architekturphoto

In designing the Christ Pavilion for Expo 2000 in Hanover, Meinhard von Gerkan wanted to create the same kind of atmosphere as in Franz Füeg's Church of St. Pius in Meggen where splendid light shines through the marble façade cladding, albeit using present-day techniques. This resulted in a finer overall construction and, most striking of all, a façade of *Steinglas*, a stone-glass laminate which in this case consisted of thin sheets of Greek Naxos marble glued to laminated glass.

Technical Aspects

Structurally speaking, natural stone, and marble in particular, is not wholly reliable. Small irregularities in the stone's surface can significantly reduce the maximum amount of force it can absorb. By gluing the stone to a laminated glass panel, this risk is eliminated and greater design freedom is attained, including the possibility of larger panel dimensions. The detailing employed in the Christ Pavilion was such that the stone itself was not required to absorb any forces. The thickness of the stone-glass panels depends on the strength desired. The glass can vary in thickness from 12 to 30 mm. The recommended thickness for natural stone veneer in sandwich constructions is normally 30 mm, but the panels used for the Christ Pavilion were only 10 mm thick. This not only resulted in immense savings in weight and cost, but also satisfied the architect's desire that the stone should admit as much daylight as possible.

Applications

In effect, *Steinglas* has *two* outer surfaces: the panel can be positioned with either the glass or the stone on the outside. The advantage of having glass on the outside is that the stone is still visible but shielded from the soiling effects of weather and air pollution; in addition, glass is easier to maintain than stone. It also means that many limestone types, such as marble, which have a poor resistance to acidic environments can be used in façades, although this also depends to some extent on the background construction. Vulnerable stone types must also be protected from polluted rainwater by means of very efficient ventilation or joints so tight that no moisture can penetrate the façade construction. *Steinglas* can however be used with both a ventilated and non-ventilated cavity.

Colour	**variable**
Glossiness	**glossy**, **satin**, **matt**
Translucence (%)	**0** – 20 – 40 – 60 – 80 – 100
Texture	sharp, **medium**, **dull**
Hardness	**hard**, soft, depressible
Temperature	warm, **medium**, cool
Odour	strong, moderate, **none**
Acoustic opacity	good, moderate, **poor**

Natural Stone
Sandwich Constructions

Sandwichkonstruktionen | Construction en sandwich | Construcciones en sándwich | Construzioni sandwich o compositi della pietra naturale | Samenstellingen steen

Natural stone is costly. It is both heavy and hard, but at the same time brittle. It is a natural product and consequently always liable to contain hidden flaws which could negatively affect its performance. Finally, erecting a natural stone façade is labour intensive and thus expensive. Reasons enough to search for more practical and perhaps also more efficient ways of using natural stone. This research resulted in several sandwich constructions.

The Development of Sandwich Panels

Prefabricated façade elements with natural stone outer leaves and inner leaves of concrete, have been around now for some forty years. Initially, the two materials were rigidly fastened together. This made it impossible for them to move independently of each other, something which is necessary given that concrete is subject to creep and shrinkage while stone expands at a different rate from concrete. Not only is stone's coefficient of expansion different, but, mounted on the outer side of a sandwich panel, it is also exposed to different temperatures from the concrete backing.

This problem became even worse in the second generation of sandwich panels. In order to satisfy new thermal requirements, an insulating layer had to be inserted between the stone and the concrete. The stone was once again fastened directly and rigidly. The natural stone was exposed to outdoor conditions, however, whilst the concrete remained relatively protected, but the rigid connection of the layers prevented the stone from expanding and contracting freely. The stone reacted by bulging and eventually even cracking.

The stone was accordingly detached from the concrete by connecting it by means of anchors, through the insulating material, to the concrete behind. It should be noted that the stone for such façade elements cannot not be much thinner than traditional stone cladding panels, for not only must the stone be able to withstand the vibration to which the concrete mould is subjected, but it must also be able to bear the weight of the layer of concrete while it is hardening: in the factory the sandwich element lies stone side down in the mould.

The direct contact between the back of the stone panel and the hard insulation gave rise to other problems. The insulation prevented the moisture that penetrated the natural stone from draining away quickly. This resulted in unsightly staining, especially in light coloured stone. The best solution, it was discovered, is to have a cavity behind the stone.

A prefabricated façade element is much quicker and, as a result, cheaper to install than individual slabs. Not only are support, insulation and finishing all mounted at the same time, but each façade element contains a number of natural stone slabs. A sandwich panel is typically one storey high and can be up to 10.7 metres wide. Finally, the quality of workmanship is higher as the natural stone is mounted in a controlled environment and therefore not dependent on weather conditions. One disadvantage of this method is that damaged façade panels are much more difficult to replace. In addition, wider joints are necessary between the elements. Whilst a joint of 8 to 10 mm is sufficient to absorb the sawing tolerances and

Project Town Hall, Den Bosch (2003)
Architect Dirk Jan Postel, Kraaijvanger . Urbis
Photographer Christian Richters

suitable for use in the environment and under the specific conditions for which it is intended. If a new and untried stone type is selected, it has to be subjected to a rigorous battery of tests to determine its frost resistance, weather resistance, expansion coefficient, et cetera. In *Steinglas*, a stone-glass laminate, the type of stone used is less critical. This sandwich construction was first used in the façade of Meinhard von Gerkan's Christ Pavilion at Expo 2000 in Hanover. The unique feature of this combination of materials is that it not only makes the stone much stronger, but also more or less translucent. Another advantage is that either side, glass or stone, can be turned to the outside, which means that environmentally vulnerable stone types like marble can still be used in acid environments.

expansions between individual façade slabs, with prefab elements this can easily increase to 30 to 40 mm, a width many architects find aesthetically unacceptable.

Other Backing Materials

In addition to sandwich panels with concrete backings – which are still quite heavy – other types have, in the course of time, been developed in an effort to make natural stone more practical. For example, another material is frequently glued to the back of the stone to compensate for the stone's negative properties. Since the forces on the façade are absorbed by the backing material, thinner slabs of stone can be used.

However, the problem of expansion coefficients is even more acute with such sandwich panels than with the original concrete-backed ones. Ideally, the backing material should have the same coefficient of expansion as the stone because while traditional fixing methods always allow a certain amount of independent movement, this 'escape route' is all but absent from such direct connections. When the expansion coefficient of the backing deviates sharply from that of natural stone, serious problems can arise, as happened in the past when aluminium honeycomb panels were glued to natural stone. It seemed like a good combination, as aluminium is strong and extremely light, but aluminium's far greater expansion coefficient initially proved problematical. These problems seem to have been largely resolved by inserting fibre-reinforced films between the aluminium and the stone veneer. The resulting panels are only 24 mm thick and some 80% lighter than natural stone panels. Against these advantages is one big subjective disadvantage: these panels look like natural stone but do not feel like it – they sound too hollow.

Façade Applications

In principle, the same constraints apply when selecting the stone for a sandwich construction with a concrete or aluminium backing as for traditionally fixed façade panels. It must be proven that the stone is

Sandwich Façade Panels

*Sandwich-Fassadenpaneele | Panneaux de façade en sandwich | Paneles sándwich de fachada | Pannelli sandwich per facciata |
Sandwich gevelelementen*

Project Addition to Joslyn Art Museum, Omaha (1994)

Architect Foster and Partners

Photographer Patrick Drickey

Although Sir Norman Foster nearly always seeks to adjust his buildings to their surroundings, he does so in his own unique way. For example, the context of the extension to the Joslyn Art Museum in Omaha pretty well dictated the use of natural stone. Foster duly opted for the same American marble, Etowah Fleuri, as that used in the main museum building, an Art Deco structure dating from 1931. However, instead of the blocks used in the older building, Foster elected to use sandwich panels with a concrete carrier for his Scott Pavilion – a smarter and more economical use of natural stone.

Technical Aspects

When used in sandwich panels, marble is an even more problematical façade material than it normally is. The slabs' relative thinness makes the marble more vulnerable. Exposure of such slabs to a large number of thermal cycles can have a detrimental effect on the stone's crystalline structure causing the stone to expand irreversibly. If the joints between the slabs are too narrow, the thin marble slabs may start to bulge. With thicker slabs, the effect is of little or no consequence. However, the thinness of such panels promotes not only greater moisture penetration, but also quicker saturation. Aside from the aesthetic problems this entails, moisture penetration can also reduce the strength of thin slabs of stone.

Applications

In principle, any natural stone type that can be used as façade cladding can also be used in a sandwich construction, provided the detailing is tailored to the characteristics of thin slabs. Naturally, in addition to problems specific to sandwich constructions, the problems associated with each natural stone type must also be taken into account. For example, Etowah Fleuri would have been an inappropriate choice for a Dutch façade – in moist and acid environments its vivid colours are soon obscured by 'lime bloom'.

Colour	variable
Glossiness	**glossy**, **satin**, **matt**
Translucence (%)	**0** – 20 – 40 – 60 – 80 – 100
Texture	sharp, **medium**, **dull**
Hardness	**hard**, soft, depressible
Temperature	warm, **medium**, cool
Odour	strong, moderate, **none**
Acoustic opacity	good, moderate, **poor**

Natural Stone Granulate

Natursteingranulat | Granulat de roche naturelle | Granulado de piedra natural | Granulati in pietra naturale | Natuursteengranulaat

Project Convent of Sainte-Marie-de-la-Tourette, Eveux-sur-Arbresle (1960)

Architect Le Corbusier

Photographer © Thomas A. Heinz | Corbis | TCS

The façade of Le Corbusier's La Tourette monastery could be said to be an example of the use of natural stone granulate in its most primitive form. For the façade elements of this building, Le Corbusier combined the traditional method of piling boulders on top of one another with the modern technique of precast concrete. Actually, it was a rather clever use of such façade elements in that they simultaneously functioned as a kind of permanent formwork.

Technical Aspects

The quality of a façade in which natural stone granulate is used, does not depend directly on the properties of the stone used. In principle, the stone is nothing more than a finishing for the concrete. One potential difficulty lies in the fact that the outer layer of cement paste must be removed in order to reveal the stone. This robs the concrete of its covering and raises the risk of reinforcement corrosion. To prevent this, an extra 10 mm covering is generally recommended.

Removal of the cement 'skin' can be done in a number of different ways, which in turn produce a variety of effects. Abrasive blasting will remove only a part of the skin, such that the stone becomes only vaguely visible. If hydration of the surface cement is retarded, the cement paste can be rinsed away leaving the granulate fully exposed. If the stone is then polished, a fascinating effect is obtained, approaching that of 'genuine' natural stone.

Applications

Not all natural stone is suitable for use as a granulate. Much the same rules apply here as for natural stone façade panels. Limestone, for example, is not suited for use in façades in an acid environment such as that prevailing in many West European countries. However, other stone types, such as granite or quartzite, lend themselves well to such applications. Precast concrete elements with a top layer of stone granulate work well in façades. A comparable technique can also be used for finishing floors; formerly referred to as *granito*, it is today known as *terrazzo*.

Colour	variable
Glossiness	**glossy**, **satin**, **matt**
Translucence (%)	**0** – 20 – 40 – 60 – 80 – 100
Texture	**sharp**, **medium**, **dull**
Hardness	**hard**, soft, depressible
Temperature	warm, **medium**, cool
Odour	strong, moderate, **none**
Acoustic opacity	good, moderate, **poor**

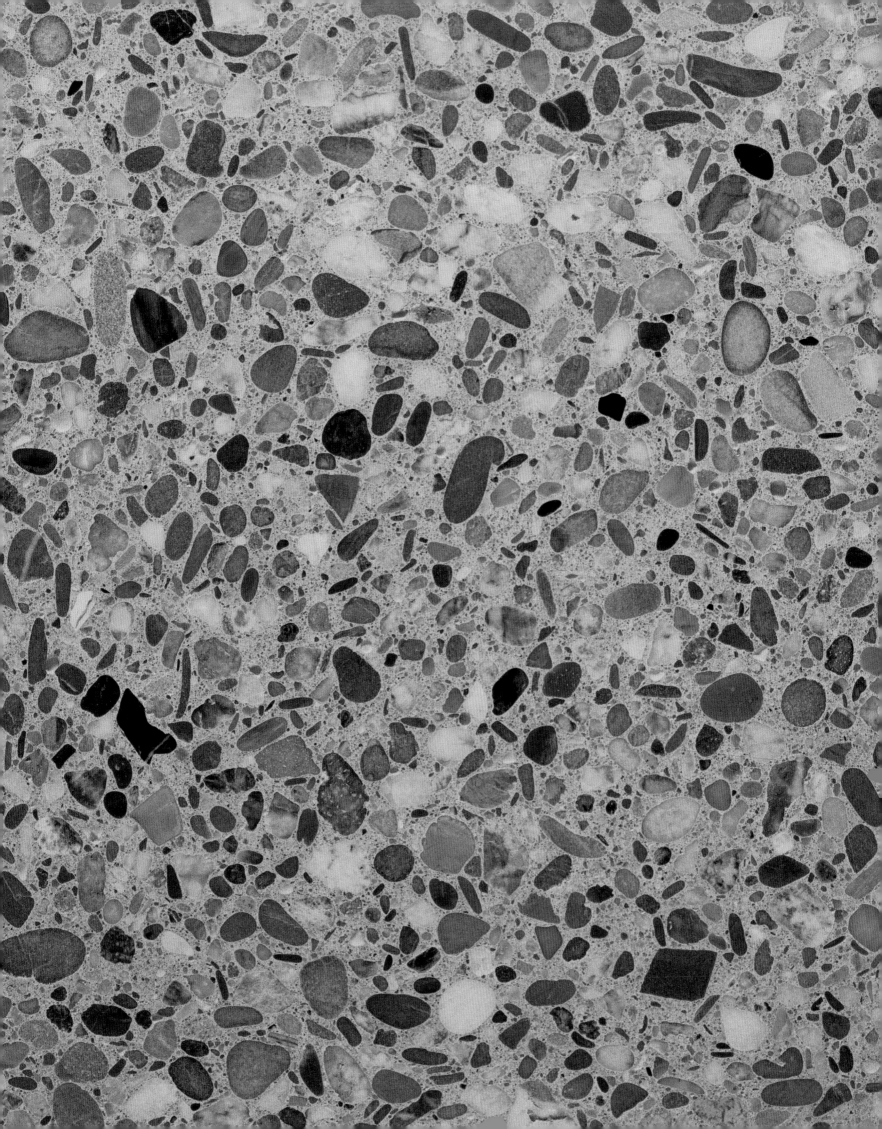

Working with Natural Stone

Natursteinbearbeitung | Construire avec roche naturelle | Trabajo con piedra natural | Lavorazioni con la pietra naturale | Bewerkingen natuursteen

Natural stone has been worked ever since it was first used as a construction material. Strictly speaking, the working of natural stone goes back even further, since many of primitive man's tools consisted of stones fractured and flaked to a usable shape. However, such pure functionality was not the only motivation involved when it came to using stone as a building material. After all, natural stone is not the easiest of building materials. It is hard, heavy, temperamental and consequently extremely difficult to extract, transport, handle and work – especially if you only have primitive tools at your disposal.

Description Perforated marble in Juna Mahal Palace, India (13th century)
Photographer Thomas Dix

Yet it was for just these reasons that the Pharaohs of Egypt chose to build in natural stone. Of course at that time monumental structures could not have been realized in anything other than natural stone, but this special, exotic material made their projects even more special precisely because of the difficulties it entailed. These prestigious edifices were intended to impress contemporaries and, in addition, to withstand time. For both these reasons, it was not enough simply to pile stone blocks on top of one other. The capricious material had to be 'tamed'. Endless hewing, sawing and grinding of the stone (in this case, granite) produced striking forms, laborious polishing accentuated the fascinating structures in the stones, and long texts were incised with great precision in the surface of the stone.

From ancient times until the end of the 19th century, little changed in how natural stone was used. Stone blocks were carved into huge works of art or hewn into simple blocks and stacked to form impressive buildings. The ornamental richness in and around churches, palaces, commercial buildings and villas was seen as a symbol of power, wealth and/or religious devotion. But at this point, everything changed. From a strategic point of view, massive walls of natural stone no longer afforded any added protection against the latest, more powerful weapons. In addition, it was becoming socially more difficult to realize such extravagant projects. The Viennese architect Adolf Loos, for example, took issue with the non-functional ornamentation in and on buildings in an essay entitled 'Ornament und Verbrechen' ('Ornament and Crime', 1908) in which he castigated such decoration as a waste of money, material and above all, labour. Last but not least, new construction materials were being discovered. Steel, but even more importantly, reinforced concrete, eliminated the need for those vulnerable, heavy and costly massive stone walls. It was now possible to use stone more efficiently – as a thin facing for the supporting structure – while retaining its aesthetic effect and status. Otto Wagner, for one, was very enthusiastic about these thin, and consequently less expensive, slabs which brought the more costly natural stone varieties within reach.

The combination of Loos's strictures and the new thin slabs had a major impact on the way natural stone was used and finished in the 20th century. The new slabs had scarcely any depth and besides, decoration was now taboo. Rather than 'carving' a building with all its frills very precisely out of stone as if it were a piece of sculpture, stone 'dressing' was increasingly confined to the surface. Sanding and polishing stone made it very smooth. Alternatively, it could be textured by means of chipping (using a chisel to introduce isolated striations), fluting (using a chisel to add grooves), bush hammering (roughening the surface), boasting (using a tooth chisel to make parallel, relatively wide grooves) or tooling (using a milling cutter to create grooves of varying widths).

During the 20th century, such processing was increasingly done by machine. The traditional stonecutter virtually disappeared from everyday building practice and his skills are only called upon nowadays in connection with the restoration of historical monuments. Although some of the vitality of traditional methods has been lost through machine processing, automation has yielded several interesting innovations as well. Examples are the 'frost flower' effect, obtained by five chisels rotating over the surface, and flaming, whereby a blowtorch is applied to the surface and the stone rapidly cooled, whereupon the surface cracks to produce a rough texture.

Machines have also enabled architects and builders to attain a higher degree of perfection in stone working than hitherto possible, especially since the advent of CAD programs and computer-controlled stone working. Robots with industrial diamonds fitted to the ends of their arms are able to cut a pattern out of stone with the same degree of precision as the designer drew it. Not only can tooling and boasting be done to a tolerance of 1 mm, and with grooves of any desired depth and spacing, but even far more difficult patterns can now be realized more easily and cheaply, from parallelograms and cannelures to wavy lines.

Computer-controlled saws and milling machines have also made possible the return of the third dimension to natural stone façades as demonstrated by Frank O. Gehry in his Guggenheim Museum in Bilbao and, more especially, the Disney Concert Hall in Los Angeles, where the blocks were sawn and milled in such a way as to create volumes bent in three different directions.

Despite such dazzling techniques, there are still limits to what can be done with stone. For example, not all finishes are suitable for all stone types. Only hard stone types can be flamed or polished, while slate and quartzite, for example, cannot be tooled. Then again, the

country of origin or the supplier may make the cost of certain finishes prohibitively expensive. Finally, not every finish is suitable for façade applications. Grooved surfaces channel rainwater along the same paths, while the open structure allows it to penetrate deeper into the stone. Algae, moss and streaks of dirt are the result. Smooth surfaces are usually less susceptible to soiling and easier to maintain.

In short, the same procedure applies to selecting a finish as to deciding on a stone type: it is necessary to ascertain whether the struc-

Project Guggenheim Museum, Bilbao (1997)
Architect Frank O. Gehry
Photographer © Ralph Richter | Architekturphoto

ture, hardness and composition of a stone will allow a given finish, whether this will achieve a long-lasting effect and, not least, whether it is affordable.

Rough Dressing | Splitting

Bossieren - Spalten | Taillage – fendage | Tallar toscamente – Cortar | Sbozzatura – Spacco | Ruw behakken – Kloven

Project Getty Center, Los Angeles (1997)
Architect Richard Meier & Partners
Photographer Joery Jordanov

On the Czech-German border, the German architects Brückner & Brückner designed a small complex whose walls consist of layers of different materials: glass, larch wood and granite. In themselves three materials with totally different textures. Yet by simple stacking the granite slabs, the wood and the glass and rough dressing the edges, while at the same time polishing the wood to a high gloss, the architects succeeded in generating an intriguing confusion as to which layer is made of which material.

Technical Aspects

The technique of splitting stone is as old as stone working itself. Originally, it was used primarily for reducing large blocks of stone to a size suitable for construction. More than any other type of treatment, splitting lays bare a stone's 'soul', enabling one, as it were, to look inside the stone and revealing a surface scattered with large flakes and cavities. Splitting can be done by hand or with a hydraulic press which splits the sawn stone blocks in two. Rough dressing can help to accentuate the effects obtained through splitting and it, too, can be done by hand (with chisel and hammer) or by machine.

Applications

Naturally, rough dressing is only feasible with thicker blocks of stone. Its special attraction is also its great drawback: cutting away a stone's surface leaves it more exposed to the environment. Laminated stone types, like slate and serpentino, can only be rough-hewn on their sides, as otherwise the stone would split. Many sandstones and limestones are also unsuited to rough dressing, at least in a northern European climate. Stones with dense structures, like granite and gneiss, are ideal candidates for rough dressing. One aesthetic disadvantage is that dirt clings more tenaciously to a rough surface. To avoid this, the rough, cleft-cut blocks of travertine Richard Meier used for his Getty Center in Los Angeles, were treated with a silicone-based water repellent.

Colour	**variable**
Glossiness	glossy, satin, **matt**
Translucence (%)	**0** – 20 – 40 – 60 – 80 – 100
Texture	**sharp**, medium, dull
Hardness	**hard**, soft, depressible
Temperature	warm, **medium**, cool
Odour	strong, moderate, **none**
Acoustic opacity	good, moderate, **poor**

Sanding and Honing

Schleifen und Honen | Ponçage et affinage | Limpieza con chorro de arena y alisado | Sabbiatura e levigatura |
Schuren en zoeten

Project La Grande Arche, Paris (1990)
Architect Johann Otto von Spreckelsen
Photographer Kees Hummel

It makes little sense to use polished marble on exteriors, since the high gloss inevitably vanishes after only a few years. Besides, a smooth surface can also be obtained through sanding or honing. Architect Johan Otto von Spreckelsen wanted the façades of his Grande Arche in Paris to be as smooth as possible. In view of the building's shape (a hollowed-out cube) and height (110 metres), a metal façade might have been more logical. In fact, natural stone was an inevitable choice given that the Grand Arche forms the end of an axis that begins at the Louvre and ends, by way of Arc du Carrousel, Place de La Concorde and Arc de Triomphe, at La Défense – all monuments in natural stone. Hence the decision to use super-smooth Carrara marble for this colossal structure.

Technical Aspects

The first objective of sanding is to remove the grooves left by sawing. It can be done dry using diamonds or carborundum, or with the addition of water. Sanding leaves the surface smooth although fine, circular marks may still be visible. These have a depth equal to that of the abrasive used (i.e. a maximum of 0.2 mm).

To obtain an even smoother surface, the stone can be honed using a finer abrasive and the addition of water. A series of sanding wheels make the surface progressively smoother. Honing can be done on a conveyor belt, but smaller surface areas can also be honed manually. Honing and fine honing can be followed by a final polishing, often using a felt disc and various polishing agents.

Applications

Many stone types can be sanded and honed. For coarse-grained stones like sandstone, and some laminated types like slate, this is either infeasible or ineffectual. In general, though, sanding and honing enable stone to retain its beauty for a longer period of time. The smooth surface makes it more difficult for dirt or moss to adhere and also absorbs water less readily than a rough surface.

Colour	**variable**
Glossiness	glossy, **satin**, matt
Translucence (%)	**0** – 20 – 40 – 60 – 80 – 100
Texture	sharp, medium, **dull**
Hardness	**hard**, soft, depressible
Temperature	warm, **medium**, cool
Odour	strong, moderate, **none**
Acoustic opacity	good, moderate, **poor**

Flaming

Flammen | Flammage | Abrasar o reducir | Trattamento superficiale alla fiamma | Branden

Project Van Gogh Museum new wing, Amsterdam (1998)
Architect Kisho Kurokawa
Photographer Kees Hummel

Project Aquarium Artis, Amsterdam (1997)
Architect G.B. Salm and A. Salm
Photographer Fred Nordheim

Given that the work of Kisho Kurokawa is usually dominated by shades of grey (a reference to the grey skies above his native city, Kyoto), his choice of Red Deer Brown granite-porphyry for the façade of the extension to Amsterdam's Van Gogh Museum seemed rather out of character at first. As the name suggests, red-brown hues predominate in the polished version of this costly Canadian stone. When the stone is flamed, however, its markings become paler. From a distance, the stone now appears greyish in colour; from close at hand, or after rain, its red, grey and brown nuances become visible.

Technical Aspects

Flaming involves working the surface of the stone with a hot welding flame. The treatment takes place before the slabs are cut to size. After flaming, the stone is cooled rapidly. The thermal shock causes its top layer to crack. This not only makes the surface rougher but also renders its markings less pronounced and more subtle. Yellow hues turn a pinky orange under the influence of the hot flame.

Applications

Flaming is only possible on a limited number of hard stone types. The roughened surface resulting from flaming makes it easier for dirt to adhere and, more problematical still, makes it easier for rainwater to penetrate the stone. While this is not a problem for several hard, dense stone types, for many others, it is certain to lead to extensive frost damage. All the granites, a limited number of quartzite, orthogneiss and migmatite varieties as well as a very small number of paragneisses and hard limestones are suitable for flaming. The treatment is especially popular for stair treads, as the roughness obtained through flaming significantly reduces the danger of slipping. Flaming can also be used to create special effects for façade cladding. For example, flamed blue limestone appears greyer from a distance, while closer inspection reveals white, faintly glistening specks; if machine-brushed after flaming, it acquires a bluish-grey hue.

Colour	**variable**
Glossiness	glossy, satin, **matt**
Translucence (%)	**0** – 20 – 40 – 60 – 80 – 100
Texture	sharp, medium, **dull**
Hardness	**hard**, soft, depressible
Temperature	warm, **medium**, cool
Odour	strong, moderate, **none**
Acoustic opacity	good, moderate, **poor**

Bush Hammering

Scharrieren | Bouchardage | Martillo con cantero | Bocciardatura | Boucharderen

Project Beyeler Foundation, Riehen (1997)
Architect Renzo Piano
Photographer Thomas Dix

Project Humana Building, Louisville (1982)
Architect Michael Graves
Photographer © Raymond Gehman | Corbis | TCS

Bush hammering stone causes a pattern of white spots to appear on its surface, an effect totally different from that obtained with any other treatment. Michael Graves used this effect in his Humana Building in Louisville. His design was chosen ahead of those by Sir Norman Foster and Helmut Jahn because it struck the jury as 'familiar', which was odd since the design includes typical exaggerated Gravesian elements that are totally at odds with 'traditional' skyscrapers. The jury was probably influenced in part at least by the choice of material. Graves chose to clad the building in pink granite which he handled in a remarkable way. By polishing some areas of granite and bush hammering others, he created totally different effects with the same material.

Technical Aspects

Nowadays, bush hammering is done using a pneumatic or hydraulic hammer fitted with a special head. The texture of the finished stone depends on the width of the hammer head and the number of points. Eight to sixteen points will yield a coarse effect, twenty-five, a fine one. The bush hammer makes small depressions, one to three millimetres deep, in the stone. Whilst with manual bush-hammering it was often possible to detect the craftsman's touch, the result of pneumatic bush hammering is much more even. The manual technique is nowadays used only in restoration work, where a pattern must be copied exactly.

Applications

Bush hammering is mainly used on granite and dark limestones, like Belgian blue limestone. The rough surface finish complements the texture of granite and imparts a fascinating haze of fine white dots to dark limestone. As well as giving stone a specific appearance, bush hammering can also be used to make the stone less smooth and consequently safer when used for stair treads and other trafficable surfaces. On façades, however, the roughened surface can lead to accelerated soiling.

Colour	**variable**
Glossiness	glossy, satin, **matt**
Translucence (%)	**0** – 20 – 40 – 60 – 80 – 100
Texture	sharp, **medium**, dull
Hardness	**hard**, soft, depressible
Temperature	warm, **medium**, cool
Odour	strong, moderate, **none**
Acoustic opacity	good, moderate, **poor**

Polishing

Polieren | Polissage | Pulido | Lucidatura | Polijsten

Project Barcelona Pavilion, Barcelona (1930)

Architect Mies van der Rohe

Photographer © Ralph Richter | Architekturphoto

The heart of Ludwig Mies van der Rohe's famed Barcelona Pavilion consists of a 3.1 metre high, 5.86 metre long wall of onyx. True onyx is a non-crystalline, amorphous quartz and very expensive. However, green marble is often mistaken for onyx. Mies' use of genuine onyx was no accident; his father was a stonecutter by trade and his oldest brother worked for a monumental mason. For his pavilion, Mies selected the most costly variety of onyx and had it polished until the wall's gleaming surface could play an important role in the effects of perspective and reflection that formed an integral part of the design.

Technical Aspects

Polishing a stone accentuates its mineral composition as well as any other structures that may be present. Normally, polishing takes place after the stone has been sanded and honed. A 'gantry' machine is used throughout this process while the actual polishing is done with a felt disc. In addition to the slab's surface, its sides can also be polished and honed. As with sanding and honing, polishing can increase a stone's durability, since the smooth surface is more resistant to dirt. However, this only applies to the harder stone types; in the case of those containing calcium carbonate (all limestones) acid rain attacks the calcium, causing the lustre obtained through polishing to disappear.

Applications

Successful polishing is only possible with dense stone types since it requires a hard stone and the presence of certain minerals. Quartz and calcite are suitable for polishing, for example, whereas limonite and muscovite are not. Equally important is the fact that while all marbles will take polishing, they soon lose their lustre when exposed to the outdoor air, especially if it is damp or polluted. There is little point therefore in polishing limestone (including travertine) and marble types for external use. When used for internal walls, most marbles, travertines and other dense limestones are quite suitable for polishing. Polished floor surfaces lose their shine through constant traffic. Sandstone's coarse structure makes it completely unsuitable for polishing.

Colour	**variable**
Glossiness	**glossy**, satin, matt
Translucence (%)	**0** – 20 – 40 – 60 – 80 – 100
Texture	sharp, medium, **dull**
Hardness	**hard**, soft, depressible
Temperature	warm, **medium**, cool
Odour	strong, moderate, **none**
Acoustic opacity	good, moderate, **poor**

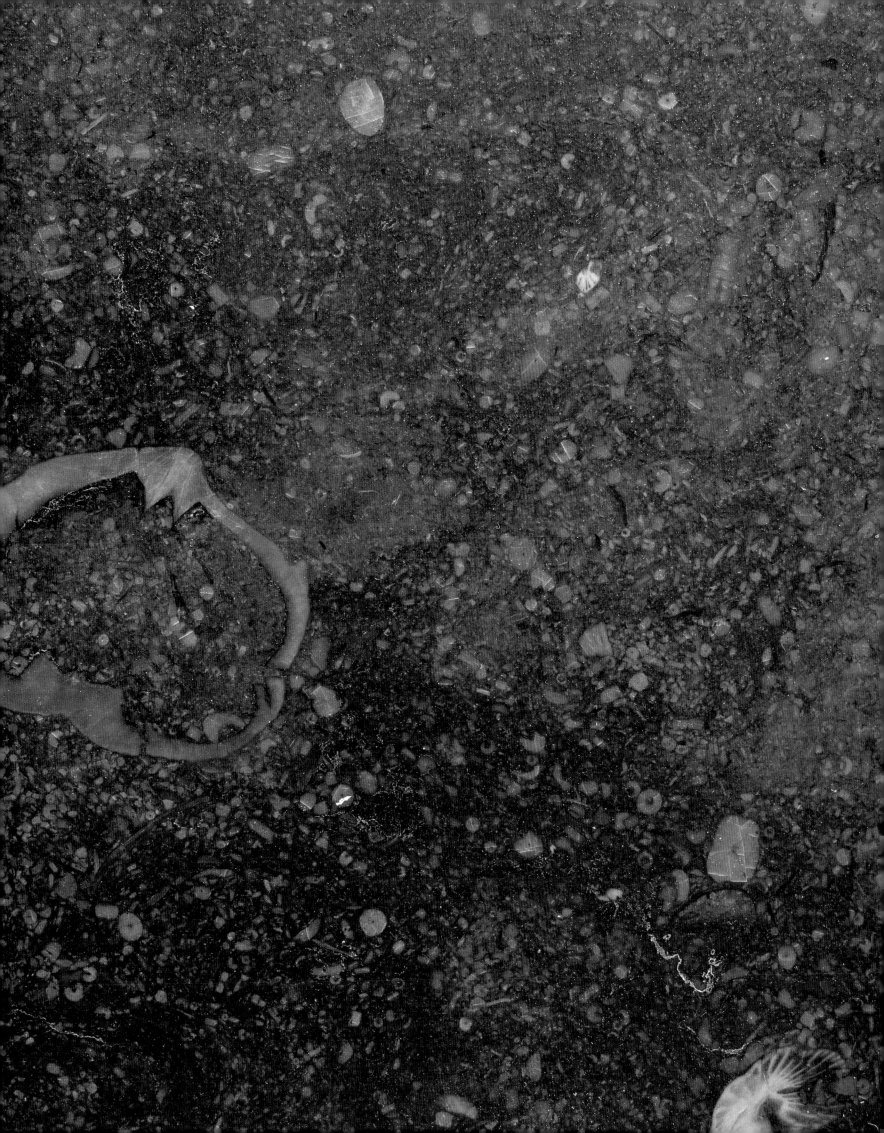

Milling

Fräsen | Fraisage | Laminado | Fresatura | Frezen

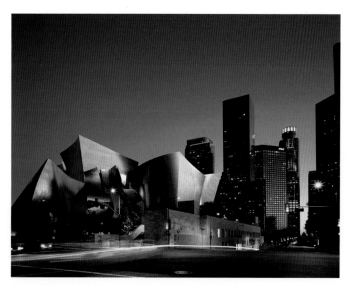

Project Walt Disney Concert Hall, Los Angeles (2004)
Architect Frank O. Gehry
Photographer © Architekturphoto

With his Guggenheim Museum in Bilbao and Disney Concert Hall in Los Angeles, American architect Frank O. Gehry reinvoked the sculptural potential of natural stone. In order to realize precisely in stone the bizarre geometries of Gehry's designs, a 3D modeller was used to control various machines. First, rough shapes were sawn out. Then, the definitive slabs were 'bent' in three different directions with the help of milling machines.

Technical Aspects

A milling machine is a cylindrical grinding wheel studded with industrial diamonds that rotates at extremely high speeds. The wheel is attached to an arm which can move in three different directions. In the case of Gehry's buildings, the arm's manoeuvres were computer-controlled. Wherever the grindstone is pressed hard against the stone, it grinds away the excess stone. This is done with the addition of large quantities of water. Different grindstone forms can be used depending on the effect required. As well as working the slab as a whole, milling machines can also be used to carve patterns, such as cascades or cannelures, in a slab's surface.

Applications

Extremely hard stone is difficult to mill. Gehry's choice of limestone was no accident, therefore, even though the Grenada limestone used in the Guggenheim is one of the hardest limestones. Granite is much more difficult but not impossible to mill. For other, obvious, reasons laminated stone types (slates and quartzites) are unsuitable for milling.

Nowadays, floor tiles are also increasingly being milled (calibrated) to the desired thickness. Although more expensive than merely sawing to size, this method produces tiles of exactly the same thickness.

Colour	**variable**
Glossiness	**glossy, satin, matt**
Translucence (%)	**0** – 20 – 40 – 60 – 80 – 100
Texture	sharp, **medium, dull**
Hardness	**hard**, soft, depressible
Temperature	warm, **medium**, cool
Odour	strong, moderate, **none**
Acoustic opacity	good, moderate, **poor**

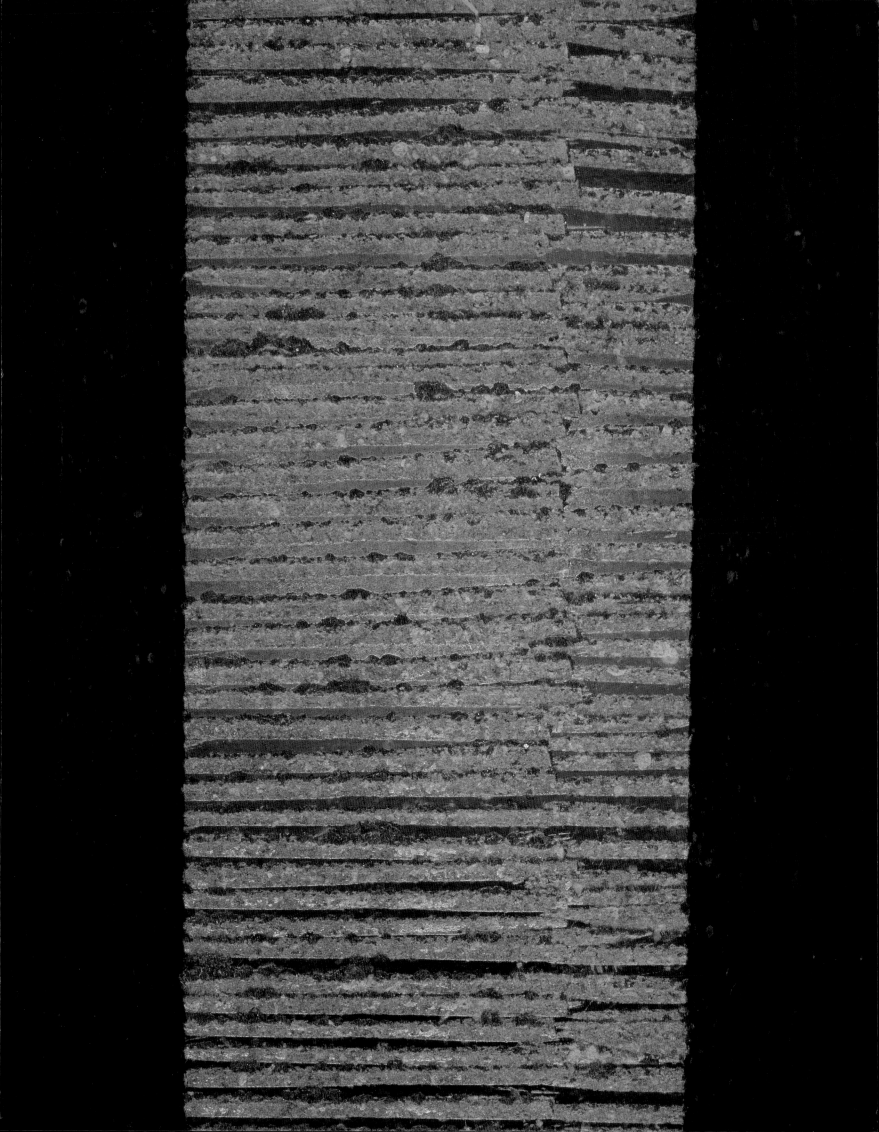

Chipping and Tooling

Meisseln und Kröneln | Gravillonnage et ouvrage | Cerrar bloques de piedra natural en tableros | Scalpellatura e lavorazione con utensili | Bikken en frijnen

Project ETH, Zürich (1858)
Architect Gottfried Semper
Photographer Evert Ypma

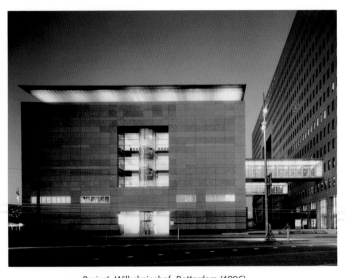

Project Wilhelminahof, Rotterdam (1996)
Architect Rob Ligtvoet, Kraaijvanger . Urbis
Photographer Sybolt Voeten

"Es spreche das Material für sich und trete auf, unverhüllt, in der Gestalt, in den Verhältnissen, die als die zweckmäßigsten für dasselbe durch Erfahrungen und Wissenschaften erprobt sind. Backstein erscheine als Backstein, Holz als Holz, Eisen als Eisen…" ('Let each material speak for itself and appear uncovered, in a form and in proportions which, through experience and science, have proven to be the most appropriate for it. Let brick appear as brick, wood as wood, iron as iron…') That Gottfried Semper also put his ideas concerning the appropriate use of materials into practice is demonstrated by, among others, his ETH building in Zurich. This sandstone building is 'authentic' in every pore. An 'ornamental' effect was obtained by finishing successive rows of stone in a different manner. The stones were rough-dressed, chipped or tooled.

Technical Aspects

As one would expect, most stone finishes are today done by machine. In Semper's time, chipping was done with a pointed chisel and the stone was generally only sawn or split. This resulted in a pattern of isolated, roughly parallel grooves. Chipping done by hand results in a rougher surface and less regular grooves than machine chipping. Mechanically chipped surfaces strongly resemble those which have been mechanically tooled.

Manual tooling is the almost classic method of dressing stone and was done with a chisel, boaster and wooden mallet. In large façade slabs these have now been replaced by a multi-mill with diamond teeth which produces exactly parallel grooves; the human hand was less consistent. The lines on some of the stones in the ETH building almost describe quarter-circles (incidentally, an intentional effect).

Over time, a number of different tooling patterns have been developed, such as the herringbone, cathedral stroke and draught board. In addition, stone can be boasted, a finish in which the slanting strokes are discontinuous.

Applications

Fine tooling has hardly any effect on the coarser varieties of sandstone and is completely impossible on granite, as this stone is much too hard and its coarse crystals do not permit the carving of extremely precise lines.

Tooled finishes roughen a stone's surface thereby making it easier for dirt to adhere to it. Another undesirable effect is that rainwater is channelled along the grooves, resulting in weathering and streaks of dirt.

Colour	variable
Glossiness	glossy, satin, **matt**
Translucence (%)	**0** – 20 – 40 – 60 – 80 – 100
Texture	sharp, **medium**, dull
Hardness	**hard**, soft, depressible
Temperature	warm, **medium**, cool
Odour	strong, moderate, **none**
Acoustic opacity	good, moderate, **poor**

Fired Man-made Stone

Gebrannter, künstlicher Stein | Roche artificielle cuite | Piedra artificial cocida | Manufatti per cottura | Gebakken kunststeen

Fired man-made stone has earned itself a permanent place in the repertoire of architects and artists. Long burdened by the stigma of traditionalism, this ceramic building product was rediscovered in the 1990s as an instrument that can be used to influence the visual quality and design of the built environment. Architect Koen van Velsen symbolically bridged the gap between traditional clay products and high-tech architecture in steel and other metals by using aluminium-coloured bricks for his Kennispoort building in Eindhoven.

Products made from fired clay have long been a part of the built environment in the West. The extent to which this occurs varies greatly, however. In areas with an abundance of natural stone, clay is mainly used for roofing materials and tiles. In areas with no natural stone quarries, walls are also made of fired clay. Dutch, North German and Flemish streets have been characterized by brick façades since the Middle Ages, while in more southern regions plastered façades have predominated.

It was practical and economic motives that made brick the material of 19th-century town expansions not only in the Netherlands but also in France and Great Britain. If brick production was still a traditional, labour-intensive process around 1850, barely two decades later the greatly increasing demand had resulted in the mechanization of the production process. Not only did production capacity increase, but the quality of the product clearly improved too. The manufacture of ceramic roofing tiles and tiles in general enjoyed a similar growth. In areas where there are no quarries, natural stone has always been a relatively expensive material, its use restricted to the most high-profile buildings and to special features such as keystones.

Around 1900, architecture was marked by a wealth of ornamentation. This applied both to the then popular revival styles and subsequently to Art Nouveau. Brick façades were not exempted from this trend, witness the architectural sample books that started to appear at this time. As well as drawings of entire buildings, they also offered studies of colourful brick patterns and ornaments of fired clay as a source of inspiration for contemporary architects. This period also saw the emergence of an international style in specific brick applications.

It took the Netherlands until the second half of the 19th century to begin producing tiles, certain types of brick and other ceramic building products from imported clay of a higher quality. This aside, fired clay products have remained closely tied to the properties of local clays and to regional building traditions. Because such ties make it impossible to generalize, this text focuses mainly on the country where, more than anywhere else in Europe, bricks and roofing tiles have for centuries characterized the streetscape.

The great potential of ceramic building materials is particularly evident now that they are no longer used exclusively in accordance with traditional patterns. Increasingly, ceramic brick is developing from a material used to make loadbearing walls into one for cladding façades. The fact that ceramic products are chosen for this role is due to the range of shapes, colours and textures they have to offer. The

significance of ceramic building materials is further positively influenced by the fact that the façade and the roof, together the skin of the building, have become equals. The design of this skin usually derives from a combination of desired appearance and performance requirements.

Lastly, ceramic building materials constitute the pre-eminent realm where the worlds of architecture and the visual arts merge. It is to this union that we owe the refinement of our living and working environment as well as an increase in its diversity and expressive force. The synthesis of art and architecture, which marked the work of Antoni Gaudí and that of the architects of the Amsterdam School, faces a rosy future as continuing technological development of the material eliminates more and more practical obstacles to its use.

Types of Clay

Clay is produced by the erosion of igneous rock. Clay minerals are only produced when the rock has fully eroded. A layer of water can form around these minerals, giving clay its plasticity. The flat clay minerals can be compared to sheets of glass. Laid one on top of the other unmediated, they are almost impossible to separate. However, if there is a thin film of water between the sheets of glass, only the slightest effort is required to shift them out of alignment.

There is a distinction between primary, secondary and tertiary clay, depending on the erosion process and where the clay particles have been deposited. Primary clay contains the highest percentage of clay minerals and is the least contaminated, since primary clay (china clay or porcelain) was formed where it is found. Primary clay, which is always more than 40,000 years old, is fired at temperatures between 1250 °C and 1400 °C and results in a white product. In the Western world, porcelain is used mainly for crockery and for applications in the electrical industry.

Secondary clay is clay that was in the process of becoming primary clay before this process was halted by a natural disaster, an earthquake for example. Secondary clay, therefore, contains a smaller

Project Het Schip, Amsterdam (1921)
Architect Michel de Klerk
Photographer Kees Hummel

Project Kennispoort, Eindhoven (2002)

Architect Koen van Velsen

Photographer Royal Tichelaar

percentage of pure clay minerals and more feldspar, an erosion product somewhere between clay and sand. Secondary clay is fired at between 1150 °C and 1250 °C and gives a product with a compact structure. This clay type is used for applications collectively designated as stoneware. In France it is known as *grès*. Technically they are one and the same type, even though *grès*, which contains substantial amounts of iron oxide and manganese, fires to an orange-red, while German Westerwalder clay, for example, fires to a white colour.

In tertiary clay, the product of erosion has been carried along by seas, rivers and even glaciers. Particles are deposited at places where the current slackens or the glacier melts. The eroded rock may also be blown by the wind. Tertiary clay is the most contaminated type and contains relatively large amounts of iron, lime and feldspar. It is fired at between 850 °C and 1050 °C. This clay type is mostly used for bricks and roofing tiles, with a slightly purer clay being preferred for the latter. In the Netherlands, tiles were made from tertiary clay until late into the 19th century, not from choice but because a better, secondary clay was not available.

The thickness of the layer of clay depends on how it has been deposited. In relatively flat regions, where river courses have been channelled by man only since the Middle Ages, the deposits of river clay, such as those found in water meadows, will be of only limited thickness. In other locations the layers are sometimes dozens of metres thick.

Clay in its natural state basically consists of small particles of silt and larger grains of quartz. The fine silt particles are mainly clay minerals (aluminium oxide) with the capacity to bind with water. It is this which gives clay the plasticity that is so essential to its processing. The quartz component consists of silicic acid or silica. Unlike silt particles, grains of quartz are unable to bind with water. The ratio between the two main components, aluminium oxide (Al_2O_3) and quartz (SiO_2), that is to say between the clay component and the quartz component, has a palpable effect on the clay's workability

and on the behaviour of the fired product. Tertiary clay contains about 15% Al_2O_3 and 65% SiO_2. In secondary clay, the clay component (Al_2O_3) increases to 20% while the quartz component (SiO_2) decreases to 50-60%.

Clay with a relatively high aluminium oxide content and a high percentage of fine particles (smaller than 10 μm) is called fat clay. A high content of fine particles, known traditionally as the loam content, increases the clay's plasticity, but at the same time makes the product susceptible to shrinkage and cracking. Fat clay is used to produce machine-pressed bricks and ceramic roofing tiles, as well as for stoneware and floor and wall tiles. Clay with a relatively high quartz content and a low loam content exhibits exactly the opposite properties. Lean clay (of low to medium plasticity) is used mostly to produce hand-moulded bricks and sanded facing bricks.

Fired Colours

The various types of clay are categorized not only according to their purity, but also according to their colour after firing. Primary clay types (china clay or porcelain) fire to white, as do some of the purer secondary types. Since it contains none of the contamination that lowers the sintering point of other types of clay, white-firing clay can be fired at a higher temperature. The fact that the sintering point is only reached at a relatively high temperature means that white-firing

Project Janssen Precision Engineering office building,

Maastricht-Aachen Airport (2001)

Architect Bruls and Co.

Photographer Arjen Schmitz

clay is particularly suitable for heat-resistant applications. White clay is often used as the base for clay products coloured with natural pigments. The neutral white colour is the most favourable starting point as it allows the colouring process to be most accurately controlled. On the other hand, white-firing clay is relatively expensive.

Red-firing clay (secondary or tertiary clay) contains a comparatively large quantity of iron oxide which not only produces the red colour but also fuses easily. Red-firing secondary clay, such as stoneware, gives a very dense product if a high enough temperature is used. Red-firing tertiary clay contains so much iron oxide that the sintering point is reached at a relatively low temperature.

Yellow-firing clay (secondary or tertiary clay) also contains iron oxide, but to a much lesser extent. Unlike red-firing clay, it has a high natural lime content and it is this which gives it its yellow colour. The colour is the result of a chemical reaction between the lime, iron and aluminium.

Red-firing and yellow-firing clay are common forms that give fired products of the same technical quality. The fact that yellow bricks once predominated in the buildings of one region and red bricks in another is simply a reflection of the composition of the local clay. Besides the red-firing and yellow-firing clays, there are also less

Project Michaelis Quartier, Hamburg (2001)
Architect Steidle + Partner
Photographer Reinhard Görner

material used for chamotte has a high clay content and is therefore rich in aluminium oxide. To this fat clay, which would normally be used for stoneware among other things, a fat-reducing agent known as 'chamotte' is added. The chamotte, which consists of ground particles of fired clay, ensures that the fat clay shrinks less.

Project Dona Nobis Panem, Enkhuizen (1997)
Architect Min2 bouw-kunst
Photographer Elly Valkering

prevalent types that contain other metal oxides and consequently result in a different colour. The clay found in the Thames estuary, for example, contains cobalt which turns it blue during the firing process. In other areas the clay contains chrome, which produces a green colour when fired.

The more finely the colour-determining metal oxides, such as iron oxide but also lime, are distributed throughout the clay mixture, the more homogeneous and intense the colour. This is because smaller particles produce a chemical reaction more quickly than larger ones.

Chamotte occupies a special place in the list of clay types as it consists of a mixture of raw materials and an additive. The pure raw

Bricks

Ziegel | Briques | Ladrillos | Mattoni | Bakstenen

Bricks were used as early as the fourth millennium BC to build temples and palaces between the Euphrates and the Tigris rivers in Mesopotamia. The well-preserved temple tower (ziggurat) of Chogha Zanbil, located in the westernmost part of Iran, dates from the mid 13th century BC. The terraced tower measures 100 metres at its base and has a core made from unfired clay. A more weather-proof kiln-fired brick was used for the two-metre-thick outer shell. The austere, angular brick architecture and consistent use of stretcher bond give the ziggurat a contemporary look.

The first large-scale use of fired bricks for building houses occurred during Roman times. Initially the Romans used brick only for strengthening the corners and posts of walls, while the remainder was made from rubble. Brick was otherwise used as a more afford-able alternative to natural stone. For example, instead of carving columns from marble or tufa rock, these were built from segment-shaped bricks designed specially for the purpose. This application was hidden from view, however, since it was always covered with a coat of plaster. Such use of brick is well documented in Pompeii, which was buried by the eruption of Mount Vesuvius in 79 AD.

A true brick industry only emerged towards the end of the first cen-tury AD, when businesses were set up specifically to produce bricks for the construction of numerous apartment complexes. There was a great demand for such accommodation, particularly in Rome and its seaport, Ostia. Contrary to previous practice, the brick used in the façades remained visible. The Romans used fattish clay, both red-firing and yellow-firing, to make bricks measuring approximately 60 x 60 cm. These were used either whole or split into smaller dimensions in the forerunner of medieval rubble-core walls. Only the outer layer was made of brick; the core was filled with a combi-nation of mostly fist-sized chunks of natural stone and a concrete-like mortar.

Developments in the North

The Roman architectural style also penetrated northern regions, as is demonstrated by the Basilica in Trier, Germany, built as a throne room by the emperor Constantine in the fourth century AD. Later, during the Carolingian period, there was some reuse of Roman bricks but also the production of new bricks in the Roman style. It was not until the end of the 12th century, however, that a significant brick tradition developed in northern Europe. Its beginnings are linked to the spread of Cistercian monasteries into the northern regions. Consequently, the first brick makers were monks and the kilns were owned by the monasteries. At first local clay was used, but when it became obvious that the supply in some regions was limited, it was decided to concentrate extraction in the more productive locations, such as along the banks of large rivers, where it is often still mined today. Both fired and unfired clay bricks were used to infill timber frames. In the 13th century and part of the 14th, bricks were used, as they had been during Roman times, for facing mortared rubble-core walls. Only during the course of the 14th century did it become common practice to build solid brick walls.

Medieval bricks were initially very large, measuring approximately 35 x 17 x 10 cm, which meant that they required quite a long period of firing before they were strong enough for construction work. Another disadvantage was their great weight. The façades of castles and monasteries were sometimes decorated with Christian symbols, such as diamonds or the Saint Andrew's cross, using sintered bricks. Yellow and green glazed bricks were incorporated as decorative touches in both civic buildings and houses.

The pressure to produce enough bricks to meet the rapidly swelling demand led to the production of progressively smaller sizes with much shorter firing times. This pursuit of efficiency went too far, however, leading to the manufacture of bricks so small that they could no longer be used to produce sound masonry. Therefore, guidelines governing the size of bricks were drawn up. From the beginning in the 12th century bricks were laid in special patterns or bonds. The structure of masonry gradually became more regular. The bricks became progressively flatter and the joints progressively thinner so that façades took on a planar aspect.

Mass Production

It was not until the 19th century that bricks, which by this time were being produced by machine, regained their former eloquence. This was partly due to a newfound respect for craft traditions. Berlage's Stock Exchange in Amsterdam, built in 1903, is probably the best-known example of this attitude. However, at that time ornamental brickwork made from specially shaped, coloured and sometimes glazed brick was also being used for housing. Such bricks were used to apply visual accents, such as orange-red flat arches and brick mosaic tympanums above windows frames. In view of the cost involved, this was almost exclusively restricted to the main façade. During the period in which the Amsterdam School held sway, another form of brick ornamentation appeared in which the emphasis was far more on sculptural effects which were further enhanced by the use of different coloured bricks. From the 1920s on, the external walls of houses were usually built with a cavity, resulting in a considerable improvement in domestic comfort. Cavity walls had first made their appearance in 17th-century country houses.

Bricks continued to dominate the Dutch building industry after the Second World War, although their dominance in the streetscape was now challenged by other materials and techniques ushered in by the post-war faith in progress and the related modernist architectural style. High-rise projects and large public buildings in particular were increasingly being erected in the 'new materials', while housing remained almost exclusively the domain of the 'bourgeois' brick architecture. This was mainly because this style was so firmly anchored in Dutch tradition and the Dutch construction industry and because it was also the cheapest solution.

Since the 1960s, brick has played a relatively low-key role as the most appropriate material for the façades of street-access dwellings. During the 1970s and 1980s in particular, more attention was given to urbanistic aspects than to the architectural treatment of individual dwellings for which there was often little or no money. The use of brick in high-rises and offices was not exactly imaginative either. One exception to this is the organic architecture of Ton Alberts and Max van Huut, who, in the mid 1980s, housed the headquarters of a

leading bank, NMB, in a brick sculpture in Amsterdam-Zuidoost. Later examples of their organic style include the large office buildings of KPMG in Amstelveen (1991) and the Gasunie headquarters in Groningen (1994).

In the 1990s, the primarily pragmatic choice of brick for façade cladding made way for a more deliberate use motivated by brick's unique aesthetic and expressive qualities. Brick has become an instrument for attaining a particular visual quality. Brick has also made a comeback in the office construction market.

Production Process

A brick factory is seldom able to produce brick from one and the same clay source. For the most part, bricks must be manufactured from different, often small batches of clay. Yet the manufacturer is required to produce bricks of a constant colour. It is therefore im-

Project Ammersoyen castle (14th century)
Commissioner Arent van Herlaer
Photographer Jan Derwig

portant to understand the properties of the resulting mix. For this reason, the clay is tested before being extracted in order to determine its suitability and precise composition. Although the iron content and amount of lime play a key role in determining the colour, the distribution of the particles is important too. Each factory therefore has its own formula, determined not only by a careful matching of pure clay batches, but also by additions, for example of natural pigments.

Once extracted, the clay is usually stored in a depot in horizontal layers. The advantage of this is that any possible differences in the com-

position of the various batches of clay are distributed over the entire area. By removing the clay vertically from the depot, the batches are always mixed in a constant ratio so that the composition of the clay remains constant too.

Before the clay is made into bricks, the raw materials are kneaded and mixed into a homogeneous, plastic mass. The pre-processed clay is placed in a long narrow tray that acts as a buffer and a dosing unit. The clay is then treated to remove any contamination and to enhance the homogeneity. A brick factory uses various machines for this purpose, such as clay shredders and edge-runner mills. The shredder reduces the size of any lumps and removes any plants left in the clay. In the edge-runner mill, two rollers spread the clay over a sieve and subsequently push it through.

The pre-treated clay is nearly always shaped by machine. Generally speaking, there are two ways of doing this. One method uses moulds in which the clay is thrown (handmade) or pressed (press-moulded and table-moulded). In the other method the clay is pushed through a die (extruded).

After the clay product has been shaped, the bulk of the water must be removed before it can be fired. This is important because other-

Project Pawnbroker's, Nijmegen (1889)
Architect J.J. Weve
Photographer Pansa bv

Project NMB Headquarters, Amsterdam (1986)
Architect Ton Alberts & Max van Huut
Photographer Kees Hummel

wise steam would form in the clay product during the firing process that might cause it to explode. Drying is usually an automated process that makes use of residual heat from the cooling phase of the firing process. The unfired product shrinks during the drying process, an outcome the manufacturer will have taken into account, tied as he is to a fired product of fixed dimensions. The firing process can begin as soon as the shaped brick has dried sufficiently. It is during this process that the brick obtains its strength and the desired colour. The temperature in the kiln containing the dried brick is slowly stepped up to remove any moisture still present in the form of unabsorbed water. As the temperature rises, water from the clay is also removed from the clay minerals. The clay then loses its plasticity and becomes gritty. With the temperature still rising, the clay reaches its sintering point. This is the moment when a fraction of the clay particles starts melting and begins to behave like glass. The melted particles seal the non-melted particles together into a solid, densely structured mass. If the temperature is increased after reaching the sintering point, the product will exhibit glass-like bubbles; when melting point is reached, lack of stability will cause it to lose its shape. For tertiary clay in particular, where the sintering point and the melting point are very close together (usually within a range of only 20 °C), the temperature must be very closely monitored. For secondary and primary clay with ranges of around 70-80 °C and 150 °C respectively, the margin is significantly greater.

The colour of the fired clay product is determined not only by the composition of the clay and the additives, but also by the firing temperature and conditions. Soft-fired clay products are always greyish-red regardless of the exact ratio of iron oxide to lime. On the other hand, if the clay product is fired at a higher temperature than normal, yellow-firing clay gives a greenish colour while red-firing clay becomes a darker red. If the bricks undergo continued sintering, they turn purple. Nuances in colour result from an inconsistent exposure of the bricks to the fire during the firing process.

Hand-moulded Bricks

Manuell geformte Ziegel | Briques faites à la main | Ladrillos de tejar | Mattoni formati a mano | Handvorm

Project Brandevoort, Helmond (2001)
Architect Lanfermeijer Seelen, Van der Laan, Saanen-Knoups Architects
Photographer Kees Stuip

Project El Pi High School, Barcelona (1996)
Architect Roldán + Berengué
Photographer Eva Serrats

Hand-moulded bricks are the oldest and most commonly used type of brick in the Netherlands. They have a more irregular shape and are more textured than the other types. Hand-moulded bricks are only actually made by hand in special cases. Since the 19th century, this gruelling work has been performed by a machine as was already the case for press-moulded bricks. The mechanical production of hand-moulded bricks only really gathered momentum after the Second World War. In principle, the effects of the manual process have been maintained although both the colour and texture of mechanically produced bricks are more homogeneous than those made by hand. Mechanical production gives the manufacturer more control over the quality and consistency of the product.

In mechanical production, pre-treated clay of medium plasticity is rolled into balls, each of which contains more than enough material for one brick. After being sanded, they are thrown one by one into a sanded mould. This is done with such force that the mould is filled at a single throw. All clay protruding beyond the top is cut away with a steel wire.

The surface of hand-moulded bricks, except for the side not touching the mould, is textured and pleated as well as sanded. This surface texture can be influenced by altering the plasticity of the clay. Thrown with the same force, clay that is more plastic will fill the mould better and therefore produce a finer surface texture.

Hand-moulded bricks, like all other brick types, are used for both loadbearing and non-loadbearing exterior walls. The current popularity of the hand-moulded brick is mainly due to the fact that of all types it is the one most strongly associated with traditionalism, a design syntax that is increasingly gaining ground in contemporary Dutch architecture. In the new Brandevoort housing estate in Helmond, all the façades boast hand-moulded bricks. Instead of being just another suburban development, Brandevoort was required to resemble a village that has grown naturally through the ages, making hand-moulded bricks the appropriate choice.

Colour	variable
Glossiness	glossy, satin, **matt**
Translucence (%)	**0** – 20 – 40 – 60 – 80 – 100
Texture	sharp, medium, **dull**
Hardness	**hard**, soft, depressible
Temperature	**warm**, medium, cool
Odour	strong, moderate, **none**
Acoustic opacity	good, **moderate**, poor

Press-moulded Bricks

Vorgefertigte Ziegel | Briques préformées | Ladrillos o bloques cerámicos preformados | Mattoni preformati | Vormbak

Project Beurs van Berlage, Amsterdam (1903)
Architect H.P. Berlage
Photographer Kees Hummel

Project Smetana House, Vonoklasy, Czech Republic (2000)
Architect Jan Jehlik Architectural Office
Photographer Jan Brodsky

Press-moulded or pressed brick has been produced since the first half of the 19th century, when machines like the mould press of the Dutch firm of Aberson in Olst took over part of the physically onerous duties in the brick factory. To produce press-moulded bricks, pre-treated clay of medium plasticity is mechanically compressed into a sanded mould and the excess clay removed. Bricks produced by this mould method have a much sleeker and more uniform surface than the hand-moulded variety.

Machine-moulded brick has been used on a large scale since the end of the 19th century. Besides the late 19th-century town expansions, buildings of the Amsterdam School period and housing projects of the 1930s were largely built in press-moulded brick. So was most Dutch subsidized housing of the 1960s, '70s and '80s. This was due to the favourable price in those decades and to the fact that architects wished to distance themselves from traditional architecture, of which hand-moulded bricks were considered to be a part. Nowadays, press-moulded brick is mainly used for its sleek shape and uniform, sanded surface and because it is cheaper than hand-moulded brick.

Sited where two streets meet at the corner of a large square, the Ransila I Building in Lugano, Switzerland (1985, Mario Botta), has expressive façades of red press-moulded brick. On the one hand they continue the two street elevations, on the other they firmly emphasize the building's location on the corner of the square. The honeycomb structure includes deep recesses at regular intervals to contain the windows. The ribs of this structure are uniform stretcher bond courses that meet in a mitre joint.

Table-moulding System
The table-moulding system is related to the press-moulded brick method. It is still quite widely used particularly in Denmark. Here the pre-treated clay bricks are shaped using a moulding table. Unlike the press-moulded brick method, the shaped bricks are not sanded but are removed from the mould using water. These so-called Wasserstrich bricks have an intense colour as the natural colours are not softened by sanding.

Colour	variable
Glossiness	glossy, satin, **matt**
Translucence (%)	**0** – 20 – 40 – 60 – 80 – 100
Texture	sharp, medium, **dull**
Hardness	**hard**, soft, depressible
Temperature	**warm**, medium, cool
Odour	strong, moderate, **none**
Acoustic opacity	good, **moderate**, poor

Extruded Bricks

Strongpress (Ziegel) | Briques pressées | Ladrillos o bloques hechos por extrusión | Mattoni estrusi | Strengpers

Project American Hotel, Amsterdam (1900)
Architect W. Kromhout and H.G. Jansen
Photographer Kees Hummel

Bricks produced by means of the continuous extrusion method are made from a plastic mass of fattish, tough pre-treated clay forced through a die the size of a single brick. The wet clay reappears in one continuous strand that is then cut by machine into slices the thickness of a brick. The resulting bricks are taut and angular with a smoother surface than both hand-moulded and press-moulded bricks. The extrusion technique means that these bricks can be easily perforated using a special die. This is done to reduce their weight and to improve the drying properties. This last-named is desirable, as a dense extruded brick of fat clay is more sensitive to shrinkage and cracking than a hand- or press-moulded brick. The surface of an extruded brick, which normally speaking is smooth, can be sanded if desired or given a motif or texture using a roller. This is also done to produce imitation hand-moulded bricks.

The extrusion technique was formerly used to make shaped bricks using a special die. In order to produce a smoother brick and increase the density, these 'profiled' bricks were sometimes re-pressed by placing the dryish extruded bricks in a stamping press. Smooth facing bricks of German origin were also dry pressed twice at first. Both profiled and facing bricks were used for decorative brickwork. This was particularly the case in the eclectic architecture of the years leading up to 1900 and in Jugendstil and Art Nouveau buildings. One of the many examples is the American Hotel in Amsterdam (1898-1900) designed by W. Kromhout and H.G. Jansen, with its cladding of yellow facing bricks. Nowadays, such high quality facing bricks are used primarily for glazed work.

Extruded brick is still used to a large extent because of its sleek form, smooth surface and intense colour. Soeters Van Eldonk Ponec Architects chose it for Nijmegen's municipal records office as part of the Mariënburg project. The façade, made from extruded bricks inconsistently fired with a brownish-black slip, is held in a galvanized steel frame.

Project Mariënburg, Nijmegen (2000)
Architect Soeters Van Eldonk Ponec Architects
Photographer Pansa bv

Colour	**variable**
Glossiness	glossy, satin, **matt**
Translucence (%)	**0** – 20 – 40 – 60 – 80 – 100
Texture	sharp, medium, **dull**
Hardness	**hard**, soft, depressible
Temperature	**warm**, medium, cool
Odour	strong, moderate, **none**
Acoustic opacity	good, **moderate**, poor

Ceramic Roofing Tiles

*Keramische Dachziegel | Tuiles céramiques | Tejas de cerámica |
Tegole in ceramica | Keramische dakpannen*

Ceramic roofing tiles have long left an important mark on our built environment, as roof architecture is generally visible in the streets and the landscape. In today's building projects, the significance of the sloping roof as an instrument of architecture and urbanism is fully recognized. Partly because of this, the roof has formally been upgraded to a fifth façade.

The oldest ceramic roofing tiles were made by the Greeks. The Greeks covered their roofs with large terracotta pantiles, which had flanges on the two long sides. These tiles were placed side by side and the seam was overlaid with a tapering semi-cylindrical cover tile. Besides these tiles, the Greeks incorporated other ceramic products in their roofs such as gargoyles in the shape of lion's heads and fired-clay images of the gods. Sometimes the roofing tiles were made of marble instead of clay, as in the case of the Parthenon.

The Greek method of making roofing tiles was also employed by the Etruscans and the Romans. The excavations at Pompeii show that the space between the flat tiles and the convex cover tile was filled with loam. The Romans used similar roofing tiles in our region,

Project Casa Batlló, Barcelona (1906)
Architect Antoni Gaudí
Photographer El Poder de la Palabra © epdlp.com

although roofs there were also covered with natural stone slates and shingles. Two systems prevailed during the Middle Ages. One was an alternation of interlocking concave and convex tiles variously known as 'over and unders', 'Spanish tiles' or even 'monks and nuns.' The space under the convex tile was filled with mortar reinforced with cow hair or horsehair. In the Netherlands, this roof covering was used particularly in the northeast. It still dominates the rooftop landscape in many parts of the Mediterranean region. The other system used flat roofing tiles, also known as slate tiles. The earliest instances of this last-named method in the Netherlands date from around 1300.

Modern Roofing Tiles

The predecessors of the modern Dutch ceramic roofing tile date back to the 15th century, when the first S-shaped tiles were made from river clay of tertiary origin. These so-called pantiles were produced by hand for many centuries. They were made from fattish clay that was either red base or blue through reduction firing. Since about 1850, many types of roofing tile have been mechanically produced, sometimes with an extruder but for the most part using a stamping press. The first mechanically produced roofing tiles in the Netherlands were imported from France.

Pantiles have long been used on roofs, including most of Amsterdam's canal houses, whose slope was more or less constant. In order not to overtax their water-repellent qualities, such roofs could in principle not be pitched less than 35 degrees, while it was assumed that a slope of more than 45 degrees would considerably increase the risk of tiles being lifted by the wind. This relatively great slope means that the roofs of many old houses are visible from the street. Amsterdam and many other old towns owe their street image with its characteristic gables to this phenomenon.

That ceramic tile roofs have an aesthetic as well as a technical side has been acknowledged for some time, as exemplified by the coloured roofs found in such cities as Prague and Vienna. Possibly the best example of the opulence of ceramic roof architecture is to be found in the work of Antoni Gaudí. In the Casa Batlló (1904-1906) he combined broken tiles, slates and fantastic excrescences to create a true roof sculpture.

Yet, in the main, ceramic roof coverings and tiles in particular obey a somewhat rigid and traditional pattern. Certainly the shape of the roof and the distinction between vertical walls and pitched roof have changed little through the ages. It was only during the Amsterdam School era that roofing tiles were upgraded to a expressive visual resource and the line drawn between façade and roof became fainter. Roofing tiles were then used to clad façades as well as to give them a decorative crown.

These days there is an awareness among architects that the roof place and its ceramic covering are instruments that can be used in various ways to achieve urbanistic and architectural aims. For a housing scheme in Bleiswijk, architect Wilma Kingma raised the tiled roof to the status of leitmotif. The gutter height and roof slope as well as the street profile and the fact that roofing tiles were to be used, had all been laid down in the brief. In order to achieve a gentle incidence

Project Private houses, Bleiswijk (2000)
Architect Atelier Kingma & Van Mameren
Photographer Kees Stuip

of light in the narrow streets and to obstruct it as little as possible, Kingma gave the houses a curved section in which façade and roof became one. The resulting skin was covered with blue ceramic roofing tiles, a move prompted by the quality of the material and the product as well as by the expressiveness the undulating tiles contribute to the design.

Pantiles

Gewölbte Dachziegel | Tuiles ondulées | Tejas onduladas | Tegole curve | Gegolfde dakpannen

Project Het Nieuwe Glas, Hoorn (2001)
Architect Rien van Geluk, Zeeman Architecten
Photographer Pansa bv

Project Leesten, Zutphen (1998)
Architect Min2 bouw-kunst
Photographer Harry Noback

Given the roof's significance as fifth façade, it is useful to make a distinction between the visual effects produced by the various types of roofing tile. With their S-shaped cross section, the family of pantiles gives the strongest impression of a scaly skin and produces the most shadow effect. Pantiles have a concave and a convex area. The convex area of the one acts as a downturn and overlaps the upturn of the next tile in the course. Pantiles are made from thoroughly pre-treated tertiary clay using a stamping press.

The earliest pantile in the Netherlands (the *Hollandse pan* or *holle pan*) had no flanges or grooves. These were developed later to improve the tile's resistance to water and dirt. The first generation of improved roofing tiles had a side flange so that the downturn locked into the upturn of the neighbouring tile. Roofs covered with these improved pantiles are easily recognized by the taut line of the underlying groove visible alongside the upturn. In the next generation the flange on the upturn not only locked into the groove of the next tile but extended over it. This new improvement not only gave a greater shadow effect but a much stronger impression of an unbroken succession of waves.

In Het Nieuwe Glas, a new residential development in Hoorn, architect Rien van Geluk of Zeeman Architecten used red pantiles on mansards and curved roofs. The downturn of the roofing tiles used here locks into and extends past the groove of the neighbouring tile. The project alludes to a more rural version of Amsterdam School architecture such as is found in Bergen in the province of North Holland.

Colour	**variable**
Glossiness	glossy, **satin**, **matt**
Translucence (%)	**0** – 20 – 40 – 60 – 80 – 100
Texture	sharp, medium, **dull**
Hardness	**hard**, soft, depressible
Temperature	**warm**, medium, cool
Odour	strong, moderate, **none**
Acoustic opacity	good, **moderate**, poor

Plain Roofing Tiles

Biberschwanzziegel | Tuiles plates | Tejas planas | Tegole piane | Vlakke dakpannen

Project Steijling dune house, Bergen aan Zee (1999)
Architect Min2 bouw-kunst
Photographer Min2 bouw-kunst

Plain roofing tiles have a flat middle section, usually a bent or curved downturn on one of the sides and a groove in the side opposite. Some types of plain tile have a sunken groove and can therefore be laid completely flat. Plain roofing tiles are shaped in a stamping press from tertiary clay that has been carefully pre-treated. They throw less shadow on the roof and are therefore much less expressive. Some types of plain tile can be used to cover large areas where individual tiles can barely be distinguished. This quality makes plain tiling useful in architecture of an abstract nature. The generation of modern plain tiles was preceded by three types originally imported from France: Mulden (from Marseilles), Tuile du Nord and Boulet.

Architects Leon Their and Allard Assies of Atelier Pro have clad the gymnasium of the Euro College in Maastricht (1999) with orange-red Tuile du Nord tiles. These were laid above a manganese brick plinth rising to slightly below head height and topped by a precast concrete moulding. Here the type of tile and the use of roofing tiles as façade cladding are a reference to Amsterdam School architecture.

In Ypenburg, a new housing development near The Hague, De Architectengroep deliberately opted for a plain roofing tile. This Amsterdam practice designed terraced houses in a layout prompted by the masterplan. The blocks of houses forge a link between existing traditional development and the natural surroundings. The closer they get to the surrounding nature, the more expressive they become. This is most notably achieved by the roof, which has a variable slope and a diagonal ridge. The blocks were not designed as a chain of individual units but as street elevations with unbroken roof planes appropriately covered with plain ceramic tiles in a stretcher bond.

Project Hageneiland, Ypenburg (2001)
Architect MVRDV
Photographer Rob 't Hart

Colour	**variable**
Glossiness	glossy, **satin**, **matt**
Translucence (%)	**0** – 20 – 40 – 60 – 80 – 100
Texture	sharp, medium, **dull**
Hardness	**hard**, soft, depressible
Temperature	**warm**, medium, cool
Odour	strong, moderate, **none**
Acoustic opacity	good, **moderate**, poor

Ceramic Slates

Keramische Platten | Ardoise céramiques | Losas de cerámica | Lastre ceramiche | Keramische leien

Project LUX Theatre, Nijmegen (2000)
Architect Soeters Van Eldonk Ponec Architects
Photographer Pansa bv

Ceramic slates are usually made from iron-rich tertiary clay, which nonetheless has a purer composition than clay used to make bricks. They are used to cover vertical roof elements and are therefore used in combination with ceramic roofing tiles. Around 1900 it was normal practice for the sides of a dormer window to be clad with ceramic slate, while the roof itself was covered with tiles.

Nowadays, ceramic slate is often used where a roof, façade or combination of the two needs expressing as the building's skin. In their contribution to the Ypenburg housing development, Karelse Van der Meer Architecten designed terraced houses of which the façade and the roof constitute a single unit. Both are covered with an orange-brown ceramic slate, creating the image of a volume encased in a scaly snakeskin jacket.

Soeters Van Eldonk Ponec Architects covered one side of the LUX theatre and film centre in Nijmegen with ceramic slate deliberately laid in a visually unsettling bond. This was done in order to maximize the shadow effect and to throw up diagonal lines.

Project Housing development, Ypenburg (1999)
Architect Karelse Van der Meer Architects
Photographer Freek Goos

Colour	**variable**
Glossiness	glossy, **satin**, matt
Translucence (%)	**0** – 20 – 40 – 60 – 80 – 100
Texture	sharp, medium, **dull**
Hardness	**hard**, soft, depressible
Temperature	**warm**, medium, cool
Odour	strong, moderate, **none**
Acoustic opacity	good, **moderate**, poor

Wall Tiles

Wandfliesen | Carrelages pour murs | Azulejos pared |
Piastrelle per pareti | Wandtegels

The use of glazed tiles in architecture originated in Persia. From there this technique spread throughout the Mediterranean region on the heels of the Moorish conquest. Glazed tiles finally reached the Netherlands by way of Spain and Italy. Tiles have been used in the Netherlands to clad the interiors and exteriors of buildings since the 17th century. One reason for doing so was to make an enduring yet attractive plinth in damp stonewalled rooms whose floors were regularly doused with water. Tiles were also placed on surfaces behind fireplaces to hide unsightly brick walls smeared with soot. In 17th-century households, the fireplace was not only a cooker and a source of heat but also the most important source of light. White glazed tiles were a means of enhancing this aspect.

Seventeenth and eighteenth-century wall tiles were made from a plastic red – or yellow – firing tertiary clay. This was rolled out in an iron mould, dried and fired once. The tile was then coated with a tin glaze in paste form, known as a slip. Once this had dried, a drawing was made on the tile in pigments obtained from metal oxides and other sources. Originally this was done by scratching through the slip, though zinc templates were also used from the 19th century on. The tile was then fired for a second time causing the tin glaze and the drawing to fuse in a single glassy layer.

Improved Production

In the mid 19th century, another production procedure was adopted, first in Great Britain (by the Johnson company in about 1850) and then in Germany. This procedure did not use moulded tiles but rather a so-called biscuit tile made from a compressed, almost dry powder of secondary clay. The result was a compact, white-fired tile that could be painted without the need to apply a tin glaze. At that time too, the colouring agents were improved and a wider choice of colours became available. For this technique, which quickly caught on in the Netherlands, the painted tile was first fired at a high temperature. Next, a lead glaze was applied, after which the tile was fired a second time at a lower temperature. For some colours, such as bright red or gold, the tile underwent further firings, each time at a lower temperature. Known as the underglaze technique, this method produced a tile that looked like a painting or part of a painting. These tiles were used to build up entire panels which were commissioned to commemorate company anniversaries and the like. Panels made from underglazed tiles were also used for advertisements in shops or to wainscot ceremonial or public rooms.

Wall tiles were often applied to exteriors, particularly in the years between 1900 and 1920, and for this a less porous biscuit was required. One example are the so-called sectile tiles developed by De Porceleyne Fles, in which the top layer was completely permeated by the colouring agent. Apart from exterior applications, sectile tiles were also used for Stations of the Cross in churches. The technique, in which the tile joints follow the lines of the composition, was inspired by leaded windows. It was in the first decades of the 20th century that renowned manufacturers such as Rozenburg in The Hague and De Porceleyne Fles in Delft reached their peak.

Another technique was that of 'tube lining', whereby a drawing was first made by trailing lines of slip onto the surface of the tile, after

Project Huize Kareol, Aerdenhout (1911)

Artist Max Läuger

Photographer Nederlands Tegelmuseum

which the areas between the lines were filled in with a colour. During the firing process, the glaze flowed until it reached the lines of slip. Although this ancient technique has been modernized, ceramicists do not always resort to the latest technological innovations. Take the tile pictures that once graced the exterior of Kareol, a country house in Aerdenhout near Haarlem designed by the Swedish architect Anders Lundberg and built between 1908 and 1911. This artwork was created by the German Jugendstil ceramicist Max Läuger using red-fired and yellow-fired tiles. It was intended to add to Kareol's stature as a Gesamtkunstwerk, completely in the spirit of the times. The house was demolished in 1980.

The external use of tiles and tile panels continued until the end of the Art Nouveau period. After 1920, the practice virtually ceased, a turn of events that undoubtedly had something to do with the technical problems that were increasingly coming to light. It should be remembered that until shortly before 1900 all tiles made in the Netherlands had been produced from tertiary clay. These tiles were always slightly porous and therefore vulnerable to frost damage. The problems were scarcely evident at first, but over time more and more

water penetrated the pores of the fired clay, increasing the possibility of cracking during heavy frosts.

Since the 1950s, tiles have made a sporadic reappearance on the outsides of buildings, thanks in part to the artists of the Cobra movement. Karel Appel, for example, enriched the entrance to the Netherlands Congress Centre in The Hague with two large tile pictures. Ceramic tiles were often used as a façade cladding in social housing of the 1950s, but the practice did not extend into subsequent decades. The use of tiles as a façade cladding reached an absolute low in 1980.

Tiles and Design

Since then, a lot has changed in the architectural application of tiles. Production and glazing techniques have improved and the tile is becoming increasingly popular among designers. Collaborations between designers and renowned ceramic companies are producing technically and aesthetically high-quality and innovative products. For example, Koninklijke Tichelaar in Makkum produced a range of glazed wall tiles for the designer Ettore Sottsass. For interior use, the same company produced artist Baukje Trenning's TacTiles, Babs Haenen's Wad Tiles and Erik Jan Kwakkel and Arnout Visser's Drop Tiles.

In the last few years, the exterior use of tiles has gained an extra dimension. In deprived districts and unsafe areas such as underground railway stations and viaducts, tile pictures are used to enhance social safety and increase the involvement of residents in their living environment. In the Wippolder district in Delft, artist Ben Hosman and the residents, children and adults alike, have made dozens of tile pictures for fitting into the boarded-up windows of old houses. The paintings were made on white biscuit tiles (15 x 15 cm) which were then given a second firing. In Lisbon, it has been standard practice since 1959 to commission artists to tile the city's underground railway stations. Thus, Julio Pomar enriched the Pessoa station (1988) with panels of white tiles, each inscribed with a line portrait in black. This idea has been imitated, with variations, in underground railway stations in Brussels (1992), Tokyo (1993), São Paulo (1994) and many other cities including Moscow.

Project Netherlands Congress Centre, The Hague (1969)

Artist Karel Appel

Photographer Wim de Jong

Ceramic Tiles

Keramische Fliesen | Carrelages double cuisson | Azulejos cocidos dobles | Piastrelle in bicottura | Dubbelhardgebakken tegels

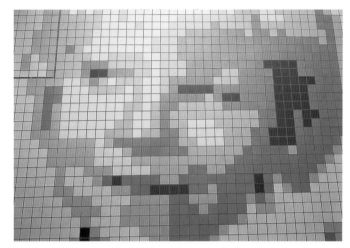

Project De Vrolike Eik, Amsterdam (1997)

Architect M3H Architects

Photographer Kees Hummel

Ceramic tiles are common within the Dutch construction industry. Made from secondary clay, they usually measure 10 x 10 cm. They have a matt surface and are available in various colours and textures.

Technical Aspects

The biscuit tiles, fired at 1000 °C, are given a matt finish and fired again at 1200 °C. A few decades ago, ceramic tiles were often given a characteristic flame pattern. This effect was achieved by irregularly subjecting the surface of the tile to the kiln's flame and the reduction atmosphere during the firing process.

Applications

Since the 1950s in particular, ceramic tiles have been used more or less as the standard for floors in wet rooms such as the changing rooms of sports complexes and the bathrooms of simply decorated apartments. This custom continues to the present day. Ceramic tiles are also used eternally as a façade cladding. Many houses built in the 1950s and '60s with a 'through room' have a tableau in ceramic tiles between the large living room window on the ground floor and the large window of the master bedroom directly above it. These specific uses gave ceramic tiles a bad name among designers for many years. This attitude changed when they began making full use of the potential of ceramic tiles as floor mosaics. A notable example can be found in the trendy Café de Jaren (converted 1990) in Amsterdam.

Project Café De Jaren, Amsterdam (1990)

Photographer Kees Hummel

Colour	variable
Glossiness	glossy, satin, matt
Translucence (%)	**0** – 20 – 40 – 60 – 80 – 100
Texture	sharp, medium, **dull**
Hardness	**hard**, soft, depressible
Temperature	**warm**, medium, cool
Odour	strong, moderate, **none**
Acoustic opacity	good, **moderate**, poor

Glazed Stoneware Tiles

Glasierte Steinzeugfliesen | Carrelages en grès vitré | Azulejos de piedra vidriada | Piastrelle in gres porcellanato | Grestegels

Project Tiled picture A. Bloemaertstraat, The Hague (c. 1990)
Artist Berry Holtslag
Photographer Ingeborg Nefkens

Technical Aspects

Glazed stoneware tiles are made from red-firing secondary clay with a high iron and manganese content. They are usually produced by the extrusion method as a split tile and fired at a high temperature (1100-1200 °C). Since they range from barely porous to non-porous, glazed stoneware tiles are suitable for external uses and in chemical (acidic) environments. They are also very wear-resistant.

Applications

For external applications there is a standard tile size, but glazed stoneware is increasingly also used to make mosaic stoneware. These mosaic tiles are cut from large panels using a high-pressure water jet.

In the 1990s, artist Berry Holtslag made a large mosaic on Abraham Bloemaertstraat in the Schilderswijk district of The Hague. Covering the entire side elevation of an old block of houses, it shows a perspective view of the part of the street that was demolished before the mosaic was installed. The work is in two colours, with white glazed stoneware panels standing out against the dark red bricks of the houses.

Colour	variable
Glossiness	glossy, **satin**, **matt**
Translucence (%)	**0** – 20 – 40 – 60 – 80 – 100
Texture	sharp, medium, **dull**
Hardness	**hard**, soft, depressible
Temperature	**warm**, medium, cool
Odour	strong, moderate, **none**
Acoustic opacity	good, **moderate**, poor

Extrusion Panels

Stranggepresste Paneele | Panneaux de carrelage extrudés | Paneles de extrusión | Pannelli ad estrusione | Extrusiepanelen

Project Centre Pompidou, Paris (1977)
Architect Renzo Piano + Richard Rogers
Photographer Kees Hummel

The façades of high-rise buildings were usually made from 'new' materials such as glass and steel. This has changed with the development of ceramic elements extruded from chamotte clay.

Technical Aspects

These elements are lightweight and dimensionally very stable. The extruded elements are placed in aluminium frames as lamellae or strips using special fasteners. These frames are then mounted on façade supports usually of steel. This technique makes it possible to integrate the specific material qualities and visual resonance of ceramic products in new façade concepts.

Applications

Since the extrusion elements fit into frames, there are many different compositions open to designers. The elements can be used both vertically and horizontally and the frames need not be filled in identically. An important example of this technique can be found in Berlin where architects Renzo Piano and Christoph Kohlbecker used terracotta cladding elements in the 27-storey Debis Tower (1998) located on Potzdamer Platz. Held in aluminium frames, the terracotta elements are not only a cladding but also function as shading devices and decoration. A ceramic cladding has also been prescribed for the adjoining buildings.

Colour	**variable**
Glossiness	glossy, **satin**, **matt**
Translucence (%)	**0** – 20 – 40 – 60 – 80 – 100
Texture	sharp, medium, **dull**
Hardness	**hard**, soft, depressible
Temperature	**warm**, medium, cool
Odour	strong, moderate, **none**
Acoustic opacity	good, **moderate**, poor

Additives and Treatments

Zuschlagstoffe und Bearbeitung | Additifs et traitements | Aditivos y Tratamientos |
Additivi e trattamenti | Toevoegingen en bewerkingen

To this day, clay products are usually produced in locations close to where the clay is extracted. The disadvantage of this is that the colour of the clay product is largely dependant on the colour the clay naturally acquires after firing, and on its other properties. For example, red-fired bricks and roofing tiles are traditionally produced in an area where red-firing tertiary clay is extracted. The colour can only be influenced during the firing process by reduction, which gives the product a dark blue to purple colour. There are two ways of producing a different colour. The first, in which the clay is mixed with an additive, is what concerns us here. The second method, which will be explained later, involves treating the already shaped, and sometimes already fired, clay product.

An additive can also be used to influence the physical properties of a fired clay product. An example already referred to in another context is the addition of chamotte clay to pure, fat clay in order to reduce shrinkage. Another reason for using an additive is to reduce the weight or improve the noise and heat insulation properties.

It is by no means the intention that the fired clay should remain visible in all applications of ceramic building materials. The clay product often merely provides a suitable ground for a visually defining treatment. This is particularly true of glazed tiles but also of slip-coated roofing tiles and bricks. In such cases the natural colour of the fired clay is of little consequence.

Project National Trade Unions Museum, Amsterdam (1900)
Architect P.H. Berlage
Photographer Jeroen van Amelsvoort

Other treatments go less far in this respect and merely give the natural colour of the fired clay product a slightly different shade. Sanding wet-shaped bricks greatly influences the texture of the brick and the intensity of the colour, while added combustible materials impact on the surface. Reduction during the firing process of clay products is in a category of its own. This is not strictly speaking a treatment and although the effect on the colour is quite profound, the change occurs within the product itself and does not involve the use of additives.

Project Noorderhof, Amsterdam (1999)
Architect Rob Krier
Photographer Kees Hummel

Project Private house, Warmenhuizen (2002)
Architect Liong Lie, 123DV
Photographer Roos Aldershoff

Colour

Farbe| Couleur | Color | Colore | Kleur

Project Private house, Heusden-Zolder (1992)
Architect Kristien Ceyssens
Photographer Jan Derwig

Project Piraeus building, Amsterdam (1994)
Architect Hans Kollhoff and Christian Rapp
Photographer Kees Hummel

There are various ways of influencing the colour of brick and other ceramic products. One is the addition of pigments. This is done during pre-treatment of the clay when the colouring agent is thoroughly mixed with the raw material. Adding iron oxide will give the brick a more intense red colour, while adding finely ground quarried lime produces a yellower brick. Adding liquid pyrolusite (natural manganese) to clay containing iron oxide will turn the brick a dark brown to black colour.

Manganese-coloured brick is normally used for purely architectural reasons. Two variations are to be found in Amsterdam. The Noorderhof district designed under the supervision of Rob Krier uses manganese-coloured brick for special emphasis. The plinth of the blocks of rental units has been darkened to make it look heavier. Here, every seventh brick course in the plinth has been moved back two centimetres to give it a rusticated look. Dark pointing further emphasizes this effect, so that the bricks and the pointing present a single plane.

A different approach is discernible in the Piraeus housing block on KNSM Island, designed by Hans Kollhoff and Christian Rapp. The use of manganese-coloured brick and darker pointing accentuates the monolithic and abstract shape of the block. The black Piraeus building hit the Dutch architectural world like a bombshell and its use of manganese-coloured brick has been much imitated.

Colour	variable
Glossiness	**glossy**, **satin**, **matt**
Translucence (%)	**0** – 20 – 40 – 60 – 80 – 100
Texture	sharp, medium, **dull**
Hardness	**hard**, soft, depressible
Temperature	**warm**, medium, cool
Odour	strong, moderate, **none**
Acoustic opacity	good, **moderate**, poor

Porosity

Porosität | Porosité | Porosidad | Porosità | Porositeit

Project De Laatste Eer funeral home, Delft (1998)
Architect Molenaar & Van Winden Architects
Photographer Tom Croes

Porous brick is made by adding a combustible material to reasonably fat tertiary clay. The brick is then shaped by the press method during which the core usually becomes perforated. During the firing process, the additive is burned away leaving coarse pores in the clay product. This makes the brick lighter and gives it other favourable properties such as better sound absorption and insulation, improved heat insulation and greater fire-resistance. This intentionally porous brick has been in use since the 1920s. It was initially introduced to save weight and because porous brick provided an excellent surface for plasterwork. The aesthetic potential of porous ceramic brick was only recognized much later. Since then it has also been produced for use in facing brickwork, although its application is limited to the interior.

Poriso, Fimon, and Poroton are types of porous brick produced from ceramic materials. The Poriso brick is made from 'Brunssum' clay with sawdust and fly ash added for combustion. Until recently, the Fimon brick was made from fat Groningen clay co-fired with sawdust. This solid core brick is no longer produced. The Poroton brick consists of clay fired with polystyrene grains and is used almost exclusively for concealed brickwork. The surface of the brick has vertical grooves for improved bonding with the plasterwork.

Colour	**variable**
Glossiness	glossy, satin, **matt**
Translucence (%)	**0** – 20 – 40 – 60 – 80 – 100
Texture	sharp, medium, **dull**
Hardness	**hard**, soft, depressible
Temperature	**warm**, medium, cool
Odour	strong, moderate, **none**
Acoustic opacity	good, **moderate**, poor

Printing

Bedrucken | Impression | Impresión y serigrafía | Stampa | Printen

Project Printed bridge Elfstedentocht, Leeuwarden (2000)

Artist Maree Blok, Bas Lughthart

Photographer Royal Tichelaar

All kinds of decorative patterns, such as geometric shapes or a company logo, can be applied to the facing side of an extruded brick either by using a roller, or by carving the pattern out of the material. This printing technique is also used to make extruded bricks look like hand-moulded ones.

Another printing technique is photo transfer whereby a photograph is transformed into a print composed of pigments and then applied to a panel of biscuit tiles before firing. This technique was used by artist Tessa van der Waals in the washrooms of the Faculty of Communication and Journalism in Utrecht. Each tile picture is three tiles across and four high and portrays an employee or a student. Artists Maree Blok and Bas Lughthart used the same technique when designing the cladding of the last bridge in the Elfstedentocht ice skating marathon in Friesland. Close up, each tile can be seen to depict one of the skaters who have at one time or another completed the marathon. From a distance, the individual tiles merge to present a different picture, that of a line of skaters – a scene that can easily become a reality here in the winter months.

Colour	variable
Glossiness	glossy, satin, **matt**
Translucence (%)	**0** – 20 – 40 – 60 – 80 – 100
Texture	sharp, medium, **dull**
Hardness	**hard**, soft, depressible
Temperature	**warm**, medium, cool
Odour	strong, moderate, **none**
Acoustic opacity	good, **moderate**, poor

Sanding

Schleifen | Ponçage | Acabado con chorro de arena | Insabbiatura | Bezanden

Project Brandevoort, Helmond (2001)

Architect Lanfermeijer Seelen, Van der Laan, Saanen-Knoups Architects

Photographer Kees Stuip

To sand an unfired clay product, a thin layer of sand is applied to the still wet surface. The sand sticks to the wet clay and is fired in the kiln with it. For the production of hand-moulded and press-moulded brick, the ball of clay and the mould are sanded beforehand to prevent the clay from sticking to the mould. The other use of sanding is for visual effect. Wet hand-moulded and press-moulded bricks are always sanded after being shaped, and wet extruded bricks are occasionally given a thin layer of sand.

Sanding has a major influence on the colour and texture of the brick. Using sand of a neutral colour tempers the colour, softening bright red for example to a pastel shade. This shading or toning down of the colour is standard for hand-moulded and press-moulded brick. The precise colour of the sand and the size of the grains are parameters that influence the brick's colour and texture. Coloured sand can be substituted for the neutral variety, in which case it is the sand and not the brick that determines the colour.

Colour	**variable**
Glossiness	glossy, satin, **matt**
Translucence (%)	**0** – 20 – 40 – 60 – 80 – 100
Texture	sharp, medium, **dull**
Hardness	**hard**, soft, depressible
Temperature	**warm**, medium, cool
Odour	strong, moderate, **none**
Acoustic opacity	good, **moderate**, poor

Combustible Additives

Brennzusätze | Poussière de charbon, sciure | Aditivos de fuel | Materiali combustibili | Uitbrandstoffen

Project Mariënburg centre, Nijmegen (2000)
Architect Molenaar & Van Winden Architects
Photographer Pansa bv

Formerly, when sanding was not desired because of its effect on the colour but the percentage of fine particles was too high for the clay to emerge intact from the mould without further precautions, sawdust or coaldust was added to the top layer of the brick as an alternative to sand. The look of the fired brick barely altered as the sawdust or coaldust was burned away in the kiln.

Nowadays, a combustible material is often added for the visual effect it produces. The surface has a more irregular texture as a result of the combustion and slight differences in colour may occur. With coaldust the brick acquires the effect of continued sintering in places, as often occurred in the past in old coal-fired kilns. Nowadays, such brick is produced for restoration work as well as to meet nostalgic needs for a traditional product.

Molenaar & Van Winden Architecten have built the façade of a shop on a square (Koningsplein) in Nijmegen, using extruded brick in horizontal and vertical lines around large openings in the façade. The places where the lines meet have been made to look like thick knots. These consist of a border of perforated extruded bricks, the top layer of which has been sintered in places by the coaldust added during the firing process. At the centre of each knot is a ceramic relief made by St. Joris Keramische Industrie in a white-firing secondary clay (Westerwalder) to which chamotte has been added.

Colour	variable
Glossiness	**glossy, satin, matt**
Translucence (%)	**0 – 20 – 40 – 60 – 80 – 100**
Texture	sharp, medium, **dull**
Hardness	**hard**, soft, depressible
Temperature	**warm**, medium, cool
Odour	strong, moderate, **none**
Acoustic opacity	good, **moderate**, poor

Slip

Engobieren | Engobes | Engobes / antideslizantes | Ingobbiatura | Engoberen

Project Broekpolder, Heemskerk (2002)
Architect Min2 bouw-kunst
Photographer Min2 bouw-kunst

Local clay types are often unable to produce an unlimited range of colours. Since it is unrealistic to import special types of clay, an after-treatment has been developed whereby a solution of the desired clay is applied to the dry but as yet unfired brick or roof tile. This solution or slip contains the metal oxides that will produce the desired colour. The layer of clay can be applied by spraying it onto the brick or by immersion. The slip has a melting point that is slightly lower than that of the brick. During the firing process, therefore, the slip has already begun to sinter and thus to lose its cohesion by the time the brick reaches its sintering point. The slip is distributed evenly and regularly over the brick, giving a fired product with a dense surface. Applying the slip irregularly will produce a more subtle colour effect.

Soeters Van Eldonk Ponec Architecten used a red extruded brick with a subtly applied brownish-black slip for their municipal records office on the new Mariënburg square in Nijmegen. In the adjoining Marikenstraat, the architect Vera Yanovshtchinsky used the same brick on the façade of the lowest level of shops to convey an impression of weight.

Colour	**variable**
Glossiness	glossy, **satin**, matt
Translucence (%)	**0** – 20 – 40 – 60 – 80 – 100
Texture	sharp, medium, **dull**
Hardness	**hard**, soft, depressible
Temperature	**warm**, medium, cool
Odour	strong, moderate, **none**
Acoustic opacity	good, **moderate**, poor

Glazing

Glasieren | Glaçure | Vidriado | Smaltatura | Glazuren

Project P. de Gruyter shop, Nijmegen (1919)
Architect W.G. Welsing
Photographer Pansa bv

Project Noorderhof, Amsterdam (1999)
Architect Joris Deur
Photographer Kees Hummel

Glazing a clay product not only gives it a glossy or semi-glossy appearance, but also renders the surface hard and dense. A glaze is a mixture of fine clay and pigments, including metal oxides. Together they form a paste that is used to coat the dried or once-fired clay product. Alternatively, the glaze can be sprayed on or the product immersed in it. Glazes used to be made with tin or lead. Lead glaze is transparent and has a yellowish colour, while tin glaze is opaque and gives a shiny, even white surface.

Tin glaze was used as a base for glazed tiles and bricks. The glazed surface could be decorated using a special paint containing other metal oxides. During firing, the decoration formed a single layer with the underlying surface. Tin glaze has always had the disadvantage that it does not behave like water, so the dissolved metal oxides are not able to oxidize properly and the colours are less than perfect.

When the painting was done on a white-fired product, the tin glaze ground was no longer necessary. After the painting had been fired, the lead glaze was applied as a varnish and the product was fired once more. Toxic lead and tin have since been replaced by environmentally-friendly additives such as feldspar or frits of lead or tin.

During the glazing process it is important that the glaze (or more accurately, glass frits) has a sintering point slightly lower than that of the clay product. This means that the glass frits will have already melted and spread into a homogeneous layer by the time the clay particles begin to bond but have not yet reached the vitreous phase. The clay is then still strong and non-brittle. If the pigments have to be added to different layers of the glaze because of a difference in melting points, the layer with the highest melting point is placed in the kiln first.

In the Netherlands, glazed ceramic products were particularly popular in building construction around 1900. The shops of the De Gruyter grocery company had a readily identifiable house style of blue glazed tiles with the company name inscribed in gold glaze. Architect W.G. Welsing designed the De Gruyter shop in Nijmegen (1919). In the Noorderhof project (1998) in Amsterdam, architect Joris Deur decorated the houses he designed with blue, green and black glazed facing bricks. These he worked into columns and façades characterized by continuous cross joints.

Colour	**variable**
Glossiness	**glossy**, satin, matt
Translucence (%)	**0** – 20 – 40 – 60 – 80 – 100
Texture	sharp, medium, **dull**
Hardness	**hard**, soft, depressible
Temperature	warm, **medium**, cool
Odour	strong, moderate, **none**
Acoustic opacity	good, **moderate**, poor

Reducing

Reduktionsverfahren | Réduction (d'oxygène) | Reducción (alisamiento o matificación) | Deossidazione | Reduceren en smoren

Project Hunebed, Assen (1999)

Architect Min2 bouw-kunst

Photographer Min2 bouw-kunst

Normally speaking there is an unhindered supply of oxygen during the firing process, which produces red Fe_2O_3. Restricting the oxygen supply means that oxygen is extracted from the iron in the clay during that process. As a result, the fired clay product turns dark blue or dark purple. Nowadays, the reduction process takes place automatically in state-of-the-art kilns. In the past, the kiln was heated to the maximum allowable temperature and the air supply shut off after adding a large amount of carbon-rich fuel to the fire. The oxygen can also be restricted during the cooling phase of the firing process. Known as reduction, this give the clay surface a denser structure. Roofing tiles produced using this method are less liable to become overgrown with moss.

In Het Nieuwe Glas, a new residential development in Hoorn, architect Rien van Geluk of Zeeman Architecten was inspired by the formal syntax of the Amsterdam School. He sought to create an expressive housing project using narrative architecture; a living environment that conveys a sense of having been crafted with care and attention to detail. This effect is in part due to the use of reduction-fired blue roofing tiles as a façade cladding.

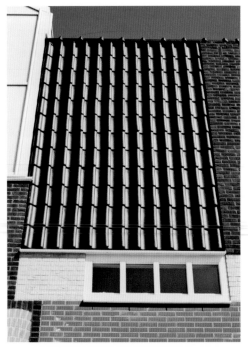

Project Het Nieuwe Glas, Hoorn (2001)

Architect Rien van Geluk, Zeeman Architecten

Photographer Pansa bv

Colour	**variable**
Glossiness	glossy, **satin**, matt
Translucence (%)	**0** – 20 – 40 – 60 – 80 – 100
Texture	sharp, **medium, dull**
Hardness	**hard**, soft, depressible
Temperature	**warm**, medium, cool
Odour	strong, moderate, **none**
Acoustic opacity	good, **moderate**, poor

Applications

*Verwendung von gebranntem Stein | Applications de roche artificielle cuite |
Aplicaciones de piedra artificial cocida | Applicazioni dei manufatti per cottura |
Toepassingen gebakken kunststeen*

Although each brick and roofing tile has its own properties of shape,
size, colour and texture, the aesthetic quality of the wall or roof
plane in which the bricks or tiles have been combined is determined
by a combination of factors. The architectural impact of brick cannot
therefore be seen in isolation from the bond in which the bricks are
laid or from the joints between the bricks. Roofing tiles, too, are
architecturally speaking only one part of a larger whole.

Bonds and Patterns

Brick bonds have been around since the very first brick was laid.
In the aforementioned Chogha Zanbil temple in present-day Iran,
bricks were consistently laid in a stretcher bond – that is, with the

Project Het Nieuwe Glas, Hoorn (2001)
Architect Rien van Geluk, Zeeman Architecten
Photographer Pansa bv

vertical or cross joint of each layer staggered half a brick. This was
done to increase the strength of the brick construction, which
required that cross joints should not be aligned vertically. This hard-
and-fast rule also applied to walls of natural stone. The bond was
usually laid side on as well as in the wall plane itself. In rubble-core
walls this joined the wall's exterior to the filling behind it, while in
solid masonry facing and backing bricks were bonded at regular
intervals by headers, bricks with their shorter edge parallel to the
surface.

Many different types of bond have been developed through the ages. Aside from the stretcher, the use of a particular bond was regional in origin. This is often evident in the name, such as Flemish bond or English bond. Architects, having realized that brickwork bonds can do much to articulate a façade, use them as an architectural device. Michel de Klerk (1884-1923) did so for the street frontage of the houses on Vrijheidslaan (1921-1922) in Amsterdam South. These buildings sport a characteristic block pattern created by alternating horizontal courses with bricks set upright with the broad face exposed (in sailor position).

One way of introducing metaphorical relief to brickwork bonds is to vary the colour of the bricks. In the Noorderhof project in Amsterdam (1998), architect Mark Tuerlings emphasized the entrances to the houses by placing them inside a double-height frame of brick in a contrasting colour, sometimes accompanied by a small window. The rest of the façade within the frame is laid in a Flemish bond (alternating stretchers and headers) in which one layer has yellow stretchers and brown headers and those above and below have brown stretchers and yellow headers. The result is a pattern of yellow crosses.

While Tuerlings' colour pattern coincides with the brickwork bond, a subsequent step is to introduce colour motifs that are all but independent of the brickwork. Only the size of the course and the heads affects the pattern. An exuberant example of this is the side of Marikenstraat in Nijmegen designed by Molenaar & Van Winden Architecten: this 'tattooed' façade is composed of white and brownish-red extruded bricks.

Since the 13th century, colourful geometric patterns have been applied to the roofs of buildings using glazed plain tiles. This practice originated in Central Europe, one example being St Stephen's Cathedral in Vienna. Coloured roofs became very popular and were soon adopted elsewhere, such as in Burgundy. A particularly fine example is the Hôtel-Dieu in Beaune, built in 1443. Glazed coloured roofing tiles were used in the Netherlands too. Remnants found in Utrecht indicate that such tiles were being produced around 1300. It was not until later that roofing tiles were arranged into patterns, though often only in two colours. For example, red tiles would be used to inscribe the name of a company in a field of reduction-fired blue tiles. Brick factories often did this. The artist Clara Froger thus designed coloured roofing tile patterns for a Dutch roofing tile manufacturer (KDN-Teewen Dakpannen, now Lafarge Roofing) in which she makes a distinction between geometric, amorphous and organic patterns.

Pointing
The architectural impact of brick is inextricably bound up with the structure, shape and colour of the pointing. Pointing as we know it today was not used in Dutch building construction until the 17th century. The oldest joints were of lime mortar and as it dried fairly slowly it could be easily worked using a jointer. During the 18th century, joints steadily became thinner and brick façades were sometimes ground down to produce a homogeneous surface. Wider bed joints arrived in the 19th century, though cross joints remained extremely thin. Tuck pointing was preferred until the late 1930s,

Project Noorderhof, Amsterdam (1999)
Architect Mark Tuerlings
Photographer Kees Hummel

although other types had become current by this time. The architect Willem Marinus Dudok used weather-struck joints for such building projects as the City Hall in Hilversum (1924-1931). These are inclined mortar joints where the bottom of the joint lies flush with the façade whereas the top is set a few millimetres back. Full brickwork became very popular in the 1950s. The often ragged jointing, which sometimes spills over onto the façade, gives such brickwork great character. With this one exception, the use of jointing in Dutch architecture was long neglected after the Second World War. It is only since the revival and revaluation of brickwork in the 1990s that it has received more attention, particularly as regards colour.

In the Noorderhof project in Amsterdam, architect Mark Tuerlings gave his houses (1998) a distinctive entrance area in a pattern of brown and yellow bricks. Yellow pointing was used for the yellow brick, dark pointing for the brown brick. Whereas Tuerlings chose a treatment that allows the brickwork to register as a surface, Soeters Van Eldonk Ponec Architecten opted for a more expressive effect in the plaza façade of the LUX theatre and film centre in Nijmegen. This they achieved by raking out the mortar from between the orange-red hand-moulded brick to a depth of about 1.5 cm and leaving it unpointed.

Unfired Man-made Stone

Ungebrannter, künstlicher Stein | Roche artificiel non cuite | Piedra artificial no cocida | Pietre sintetiche | Ongebakken kunststeen

Ancient Civilizations

The foundation for the artificial production of stone-like materials was laid by ancient civilizations long before the Christian era. One of the oldest building materials is mud, which hardens as it dries in the open air. Impressive, delightful mud-brick structures in natural ochre or terracotta colours can be found in Africa. One example is the mosque at Djenné in Mali, which is given a new mud finish every year after the rainy season because mud cannot withstand protracted exposure to water.

The hydraulic effect of lime as a binding agent has been known for thousands of years in the Middle and Far East. Lime-based plaster-work crops up in many ancient cultures as an aesthetic wall finish. The Greeks, for example, mixed lime with finely ground marble for a decorative and colourful plasterwork for temples and palaces.

Description Mosque Djenné, Mali (1907)
Architect Ismaila Traoré
Photographer Miguel Cruz

Polishing such plasterwork resulted in walls that looked like natural stone and were also fairly water resistant. Another well-known example is the fifth-century Mirror Wall in the Palace of Sigiriya in Sri Lanka, which owes its name to the gleaming finish of polished plasterwork. The Romans discovered cement as a binding agent for their *opus caementitium*, the predecessor of modern concrete.

Opus Caementitium

Human beings have always used materials from their immediate sur-roundings to build their shelters. Limestone occurs abundantly in nature. When heated to about 900 °C, the stone disintegrates into a powder. As soon as the 'burnt' lime comes into contact with water, it hardens again into stone. It is not so surprising, then, that this process should have been known in ancient times. The ancients mixed lime with sand or clay into lime mortars that were used for building sturdy walls. The discovery of cement by the Romans sprang from the combination of lime mortars with other raw materials like pozzolana, natural stone rubble or shards of earthenware, that were mixed into a compression-resistant artificial stone. In Latin, *opus cae-mentitium* means a *caementum* work, which is to say undressed stones in a bedding of cement. In his ten-volume work on architec-

ture written in the 1st century BC, Vitruvius described the Roman use of *opus caementitium* for building walls. Two masonry walls were erected at a certain distance from each other. A mixture of crushed stone and hydraulic lime mortar was poured into the space between and firmly tamped down. The result was a sturdy wall that could withstand high compressive forces. The outer skin of walls, excepting those of utilities like aqueducts and water reservoirs, was often given a richly decorated finish. The Romans succeeded in building impres-sive structures with this predecessor of our modern concrete. One of the best-known and still intact structures from the 1st century BC is the Pantheon in Rome. The spectacular dome, with a span of 43 metres, is made of Roman concrete of varying compositions. For the upper part of the dome, for example, a lightweight aggregate of pumice was used instead of heavier marble or tuff granules. By con-trast, the base of the circular wall on which the dome rests has a core made entirely with a heavy natural stone aggregate. The Romans adapted the composition of the concrete to the calculated play of forces in the construction. Recent research suggests that as well as pouring concrete on site, the Romans also used moulds to precast some elements for things like water channels. Although technical expertise with respect to building and building materials was fairly advanced in Roman times, much of this knowledge was lost with the fall of the Roman Empire.

Industrial Revolution

The method for producing cement was not rediscovered until the industrial revolution. Towards the end of the nineteenth century, with building production soaring, there was a great and urgent need for new, inexpensive building materials and building methods to meet the enormous demand. During this period, many ingenious processes

Description Rammed earth Tameclost, Morocco (c. 1650)
Photographer Carl Gispen

Project De Hoep, Castricum (2003)
Architect Min2 bouw-kunst
Photographer Min2 bouw-kunst

were patented for the industrial production of materials based on binding agents such as cement, lime and plaster. Sand-lime brick started to be produced as an alternative to fired brick. The large-scale production of Portland cement as basic ingredient for concrete was also of tremendous importance for the development of construction technology. The first decades of the twentieth century in particular were dominated by tremendous and exciting sense of progress. It was in this fertile climate for new inventions that the idea of combining the strength properties of steel and concrete arose, giving birth to ferroconcrete. Ferro, or reinforced, concrete sparked a revolution not only in the construction world, but also in the world of architecture.

In the 1920s and '30s, concrete was regarded as a symbol of modernization. The increasing interest in health led to a greater demand for space, light and air. Proponents of modern architectural movements, such as Le Corbusier, Mies van der Rohe, and the Dutch 'Nieuwe Bouwen' architects, Duiker and Rietveld, regarded the structural performance of concrete and the opportunities it afforded for 'free' design as quite literally a liberation from the cheerless, insalubrious nineteenth century. Concrete made it possible to separate supporting structure, façade and internal partitioning, thus allowing architects to design large areas of glass that flooded the interior with daylight. The Expressionists, too, were attracted to concrete because it made it possible to realize the continuous flowing movements of their quick sketches.

In the 1930s, the modern architecture movement was focused on industrial developments in America. Lightweight building became a fashion that resulted in a booming business for the manufacturers of pumice and aerated concrete and of sheet materials like fibre cement and wood-wool cement. Know-how from America and Europe was exchanged by way of lectures and articles in professional journals like *De 8 en Opbouw*. Experiments with reinforced stucco façades, like

that in Duiker's Zonnestraal Sanatorium, met with varying success. For the façade of his Retraitehuis in Heerlen (1932), Dutch architect F.P.J. Peutz even went so far as to import a special American reinforcement. Steeltex, which originated in the timber-frame construction industry, consisted in those days of a mesh reinforcement of galvanized steel and asphalt paper. Several layers of concrete mortar were applied to the mesh, resulting in a thin, reinforced cavity leaf. Compared with the poor condition exhibited by the Zonnestraal façade not long after construction, the Steeltex-based walls are still in remarkably good condition. Not everyone was impressed by the use of these new materials, however, and there were heated discussions between the modernists and the 'traditionalists', which is to say the architects of the Amsterdam School. The contrast between the monumental ornamentation in brick and natural stone of the established order and the austere design in concrete, glass, and steel of the avant-garde was indeed very great. The Depression and the war put an end to this brief period of optimism and high expectations.

After the War

Before the Second World War, concrete surfaces were often hidden behind a layer of light coloured rendering, whereas after the war in the 1950s and '60s, it was precisely the raw, abstract quality of the concrete skin that was appreciated. In Le Corbusier's post-war buildings, like the Unité d'Habitation or the La Tourette monastery in Evreux, France, the outlines of the formwork planks are obviously part of the aesthetic design. The Salk Institute in California by Louis Kahn (1965) is a source of inspiration to many architects because of the contrasting combination of rough concrete and wood. In the

Project Office space, Vlaardingen (1997)
Architect Moen and Van Oosten Architects
Photographer Jan Derwig

1970s, the Dutch architect Herman Hertzberger used concrete blocks as a 'statement' of his structuralist approach to architecture. He realized a number of now famous projects in which the colour (pale grey) and shape of the concrete block are prime determinants of the design.

During the same period, Swiss architect Mario Botta realized remarkable buildings with 'striped' façades of coloured concrete block.

Colour and material are clearly subject to swift-changing fashion. In a reaction against the nostalgic brown that had dominated domestic interiors in the 1970s, for example, pastel shades and a sunny Mediterranean ambience were all the rage in the years thereafter. Manufacturers of concrete block and sand-lime brick catered to this change of fashion by producing bricks in candy-coloured shades which duly turned up in the façades of many a new suburban development. New techniques for finishing façades were introduced, such as insulating polystyrene panels to which stucco in varying textures and fresh colours could be applied. In the meantime, pastel shades have in turn given way to darker tints, and many architects now prefer brick to concrete block and sand-lime brick in façades.

New Developments
While the use of concrete block and precast elements is highly susceptible to architectural trends, this seems to apply much less to cast in situ fair-faced concrete. Since Le Corbusier and Louis Kahn, there

Project School for Spiritual Science, Basel (1928)
Architect Rudolf Steiner
Photographer Thomas Dix

have always been avant-garde architects who have chosen to express their architectural and aesthetic ideas in concrete. Grandmasters of concrete architecture can be found in Japan. The quiet and austere 'Zen architecture' of Tadao Ando commands worldwide admiration because of its consistent detailing and superlative fair-faced concrete. The same is true of Santiago Calatrava whose works inspired by organic forms look as if they might spring to life at any moment. At the same time, the expressive deconstructivism of Zaha Hadid in Weil am Rhein, Germany, and the remarkable design of the Jewish Museum in Berlin by Daniel Libeskind, arouse amazement with their seemingly impossible constructions.

A lot has indeed happened in the field of construction since the discovery of reinforced concrete. But even the early years saw some impressive feats in terms of huge spans, dome constructions and shell roofs, such as the concrete 'spider webs' of Pier Luigi Nervi

(Palazetto del Sport, Rome 1957) and the iconic, curving roofs of the Sydney Opera House. The development of prestressed concrete, high-strength concrete (strength classes B65 through 105) and self-compacting concrete have led to stronger, sleeker constructions, even larger spans and finer detailing, as demonstrated by Calatrava's spectacular designs and the wafer-thin, free hanging concrete roof of the Portuguese Pavilion at Expo '98 in Lisbon by Alvaro Siza.

Developments in concrete technology allow specialists to tailor the concrete formula precisely to the specified properties. Chemical additives control the plasticity or density of the surface. The addition of steel or artificial fibres enhances the resistance of the concrete mortar to plastic shrinkage cracks. And the days are long past when concrete was available in grey only. Pigments are now used to produce a wide spectrum of colours. Pre-casting offers extensive possibilities for controlling the texture and colour of a concrete surface. Surface treatments such as polishing give concrete the lively appearance of natural stone.

In sharp contrast to these potential qualities and some astoundingly beautiful projects, is the stubbornness of everyday practice. Fair-faced concrete is not an easy material to produce. The quality depends largely on careful attention and craftsmanship in both design and execution. For this reason, the cement and concrete industry has set about disseminating knowledge about fair-faced concrete and standardizing information about quality control by means of special publications and a web site. To this day, the technical and architectural limits of reinforced concrete have still not been reached. Concrete is not only a material with a long history, but most probably one with a very long future as well.

Cement-bound Man-made Stone

*Zementgebundener, künstlicher Stein | Roche artificielle liant ciment |
Piedra artificial de cemento | Pietra sintetica con legante cementizio |
Cementgebonden ongebakken kunststeen*

The production process for cement and its use as a binding agent for
the production of a type of concrete, was known to the Romans as
opus caementitium. This knowledge was lost in the Middle Ages and
only rediscovered in England at the beginning of the nineteenth century. Since the rediscovery of cement as a raw material for the production of concrete, the development of concrete as a building
material has boomed. The discovery of reinforced and pre-stressed
concrete, in particular, caused a revolution in the construction world
that is still ongoing. For architecture, the discovery and constant
development of concrete has proved an inexhaustible source of
spatial, aesthetic and structural innovation. At the start of the twentieth century, this new material was regarded by many architects,
such as Le Corbusier, Oscar Niemeyer, Mies van der Rohe and Gerrit
Rietveld, as synonymous with Modernism. Now, in the 21st century,
leading international architects continue to use concrete as an aesthetic and structural material for producing innovative architecture.

History
In 1824, the English bricklayer, Joseph Aspdin, took out a patent for
a cement he had developed. The production process was simple. In
his kiln, he heated a mixture of finely crushed limestone and clay
until it turned into sintered balls. Grinding these balls into a powder

Project Bijvoet Centre, NMR Facilities, Utrecht (2000)
Architect UN Studio
Photographer Christian Richters

gave rise to the hydraulic binding agent, cement. When mixed with
water, cement hardens into a stone-like material that no longer dis-
solves in water. Aspdin called his discovery Portland cement because
of its resemblance to natural stone from the island of Portland. This
discovery formed the basis for today's cement industry.

The Production Process for Portland cement
The raw materials for Portland cement are supplied by nature, the
main ingredient being limestone. In the Netherlands, limestone (marl)
is extracted from the St. Pietersberg quarry near Maastricht. The
principle of Portland cement production is still very similar to that of
Aspdin's discovery. Silicic acid, aluminium oxide and iron oxide

derived respectively from sand, fly ash and a ferrous aggregate, are added to the marl. A tall (180 metre high) rotating kiln heats the mixture to 1450 °C, at which temperature calcium oxide combines with the additives to form dark coloured balls: Portland cement clinker. Portland cement is produced by grinding the clinker. The reactivity of the cement is reduced by adding a small percentage of gypsum. This makes it possible to produce cement mortar with sufficient plasticity and time for transport and pouring. Mixing Portland cement with granulated blast furnace slag and then grinding it produces blast furnace cement.

Cement forms the basis of many building materials and products of which concrete is by far the most important. The various types of cement are categorized according to their composition and the relative proportions of the main ingredients. For example, CEM I stands for European Portland Cement that contains 95-100% Portland cement clinker. CEM III is called blast furnace cement because a large quantity of blast furnace slag is added to the Portland cement. The cement types are available in three strength classes. The strength class are preceded by a name code: N indicates a normal early strength, and R indicates a higher early strength.

Concrete Formula

In principle, concrete consists of cement, sand, gravel and water. Portland and blast furnace cement are the most commonly used types of cement. Additives and fillers are added in order to adjust the properties of the concrete to the required quality. Steel fibres make the concrete extra 'tough'. In effect, concrete technologists tailor the formula for a specific project in consultation with the architect, the engineer and the building contractor.

A special type of cement is white Portland cement, the only cement that comes with a colour guarantee. Its near-white colour is achieved by selecting extremely light-coloured ingredients that are free from iron oxides. For coloured concrete, only white Portland cement in combination with light-coloured pigments results in true colours. White Portland cement is also used for the production of precast elements in fair-faced concrete. Since white Portland cement is expensive, standard cement in combination with white pigments and/or limestone powder is generally used for cast in situ concrete that is required to look like light-coloured fair-faced concrete. Blast furnace cement gives a lighter grey result than do most Portland cements.

Concrete in Architecture

The aesthetic quality of cast in situ concrete depends on many factors. The result is determined not only by the composition of the concrete, but also by the care with which it is poured. For example, concrete does not have a constant, precisely reproducible grey colour. It is therefore necessary to make trial walls on site in order to test the quality, the greyness, the impression of the formwork, the surface density, the profile of the construction joints, the marks left by the form spacers, et cetera.

Fair-faced concrete is not an easy material. Nevertheless, many examples from Japan, Switzerland, France and Germany demonstrate that it is possible to achieve a high quality. In Switzerland, for exam-

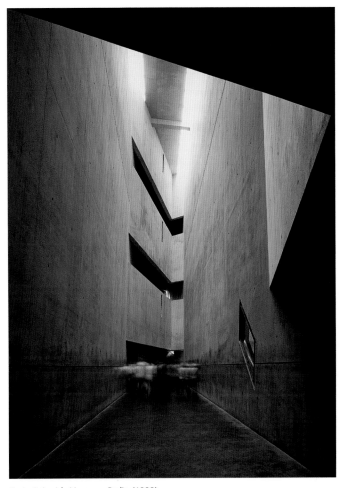

Project Jewish Museum, Berlin (1999)
Architect Daniel Libeskind
Photographer Bitter + Bredt Fotografie

ple, there are a number of exceptional projects where large monolithic façades without expansion joints have been cast in situ. By selecting a relatively thick outer cavity wall in combination with a fine-meshed reinforcement mat and a modified composition with a maximum particle size of 16 mm and a low water/cement ratio, no cracks appear on the outer surface.

Concrete

Beton | Béton | Hormigón | Calcestruzzo | Beton

Project Gymnasium, Monte Carasso (1984)
Architect M. Arnaboldi, G. Mazzi
Photographer Jan Derwig

Project Noorderpoort college, Groningen (2000)
Architect Henri Ciriani, Team4 Architects
Photographer SAPh, Rob de Jong

Since the early 20th century, the design potential and appearance of concrete have inspired architects to the creation of unique, high-quality architecture. The material is ideally suited to realizing progressive constructional and architectural ideas. Every architectural movement boasts examples of the important role played by concrete in the 'look' of the design. Although it has often been chosen for its austere, rough character or for the possibility of creating monolithic structures, concrete can also be very subtle and elegant, witness the organically shaped, airy constructions of Santiago Calatrava (TGV Station Liège, Belgium). Recent progress in concrete technology and developments in formwork techniques indicate that there is still plenty of scope for innovation in concrete design and aesthetics.

Technical Aspects

Concrete basically consists of cement, sand, gravel and water. Increasingly, this basis is supplemented with various additives and fillers that affect the properties of the concrete in both the plastic and hardened phases. Whilst the structural properties of concrete are precisely defined and accurately predictable, this is not true of its aesthetic properties. The greyness, density and soundness of the surface depend not only on the raw materials, but also on human factors such as the skill of the pouring team and the careful handling of the vibrator. An unusual feature of fair-faced concrete is that it is both a structural and a finishing material. Achieving the desired aesthetic quality calls for good communication between the designer, building contractor and concrete technologist. Details like the location and detailing of construction and slab joints, the finishing of tie holes and the desired form tie pattern, must be established by the designer early on. Standard formwork systems do not allow for deviating form positions. On-site test pieces (possibly in the foundations or the basement wall) are necessary to check the aesthetic quality of poured concrete. Although it is easier to oversee the quality of concrete elements under factory-controlled conditions, the assembly of pre-cast elements inevitably entails a visible joint pattern. Architects aiming at a monolithic look consequently prefer cast in situ concrete.

Applications

Fair-faced concrete, both pre-cast and in situ, is a distinctive material that can make a special contribution to the architectural and spatial design of structures with a wide variety of functions, from sacred spaces to school buildings and housing.

Colour	grey
Glossiness	glossy, satin, **matt**
Translucence (%)	**0** – 20 – 40 – 60 – 80 – 100
Texture	sharp, **medium**, dull
Hardness	**hard**, soft, depressible
Temperature	warm, **medium**, cool
Odour	strong, moderate, **none**
Acoustic opacity	good, moderate, **poor**

Non Cement-bound Man-made Stone

Nichtzementgebundener, künstlicher Stein | Roche artificielle liant sans ciment |
Piedra artificial sin cemento | Pietre sintetiche senza legante cementizio |
Niet-cementgebonden ongebakken kunststeen

There are other binding agents besides cement which can be used to manufacture unfired artificial stone, such as lime, gypsum or plastics (for example, polyester resin). The best known artificial stone types are sand-lime bricks and products with a gypsum base. Artificial stone also includes composite sheet materials with a stone-like surface, such as plasterboard and various types of plasterwork with a lime and gypsum base. A special type of 'unfired' stone-like surface is clay plaster. This is plasterwork with a sand and clay base which hardens on drying. In contrast to other binding agents which harden due to a chemical process, clay hardens as a result of the natural drying process.

Sand-lime Bricks

This material has been used on a large scale since it was first mass-produced at the end of the 19th century. The use of sand-lime bricks as a facing brick reached its peak in the 1970s when there was an architectural trend in northern Europe, especially in suburban housing developments, for a light, Mediterranean appearance. The originally light palette was augmented with soft yellow, pink, light blue and pale grey facing stones. Nowadays, the architectural trend is more towards the use of darker, more natural-looking bricks and the demand for sand-lime bricks has declined accordingly.

The industrialized production of sand-lime bricks is based on the chemical reaction between lime ($Ca(OH)_2$) and sand in the presence of water. Water is added to a mix of lime and sand, after which the lime is slaked for four hours. The resulting lime paste is first compressed into the desired shape and then hardened under steam pressure at about 180 °C in an autoclave. The production technique has been so optimized over the years that the cheap price of the bricks has led to their general use in the construction industry. Having originally been developed as a cheap alternative to fired bricks, sand-lime bricks were only available in three standard sizes. They were manufactured in three qualities of ascending compressive strength: standard, clinker and façade quality.

For exposed brickwork in the interior, bricks with one smooth surface without stains, pitting or variations in colour are used. For external applications there are, in addition to the standard smooth, white bricks, coloured facing bricks and bricks with a surface texture of fine sand. The 'sanded' texture is created by working the stretcher or header face with coarse steel brushes. Another type of facing brick is the split-faced brick whose rough surface texture is achieved by a special production technique.

The range has now been expanded with building blocks (glued and mortared) and large elements. These 'new' products are usually hidden from view behind coats of plaster. The large elements are always glued together and are not suitable for exposed brickwork. A recent development is the production of chamfered blocks, which can be used as two-sided facework for decorative loadbearing internal walls in non-residential buildings.

Gypsum Plaster

The production not only of sand-lime bricks, but also of gypsum plaster powder increased greatly at the end of the 19th century. For a long time this was made from natural gypsum ($CaSO_4.2H_2O$) in a simple process that involved heating the gypsum rock. The addition of water triggers a chemical reaction that causes the plaster to set rock hard. This material property of gypsum powder makes gypsum plaster suitable for plasterwork and the production of building materials.

Since the early 1980s, flue gas desulphurized (FGD) gypsum has been added to the raw materials used for manufacturing this plaster. FGD is a by-product of the desulphurization of flue gases in coal-fired power stations and not only has the same composition and properties as naturally formed gypsum, but also contains fewer impurities. In time, the very pure FGD gypsum will replace natural gypsum as a raw material for plaster.

Gypsum plaster is best known in architecture worldwide for its decorative interior uses. The aesthetic possibilities of gypsum plaster, whether or not mixed with lime or other additives, appear to be limitless and suitable for every architectural style, from exuberant rococo to chaste minimalism. The appearance of the plastered wall or ceiling depends on the composition of the mix and the method of application. According to individual taste, its look can vary from expensive marble-like or exotically coloured and smoothly polished, to a simple rough or fine texture.

Mixed with water, gypsum plaster can be cast into any desired shape using moulds. Ornaments made in this way adorned many a Renaissance ceiling or wall in the palaces and villas of the well-to-do. Less spectacular is the most common and widespread modern-day use of cast plaster, for elements and blocks for non-bearing interior walls. These functional plaster elements are usually hidden from view by a finishing coat.

Since the 1930s, gypsum plaster has also been available in the form of sheeting which is produced by pouring a mix of water and plaster onto a layer of recycled cardboard. The layer of plaster is then covered with a second layer of cardboard (the 'back') and the whole is then hot-pressed to the required thickness. The sheets are then

Project Private house, Le Deux Tour (2002)
Architect Bokara
Photographer Carl Gispe

turned over and dried in a drying kiln with the visible side facing upwards. Gypsum plasterboard comes in many different shapes and sizes – as a backing for wall and ceiling finishes, but also in the form of tiles for system ceilings. The tiles are available in many sizes and with perforations, graphic patterns, surface structures and textures.

Clay Plaster

As a result of current environmental awareness and the encouragement of user- and environmentally-friendly products, one of the oldest wall finishing materials, clay plaster, has been given a new lease of life. Clay plaster is nothing more than a mixture of sand, clay and straw which becomes hard on drying. New processing methods and compositions make it possible to create wall surfaces in attractive, natural colours and textures.

Polyester Concrete

The use of modern plastics as binding agents is also resulting in innovative stone-like building materials. Polyester concrete is produced by adding polyester resin, instead of cement, to a mixture of sand, gravel or natural stone granules. This material opens up many new possibilities for the architectural design of façades and interior elements. Polyester concrete can be easily cast in complex shapes and can be given many kinds of surface texture.

Description Loam city Sadaa, Yemen
Photographer Jan Derwig

Sand-lime Bricks

Kalksandstein | Brique en chaux et sable | Ladrillos de sílice (cal y arena) | Mattoni silico-calcarei | Kalkzandsteen

Project Twiske, Amsterdam (1994)
Architect Gert-Jan Hendriks, de Architectengroep
Photographer Jan Derwig

Project Cayennepeper, Almere (1992)
Architect VVKH Architects (Verheijen Verkoren Knappers de Haan)
Photographer Ger van der Vlugt

One of the most striking properties of a wall made from sand-lime bricks is its smooth, even appearance. Since sand-lime bricks are extremely dimensionally stable and show little colour variation, they lack the liveliness associated with a natural material. Without additions to the basic ingredients of lime, sand and water, the colour of this material varies from white to a light, sandy colour. In the 1970s, this original Mediterranean palette was supplemented with anthracite by adding iron oxide to the mix. Some variation is also possible in the surface texture from a smooth, finely sanded surface to a rough, split-faced texture. A recent innovation is the production of chamfered blocks for two-sided exposed brickwork inside buildings. The pattern of V-shaped joints in walls of glued chamfered blocks is reminiscent of natural stone blocks stacked on top of each other.

Technical Aspects

Sand-lime bricks are an 'environmentally friendly' building material that complies fully with the standards of the Dutch Building Materials Decree (Bouwstoffenbesluit). Moreover, the production process requires little energy compared with that for standard building bricks. The material properties (good sound insulation, the ability to accumulate heat, high fire resistance and breathing properties) make sand-lime bricks suitable for many different uses. The bricks are available in three different qualities, namely standard, clinker and facing brick, with a respective compressive strength of 15 N/mm^2, 25 N/mm^2 and 30 N/mm^2. Their dimensions in the Netherlands correspond to standard Waal, Amstel and Maas brick measurements. Larger bricks and blocks are also available. Exposed bricks and blocks are usually bonded using cement mortar whereas a glue mortar is usually preferred for chamfered blocks. To prevent cracks due to contraction, long walls, whether cemented or glued, must be provided with expansion joints. The maximum permissible wall length depends on the brick size and the method of laying.

Applications

Sand-lime bricks can be used for exposed brickwork both internally and externally. Depending on the type of brick chosen, they can also be used in loadbearing façades or interior walls. The chamfered blocks are particularly suitable in non-residential construction as an inexpensive solution for large, decorative wall surfaces, such as in sports halls and schools.

Colour	**white**
Glossiness	glossy, satin, **matt**
Translucence (%)	**0** – 20 – 40 – 60 – 80 – 100
Texture	sharp, **medium**, dull
Hardness	**hard**, soft, depressible
Temperature	warm, **medium**, cool
Odour	strong, moderate, **none**
Acoustic opacity	good, moderate, **poor**

Polyester Concrete

Polyesterbeton | Béton de polyester | Cemento de poliéster | Calcestruzzo di poliestere | Polyesterbeton

Project NUVO 2000, Arnhem (2000)
Architect Kjell Kuizenga
Photographer Prepoton Panelcraft

Even when produced with meticulous attention to detail and quality, concrete remains a 'coarse-grained' building material with a characteristic, rough appearance which does not on the whole lend itself to very subtle detailing. Polyester concrete has been developed for the manufacture of lightweight façade elements to compensate for the disadvantages of concrete as an outer skin. The attraction for designers is that intricate, round shapes or delicate mouldings are easy to achieve with polyester concrete. The untreated surface of polyester concrete is smooth and flawless. However, like cement concrete, it can be surface finished in many different ways, including sandblasting and polishing. Fine surface textures and patterns are easily applied. In addition, all kinds of objects or materials, such as broken shells or glass, can be added to polyester concrete to give the surface an interesting and lively appearance.

Technical Aspects

Despite what its name might suggest, polyester concrete lacks one of the most important ingredients of concrete products, namely cement. Instead of cement, polyester is used as a binding agent to create a strong, smooth material which can easily be moulded into the desired shape. In contrast to cement concrete, polyester concrete is not capillary, so neither water nor dirt can penetrate it. Polyester concrete can be made into thin panels which are consequently much lighter than precast cement concrete panels. This in turn makes for a lighter façade construction. Reinforcing polyester concrete with glass fibres creates an extra strong material that can be used to produce hard wearing, three-dimensional façade elements. A special property of polyester concrete is that it contracts a great deal whilst drying. As a result, any objects added to the liquid mixture, such as shells, pebbles or broken glass, are firmly enclosed in the surface.

Applications

Apart from the creation of durable façades with a traditional appearance, polyester concrete offers many scarcely explored possibilities for architectural design.

Colour	white
Glossiness	glossy, satin, **matt**
Translucence (%)	**0** – 20 – 40 – 60 – 80 – 100
Texture	sharp, **medium**, **dull**
Hardness	**hard**, soft, depressible
Temperature	warm, **medium**, cool
Odour	strong, **moderate**, **none**
Acoustic opacity	good, moderate, **poor**

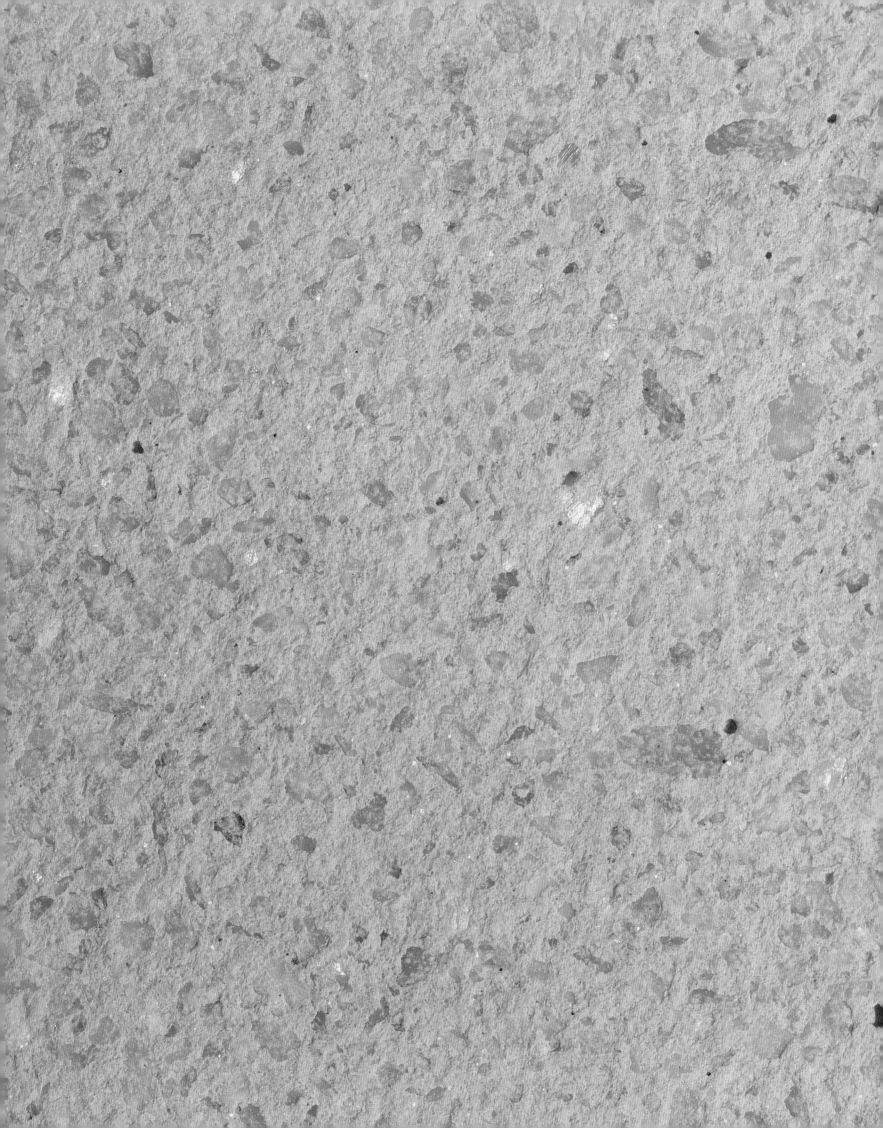

Gypsum Plaster

Gipsputz | Plâtre de gypse | Enyesados de escayola (interiores) | Malta di gesso | Gips

Project Nieuw Terbregge, Rotterdam (2001)
Architect Mecanoo
Photographer Bruynzeel

Gypsum plaster is a material that has been used for centuries for decoration and embellishment in architecture. The Romans were masters in casting 'marble' statues in plaster. The decorative possibilities of this material continue to be exploited in interior architecture where there is a renewed interest in plaster ornaments, statues, wall and ceiling decorations. Without additives, the surface of cast gypsum plaster is smooth and white. For casting ornaments, the plaster is poured into moulds in layers interspersed with non-woven glass fibre mats to provide extra strength. The mixing water is reinforced with polymers and a flow control agent. Apart from being used to make the desired shape, plaster can also be used to create the desired surface texture and colour. The mass production of standard plaster elements has increased greatly in recent decades. Walls made up of plaster elements are usually given a finishing coating. As well as its use in the production of plaster elements, gypsum, sometimes mixed with other raw materials like chalk, is also used to make gypsum mortar. Gypsum plaster is sandwiched between cardboard to make plasterboard. Produced in a wide variety of forms and with special textures, patterns or perforations, plasterboard wall and ceiling panels can make an important contribution to the appearance of interiors.

Technical Aspects

Since gypsum plaster has a low resistance to water, plaster products are not suitable for external uses. However, the material properties of plaster make it very suitable for interior uses. Non-structural internal walls are easy to make using plasterboard panels. They are lightweight, handle well and do not shrink, so the design does not have to allow for expansion joints. The panels have a 'tongue and groove' profile and are glued together without any visible seams. The layers of glass fibre reinforcement make moulded plaster decorations strong and impact resistant.

Applications

Plaster ornaments are used in all kinds of monumental projects, ranging from the classic to the abstract-modern look.

Colour	**white**
Glossiness	glossy, satin, **matt**
Translucence (%)	**0** – 20 – 40 – 60 – 80 – 100
Texture	sharp, **medium**, dull
Hardness	**hard**, soft, depressible
Temperature	**warm**, medium, cool
Odour	strong, moderate, **none**
Acoustic opacity	good, moderate, **poor**

Clay Plaster

Lehmputz | *Plâtre d'argile* | *Morteros monocapa o escayola a la intemperie (exteriores)* | *Malta di argilla* | *Leemstuc*

Project City Hall, Zutphen (1999)
Architect Rau & Partners
Photographer Herman van Doorn

Clay plaster is one of the oldest building and wall finishing materials. The attention currently being given to environmentally friendly materials that contribute to a healthy social climate in buildings, has led to renewed interest in clay plaster as a wall finishing material. Whilst clay was traditionally used for the exterior walls of buildings, modern clay plaster is only suitable for interior wall finishings. Natural, earthy hues and special textures give wall and ceiling surfaces made from clay plaster a warm, natural appearance. Without the addition of pigments, the colour of clay plaster varies from off-white to yellow ochre, depending on the raw materials used. The addition of straw makes the wall surface rough and fibrous. The addition of fine shell grit to the mixture of clay plaster gives the surface a glittery effect due to the mother-of-pearl particles in the shells.

Technical Aspects

Clay plaster is based on a mixture of clay, sand and water. When dry, it has a stone-like surface similar to traditional lime and gypsum plaster, but softer to the touch. The plaster is usually applied in two coats, a bottom (scratch) coat of no more than 10 mm thick, and a finishing coat up to 4 mm thick. A clay plaster wall can only be used in interiors and is not suitable for extremely damp conditions. Since clay plaster absorbs and releases moisture, it helps to regulate the humidity of the indoor climate. Its heat accumulating properties contribute to a pleasant indoor temperature, warm in the winter and cool in the summer. The surface is prone to damage, but easy to repair. Depending on the method of application and the choice of raw materials, the surface texture varies from smooth to fibrous.

Applications

A remarkable example of the aesthetic possibilities of clay plaster is the staircase in the Küppersmühle Museum in Duisberg, Germany, designed by Herzog & De Meuron.

Project Rijkswaterstaat Directie Noord-Holland
Dienstkring Noordzeekanaal, IJmuiden (1999)
Architect Atelier Z | Zavrel Architects
Photographer Jan Derwig

Colour	**variable**
Glossiness	glossy, satin, **matt**
Translucence (%)	**0** – 20 – 40 – 60 – 80 – 100
Texture	sharp, **medium**, dull
Hardness	**hard**, soft, depressible
Temperature	**warm**, medium, cool
Odour	strong, moderate, **none**
Acoustic opacity	good, moderate, **poor**

Unfired Man-made Stone
Treatments and Finishes
Bearbeitung und Veredelung | Traitements et finissages | Tratamientos y acabados | Trattamenti e finiture | Bewerkingen en afwerkingen

Introduction
The artificial creation of stone-like surfaces starts with the mixing of liquid mortar. The possibilities for manipulating the surface – for giving it shape, texture or changing its appearance – can be roughly divided into treatments applied before and after the liquid mortar has hardened. The appearance of the usually grey concrete surface can undergo a spectacular metamorphosis as a result of various treatments. In addition to attractive textured surfaces, finishing techniques can also produce surprisingly colourful and smooth surfaces.

Treatment before Hardening
The rediscovery of cement as a raw material for the production of concrete at the end of the 19th century opened up a whole new world of structural and aesthetic possibilities for architects. Liquid concrete mortar is relatively easy to cast into shape with the aid of a mould. This characteristic is utilized for the in situ casting of load-bearing constructions and for the industrialized production of building components. Concrete is a versatile material that is at home in a wide range of architectural styles from historicism to futurism. Furthermore, concrete is an important source of inspiration for new developments in modern architecture. Its austere, pure appearance has inspired architects like Tadao Ando to design minimalist, monolithic buildings in which the only decoration is a meticulously con-

Project Appartments, Monte Carasso (1995)
Architect Mario Botta
Photographer Jan Derwig

trived pattern in the surface of the concrete, left behind by the formwork. Other architects, such as Calatrava and Nervi, utilize concrete's ability to be cast into almost any desired shape to create complex organic shapes and structures.

One of the defining features of cast concrete is that the form into which it is poured leaves traces on the surface. The simplest method of applying texture to a concrete surface is to use the surface of the form. For example, rough, unplaned planks leave a pattern of planks with a woodgrain structure in the surface. Nowadays, every imaginable structure can be created using specially designed, flexible rubber form liners. The polyurethane moulds developed for making large

Project LF one, Weil am Rhein (1999)

Architect Zaha M. Hadid

Photographer Thomas Dix

ornaments and decorative precast façade elements allow very finely detailed mouldings and shapes to be created in concrete.

Treatment after Hardening

Once the liquid mortar has hardened, the options for influencing the appearance of the surface are comparable to the finishes applied to natural stone. Mechanical tooling of the surface with a bush hammer, chisel or saw creates an artificial texture with the particular character of the tool used. Grinding, usually followed by polishing, is a technique that removes several millimetres of the concrete surface to reveal the colourful pattern of the ingredients of the concrete mortar. The result of this kind of treatment is often spectacular and gives the concrete the satin-smooth surface of costly natural stone. Techniques like sand blasting, washing or treating with acid are designed to remove all or part of the grey layer of cement from the surface so as to expose the structure of specific aggregates, such as gravel. A simple method for changing the appearance of the grey concrete surface is to apply a coating. Transparent coloured stains and coatings impart colour without affecting the stone-like character of the concrete. A most unusual concrete surface treatment is the one devised by Herzog & De Meuron for the Atelier Rémy Zaugg in Mulhouse, France, where rainwater from the roof is deliberately channelled to flow over the concrete wall surface, leaving trails of rust on the surface.

Prefabrication

Although all but a few of these methods can be applied to in situ cast concrete, many more options are available in a controlled factory environment. Precast façade elements can be given delicate ridged patterns or an aesthetic top layer through the addition of special ingredients such as crushed shells or brightly coloured marble granules. A relatively new technique, which was first used ten years ago, is photographic printing of a concrete surface in which a graphic pattern or a photographic image is applied to the concrete surface.

In the 1950s, concrete blocks and bricks were developed as an alternative to standard bricks for exposed brickwork. Since the introduc-

tion of white-grey modular concrete blocks, made famous in the Netherlands by the work of Herman Herzberger, the range of concrete façade bricks in particular has increased considerably, with countless decorative variations that cater to current architectural and environmental trends. One recent addition to the palette, for example, are bricks that give the impression of a clear, white, sandy beach covered with cockleshells.

A special type of concrete stone is the split-face block whose rough surface is due to being split in two during a manufacturing process similar to that used for splitting sand-lime bricks, which also produces a craggy, fractured surface. Adding marble granules or other mineral aggregates to the concrete mortar results in split-face blocks with an even more varied and colourful fractured surface.

Plaster Finishes

Liquid mortars with a lime and gypsum base have been used for finishing and smoothing walls and ceilings since ancient times and are still in use today. Decorative techniques based on this finishing method are as old as building itself. Venetian and Moroccan plaster work originated from these centuries-old techniques for embellishing walls or creating a sense of opulence by polishing the hardened coat of plaster. These plasterwork techniques are related to each other, but based on different plaster mixtures and different polishing methods. Both produce an attractive, colourful and lustrous surface. Nowadays, attempts are made to recreate the aesthetic result of these traditional techniques using plastics and modern production methods. In other developments, the original technique and mortar mixture have been used to achieve new effects, such as a shiny metal-like surface.

Methods for applying texture to the surface of plasterwork all entail mortar in its liquid state. Depending on the method of application and/or the composition of the mortar, the result varies from a very fine to a rough surface texture. Modern additives even make possible concrete and cement mortars with a gypsum and lime base suitable for spraying, thus allowing the rapid texturing of large surfaces.

Project Housing Getsewoud, New Vennep (2003)

Architect 24H-Architecture

Photographer Kees Hummel

Spraying: Sprayed Concrete

Spritzen: Spritzbeton | Epandage, pulvérisation : béton | Hormigón proyectado o gunitado | Spruzzatura: calcestruzzo spruzzato | Spuiten: spuitbeton

Project Minnaert Building, Utrecht (1997)
Architect Neutelings Riedijk Architects
Photographer ENCI Media

Project Grand Café 'Colemine', It Holt (2002)
Designer Jora Vision
Photographer Jora Vision

Sprayed concrete is concrete that is sprayed at high pressure onto a substrate or formwork. The shape of the surface onto which it is sprayed determines the shape of the concrete. In this way, virtually any shape can be achieved. The surface of sprayed concrete has a rough texture.

Technical Aspects

The dry mixture of cement, sand, fine aggregate and additives is forced under pressure towards the nozzle of a hose where it is mixed with water. The liquid mixture is then sprayed at high velocity over a surface consisting of formwork or building material. The force with which it is sprayed against the surface produces a very dense and strong layer of concrete. The range of shapes attainable is almost limitless. Colour variations can be achieved by adding pigments to the mixture. The relative roughness of the surface is determined by the size of the aggregate which in turn is limited by the size of the nozzle through which it is sprayed.

Applications

Although sprayed concrete is used mostly for the structural repair of badly damaged concrete surfaces, its flexibility offers creative possibilities, especially in the leisure industry. Wherever organic shapes, such as artificial rocks, are required, sprayed concrete offers a solution. It has been used in zoos, aquariums and cafeterias, and even on the façade of the Faculty of Earth Sciences at the University of Utrecht in the Netherlands because of the expressive, rock-like character of the surface.

Colour	**variable**
Glossiness	glossy, satin, **matt**
Translucence (%)	**0** – 20 – 40 – 60 – 80 – 100
Texture	**sharp**, **medium**, dull
Hardness	**hard**, soft, depressible
Temperature	warm, **medium**, cool
Odour	strong, moderate, **none**
Acoustic opacity	good, moderate, **poor**

Formwork Texturing: Textured Concrete

Strukturieren durch Schalung: Betonschalung | Structure de coffrage : coffrage à béton | Superficies conformadas: encofrados para hormigón |
Struttura casseforme: casseforme per calcestruzzo | Structuurbekisting: structuurbeton

Project Sky Dome, Amsterdam (1995)
Architect Wiel Arets
Photographer Kees Hummel

Project KPN Building, Zwolle (2000)
Architect Martin Kleine Schaars , BDG Architects
Photographer Harry Noback

Ever since the discovery of reinforced concrete as a building material, architects have explored the aesthetic effects of textures in the surface of concrete. Le Corbusier, Tadao Ando and many other architects have used the material of the formwork itself, such as rough timber planks or sheets, to create textures and patterns in the surface, thereby turning to advantage the inevitable traces left by formwork.

Nowadays, almost any texture or pattern imaginable can be applied to the surface of concrete with the help of synthetic form liners. For example, rubber mats are available with standard patterns imitating wood grain, natural stone or bamboo, or with a custom-made pattern. When using rubber mats, the designer needs to take into account the repetitive effect of the pattern. For complex forms, polystyrene moulds offer a solution. Both types of mould can be used for cast in situ and precast concrete. In a façade composed of textured, precast elements, the designer must also take account of the pattern produced by the joints between the elements.

Technical Aspects

When textured concrete is cast in situ, it is important to ensure that the composition of the concrete mortar corresponds to the desired aesthetic effect. A coarse-grained aggregate, for example, will limit the fineness of the texture. In the case of bas relief, it is necessary to ensure that the reinforcement steel has an adequate covering of concrete. Careful workmanship, such as a good seal between the formwork joints and proper compaction, is also important in order to avoid irregularities in the surface. The formwork itself must be designed in such a way that the moulds can be removed without damaging the concrete surface. Under factory-controlled conditions, high-quality results that are comparable to sculptured natural stone can be achieved. Surface textures can render a concrete façade especially susceptible to staining and the designers of relief patterns should to take this into consideration. Horizontal mouldings, along which rainwater runs, cause more unsightly staining than vertical mouldings.

Applications

Textured concrete has many uses. The combination of sophisticated formwork and concrete technology has led to virtually unlimited design possibilities in both modern, innovative architecture and in restoration work and historicizing architecture.

Colour	variable
Glossiness	glossy, satin, **matt**
Translucence (%)	**0** – 20 – 40 – 60 – 80 – 100
Texture	sharp, **medium**, **dull**
Hardness	**hard**, soft, depressible
Temperature	warm, **medium**, cool
Odour	strong, moderate, **none**
Acoustic opacity	good, moderate, **poor**

Concrete Block

Betonfertigteile | Bloc de béton | Bloque de hormigón | Blocchi di calcestruzzo | Betonsteen

Project Private house, Benkert Konigsberg (1998)
Architect Mario Botta
Photographer Jan Derwig

Project El Pi High School, Barcelona (1996)
Architect Roldán + Berengué
Photographer Eva Serrats

Ever since the introduction in the 1950s of concrete bricks and blocks for fair-face brickwork, European architects have been inspired by the structural and aesthetic possibilities of this concrete product. In the Netherlands, a light-coloured concrete block with a slightly rough surface became the trademark of Herman Hertzberger's structuralist period. In the 1970s, coloured facing bricks were added to the range. Architect Mario Botta used them in his famous postmodernist villas whose façades boasted decorative alternating bands of terracotta and greyish-white concrete bricks. Concrete bricks are now available in a variety of surface finishes: smooth, textured and split-faced, although even the 'smooth' brick still has a slightly rough surface. The colour palette consists of a range of shades including white, dark grey, yellow, blue, green, red and mixtures.

Technical Aspects

Concrete bricks, which come in variety of brickwork dimensions, differ both in size and production method from concrete blocks. Concrete blocks are homogeneous and are produced in a single casting. Concrete bricks, by contrast, are produced in a two-stage process fed by two hoppers. During the first stage, the mould in the brick pressing machine is completely filled with a standard mortar of blast furnace cement. A 'falling' movement compresses the mortar so as to leave room for a second layer consisting of the concrete mortar mix intended for the aesthetic top layer.

Due to the low water–cement ratio and strong compaction, concrete bricks have a low drying shrinkage and a high compressive strength of 20 to 30 N/mm². Size variations are small due to the controlled production process. The composition of the concrete mortar determines the transmission properties of the concrete bricks. Although the moisture absorption depends on the type of surface structure, the composition of the top layer is such that little water is able to penetrate the brick.

Applications

Concrete facing bricks are intended for one-sided facework. There are lightweight bricks for two-sided internal facework. Although concrete facing bricks are normally laid in the traditional manner using cement mortar, they are also sometimes laid using glue mortars that produce taut façade surfaces.

Colour	variable
Glossiness	glossy, satin, **matt**
Translucence (%)	**0** – 20 – 40 – 60 – 80 – 100
Texture	sharp, **medium**, dull
Hardness	**hard**, soft, depressible
Temperature	warm, **medium**, cool
Odour	strong, moderate, **none**
Acoustic opacity	good, moderate, **poor**

Washing: Decorative Concrete

Waschen: Waschbeton | Lavage: béton décoratif | Lavado: cemento decorativo | Lavaggio: calcestruzzo con superficie decorativa |
Wassen: ruw sierbeton

Project Campus, Dessau (1996)
Architect Johannes Kister, KSH Architekten
Photographer Christian Richters

Project Cementrum, Den Bosch (1975)
Architect Zuiderhoek and Van der Veen
Photographer Gerard Monté

As many recent projects have demonstrated, the surface of concrete does not necessarily have to be a uniform grey colour. Hidden below the cement surface is a surprisingly colourful texture that is determined by the external characteristics of the aggregates in the concrete. One way of bringing this texture to the surface is to 'wash' the concrete: a few millimetres of the cement paste is removed with a jet of water, thereby exposing the gravel and other granulated material. The shape, type, colour, size and grading of aggregates all contribute to the appearance of the washed concrete surface. The rough texture that is typical of washed concrete was especially popular in the 1970s, but recent examples indicate a renewed interest in this surface treatment.

Technical Aspects

The most common technique for washing concrete involves the use of chemicals that slow down the hydration of the cement surface. The retarder is applied to the formwork face and once the formwork has been removed, the cement that has not completely hardened is washed away with water. The latest retarders have a controlled penetrative effect and bond so well that they can also be used on vertical and inclined surfaces. Although these techniques can be used for cast in situ concrete, they are more suited to controlled factory conditions. Another advantage of factory casting is that the top layer can have a different composition from the rest of the concrete, allowing more expensive types of aggregate to be chosen for the decorative facing.

Despite the rough texture, a washed concrete surface does not soil so readily. Dirt is less noticeable in a colourful concrete surface and, since it does not adhere very well to the hard aggregate, is more likely to be washed away by rain.

Applications

Owing to its rough texture, the specific aesthetic appearance of washed concrete seems to be more appropriate to large projects. Washed concrete can be used in façades and for decorative internal walls.

Colour	**variable**
Glossiness	glossy, satin, **matt**
Translucence (%)	**0** – 20 – 40 – 60 – 80 – 100
Texture	**sharp**, medium, dull
Hardness	**hard**, soft, depressible
Temperature	warm, **medium**, cool
Odour	strong, moderate, **none**
Acoustic opacity	good, moderate, **poor**

Acid Etching: Fine Decorative Concrete

Säureätzung: Feinbeton | Gravure à l'acide: béton fin décoratif | Grabado al ácido: cemento decorativo | Incisione con acido: calcestruzzo a grana fine a finitura decorativa | Zuur behandelen: fijn sierbeton

Project Boijmans Van Beuningen Museum, Rotterdam (2003)
Architect Paul Robbrecht and Hilde Daem Architects
Photographer Decomo Architectonisch Beton

Project Palace Hotel, Noordwijk (2002)
Architect Hans van Egmond Totaal Architectuur
Photographer Decomo Architectonisch Beton

A concrete surface that has been treated with acid is characterized by a fine, granular structure reminiscent of sandstone.

Technical Aspects

Concrete skin consists of hydrated cement particles. A strong acid attacks this alkaline surface and creates a micro-texture. The duration of the treatment and the properties of the granules determine the depth (up to 0.5 mm) and roughness of the texture. Siliceous granules are impervious to acid, resulting in a granular surface. Calcareous granules by contrast are attacked by acid and this produces an even, fine texture. There are two different treatment methods: immersion in an acid bath or the local application of an acidic gel. The disadvantage of the immersion method is that the entire element comes into contact with the acid, including any protruding reinforcement or suspension systems. Furthermore, the end result is more difficult to control than with a local application of gel. After treatment, the surface must be rinsed with plenty of water. Acidic gel is best applied under factory conditions which allow greater control over the end result.

Applications

Acid-treated concrete elements are suitable for use in both façades and interiors.

Colour	variable
Glossiness	glossy, satin, **matt**
Translucence (%)	**0** – 20 – 40 – 60 – 80 – 100
Texture	sharp, **medium**, dull
Hardness	**hard**, soft, depressible
Temperature	warm, **medium**, cool
Odour	strong, moderate, **none**
Acoustic opacity	good, moderate, **poor**

Abrasive Blasting

Abstrahlen mit Schleifmittel | Décapage abrasif | Chorreado con abrasivos | Pallinatura abrasiva | Stralen: gestraald beton

Project World Port Centre, Rotterdam (2000)
Architect Foster and Partners
Photographer Nigel Young | Foster and Partners

Abrasive blasted concrete is characterized by the dull, roughened texture of gravel and other aggregate in the surface. Like other treatments that impart a rough and robust appearance to concrete, this method was especially popular in the 1970s.

Technical Aspects

Steel or sand grit is blasted against the surface of the concrete at high pressure, so that the aggregate is exposed. The blasting not only removes the cement skin, but also erodes the surface of the exposed aggregate which in turn causes the sand and stone granules to appear dull. The coarseness and depth of the texture depend on the hardness of the grit and the duration of the blasting. When sloping surfaces are to be blasted, it is advisable to test a corner first so that undesirable variations in texture can be avoided.

Owing to the very dense surface of the coarser aggregates, dirt has little chance of adhering to the concrete. Rain and wind help to keep the façade clean. When this surface treatment is used in combination with vertical profiling it produces a durable and very dirt-resistant façade surface.

With an eye to working conditions and in view of the greater control over the end result, this method is best applied under factory conditions.

Applications

Given its durability, abrasive-blasted concrete is an excellent choice for façade applications.

Project Centre PasquArt, Biel (2000)
Architect Diener and Diener
Photographer Gaston Wicky

Colour	**variable**
Glossiness	glossy, satin, **matt**
Translucence (%)	**0** – 20 – 40 – 60 – 80 – 100
Texture	sharp, **medium**, dull
Hardness	**hard**, soft, depressible
Temperature	warm, **medium**, cool
Odour	strong, moderate, **none**
Acoustic opacity	good, moderate, **poor**

Grinding: Smooth Decorative Concrete

Schleifen: Glattbeton | Rabotage: béton lisse décoratif | Pulido: Cemento decorativo liso | Molatura: calcestruzzo a finitura decorativa liscia | Slijpen: glad sierbeton

Project Kunstmuseum Liechtenstein, Vaduz (2000)
Architect Morger, Degelo, Kerez
Photographer Ludwig Abache

Project Riva building, Den Bosch (2001)
Architect Boosten Rats Architects
Photographer Gerard Monté

Of all the concrete surface treatments, grinding and polishing produces the most extreme change in the material's appearance. Grey concrete undergoes a veritable transformation and acquires a colourful, glossy, smooth surface more akin to expensive natural stone than everyday concrete. The size, shape and colour of the aggregate, plus any pigments, determine the colour and the pattern of the surface. Since there is an almost limitless choice of aggregate, granules and pigments, the appearance can vary in colour from deep black to off-white. The intensity of the polishing determines whether the surface has a soft or hard high-gloss finish.

Technical Aspects

After the concrete has hardened, up to 10 mm of the surface is removed using a grinding machine, so that the materials which make up the concrete become visible. Aggregate selected for its colour and shape forms a multicoloured pattern in the smooth surface. Adding pigments to the concrete mortar affects the colour intensity of the surface. To maintain this colour intensity after polishing, a coating should be applied to the surface. The lustre of polished concrete lasts longer when the aggregate is a siliceous stone, such as granite, rather than a calcareous stone like marble. Although coatings are not usually applied to white surfaces because they make the white look yellowish, it is advisable to waterproof the surface. Given the labour-intensive, mechanical nature of grinding, this treatment is usually carried out under factory conditions where the grinding and polishing techniques are so sophisticated that they can even cope with round shapes and reveals. Monolithic poured-in-place floors may, however, be ground and polished on site.

Applications

Polished concrete has any number of uses. Façades clad with precast elements of polished concrete have the appearance of polished natural stone. Polished concrete is also suitable for interior uses as decorative, elegant wall or floor cladding.

A recent stunning example of ground and polished concrete is the monolithic, cast-in-situ façade of the Kunstmuseum Liechtenstein in Vaduz, whose glossy black surface was manually ground and polished using grinding and sanding machines. Basalt chippings and brightly coloured river gravel are responsible for the beautiful patterns in the surface.

Colour	**variable**
Glossiness	**glossy**, **satin**, matt
Translucence (%)	**0** – 20 – 40 – 60 – 80 – 100
Texture	sharp, **medium**, dull
Hardness	**hard**, soft, depressible
Temperature	warm, **medium**, cool
Odour	strong, moderate, **none**
Acoustic opacity	good, moderate, **poor**

Splitting: Split-face Concrete Brick

Spalten: Betondachstein mit Spaltfläche | Fendage: Brique de béton avec face fendue | Ladrillo o bloque con cara machihembrada |
Spacco: mattoni di calcestruzzo con superficie splittata faccia a vista | Breken/splijten: betonsteen

Project Hondsrugweg | Ermerweg, Emmen (2003)
Architect Marco Henssen, M3H Architects
Photographer Michel Claus

The distinguishing feature of split-face bricks is the rough surface of one stretcher face. In split concrete bricks, this feature acquires an additional aesthetic dimension owing to the possibility of varying the aggregates during the production process. Adding marble granules, basalt chippings, or other natural minerals of different colours and textures to the concrete mortar instead of fine gravel can produce stunning effects in the fracture surface.

Technical Aspects

What sets split-face concrete brick apart from ordinary concrete facing brick is the composition and production process. The brick mould is twice the size of that used for a single facing brick. After hardening, the brick is split in two along its length so that the shape and colour of the materials in the mortar become visible. Since it is not possible to apply a top layer in this case, split-face bricks have a homogeneous composition. The mould is still filled in two stages, as for standard facing bricks, but in this case both hoppers are filled with the same mortar mix. The material properties of split-face bricks depend on the composition of the mortar, but are comparable to those of other concrete products. For light-coloured bricks, white Portland cement is used instead of standard blast furnace cement. The colourful surface is wear-resistant, colourfast and durable.

Applications

In the exterior of projects with large façade surfaces, the shadows produced by split-face concrete bricks produce a lively effect. The colour and texture of the aggregates determine the overall impression created by the brickwork surface. That impression can vary from heavy and sombre in the darker anthracite tones, through fresh and cheerful in blue and green, to light and sunny in sandy colours.

Project Forensic Psychiatric Clinic, Amsterdam (2001)
Architect Han Westelaken, Architecten aan de Maas
Photographer Martin Thomas

Colour	**variable**
Glossiness	glossy, satin, **matt**
Translucence (%)	**0** – 20 – 40 – 60 – 80 – 100
Texture	**sharp**, medium, dull
Hardness	**hard**, soft, depressible
Temperature	warm, **medium**, cool
Odour	strong, moderate, **none**
Acoustic opacity	good, moderate, **poor**

Bush Hammering: Tooled Concrete

Scharrieren: Betonwerkstein | Bouchardage : béton ouvragé | Abujardado: hormigón picado | Bocciardatura: lavorazione con utensili | Boucharderen: behakt beton

Project Museum of American Folk Art, New York (2001)
Architect Tod Williams Billie Tsien Architects
Photographer Michael Moran

Project Court of Justice, Amsterdam (1975)
Architect Ben Loerakker
Photographer Kees Hummel

The use of precast concrete elements in façades reached a peak in the 1960s and '70s. The robust appearance of sculptured façades and the coarse, rough-textured surfaces were particularly popular in the nonresidential building sector. During this period, labour-intensive stonemason's techniques were applied to the hardened concrete surfaces in order to simulate the appearance of natural stone. These techniques have recently been rediscovered and are now used to give large concrete surfaces a lively appearance that constantly changes under the influence of light and shadow.

Technical Aspects

Once it has hardened, the surface of concrete can be treated in the same way as natural stone. Hacking away at the concrete with stonemason's tools, such as a bush hammer, a pointed or a toothed chisel, breaks the cement skin and reveals the texture and colour of the aggregate. The texture of the surface depends on the profile of the tool used. Uniform tooling of the concrete surface with a bush hammer to a depth of a few millimetres produces a roughly textured surface. When an engraving hammer is used, the hammer strokes are visible as stripes and the texture of the concrete surface is rough and irregular. Although these techniques are usually carried out under controlled factory conditions, they are also sometimes applied to cast-in-situ concrete.

The combination of formwork profiling and machine tooling after the formwork has been removed produces a stunning aesthetic effect. Vertical slats in the formwork produce deep grooves in the concrete. Whittling down the ridges after the formwork has been removed gives rise to a sculptured concrete surface in which the colourful stripes of exposed aggregate and the grey cement in the deep grooves complement each other.

Applications

Concrete walls textured with the aid of stonemason's techniques can be used for both the interior and the exterior of a building. For exterior uses, the architect must take account of the direction of the profiling in connection with soiling and weathering.

Colour	**variable**
Glossiness	glossy, satin, **matt**
Translucence (%)	**0** – 20 – 40 – 60 – 80 – 100
Texture	sharp, **medium**, dull
Hardness	**hard**, soft, depressible
Temperature	warm, **medium**, cool
Odour	strong, moderate, **none**
Acoustic opacity	good, moderate, **poor**

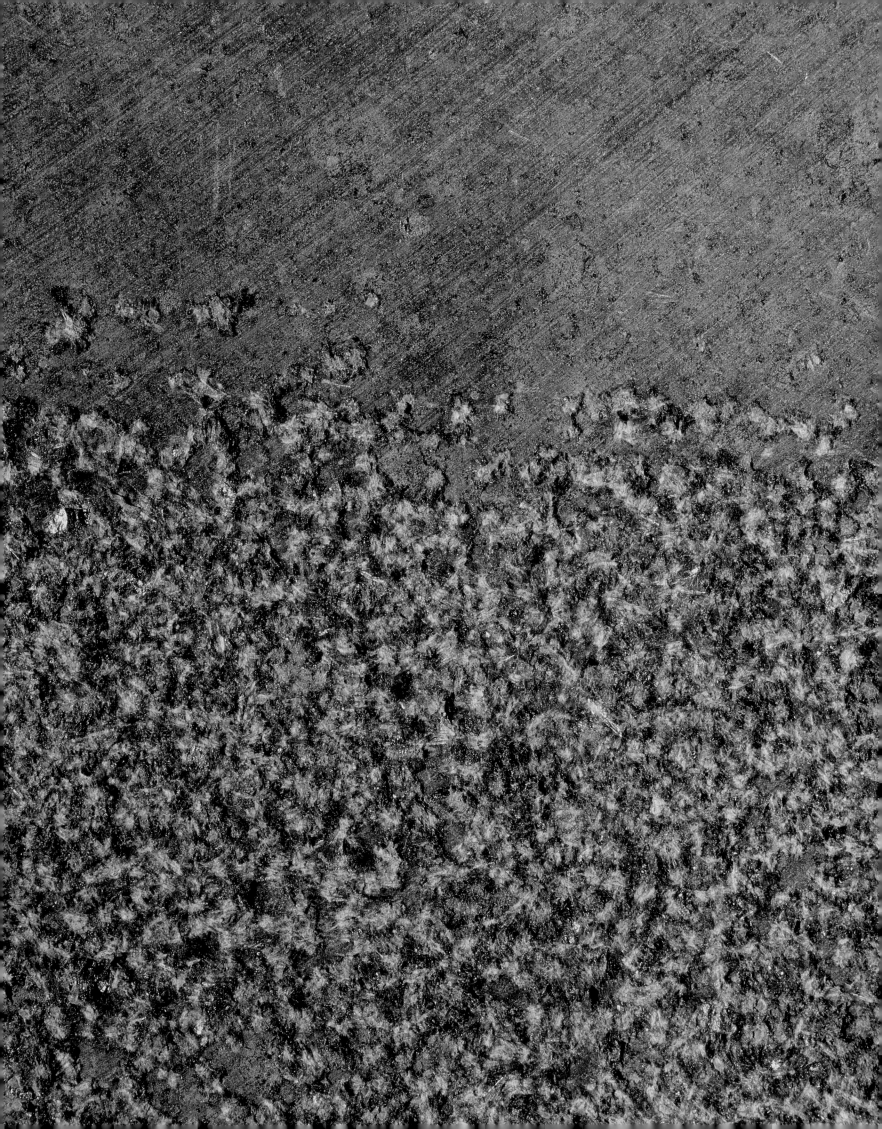

Printing: Photo-engraved Concrete

Bedrucken: Lichtdruck | Impression : béton photogravé | Dibujo impreso: cemento fotograbado | Stampa: fotoincisione nel calcestruzzo | Printen: printbeton

Project Library of the Eberswalde Technical School, Eberswalde (1999)

Architect Herzog & De Meuron

Photographer © Klemens Ortmeyer | Architekturphoto

An interesting development in the field of aesthetic surface treatments for concrete is the technique of photo-engraving. Developed in France some ten years ago, the technique has recently been used by various architects in order to lend their façade designs an extra dimension.

Technical Aspects

The photo-engraving technique makes use of retarders, chemicals which slow down the hardening process of concrete. The chosen image – a photograph, drawing or graphic design – is screen-printed, using a retarder, onto a polystyrene sheet as a layer of dots. This sheet is then placed face up in the form and the concrete poured on top. After the form is removed, the surface is washed to remove the unhardened cement paste. Wherever the retarder has been in contact with the fresh concrete, tiny concavities remain in the hardened surface. These concavities exhibit the colour and texture of the aggregate and stand out from the surrounding grey concrete: the image looks as if it has been 'burned' into the surface. The colour and structure of the raw materials and aggregates in the concrete mortar determine the appearance of the image. Since this technique requires extreme accuracy and precision, it can only be used for pre-cast elements.

Applications

The photo-engraving technique is suitable for enduring, emblematic additions to a façade, such as a company logo or an image that expresses the character or function of the building. The Swiss architects, Herzog & De Meuron, used the photo-engraving technique on the façade of the Eberswalde Technical School Library in Germany. The images, which were selected because of their historical, social and cultural character, symbolize the building's function as a source of knowledge and inspiration. The German architectural firm, Fischer, printed Ingres' famous painting, *The Source*, on the façade of the Media and Communication Centre in Mannheim in order to symbolize the theme of the centre.

Colour	variable
Glossiness	glossy, satin, **matt**
Translucence (%)	**0** – 20 – 40 – 60 – 80 – 100
Texture	sharp, **medium**, dull
Hardness	**hard**, soft, depressible
Temperature	warm, **medium**, cool
Odour	strong, moderate, **none**
Acoustic opacity	good, moderate, **poor**

Colour Coatings and Lazure

Färbungen und Lasuren I Enrobages colorés et à lazure I Capas de color y barniz o esmalte lasur I Rivestimenti colorati e a lazure I Gekleurde coatings en lazuren

Project Regenboog Area, Almere Buiten (1998)
Architect Geurst & Schulze Architects
Photographer R.K. Koopmanschap, Keim Nederland bv

Project Regenboog Area, Almere Buiten (1998)
Architect Pauw+PenningDeVries Architects
Photographer R.K. Koopmanschap, Keim Nederland bv

Brightly coloured concrete surfaces cannot be achieved by simply adding pigments to concrete mortar. If such a surface is desired, the answer is a coat of silicate paint. There are two types to choose from, transparent and non-transparent. When a non-transparent silicate paint is used, the concrete maintains its texture but the characteristic 'cloudiness' of the surface is no longer visible, whereas when a transparent coating or 'lazure' is applied, the original concrete surface remains visible through the layer of paint.

Technical Aspects

Silicate paint, which is soluble in water, has a basis of natural ingredients. It consists of liquid potassium silicate, which acts as a binding agent, mineral fillers and inorganic pigments. Silicate paint forms an insoluble bond with stone-like surfaces, such as plaster, concrete, brickwork or natural stone; the mineral paint effectively petrifies. Silicate paint is colourfast and resistant to the effects of weather, acids and UV radiation. Its microcrystalline structure means that it reflects light and heat very well. In hot climates, such as in the desert, this reflective characteristic considerably reduces the thermal load on the surface and this, in turn, limits the risk of cracks. An important property of silicate paint is its ability to breathe, allowing moisture in the underlying material to evaporate into the atmosphere. Silicate paint limits the growth of mould and bacteria. Cracking due to different expansion rates of paint and substrate do not occur, because both have the same coefficient of expansion. Thanks to all these properties, silicate paint is an environmentally-friendly and durable solution for coloured concrete. A concrete surface treated with silicate paint maintains its aesthetic quality for a very long time.

Applications

Concrete surfaces are treated with silicate paint (or lazure) when the design calls for bright colours. In the warm countries of Southern Europe and South America one comes across many projects that stand out with their bright orange, yellow, blue or purple surfaces. Apart from the aesthetic quality, the light-reflective properties play an important role in these applications. Silicate paint may also be resorted to when the aesthetic quality of the concrete is disappointing, for example, because of undesirable colour differences.

Colour	**variable**
Glossiness	glossy, satin, **matt**
Translucence (%)	**0** – 20 – 40 – 60 – 80 – 100
Texture	sharp, **medium**, dull
Hardness	**hard**, soft, depressible
Temperature	warm, **medium**, cool
Odour	strong, moderate, **none**
Acoustic opacity	good, moderate, **poor**

Special Treatments: Rust

Rost | Rouilles | Oxidos | Ruggine | Roest

Project Switching Station, Zürich (1999)
Architect Gigon & Guyer
Photographer Heinrich Helfenstein | Harald F. Müller

Project Rémy Zaugg Studio, Mulhouse (1997)
Architect Herzog & De Meuron
Photographer Klaus Kinold

As the popularity of fair-faced concrete in modern architecture has increased, so too has experimentation with the natural properties of concrete. The main objective of such experiments is not a perfect surface – smooth and homogeneous in both colour and texture – but rather irregularity due either to the composition of the concrete or external influences. Progressive Swiss architectural firms, such as Herzog & De Meuron and Gigon & Guyer, make natural processes such as rusting – discolouration due to oxidation – part of the aesthetic appearance.

Technical Aspects

If rusty rainwater flows over a vertical wall surface, it will leave rust-coloured traces on the surface. Traces of rust on the concrete surface can also occur as a result of iron particles in the concrete mortar. Irregular discolourations on the concrete surface may also arise because of the uneven mixing of colour pigments in the mortar.

Gigon & Guyer claim that the addition of copper powder or iron filings to the mortar will eventually lead to an intensification of the surface colour. Concrete technologists dismiss this effect as nonsense and believe that any colour changes that may occur are due to external influences.

Applications

A good example of intentional rust traces on a concrete surface is the south façade of Herzog & De Meuron's Remy Zaugg Studio in Mulhouse-Pfastatt, France. An abstract artwork created by nature and subject to constant change, the façade nicely reflects the function of the building.

The irregular rust-coloured concrete surface of the façades of the Seinhuis in Zurich, Switzerland, designed by Gigon & Guyer, anticipates the staining the building will undoubtedly encounter over time, situated as it is beside a railway track.

The yellow-orange speckled concrete walls of a school complex in Marseilles, France, are an example of uneven mixing of pigments in order to attain a natural effect. The walls allude to the traditional stone walls characteristic of the surrounding landscape.

Colour	**rust-coloured**
Glossiness	glossy, satin, **matt**
Translucence (%)	**0** – 20 – 40 – 60 – 80 – 100
Texture	sharp, **medium**, dull
Hardness	**hard**, soft, depressible
Temperature	warm, **medium**, cool
Odour	strong, moderate, **none**
Acoustic opacity	good, moderate, **poor**

Plaster Composites: Plasterwork

Gipsverbindungen: Putz | Composites de plâtre : plâtrage | Compuestos de escayola: enyesado | Compositi della malta: intonaco | Pleisteren: gipsstucwerk

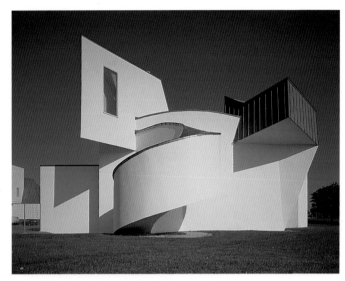

Project Vitra Design Museum, Weil am Rhein (1989)
Architect Frank O. Gehry
Photographer Thomas Dix

Whether in historical building styles, or in modern architecture from De Stijl to present-day minimalism, architects have always made grateful use of the abstract, aesthetic qualities of plasterwork. Serene white, Mediterranean pastels or, conversely, bright colours are used to accentuate either the sculptural form or the graphic composition of the architectural design. Depending on the requirements placed on the finishing, plaster consists of such raw materials as gypsum, lime or cement in varying compositions and mixing ratios. The addition of pigments and different shapes and sizes of granules determine the colour and structure of the top layer.

Technical Aspects

Cement and lime are the traditional main constituents of weather-resistant finishing coats. Nowadays, there are many types of plasters based on plastics like silicone or acrylic, which are suitable for exterior uses. Plaster is usually applied in several coats. The first should be a rough scratch coat, for example of cement and lime, which serves as a base for one or more finishing layers of variable composition. The modern silicate and silicon plasters are moisture resistant, vapour permeable and resistant to dirt. In contrast to traditional plaster, modern plasters are lightweight and can be applied in thin layers. The constructional background for plaster can be stony, such as sand-lime brick or aerated concrete, but sandwich constructions with plastic insulation material are also possible.

Applications

For interior wall and ceiling finishes, the plaster usually consists of a mix of lime and gypsum. The finishing layer can be applied over a scratch coat of cement, lime and sand or directly onto a smooth surface. Traditional gypsum-based plasters must not be directly exposed to water, although their capacity to absorb water vapour enables them to act as a temporary moisture reservoir in bathrooms and shower rooms. Special plasters have been developed for spraying, some of which are suitable for use in humid spaces.

Project Villa Rocca Pisani, Logino (1576)
Architect V. Scamozzi
Photographer Jan Derwig

Colour	variable
Glossiness	glossy, satin, **matt**
Translucence (%)	**0** – 20 – 40 – 60 – 80 – 100
Texture	sharp, **medium**, dull
Hardness	**hard**, soft, depressible
Temperature	**warm**, medium, cool
Odour	strong, moderate, **none**
Acoustic opacity	good, moderate, **poor**

Plasterboard – Perforated Texture

Gipskarton: mit Lochung | Placoplâtre : texture perforé | Yeso laminado con textura perforada | Cartongesso: struttura perforata |
Perforeren: gipsplaat structuur

Description Offices Baureferat, München (2000)
Photographer Knauf

Innovation in the field of plasterboard manufacture offers interior designers new possibilities. Perforated panels for walls and ceilings, which have been developed to improve the acoustics of a room, are available in a wide variety of perforations, patterns and textures. Panel sizes also vary widely from tile-size to panels the width or height of a room. Ceilings and walls can be lined in a continuous and apparently seamless pattern of perforations. A recent development is the production of fibre-reinforced plasterboard which can be used to make curved and seamless three-dimensional shapes.

Technical Aspects
Standard plasterboard consists of a non-flammable core of gypsum sandwiched between two layers of cardboard liner. Without special treatment or additives, plasterboard is unsuitable for extremely damp environments. However, its ability to absorb and release moisture quickly, enables plasterboard to play an active role in regulating the indoor climate. There are many different types of plasterboard available with properties geared to specific applications.

Perforated plasterboard has a high sound absorption capacity in all frequency ranges. Low tones are absorbed by the mass of the panels, the middle tones by the perforations. To absorb the high tones, an acoustic fleece or mineral wool can be attached to the rear of the panels. In general, the more perforations there are, the better the absorption. When untreated, the visible side of the plasterboard is usually ivory coloured, but it can be supplied with a variety of coloured finishes varying from a plain white coat of acrylic paint to decorative vinyl.

Applications
Apart from their acoustic properties, the perforations can also play a prominent role in the ambience of the interior. A ceiling or wall with round or square perforations of different sizes in an arbitrary pattern has a different optical effect from one with a straight, linear pattern of perforations. Linear perforations tend to accentuate the width or height of a room.

Colour	white
Glossiness	glossy, satin, **matt**
Translucence (%)	**0** – 20 – 40 – 60 – 80 – 100
Texture	sharp, **medium**, dull
Hardness	**hard**, soft, depressible
Temperature	**warm**, medium, cool
Odour	strong, moderate, **none**
Acoustic opacity	good, moderate, **poor**

Moroccan Plasterwork

Marokkanischer Tadelakt | Plâtrage marocain | Yeso laminado con acabado mudéjar | Intonaco marocchino | Marokkaans stucwerk

Project Private house, Le Deux Tour (2002)
Architect Bokara
Photographer Carl Gispen

Project Private house, Amsterdam (2003)
Decorator Carl Gispen
Photographer Carl Gispen

The shiny, lime-based plasterwork of Moroccan tradition is known as Tadelakt. The word 'tadelakt' comes from the Moroccan verb 'dellek', which roughly means 'to knead' or 'to press'. According to oral tradition, the Tadelakt technique has been around since ancient times and was used to make drinking water reservoirs waterproof. Later, the technique was used to embellish the walls of bathhouses (hammams) and to make them water-repellent. Although Tadelakt is related to the famous 17th-century Venetian plasterwork, both the composition of the plaster and the method of application are different. Characteristic of a surface treated with traditional Tadelakt are the fine cracks that give the material an 'antique' appearance. The lime mortar is often mixed with intense colour pigments so that the surface has an aesthetically pleasing and exotic appearance.

Technical Aspects

The plaster used for Tadelakt consists of a mixture of hydraulic lime, natural pigments and water. A trowel is used to apply a 4-5 mm thick layer to a sufficiently sturdy backing, such as concrete or sandstone; ordinary plasterboard is not rigid enough. Once the plaster has hardened, the surface is polished with a hard stone until it shines. It is then rendered waterproof using an olive oil-based soap. This is followed by another round of polishing until the required gloss is attained, after which a coat of wax is applied. The repeated polishing produces a rock-hard, impact-resistant and waterproof surface. Because the plaster is applied and worked by hand, colour differences appear, producing a cloudy, marble-like effect in the surface. The time-consuming application makes Tadelakt an expensive wall finishing. Nowadays, it is possible to buy various plaster mixtures with a synthetic resin base or paints with additives that attempt to emulate the aesthetic, exotically attractive appearance of Tadelakt.

Application

In Moroccan hammams, it is common to find not only walls finished with Tadelakt, but also floors, ceilings, seats and washbasins. Nowadays, Tadelakt is used throughout the interior wherever the expressive, shiny and often intensely coloured surface is desired.

Colour	**variable**
Glossiness	**glossy**, satin, matt
Translucence (%)	**0** – 20 – 40 – 60 – 80 – 100
Texture	sharp, medium, **dull**
Hardness	**hard**, soft, depressible
Temperature	**warm**, medium, cool
Odour	strong, moderate, **none**
Acoustic opacity	good, moderate, **poor**

Italian Stucco

Italienischer Stuck | Stuque Italien | Estuco italiano | Intonaco italiano | Italiaans stucwerk

Project Diligentia theatre, The Hague (2003)
Designer Art Ferro
Photographer Jeroen van Amelsvoort

Like Moroccan Tadelakt, Venetian plasterwork is based on an age-old wall finishing technique. In ancient Greece and Egypt, palace and temple walls were finished in a shiny, polished stucco based on natural minerals and water. In the heyday of Venice in the 17th and 18th centuries, this technique was rediscovered and developed into a popular type of wall decoration with the appearance of expensive, coloured marble. Stucco Antico and Stucco Lustro are only two of the terms used for this type of decorative plasterwork.

Although the old polishing techniques are time consuming and require craftsmanship, there is renewed interest in the special, expressive, aesthetic effects and properties of Venetian plaster. New ingredients for the plaster mortar have been developed so that futuristically gleaming walls can be created in metallic colours like silver, gold, bronze, and copper.

Technical Aspects

Apart from lime, Venetian plaster contains finely ground minerals like marble. Using a trowel, thin layers of plaster are applied to a strong, smooth surface and then polished. The number of layers depends on the desired pattern, gloss and appearance, and can vary from five to twelve. The repeated application of pressure carbonizes the material and creates a rock-hard coating. The marbling is due to small variations in the thickness of the various layers resulting from manual application. In Italy, there is a special type of plaster called Marmorino that contains at least 40% marble. Through the pressure applied by the trowel, it acquires the natural lustre and properties of marble and even feels like marble. Both finishes are water-repellant and able to breathe and are naturally shiny without the need of hydrophobic or protective layers of wax.

Nowadays, there is a wide selection of plaster mortars available that, with the aid of synthetic or other additives, attempt to emulate the same 'natural marble effect' without polishing. Although the aesthetic result is comparable to the original Italian technique, it does not have the same natural properties.

Applications

Venetian plasterwork can be used anywhere in the interior where a special wall finish is desired. Although Venetian plasterwork is water-repellant and suitable for damp rooms such as bathrooms, it is less suitable for uses where it will be directly exposed to water, such as in a façade.

Colour	**variable**
Glossiness	glossy, **satin**, matt
Translucence (%)	**0** – 20 – 40 – 60 – 80 – 100
Texture	sharp, medium, **dull**
Hardness	**hard**, soft, depressible
Temperature	**warm**, medium, cool
Odour	strong, moderate, **none**
Acoustic opacity	good, moderate, **poor**

Rendering: Plasterwork

Verputzen: Putz | Enduits : plâtrage | Acabados: yeso laminado | Rinzaffatura: intonaco | Schuren: gipsstuc

Project Bistro Madison, Zweibrücken (2000)
Photographer Knauf

Project Museum of Scotland, Edinburgh (1999)
Architect Benson + Forsyth
Photographer Hélène Binet

Walls and ceilings that are finished with white render are characterized by the fine texture of the plasterwork and the circular 'strokes' created by the rotating action of the float used to smooth the plaster.

Technical Aspects
White render is a traditional wall and ceiling finish using a plaster mortar on the basis of lime, gypsum, water and fine sand. A finishing layer varying from 5 to 10 mm in thickness is applied by hand on top of a base coat that usually consists of a mixture of cement, lime and sand and that is used to establish an even background. The regular, rotating movement of the float the plasterer uses to scour the plaster, creates the circular pattern. Render can theoretically be applied to any surface, although nowadays a special mortar is prepared for each type of background. There are also mortars that do not need a base coat. The size of the sand grains determines the texture of the surface which is also relatively soft and easily damaged. In damp rooms with 70% or higher humidity, and wherever a coarser, stronger texture is desired, a plaster with a cement and lime base is used. Plasterwork with a lime and gypsum base is moisture absorbent.

Applications
Fine rendering was once a common wall and ceiling finishing technique in both residential and non-residential buildings, but has now been displaced by a spray plaster that is quicker to apply. Compared with spray plaster, rendered plaster is finer-textured and smoother-looking.

Colour	**white**
Glossiness	glossy, satin, **matt**
Translucence (%)	**0** – 20 – 40 – 60 – 80 – 100
Texture	sharp, **medium**, dull
Hardness	**hard**, soft, depressible
Temperature	**warm**, medium, cool
Odour	strong, moderate, **none**
Acoustic opacity	good, moderate, **poor**

Texturing in Wet Plaster

Strukturieren in feuchtem Putz | Texturation en plâtre humide | Texturas de yeso en masa en aplicación húmeda | Struttura nell'intonaco bagnato | Structureren: structuur in natte gips

Project De Vijfhoek, Deventer (2001)
Architect Kemme van Kruysbergen Architects
Photographer Harry Noback

Decorative plasterwork usually derives its surface texture from the composition of the plaster. Fillers such as fine or coarse sand, wood chips and fibres, leave traces in the surface. Textures and patterns can also be applied to the still wet plaster with the help of special tools or objects (bottles, shells, et cetera).

Technical Aspects

The material properties depend on the composition of the plaster. Lime and gypsum plaster are used for interiors whilst cement-based plasters are used for exteriors. Since texturing in wet plaster usually results in coarse relief patterns, such finishes are especially susceptible to soiling.

Applications

Walls of coarse-textured plasterwork have a hand-crafted appearance and evoke a rural or Mediterranean atmosphere. An unusual example of austere, modern architecture in combination with hand-crafted texturing in wet plaster is a housing project by Dutch architect Thomas Kemme. Here a tiler's notched spreader has been used to create a 'patchwork' of combed areas on the outer wall.

Colour	white
Glossiness	glossy, satin, **matt**
Translucence (%)	**0** – 20 – 40 – 60 – 80 – 100
Texture	sharp, **medium**, dull
Hardness	**hard**, soft, depressible
Temperature	**warm**, medium, cool
Odour	strong, moderate, **none**
Acoustic opacity	good, moderate, **poor**

Split-faced Sand-lime Bricks

Kalksandstein mit Spaltfläche | Brique en chaux et sable face fendue liant calcaire | Ladrillos de sílice (cal y arena) con cara machihembrada |
Mattoni silico-calcarei con splittatura faccia a vista | Breken: kalkzandsteen klisstenen

Project De Landstede boarding school, Zwolle (1996)
Architect Scala Architects
Photographer Rien van Rijthoven

Project CVK building, Hilversum (1996)
Architect CVK
Photographer Kees Hummel

Façades made from split-faced sand-lime bricks are characterized by an expressive, sculptural appearance. The fractured brick face which gives the surface its relief effect is the result of a special production process. The bricks are first manufactured in a 'tile size' that is twice the width but the same length and height as a standard brick. This double brick is then split in half by a splitting machine to produce two bricks which each have one rough stretcher face along the line of fracture. Bricks with two rough edges (one stretcher and one header) are also produced for use at corners. The 'tiles' for corner bricks are 3 cm longer and are split along the long side. Split-faced bricks are available in the standard Dutch brick sizes Waal, Amstel and Maas and as blocks (326 x 102 x 102 mm). A variant of the split-faced brick is Rock Face in which the already fractured face is mechanically worked with knives to enhance the relief effect. Split-faced bricks are available in super white and anthracite.

Technical Aspects

Split-faced bricks have the same compressive strength (30 N/mm^2) as the other types of sand-lime façade bricks. During the production process, a hydrophobic agent is added to make the bricks water-resistant. To prevent cracks, dilation must be taken into account when designing a façade. Since size deviations during production are negligible, the brickwork patterns in the façade design can be accurately created from drawings and using the same drawings any non-standard filler bricks can be cut to the desired size or mechanically sawn using a diamond saw in the factory.

Applications

Split-faced bricks can be used as facing brickwork, in both residential and non-residential construction. The super white and anthracite façade bricks lend themselves perfectly to the design of façades with expressive, graphic patterns, such as black-and-white stripes.

Colour	**variable**
Glossiness	glossy, satin, **matt**
Translucence (%)	**0** – 20 – 40 – 60 – 80 – 100
Texture	sharp, **medium**, **dull**
Hardness	**hard**, soft, depressible
Temperature	warm, **medium**, cool
Odour	strong, moderate, **none**
Acoustic opacity	good, moderate, **poor**

Additives

Zuschlagstoffe für ungebrannten, künstlichen Stein | Additifs béton de roche artificielle non cuite | Aditivos de piedra prefabricada no cocida | Additivi per pietre sintetiche | Toevoegingen ongebakken kunststeen

People have always experimented with the basic ingredients of man-made building materials with a view to improving or changing the structural or aesthetic properties of existing materials, or to developing entirely new materials. A simple example is the addition of pigments to impart colour to lime- or cement-bound materials. The flood of truly revolutionary developments in this field began with the (re)discovery of cement at the beginning of the twentieth century. Since then, and partly influenced by functionalist architecture, many new materials such as aerated concrete and fibre cement have been developed. Such inventions have continued unabated to the present day and have led to materials whose structural, transmission or aesthetic properties are composed to order by the addition of chemical or other additives.

Aerated Concrete

One of the most spectacular discoveries of the early twentieth century was the method for producing aerated concrete (previously called gas concrete). Aerated concrete as we know it today was created by combining two earlier discoveries. The first was the production of water-resistant calcium-hydrate compounds by bringing a mixture of sand, lime and water into contact with saturated water vapour at high pressure. A patent was awarded for this discovery in 1880, and it still forms the basis of the production method for all building materials that are hardened under steam pressure in an autoclave, such as sand-lime bricks.

The other discovery was the 'foaming' of a mixture of fine sand, cement and water to which a small quantity of aluminium powder has been added. In the alkaline environment, the aluminium reacts with the cement to form hydrogen. The gas produced causes the concrete mass to rise like cake batter. Around 1930, these two discoveries were combined by placing the risen and stiffened foamed mixture in an autoclave and allowing it to harden there under high pressure at a temperature of 180 °C, into a material now known as aerated concrete. The same period saw the development of another material called foamed concrete which is produced by mixing foam (usually organic proteins) through a mortar of cement, fine sand and fly-ash. This is a cold process, that is, no chemical reaction takes place between the foam and the mortar. Foamed concrete is therefore essentially different from aerated concrete. Foamed concrete is still used today, in particular in lightweight foundations. While foamed concrete is unsuitable for exposed work, aerated concrete can be used to aesthetic effect. The mass production of aerated concrete elements began in Sweden in the 1950s and was swiftly followed by the production of reinforced aerated concrete. Nowadays, aerated concrete is used throughout the world as a lightweight building material. In recent years, its development has been geared more to aesthetic applications, with standard rectangular, rounded and custom-made elements.

Fibre Cement

Fibre cement was invented around the same time as the production process for aerated concrete was discovered. Around 1900, the Austrian industrialist Ludwig Hatschek developed a technique to strengthen cement-bound products with fibres. He called the material, which was intended as a cheap, strong, light and durable roof

Project Orthodontic practice, Almere (1992)

Architect Meyer en Van Schooten Architecten bv

Photographer Jan Derwig

covering, 'eternit' meaning 'forever'. The first fibre cement sheets and slates were produced in a factory in Belgium. The production methods for the various fibre cement products are almost identical, only the shaping phases differ. Portland cement, organic fibres, selected mineral aggregates and water are first mixed together in the correct quantities before being fed into a rotating sieve cylinder (Hatschek machine) which deposits thin layers of the mixture onto a forming roller where it is compressed to the desired thickness. The sheets harden on exposure to air owing to the hydraulic reaction of cement and water. Extra strong sheets are obtained by steam curing in an autoclave. After curing, the sheets can be sanded, polished, cut or sawn as required. Fibre cement is now used on a large scale in Europe as a wall, façade and roof covering.

Concrete Aggregates

The basic constituents of concrete are cement, sand, gravel and water. Sand and gravel are called aggregates. Aggregates form the supporting skeleton of the concrete and make up approximately 75% of its volume. The properties of the chosen aggregates largely determine the properties of the concrete. The bond between aggregate and hardened cement paste is crucial to the cohesion and strength of the concrete. It is obvious, therefore, that potential aggregates must satisfy stringent requirements before being used in concrete. Aggregates are divided into different categories depending on their place of origin, density and particle size. Aside from river and sea gravel, granules of hard natural stone make suitable aggregates. Natural, lightweight rock such as lava or pumice stone is used to reduce the weight of the concrete. Lightweight concrete is also created by using lightweight artificial aggregates such as expanded clay pellets. Lightweight concrete is not suitable for use as facing

concrete and needs a finishing layer. On the other hand, granules of natural stone as well as gravel can play a large role in the aesthetic appearance of fair-faced concrete if the colourful pattern of the granules is exposed by treating the concrete surface.

Self-compacting Concrete

In addition to aggregates, an increasing number of additives are being added to concrete to produce specific properties. Recent developments are high-strength concrete (HSC) and fibre-reinforced concrete (FRC). High-strength concrete (strength classes B65 – B100) gets its extra compressive strength from a very fine additive called silica fume. HSC is used to reduce weight, for example, in the construction of high-rise buildings or in extremely large spans such as bridges. Fibre-reinforced concrete is concrete to which steel fibres have been added in order to increase resistance to shrinkage cracks. The latest development in this field is an attempt to replace traditional reinforcement with steel fibres. One of the most revolutionary recent developments in concrete technology comes from Japan, where intensive research to develop self-compacting concrete (SCC) was carried out in the 1980s. At the University of Tokyo, Professor Okamura developed a method for preparing a stable mixture of self-compacting concrete. In Europe, this method was first used in the Netherlands in 1997. Self-compacting concrete is very fluid due to the combination of very fine materials and the addition of a super-plasticizer. For this new type of concrete, a fifth value has been added. Self-compacting concrete makes mechanical compaction unnecessary. This is an important consideration in precast concrete because vibration tables and formwork vibrators are a source of unpleasant noise in a concrete factory. On the building site, too, being able to dispense with internal poker vibrators leads to improved health and safety conditions. At the same time, self-compacting concrete also increases the architectural and structural design possibilities. Extremely congested areas of reinforcement and inaccessible constructions are no longer a problem because SCC flows evenly into all the corners of the most complex formwork. The high surface quality is an added advantage for aesthetic applications. Given the quality of the first projects involving SCC, such as a theatre in The Hague by Charles Vandenhove, there are high hopes for the use of self-compacting concrete as fair-faced concrete.

Project VMT office building, Enschede (1997)

Architect Min2 bouw-kunst

Photographer Elly Valkering

Superplasticizers: Self-compacting Concrete

Betonverflüssiger: Selbstverdichtender Beton | *Superplastifiant: béton autoplaçant* | *Materiales superplásticos: hormigón autocompacto* |
Superplastificanti: calcestruzzo autocompattante | *Superplastificeerders: zelfverdichtend beton*

Project Toneeltoren Schouwburg, The Hague (1999)
Architect Charles Vandenhove et Associés | HTV Architects
Photographer Jeroen van Amelsvoort

Self-compacting concrete (SCC) is an innovative development in concrete technology. By adding very fine fillers and additives such as superplasticizers to the concrete mixture it becomes possible to cast complex architectural shapes of a high aesthetic quality on site. Razor-sharp profiling, tall, narrow building sections and complex round or angular shapes are relatively easy to produce using self-compacting concrete. Furthermore, the concrete surface is remarkably smooth and flawless.

Technical Aspects

The composition of self-compacting concrete is based on a precisely determined water/cement ratio and the exact quantity of superplasticizer needed to achieve the required fluidity. Partly due to the superplasticizer, the concrete mortar flows smoothly into all the corners of the formwork even when a lot of reinforcement is used. Whereas standard concrete mortar must always be compacted (vibrated) in order to fill the formwork properly and to avoid gravel pockets and air voids, this is not necessary with self-compacting concrete. The homogeneity of hardened self-compacting concrete is much better than that of standard concrete because compaction does not depend on the skills of the workman. Apart from the correct quantity of superplasticizer, a viscosity-modifying agent can also be added to improve the viscosity of the concrete so that it is less sensitive to fluctuations in the properties of the mixture. Welan Gum, a microbiological polysaccharide, is one such agent that increases the resistance to segregation and bleeding (lime efflorescence). The cohesion of self-compacting concrete is greater than that of standard concrete, resulting in less leakage between the formwork joints. The high quality of the finished surface renders patching and repairs unnecessary. The surface of self-compacting concrete is very dense and therefore less porous, which is beneficial to the durability.

Applications

While self-compacting concrete has been used for some time in Japan and the rest of Europe, its application in the Netherlands was initially restricted to civil engineering works like the Tuibrug (cable-stayed bridge) at Zaltbommel. The reinforcement congestion in the attachments of the end anchorage of the stays was so great, and accessibility and monitoring so difficult, that standard concrete could not be used. Since then, the advantages of self-compacting concrete have also penetrated to the non-residential sector. In The Hague, self-compacting concrete was used on the façade of the Schouwburg fly tower in order to produce the razor-sharp profiling desired by the architect.

Colour	variable
Glossiness	glossy, satin, **matt**
Translucence (%)	**0** – 20 – 40 – 60 – 80 – 100
Texture	sharp, medium, **dull**
Hardness	**hard**, soft, depressible
Temperature	warm, **medium**, cool
Odour	strong, moderate, **none**
Acoustic opacity	good, moderate, **poor**

Natural Stone Granules: Decorative Concrete

Natursteingranulat: Zierbeton | Granulés de roche naturel : béton décoratif | Granulado de piedra natural: Cemento decorativo | Graniglia di pietra naturale: calcestruzzo ad uso decorativo | Natuursteengranulaat: sierbeton

Project Regional Record Office, Eindhoven (2000)
Architect Bollen Architectuur
Photographer Kees Hummel

The colour and texture of a concrete surface can easily be manipulated by exploiting the natural, aesthetic properties of the aggregate. For example, the addition of angular natural stone chippings results in a very different surface from that obtained with rounded gravel. Various types of natural stone, such as porphyry, granite, basalt, limestone and marble, are available in granular form and in a wide variety of colours, depending on their place of origin. This allows designers to compose the colour, texture and pattern of the concrete surface at their own discretion. Since the aggregate is hidden beneath a skin of hardened cement paste, the surface must be treated to expose the underlying colour and texture of the additives. Depending on the chosen treatment, the surface structure varies from rough in washed surfaces to smooth in polished surfaces.

Technical Aspects

The natural stone types are selected on colour according to their area or quarry of origin and crushed to the desired particle size. Porphyry is available in various shades of reddish brown, yellow and grey. Granites can impart a dark greyish or a predominantly light-coloured appearance to the surface. Basalt is mainly used when a black surface is desired. Concrete technologists determine the suitability of the selected stone as aggregate and the percentage to be used in the concrete mixture.

One advantage of using natural stone aggregate to create coloured concrete surfaces is the durability of the colours, which may even become more apparent over time as the concrete surrounding the aggregate slowly erodes under the influence of the wind and rain. For polished surfaces, it is advisable to apply a transparent layer of varnish to protect the surface and to intensify the colours. Marbles and soft types of limestone are easier to polish than harder types of natural stone, but are less durable. It is advisable always to have a test piece made in order to check the aesthetic effect of the concrete mixture.

Applications

Concrete to which natural stone aggregate has been added makes for a highly durable façade cladding with a superior aesthetic quality. A striking example is the precast concrete façade of the Regional Record Office in Eindhoven (Netherlands) in which the reddish-brown colour of porphyry has been exploited to suggest an expressive pattern of book spines.

Colour	variable
Glossiness	glossy, **satin**, **matt**
Translucence (%)	**0** – 20 – 40 – 60 – 80 – 100
Texture	**sharp**, **medium**, **dull**
Hardness	**hard**, soft, depressible
Temperature	warm, **medium**, cool
Odour	strong, moderate, **none**
Acoustic opacity	good, moderate, **poor**

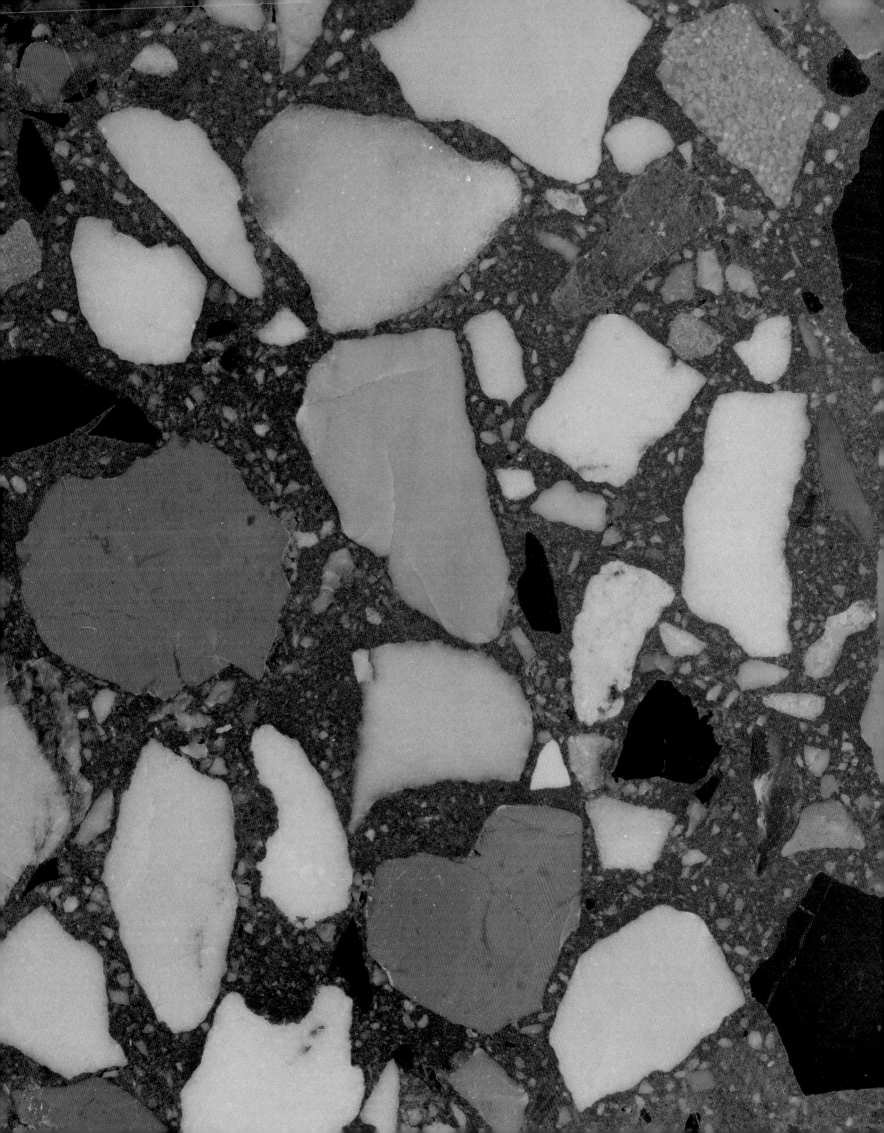

Pebbles, Crushed Demolition Waste, Glass: Decorative Concrete

Kieselsteine, zerkleinerter Bauschutt, Glas: Zierbeton I Galets, gravats de démolition concassés, verre : béton décoratif I Guijarros, material de desecho prensado, vidrio: cemento decorativo I Ciottoli, scarti di demolizione frantumati, vetro: calcestruzzo ad uso decorativo I Kiezels, basalt, glas: sierbeton

Project Schaulager Museum, Basel (2003)
Architect Herzog & De Meuron
Photographer Thomas Dix

The most commonly used raw materials for producing concrete are cement, sand, gravel and water. Gravel consists of a heterogeneous mixture of natural stone types carried down from the mountains by rivers. The flowing water rounds the chunks of natural stone into pebbles. All that is needed to utilize the colourful pattern of the river gravel for the aesthetic appearance of the concrete surface, is to remove the skin of grey cement paste. The choice of gravel and the surface treatment employed together determine the appearance and texture of the surface, which can vary from a rough blasted or washed surface to a smooth polished surface. In addition to these structurally vital ingredients, aggregates chosen purely for their aesthetic effects may also be added to the concrete mortar. Pieces of broken green glass, shells or stainless steel slugs, for example, yield surprising results in the surface of the concrete.

Technical Aspects

Gravel consists of hard pebbles of natural stone and is therefore highly suited to producing strong concrete. The pebbles are colour-fast and durable and for this reason exposure to the weather does not have a negative effect on the aesthetic appearance. River gravel from the Rhine is mostly greyish-blue in colour, while gravel extracted from the Maas tends more towards brown. Sea gravel from the North Sea contains more flint and so has more white accents. Nowadays, for economic and environmental reasons, the gravel in the aggregate is sometimes partly replaced by crushed masonry, concrete or a mixture of both. This has consequences not only for the structural properties of the concrete, but also for the outward appearance. It is necessary to check the aesthetic effect of the concrete composition and the chosen surface treatment in a test piece. Although it is possible to treat the surface of in situ cast concrete, the results are more manageable under factory-controlled conditions.

Applications

Aesthetic concrete façades, in which the textures and patterns of the gravel are visible in the surface, are suitable for both residential and non-residential buildings. An exceptionally expressive effect is achieved by the crushed wine bottles added to the aggregate for the façade of the Swiss Re Education Centre (Centre for Global Dialogue) in Rüsschlikon, Switzerland. The fragments of glass catch the sunlight and impart a green brilliance to the surface.

Colour	**variable**
Glossiness	glossy, **satin**, **matt**
Translucence (%)	**0** – 20 – 40 – 60 – 80 – 100
Texture	**sharp**, **medium**, **dull**
Hardness	**hard**, soft, depressible
Temperature	warm, **medium**, cool
Odour	strong, moderate, **none**
Acoustic opacity	good, moderate, **poor**

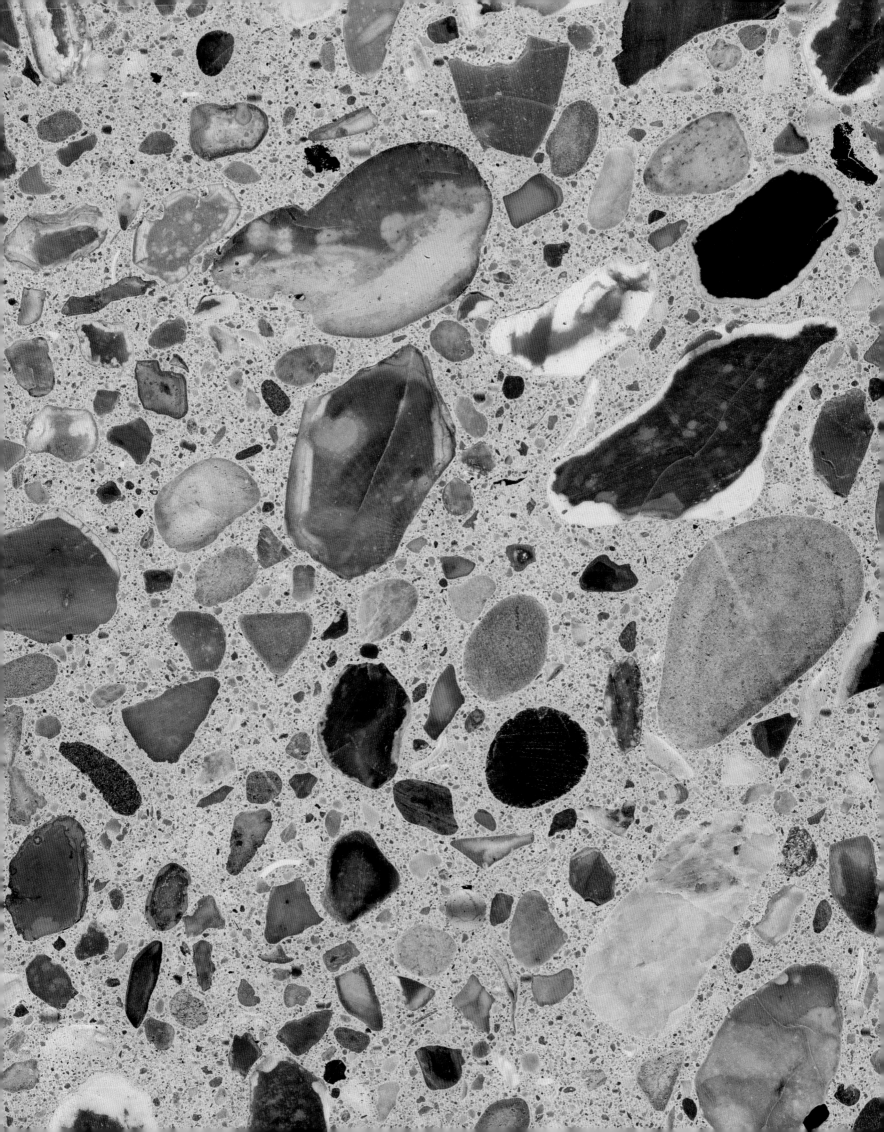

Pigments: Coloured Concrete

Pigmente: Farbbeton | Pigments: béton coloré | Pigmentos: cemento coloreado | Pigmenti: calcestruzzo colorato | Pigmenten: gekleurd beton

Project Metro station, Rotterdam (1997)
Architect M. Zwarts, R. Jansma
Photographer Marcel van Kerckhoven

Project Malburgen-West, Arnhem (2000)
Architect Marco Henssen and Frank Hemeltjen, M3H Architects
Photographer Michel Claus

Concrete can be given permanent colour by adding pigments to the concrete mixture. Coloured concrete can be produced to order in a wide spectrum of colours ranging from white, yellow, red and blue to dark grey, as well as various mixed colours. The intensity of the colour is tempered by the other ingredients in the concrete mix. Colour nuances in the surface of coloured concrete emphasize the natural character of the concrete material.

Technical Aspects

Concrete made from blast furnace or Portland cement without the addition of pigments is naturally grey. When producing coloured concrete, the choice of cement is important for the final result. White Portland cement is the only cement produced to a precise colour specification and, combined with pigments, it yields the truest colour results in concrete. Pigmented concrete is wear-resistant; minor damage to the surface does not affect the colour because it has been homogeneously mixed with the concrete mortar. Colouring agents for concrete consist of very fine powders which can be added to the concrete mix either in powdered form or as a slurry. In the slurry the pigment particles are already well mixed with water. Colouring agents must be proof against the alkaline environment of concrete, be weather-resistant, insoluble in water and adhere well to the hardened cement to prevent them from being rinsed out. Only pigments based on metal oxide meet these requirements. Red, yellow and brown tints are obtained with iron oxides. For blue and green, costly cobalt, aluminium and chromium oxides are required. Carbon black, a carbon compound rather than a metal oxide, can also be used, although it is less durable. The nearest it is possible to get to true black concrete is a dark anthracite grey.

Lime bloom, a chemical reaction to exposure to outside air, causes the 'greying' of darker concrete surfaces. Waterproofing or a coat of transparent silicate paint (lazure) can help to reduce this problem. Although there is a colour palette for coloured concrete, the outcome can never be guaranteed in advance. A test piece must always be made to check the effect of the pigment in combination with the chosen concrete mixture.

Applications

Colour imparts an extra accent to fair-faced concrete. Coloured concrete is used in residential and non-residential construction as well as in civil engineering works like bridge abutments and subway stations.

Colour	variable
Glossiness	glossy, satin, **matt**
Translucence (%)	**0** – 20 – 40 – 60 – 80 – 100
Texture	**sharp**, **medium**, **dull**
Hardness	**hard**, soft, depressible
Temperature	warm, **medium**, cool
Odour	strong, moderate, **none**
Acoustic opacity	good, moderate, **poor**

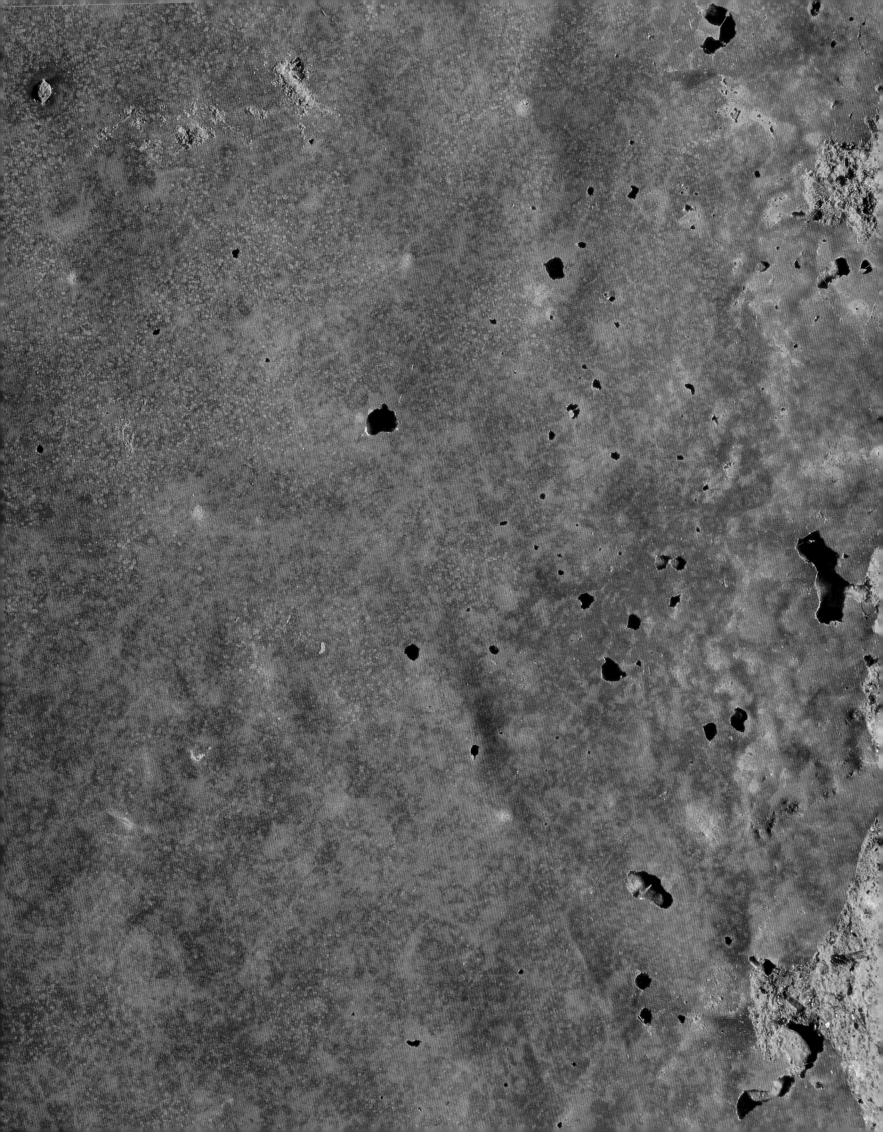

Aluminium Powder: Aerated Concrete

Aluminiumpulver: Porenbeton | Poudre d'aluminium: béton aéré | Polvo de aluminio: hormigón aireado | Polvere d'alluminio: calcestruzzo poroso | Aluminiumpoeder: cellenbeton

Project Separation panels Westpoint, Tilburg (2003)
Architect Van Aken
Photographer Wim Tholenaars

Project Living Tomorrow pavilion, Amsterdam (2003)
Architect UN Studio
Photographer Wim Tholenaars

Aerated concrete (also know as: cellular concrete, gas concrete, foamed concrete) is a lightweight material that is not strictly speaking concrete. It is produced by adding aluminium powder to cement mortar and is characterized by a homogeneous, finely textured surface in an even shade of off-white. In wall and façade surfaces composed of aerated concrete elements, the dimensions of the individual elements remain visible in the joint pattern.

Technical Aspects

Aerated concrete can only be produced under factory-controlled conditions because aluminium powder may react violently with cement if the wrong quantity is used. A tiny amount of aluminium powder is added to a precisely calculated mix of ground quartz sand, lime, cement and tap water. The chemical reaction with the cement results in millions of bubbles of hydrogen gas that cause the mixture to 'rise'. When set, the resulting 'cake' is wire-cut into blocks of the required dimensions which are placed in an autoclave where they are 'cured' under steam pressure. Aerated concrete, both reinforced and non-reinforced, is available in a wide variety of dimensions. The non-reinforced version is very brittle.

Although its compressive strength is relatively low, aerated concrete block can be used for a loadbearing wall to a maximum of three floors if the wall is sufficiently thick. Aerated concrete elements are lightweight and easy to handle. Roof and wall slabs are available in lengths up to 7.5 metres; tongue and groove joints allow them to be mounted quickly. Aerated concrete is a good thermal insulator and has excellent heat accumulation properties. For a stony material, its sound absorption is relatively high, while its fire-retardant properties make it suitable for fire compartmentation and for industrial buildings where high fire resistance ratings are specified. Interestingly, although aerated concrete can be used as is in façades, a finishing in another material is often chosen for aesthetic reasons. Recent developments indicate growing interest in the material's own aesthetic possibilities.

Applications

Aerated concrete is suitable for all types of buildings. Interest in aerated concrete as a fairly basic and insulating construction material is slowly shifting towards its more representative design potential. A tinted coating has recently been developed for aerated concrete which leaves the natural texture of the material intact while radically changing its overall image.

Colour	**off white**
Glossiness	glossy, **satin**, **matt**
Translucence (%)	**0** – 20 – 40 – 60 – 80 – 100
Texture	**sharp**, **medium**, dull
Hardness	**hard**, soft, depressible
Temperature	**warm**, medium, cool
Odour	strong, moderate, **none**
Acoustic opacity	good, moderate, **poor**

Organic and Mineral Fibres: Fibre Cement Slates | Sheeting

Organische Fasern und Mineralfasern: Faserzementplatten/-verschalungen | Fibres Organiques et Minéraux : Fibre de béton ardoises/feuilles | Fibras organicas y minerales: Pizarras/chapas de fibrocemento | Fibre organiche i minerali: tegole / lamine in fibrocemento | Organische en minerale vezels: vezelcementleien/-platen

Project Compositae, 18 private houses, Almere (1992)
Architect Frits van Dongen, de Architekten Cie.
Photographer Brakkee & Scagliola

Project Pieter Vlamingstraat, Amsterdam (1991)
Architect Zeinstra Van der Pol
Photographer Jan Derwig

Fibre cement is the basic material for the production of thin, strong façade cladding products. The products range from natural grey-beige to intensely coloured. Various surface textures are available ranging from fine to coarse – grained to smooth as glass. Fibre cement is produced in sheets, strips and slates of various sizes. Visible and concealed fixing systems allow for creative, graphic patterns in various colour combinations.

Technical Aspects

Fibre cement is composed of cement, sand, water, air, and synthetic and/or natural reinforcing fibres. The fibres strengthen the mechanical properties of the end product. Fibre cement is a durable material capable of withstanding weather and extreme temperature. In event of fire it will not propagate flames. It is also resistant to moulds and micro-organisms. The base sheet is porous and vapour-open.

Fibre cement cladding products are produced with or without a finishing coat. Without a finishing coat, the component fibres and cement are visible on the surface giving it a somewhat 'cloudy' appearance. It is naturally grey-beige in colour; grey, anthracite and red can be obtained by adding pigments to the mixture. The boards can also be given a coating of different nature. The surface of sheets with a mineral finishing coat is very hard and scratch-resistant. More recently siding planks (also called Weatherboard) with a woodgrain finish are developed.

Large fibre cement cladding panels are fastened to the façade on a wood, steel or aluminium loadbearing structure, using either visible or concealed fixings. With the visible fixing method, the panels are fastened with screws or rivets of the same colour as the panel. In the past, this method attracted the qualification 'thumbtack architecture' but since then decorative fixing elements have been developed. Nowadays, panels can also be mounted invisibly by using structural gluing.

Applications

Fibre cement sheeting is suitable for all types of constructions: residential, non-residential and civil engineering projects such as bridges, tunnels and subway stations. An example of a pleasing aesthetical effect is obtained by installing slates in different overlapping methods creating specific relief patterns.

Colour	**variable**
Glossiness	**glossy, satin, matt**
Translucence (%)	**0** – 20 – 40 – 60 – 80 – 100
Texture	sharp, medium, **dull**
Hardness	**hard**, soft, depressible
Temperature	**warm**, medium, cool
Odour	strong, moderate, **none**
Acoustic opacity	good, moderate, **poor**

Wheatherboard is a siding product of Eternit, a company belonging to the Etex Group, and almost 100 years active in the production and sales of fibre cement products all over the world.

Shells: Polyester Concrete

Muschelschalen: Polyesterbeton, Betondachstein und Betonfertigteile | Coque: béton de polyester/briques et blocs de béton |
Hormigón de poliéster/ Ladrillos y bloques de hormigón | Conchiglie: calcestruzzo di poliestere/Mattoni e blocchi di calcestruzzo |
Schelpen: polyesterbeton met schelpen

Project Kales Airline Services counter, Amsterdam (2002)
Designer Eva Krooneberg
Engineering Kors Verweij, De Geus
Photographer Kees Hummel

Project Forensic Psychiatric Clinic, Amsterdam (2001)
Architect Han Westelaken, Architecten aan de Maas
Photographer MBI

The shape and texture of mussel shells produce a remarkably attractive result in the surface of polyester concrete tiles. Cockle shells (either broken or intact) make a wall of concrete brick look like a sandy beach in summer.

Technical Aspects

Mussel shell tiles are made from glass fibre reinforced polyester concrete. Washed and dried mussel shells are added to the liquid concrete, which is then poured into a mould and left to set. Afterwards, the tile is polished. Any holes in the surface (caused by the concave shells) can, if necessary, be filled with polyester. Since polyester concrete shrinks whilst drying, the aggregate becomes exposed on the surface.

Shells can also be added to the concrete used to produce concrete bricks. In the production of split-faced bricks, the shells are evenly distributed through the cross section of the brick and become exposed when the brick is split. In the production of decorative bricks, shells (either whole or crushed) are only added to the mixture for the top layer. Washing removes the cement paste and brings the shells to the surface.

Applications

Polyester concrete tiles with a mussel shell pattern can be used for façades and floors. The expensive production process limits the possible uses. Split-face concrete brick and concrete brick with a decorative top layer of shells can be used in the façades of residential and non-residential buildings.

Colour	**variable**
Glossiness	**glossy**, **satin**, **matt**
Translucence (%)	**0** – 20 – 40 – 60 – 80 – 100
Texture	sharp, **medium**, **dull**
Hardness	**hard**, soft, depressible
Temperature	warm, **medium**, cool
Odour	strong, moderate, **none**
Acoustic opacity	good, moderate, **poor**

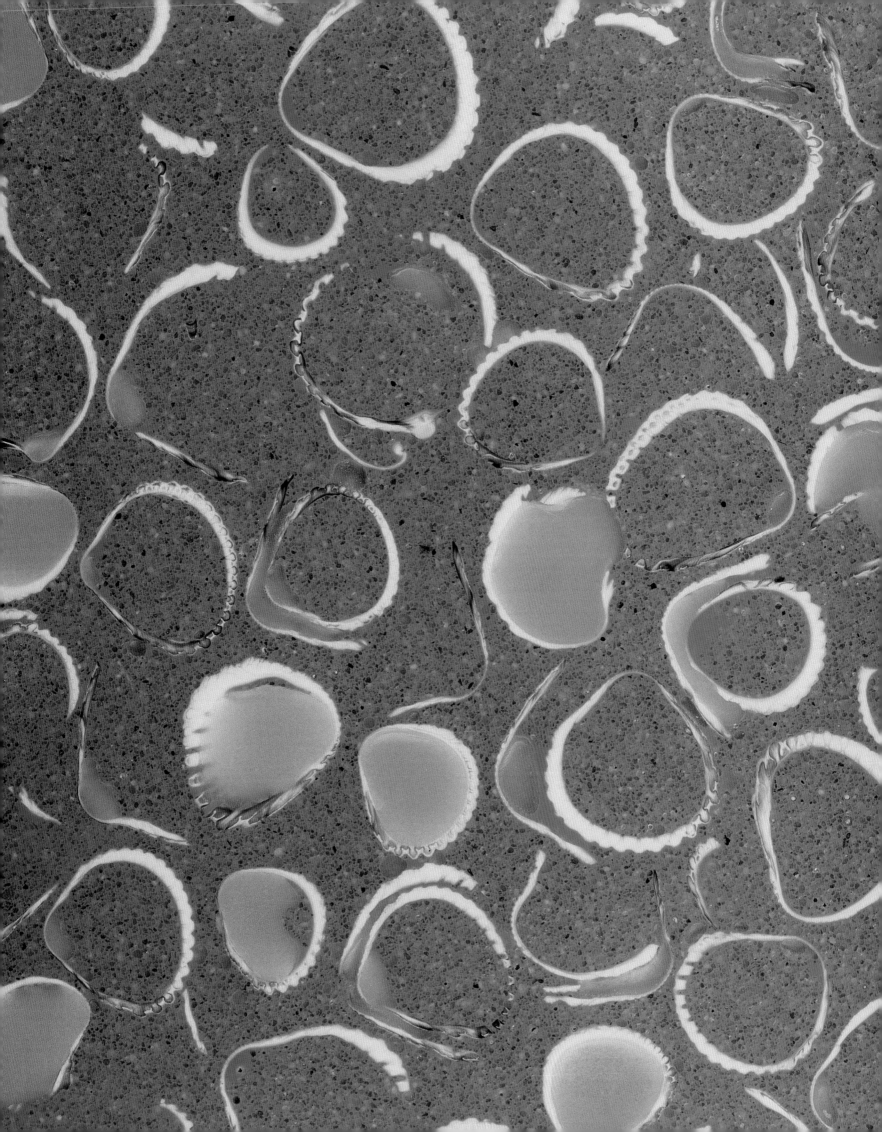

Glass

Glas | Verre | Cristal | Vetro | Glas

The expressionist writer Paul Scheerbart noted in his 1914 manifesto, *Glass Architecture*, 'Glass brings us the new age; brick culture only makes us sad'. In the same year, Scheerbart's kindred spirit, architect Bruno Taut, built his Glass Pavilion for the Werkbund Exhibition in Cologne. Commissioned by the glass industry, its purpose was to demonstrate the possibilities of glass as a building material.

However, it was not only the architects of German Expressionism and the International Style who were fascinated by the idea of glass architecture as an expression of modernity. Glass is still gaining ground as a building material, partly due to constant improvements in its mechanical properties and ever-expanding possibilities in the field of lamination, which mean that glass can now also be used as a structural element.

History

In its most basic form, glass is a natural product: vitreous lava, or obsidian, occurs in the lava from volcano eruptions, although it is translucent rather than transparent. The oldest known objects made of glass are glass pearls dating from around 5000 BC discovered in the Near East. Green glass pearls dating from 3500 BC have been found in the tombs of Egyptian Pharaohs. Objects like rings, vases and small jugs were made by pouring a liquid vitreous mass around a mould made of siliceous clay which was removed once the mass had hardened. The resulting brittle objects, which were sometimes polished and decorated with coloured glass threads, were often richly coloured but had poor transparency. This technique was employed virtually unchanged for some fifteen centuries.

Glass blowing, which made possible the production of hollow glass objects, was invented in Syria in the first century BC and because Syria was part of the Roman Empire, knowledge of this production method eventually spread to Europe. For use in buildings, the Romans made small flat panes of glass by pouring molten glass onto a table. However, the windows made in this manner were intended for only a wealthy few and were not very transparent. Excavations at Pompeii, which was buried in 79 AD, revealed a bronze window with a glass pane measuring approximately 54 x 72 cm, a huge size for that time.

In the Middle Ages window glass was produced by a method that involved inserting a rod into a viscous glob of molten glass and spinning it on its longitudinal axis. The centrifugal force spread the glass outwards into a more or less flat, round disc that was slightly thicker in the middle where the rod had been attached. Small panes were cut out of the disc, or the whole disc was used in uncut form. The central boss gave rise to names like bull's-eye or Butzenscheibe.

Blown Window Glass

In 1330, Philippe de Cacquerrai invented a new production method whereby larger and flatter discs (known as 'crown glass') could be made. A blowpipe was inserted into a glob of molten glass and blown and spun until a sphere with a flattened underside was formed. An iron rod was affixed to the flattened side and the blowpipe cut loose from the round side. Further spinning gave rise first to a goblet-like shape and, ultimately, a flat, round disc of glass. The

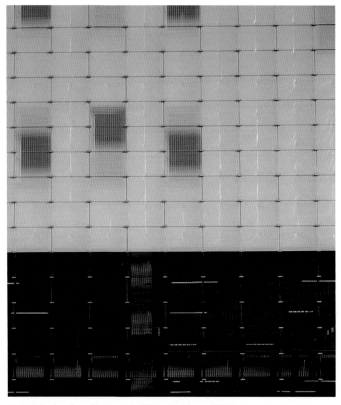

Project Beekpark multipurpose building, Apeldoorn (2002)
Architect Meyer en Van Schooten Architecten bv
Photographer Luuk Kramer

thickening in the middle was much less pronounced compared with that of discs made using the older method. In addition, the new technique made it possible to attain diameters up to 125 cm.

The technique for making another type of disc glass, known as cylinder (or muff) glass, had already been described in the 11th or 12th century by a German monk named Theophilus. It continued to be the principal method for producing sheet glass until the beginning of the 20th century, by which time glass makers were able to blow cylinders measuring two metres long and 30 to 45 centimetres across. Once the cylinder had attained the desired size, the underside was heated and blown open, and the round top portion cut off. After cooling, the cylinder was cut lengthways and flattened in a flattening oven. The result was a large, flat sheet of glass of about one by two metres.

Drawn Window Glass

In response to the construction industry's growing demand for glass and the need for ever larger expanses of glass, experiments with the mechanical production of sheet glass were carried out at the end of the 19th century. In one, an iron rod was used to draw a ribbon of molten glass out of the melting bath. The main difficulty was that the ribbon rapidly turned into a triangle before ending up as a thick thread. In 1901 the Belgian engineer, Emile Gobbe, came up with a solution, which consisted of drawing the ribbon out whilst at the same time pushing it up out of the melting bath from below. Together with glass manufacturer Emile Fourcault, after whom the process was named, Gobbe refined the technique and in 1914, the world's first automated glass factory started operation in Belgium. The Fourcault system employed a slotted block (the debiteuse) of fireproof stone. The block was pressed into the bath of molten glass and an iron rod (or 'bait') was lowered through the slot and then raised again bringing with it a continuous ribbon of glass which was allowed to cool before being cut off at the top of the machine. The

Project Invisible Box multipurpose event space, Istanbul (1999)
Architect GAD Architecture
Photographer GAD Architecture

disadvantages of this method were the undulations caused by the pulling and the stresses that developed in the glass, which made cutting difficult.

The Libby-Owens system, patented in 1905 by an American, Irving G. Colburn, brought improvement. It differed from the Fourcault system in that after rising vertically for about 750 mm, the glass ribbon was bent horizontally over a steel roller. After this the glass travelled through a 60-metre-long annealing oven where cooling took place more slowly. The resulting glass was flatter and easier to cut.

The Pittsburgh process was first employed in 1921 by the Pittsburgh Plate Glass Company in the United States. In this production method, the ribbon of glass was passed through a series of small ribbed asbestos rollers. These were internally cooled by air, which enabled the glass sheet to cool more rapidly outside than inside, which in turn resulted in greater flatness and ease of cutting. The thickness of the glass could be adjusted by varying the speed with which it was passed through the rollers.

In 1959, after more than seven years of research, the English firm, Pilkington, began producing float glass. Float glass, which is produced by a method radically different from those which had pre-

ceded it, effectively consigned to the past all older methods of glass production for architectural applications.

Glass in Architecture

Since the 19th century, glass has become increasingly important as a building material; indeed, numerous glass structures have entered the canon of great architecture. In the 19th century, steel-glass constructions of a hitherto unimaginable lightness were built, like the great Palm House of the Royal Botanic Gardens at Kew by Richard Turner and Decimus Burton (1848), London's Crystal Palace by Joseph Paxton (1851), and Amsterdam's Palace of Industry by Cornelis Outshoorn (1868).

The use of glass as a building material experienced a dramatic upsurge under German Expressionism and international Modernism, not least because of recent technological developments that had made it possible to produce greater quantities of sheet glass more economically and in larger sizes. Important German examples are the Steiff toy factory in Giengen by Richard Steiff (1903, the earliest known use of a glass curtain wall), the AEG Turbine Hall in Berlin by Peter Behrens (1909) and the workshop wing of the Bauhaus in Dessau by Walter Gropius (1926). The Modernist ideals of light, air and space were also well served by glass and examples of its use for International Style buildings included the Van Nelle Factory in Rotterdam by Michiel Brinkman and Leendert van der Vlugt (1930), the Maison de Verre in Paris by Pierre Chareau (1932), and the Lake Shore Drive Apartments in Chicago by Ludwig Mies van der Rohe (1951). The last work, together with other similar American skyscrapers, helped set the worldwide trend for tall buildings with glass façades in the second half of the 20th century.

In the meantime, technological developments in the field of glass products continue. Low-emissivity coatings (transparent coatings with a metallic base) double the heat resistance of glass façades and are expected to become standard for transparent glazing. Together with the increasing integration of glass façades with climate-control systems, this development makes possible extremely energy-efficient

Project Yamanashi Fruit Museum, Yamanashi (1997)
Architect Itsoku Hasegawa
Photographer Jan Derwig

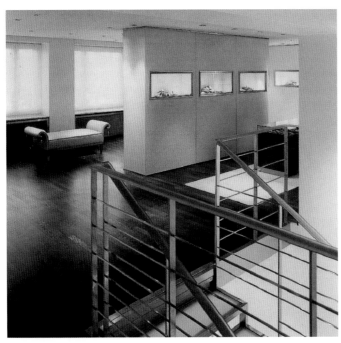

Project Embassy, Luzern (2000)
Architect König Architektur
Photographer Michael Reinhard Photography

buildings. Recent examples are Werner Sobek's R128 residential building in Stuttgart (2000) and Sir Norman Foster's London City Hall (2002).

For the rest, new processes continue to increase the material's strength while possibilities in the field of lamination, which enable it to be used as a structural material, are also growing. Recent examples of buildings in which both the construction and the façade are of glass are Kengo Kuma & Associates' villa in Atami, Japan

(1995), Dirk Jan Postel's Temple de l'Amour garden pavilion in Burgundy, France (2000) and Kruunenberg & Van der Erve's house in the Dutch glass capital Leerdam (2001, commissioned, like Bruno Taut's pavilion, by the glass industry). At present, such structures carry a connotation of daring, but within a few decades all-glass constructions seem set to be commonplace.

Project Laminata, Leerdam (2001)
Architect Kruunenberg & Van der Erve
Photographer Luuk Kramer

Float Glass

Float-Glas | *Verre flotté* | *Cristal producido por flotación* | *Vetro float* | *Float glas*

Project Van Nelle factory, Rotterdam (1931)
Architect J.A. Brinkman, L.C. van der Vlugt
Photographer Jan Derwig

Project Temple de l'Amour, Burgundy (2002)
Architect Dirk Jan Postel, Kraaijvanger . Urbis
Photographer Christian Richters

Float glass was first developed by the English firm of Pilkington, which began producing it in 1959, following a research period of more than seven years. This production process ultimately supplanted virtually all other sources of glass for the construction industry.

Technical Aspects

Although the composition of float glass varies from manufacturer to manufacturer, its basic ingredients are typically oxides of sand (silica), lime and soda. To this are added recycled glass (cullet) and – depending on the application – small quantities of other oxides, such as phosphorus, arsenic, germanium or boron. The ingredients are heated to around 1500 °C in a furnace until they form a molten mass which then flows as a continuous ribbon into a bath of molten tin. Because of the difference in surface tension between the two materials, the molten glass stays afloat on the thin and extremely smooth layer of liquid tin. Hence the term float glass. The glass's thickness is determined, amongst other things, by the speed with which it spreads over the tin. By the time the glass leaves the tin bath it has cooled to around 600 °C and is sufficiently solid to be conveyed on rollers through an annealing tunnel (lehr) where it is carefully cooled to room temperature. Float glass is available in thicknesses ranging from 0.6 to 25 mm. The standard factory dimensions are 3.2 by 6 metres, which is also the largest available size.

Applications

Glass is used in façade openings and as sheet material for open or closed façade panels. It is also used to make interior partition walls, and, in altered form, is employed increasingly as a structural material.

Colour	**none**
Glossiness	**glossy**, satin, matt
Translucence (%)	0 – 20 – 40 – 60 – 80 – **100**
Texture	sharp, medium, **dull**
Hardness	**hard**, soft, depressible
Temperature	warm, **medium**, cool
Odour	strong, moderate, **none**
Acoustic opacity	good, moderate, **poor**

Glass

Additives

Zuschlagstoffe für Glas| Additifs pour verre | Aditivos para cristal | Additivi per il vetro | Toevoegingen aan glas

Glass is made up of a number of mineral ingredients which, after they have melted, cool to form a solid material free of crystallization. It is this absence of a crystalline structure that gives glass its transparency. The same property also causes it to resemble a liquid, albeit one whose room temperature viscosity is so high that it is considered a solid.

Since antiquity, the basic ingredient of glass has been sand, or silica. Quartz was also tried, but this resulted in a product with much poorer transparency. Silica melts at 1700 °C, a temperature which can only be attained with extremely high energy consumption. This melt-

Project Pharmacological research building, Biberach (2002)
Architect Sauerbruch Hutton Architects
Photographer Gerrit Engel

ing point can be reduced through the addition of soda (sodium carbonate) or magnesium. In Western Europe, potash, which is obtained by burning beech or oak wood, was originally used for this purpose. The wood ash was leached and reduced by evaporation, leaving a brown salt which was added to the quartz or sand. Enormous quantities of wood were needed for this method of glass production: 1000 m³ of wood yields a tiny 0.43 m³ of potash. In the 17th century, the German chemist Johann Rudolf Glauber produced a salt (later named after him) which made it possible to avoid the laborious process of potash extraction. However, because it was very costly, it was never used on a large scale for the production of glass. Soda was originally made from natural soda, a by-product of common salt. The great drawback of this method of obtaining soda was the limited availability of natural soda. The first artificial soda was developed by the French surgeon Nicolas Le Blanc in 1790, but it was not until 1885 that a Belgian chemist, Ernest Solvay, achieved full-scale soda production. Soda is still produced using the Solvay process.

In addition to soda, calcium carbonate was added to the mixture in order to make the glass sufficiently hard. The addition of glass fragments (cullet) has a positive effect on the melting process, as they help to conduct the heat from the burners into the mixture. Other additives give glass properties specific to its intended use. These include borosilicate, germanium, phosphorus, arsenic and metals or metal oxides.

Sand itself typically contains small quantities of iron oxide which impart a very slight discolouration to the glass. This can be counteracted through the addition of such substances as potash, arsenic and carbon. If a totally transparent glass is required, the sand can be specially filtered in advance. If, on the other hand, a specific tint is desired, metallic compounds are added to the mix. A wide range of colours can be obtained in this way. Will Alsop's Peckham Library demonstrates how such colours can be used to a fine effect. An alternative method for colouring glass is screen-printing. A particularly colourful example of this technique is Sauerbruch & Hutton's building for Boehringer Ingelheim Pharma in Biberach, Germany.

Project Peckham Library and Media Centre, London (2000)
Architect Alsop Architects
Photographer Alsop Architects

Coloured Glass

Buntglas | Verre coloré | Cristal coloreado | Vetro colorato | Gekleurd glas

Project Funen | Sporenboog, Amsterdam (2003)
Architect Frits van Dongen, de Architekten Cie.
Photographer Jeroen van Amelsvoort

British glass designer Amy Cushing creates fused coloured glass panels suitable for use as interior partition walls. Her starting point is glass in 20 different colours: threads, rods and strips are placed on a clear sheet of glass and then heated, cut, and reheated up to four times in all. The once separate colours give rise to an inexhaustible variety of colour combinations. Cushing's experiments reveal the full potential of coloured glass.

Technical Aspects

Untreated float glass has a light green hue which is the result of a small quantity of iron oxide in the basic mixture. The smaller the angle at which the glass is viewed, the more evident its colour. A wide variety of colours can be achieved by the addition of different metal oxides: iron (green, brown, blue), chrome (green, yellow, pink), cobalt (blue, green, pink), selenium (pink, red), nickel (yellow, purple), manganese (purple), silver or sulphur (amber, brown), copper (blue, green, red). Another, special kind of coloured glass is milk glass which is produced by adding tin oxide to the mixture. Glass can also be given a colour by means of a coating or a thin film.

Applications

Coloured glass can be used for decorative purposes. However, since the early 1970s it has also been used because of its heat-absorbing properties, especially in office buildings. A disadvantage of this application is that the glass keeps out not only the heat of the sun but also a great deal of light. Further development of this application, using coatings and films, has since rendered a perceptible colour unnecessary.

Project Town Hall, Innsbruck (2002)
Architect Dominique Perrault
Photographer Thomas Jantscher

Colour	**variable**
Glossiness	**glossy**, satin, matt
Translucence (%)	0 – 20 – **40** – **60** – **80** – **100**
Texture	sharp, medium, **dull**
Hardness	**hard**, soft, depressible
Temperature	warm, **medium**, cool
Odour	strong, moderate, **none**
Acoustic opacity	good, moderate, **poor**

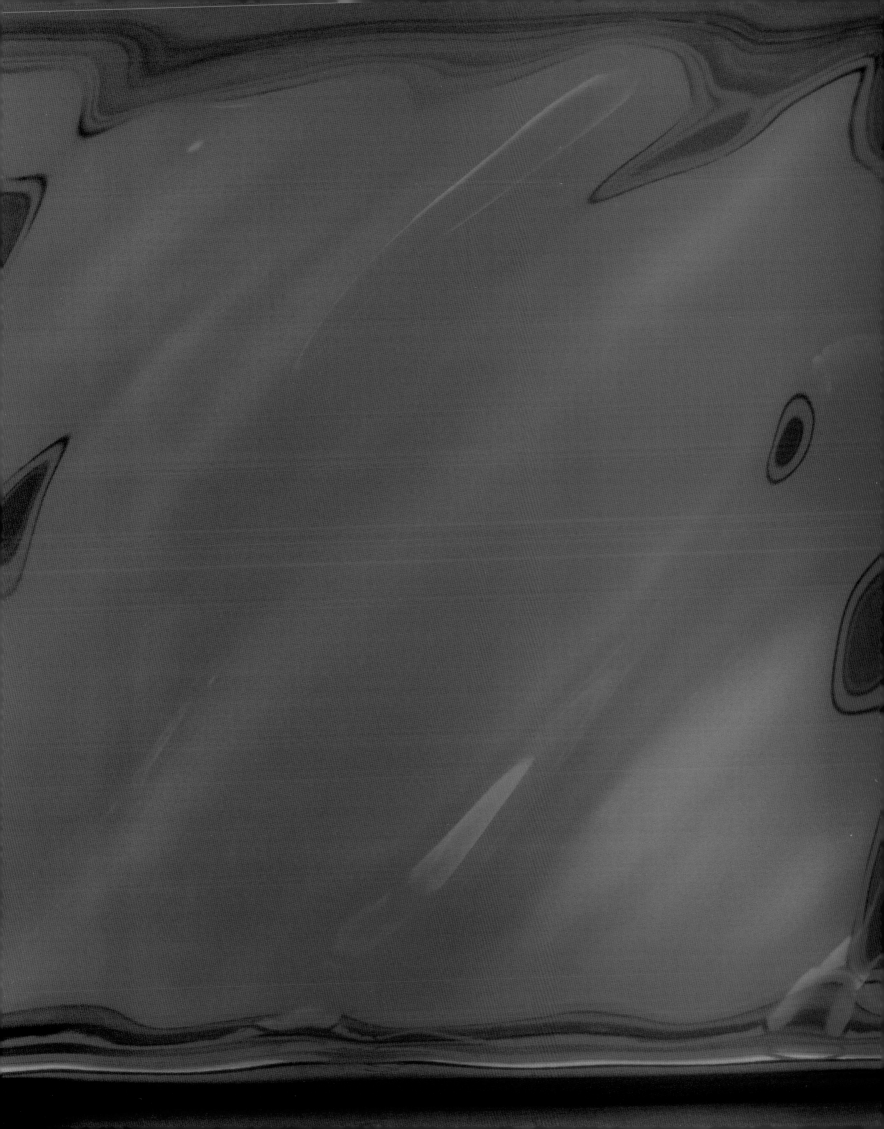

Composites

Verbundglas | Verre composites | Clases de cristal | Compositi del vetro | Samenstellingen van glas

In recent years, most innovations in the field of glass production have involved composites of glass and other materials. These, in turn, have served as the basis for a variety of new products with unique properties. Not only glass composites, but glass laminates, too, have significantly widened the choice of new materials available for architectural applications.

Composites

The term *composite* is now applied so broadly that virtually any building material can be regarded as such. In principle, a composite is a factory-made product consisting of two or more homogeneously

Project Institut du Monde Arabe, Paris (1988)
Architect Jean Nouvel
Photographer Kees Hummel

combined materials. They include fibres of wood, plastic or glass bound together with a synthetic resin, of which MDF and glass fibre reinforced polyester resin are well-known examples. However, other binding agents are also possible. Reinforced and aerated concrete, for example, also qualify as composites. Much development is taking place in the field of glass composites and while its use in the construction industry is at present limited mainly to glass wool, experiments in aerospace and other fields look very promising for future architectural applications. With their combination of light weight and high strength, materials containing glass fibre have great potential.

Laminates

Laminates consist of layers of material glued together with synthetic resin. The field of glass laminates has thrown up a great many new and interesting applications in recent decades and the end of such innovation is not yet in sight. The lamination of sheets of glass and other materials has given rise to an entirely new category of building materials that offer a wide spectrum of structural, physical and aesthetic characteristics. Many of these products have been a source of inspiration to designers. For example, holographic and dichroitic glass have the ability to change their appearance depending on the viewpoint of the observer. Architect–artist James Carpenter exploited this property in pursuit of the dream of many architects an interactive façade. The dichroitic glass in the 30 by 18 metre wall he designed for a busy Manhattan shopping street changes colour in the course of a day and as one walks past it.

It is also possible to include all kinds of 'functional' layers in laminated glass. In photovoltaic glass, photo cells are laminated between two sheets of glass from where they not only generate an electric current, but also provide sun protection for the room behind the glass. Another form of sun protection is glass fibre mats laminated to panes of glass. A relatively new product is LED glass in which electrically conductive transparent film imprinted with LEDs is laminated to glass. The result is a sheet of glass that also functions as a light source.

Laminated glass's greatest potential, however, lies in the constructional field. The combination of toughened glass and lamination produces especially strong and thin glass sheets which are used in partic-

Project 'Think Tank', Bregenz, Austria (2003)
Architect Dorner | Matt Architects
Photographer Glas Marte

ular in frameless glass façades where structural forces are absorbed by holes bored in the glass for the four-point steel connectors. Other possibilities include glass columns and fins for glass façades. Such innovations make it possible to construct buildings almost entirely of glass. A modest but pioneering example is Dirk Jan Postel's garden pavilion, Temple de l'Amour (2002), near Avalon in France. Proof that beautiful results can be attained without using factory-laminated glass is provided by Laminata, a private home in the Dutch glass capital of Leerdam, designed by Kruunenberg Van der Erve. The façades of this unusual house were constructed from thousands of layers of in-situ laminated glass, with liquid resin being used instead of PVB film. The façades vary in thickness: the thicker the wall, the greener and less transparent it becomes. The strength of laminated glass is also utilized for bullet-proof glass in which one of the layers often consists of a sheet of polycarbonate to further augment the glass's strength.

Project Office Amstelveens Vertaalbureau, Amstelveen (1999)
Architect Meyer en Van Schooten Architecten bv
Photographer Luuk Kramer

Wired Glass

Drahtglas I Verre armé I Cristal armado I Vetro retinato I Gewapend glas

Project Borneo Island, Amsterdam (1998)
Architect Heren 5
Photographer Kees Hummel

Although wired glass has traditionally been used as a fire-resistant glazing or for impact resistance purposes, architects are increasingly coming to recognize the aesthetic potential of this material. In the Netherlands, designer Simone de Waart has experimented with the incorporation of various knitted and woven wire meshes (such as those used in the filter industry) in glass, known as Deco Wired Glass.

Technical Aspects

Like float and patterned glass, wired glass is produced in one continuous, fully automated process. Wire mesh made of electrically welded, chemically treated metal is pressed into a molten ribbon of glass with a thin, ridged roller until the netting is completely surrounded by glass after which it is allowed to harden. Not all types of metal are suited for this purpose: it must be an alloy of nickel and iron and have the same coefficient of expansion as the glass. This type of wired glass has only moderate fire-resistant properties. Retardation times vary according to the size of the pane, but the maximum is 30 minutes. Wired glass is available in either rough-cast or polished form. Laminated wired glass (clear or tinted, rough cast or polished) has better fire-resistant properties, providing a retardation time in excess of 60 minutes.

Applications

Wired glass is typically used in single strength. Polished wired glass can be combined with an unwired pane to form insulating glazing, although the durability of such a unit is difficult to predict. Most manufacturers give less than a ten-year guarantee on this combination.

Project Eames House, Pacific Palisades (1949)
Architect Charles Eames
Photographer © 2004 Lucia Eames dba Eames Office (www.eamesoffice.com)

Colour	**variable**
Glossiness	**glossy**, satin, matt
Translucence (%)	0 – 20 – 40 – 60 – **80** – **100**
Texture	sharp, medium, **dull**
Hardness	**hard**, soft, depressible
Temperature	warm, **medium**, cool
Odour	strong, moderate, **none**
Acoustic opacity	good, moderate, **poor**

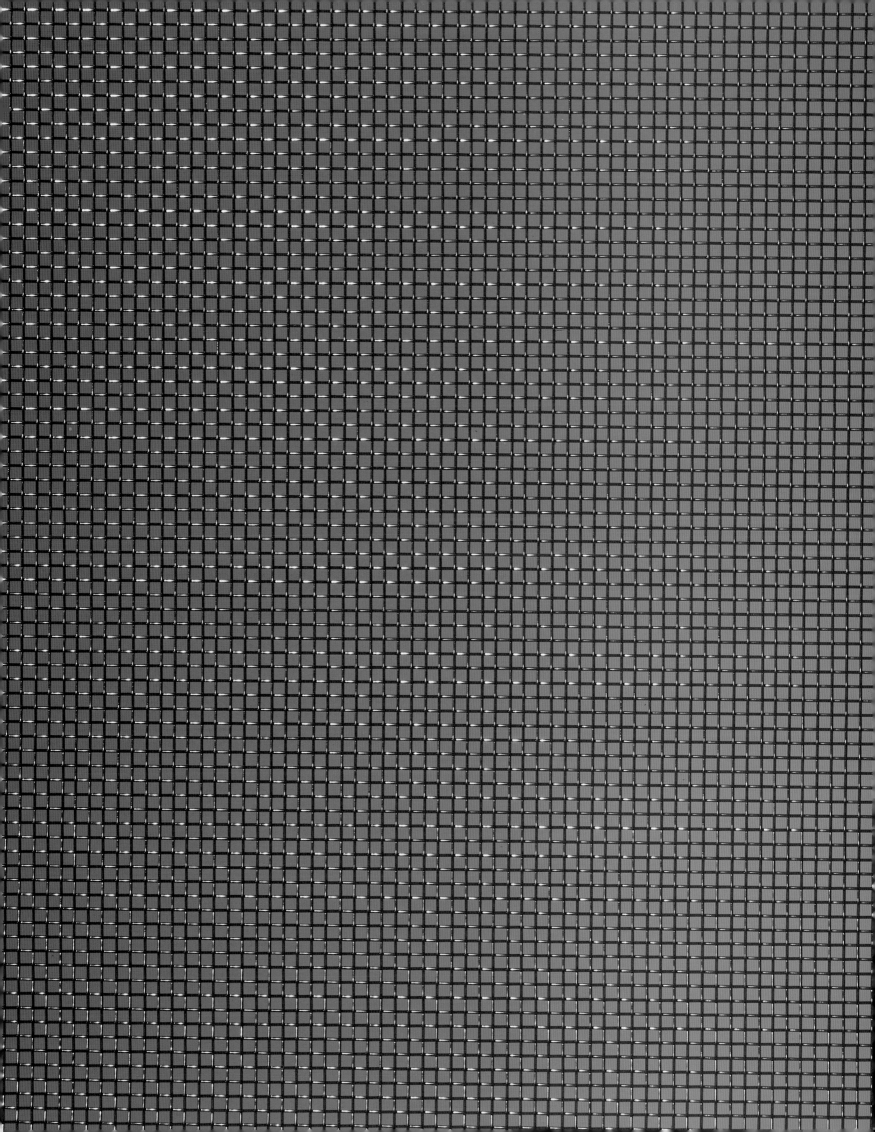

Laminated Glass

Schichtglas | Verre feuilleté | Cristal laminado | Vetro di sicurezza laminato | Gelamineerd glas

Project Media Markt, Almere (2003)
Architect Alsop and Störmer Architects with Glaverbel Solid Glass
Photographer The Media Office | DR Solutia

Laminated glass, the result of bonding several layers of glass, provides protection from impact, burglary or even bullets.

Technical Aspects

For use as safety glass, the glass sheets are usually bonded using PVB (polyvinylbutyral) film: two or more sheets of glass with a film interlayer are rolled and heated. Should such glass happen to break, the shards are held together by the plastic. The thickness of the glass sheets and the number of interlayers can be varied depending on the degree of safety required. It is also possible to replace one of the glass sheets with a sheet of polycarbonate, a material that is highly impact resistant. Using glass with a low iron content ensures that panels remain transparent, despite thicknesses up to 150 mm, as in the case of bullet-proof glass.

Epoxy resin can also be used as a bonding agent; this method is used for applying various functional interlayers such as glass fibre mats (for solar control) or electrically conductive film printed with LEDs (for glass with light-emitting dots.) Laminated glass with decorative interlayers ranging from thin wood veneers or tree leaves to photographic images on a thin film (eg Ilfochrome) is also available, while glass laminated with resin is valued for its sound insulating properties.

Applications

Laminated glass is primarily used in the cases already mentioned. However, toughened laminated glass may in some cases be used as a building material, for example as stability fins in glass façades or glass beams in glass roofs. Another, relatively new, application are laminated glass tubes used as elements in a space frame structure, or as compression bars in so-called tensegrity structures.

Project Arras bus station, Pas-de-Calais, coloured
laminated glass with Vanceva Design interlayers (2003)
Architect Cabinet TRACE, Bertrand Peretz |
Communaut urbaine d'Arras
Photographer Cyrille Dupont | DR Solutia

Colour	variable
Glossiness	**glossy**, **satin**, **matt**
Translucence (%)	0 – 20 – 40 – 60 – 80 – **100**
Texture	sharp, medium, **dull**
Hardness	**hard**, soft, depressible
Temperature	warm, **medium**, cool
Odour	strong, moderate, **none**
Acoustic opacity	good, moderate, **poor**

Vanceva Design by Solutia. Helping make your designs ... distinctive.

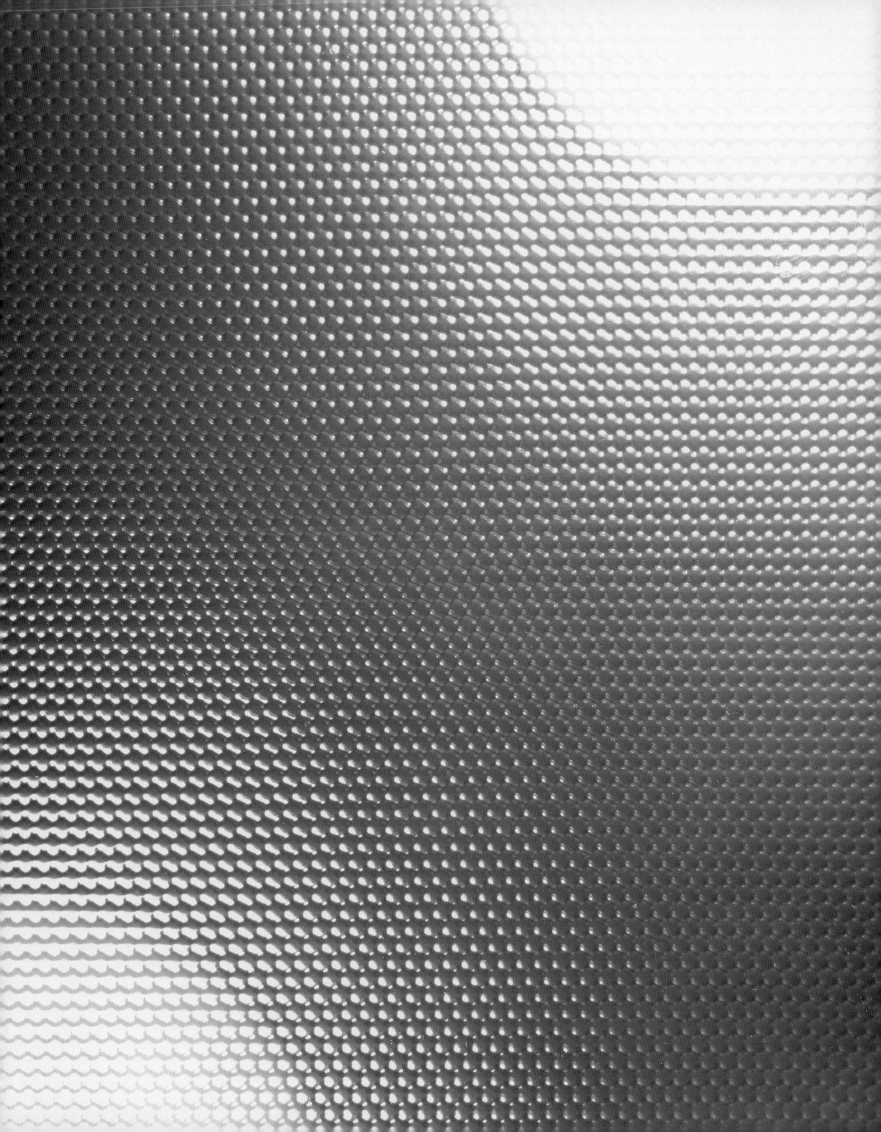

Insulating Glass

Isolierglas | Verre isolant | Cristal aislante | Vetro di d'isolamento | Dubbel glas

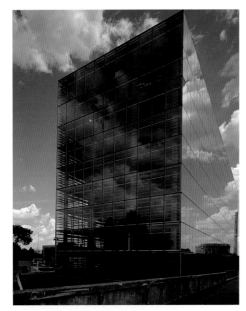

Project Hotel Industriel Berlier, Paris (1990)
Architect Dominique Perrault
Photographers Georges Fessy, ADAGP

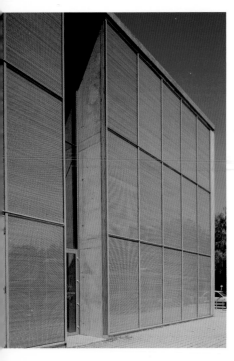

Project Technical High School, Wiesbaden (2002)
Architect Mahler, Günster, Fuchs Architects
Photographer Moshiri for OKALUX

Insulating glass consists of two or three glass plates separated by one or two hermetically sealed cavities. The panes are both connected and held apart by means of spacers. The thermal insulation of this system is far superior to that of single glass panes. The cavities can also be used for a number of functional or decorative additions. A showcase for the decorative possibilities of insulating glass was the Christ Pavilion by Von Gerkan, Marg und Partner at the Hanover Expo 2000, later re-erected in the grounds of Volkenroda Monastery in the German state of Thuringia. The cavities of the glass façade elements are filled with a variety of objects, ranging from tea strainers to sea urchins.

Technical Aspects

The cavities in insulating glass are filled with air or, for even better insulation, gases, such as argon or krypton. Insulation can be further improved by means of a low-emissivity coating on the cavity side of the inner pane. The coating consists of a very thin, usually silver-coloured foil, which minimizes heat exchange between the warm inner pane and the colder outer pane, thus increasing thermal resistance. Yet another method for improving insulation entails creating a vacuum in the cavity, but this technique needs further refinement as the glass panels have a tendency to fracture under the pressure thus created.

Functional additions to the cavity are typically for heat-absorption purposes. Insulating glass is available with cavities containing adjustable aluminium louvres, glass or plastic tubing and a variety of metallic meshes. Such additions are not only functional, but often very decorative as well.

Applications

Insulating glass is used almost exclusively as a thermal insulation for façade openings.

Colour	none
Glossiness	**glossy**, **satin**, **matt**
Translucence (%)	0 – 20 – 40 – 60 – 80 – 100
Texture	sharp, medium, **dull**
Hardness	**hard**, soft, depressible
Temperature	warm, **medium**, cool
Odour	strong, moderate, **none**
Acoustic opacity	good, moderate, **poor**

Photovoltaic Glass

Glas mit Photovoltaikmodulen | Verre photovoltaïque | Cristal fotovoltaico | Vetro per uso fotovoltaico | Fotovoltaisch glas

Project University Research Centre, Erlangen (2000)
Architect University Building Office, Erlangen
Photographer Thomas Dix

It was the physicist Henri Becquerel who discovered that light falling on a combination of materials containing silicon produces electric voltage. Laminating photoelectric cells between two glass plates offers a fascinating variety of applications: the cells not only generate electricity, but can also serve as solar shading for the rooms behind them while at the same time being remarkably decorative.

Technical Aspects

The raw material of solar cells is residual silicon, a waste product from the computer industry. This silicon is melted and moulded into bars which are then cut into wafer-thin sheets. Monocrystalline cells are roughly the size of a tile and are dull black or dark blue in colour. They are extremely efficient, converting around 15 per cent of the available solar energy into electricity. Multicrystalline solar cells, which are also tile size, are light or dark blue in colour and have an efficiency of around 14 per cent. Multicrystalline cells are also available in other colours, including silver, bronze and gold, but these cells have an even lower efficiency rate. Thin-film silicon solar cells consist of coated panels of glass ranging from tile to windowpane size. They are available in brown or black and have and efficiency of around 6 per cent.

Applications

Photovoltaic glass can be used in sun-facing façades or roofs. In addition, it is suitable for movable louvres which turn with the sun and at the same time act as solar shading.

Project Mont-Cenis Academy, Nordrhein-Westfalen (1999)
Architect Jourda Architects | Hegger + Hegger + Schleiff Architects
Photographer Christian Richters

Colour	**variable**
Glossiness	**glossy**, **satin**, **matt**
Translucence (%)	0 – 20 – 40 – 60 – **80** – **100**
Texture	sharp, medium, **dull**
Hardness	**hard**, soft, depressible
Temperature	warm, **medium**, cool
Odour	strong, moderate, **none**
Acoustic opacity	good, moderate, **poor**

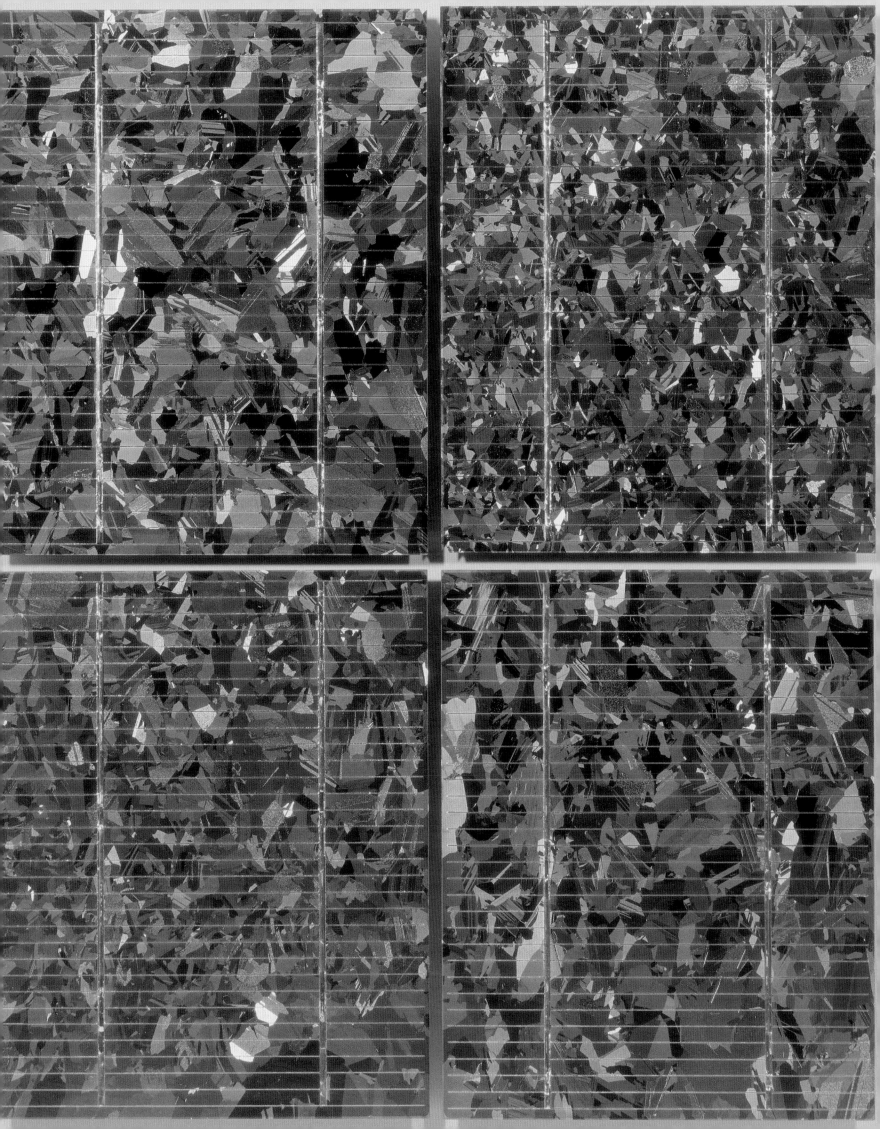

Smart Glass

Smart Glass | Verre intelligent | Cristal inteligente | Vetro 'intelligente' | Smart glas

Project ING Headquarters, Budapest (2003)
Architect Erick van Egeraat Associated Architects
Photographer Christian Richters

Project Renovation 60's flat, Amsterdam (2003)
Artist Stanislaw Lewkovicz
Photographer Jeroen van Amelsvoort

In sunglasses, smart glass that automatically darkens as the sun's intensity increases, is nothing new. Buildings, too, can be fitted with glass whose transmission increases or decreases in response to external factors. As well as light, glass can also be made to react to heat (thermochromic and thermotropic glass) or electricity (electrochromic glass). In addition, several manufacturers produce liquid crystal glazing.

Technical Aspects

Thermotropic glass changes from clear to milky white at a certain temperature. The basic material, which is laminated between two sheets of glass, consists of two different components with a different refractive index, such as water and plastic or two different plastics (a polymer mixture).

Thermochromic glass also reacts to changes in temperature. This product is based on metal oxides (such as vanadium oxide) whose transmission properties change when exposed to heat. As the temperature increases the glass becomes more metallic and reflects sunlight and heat.

Electrochromic glass changes from clear to milky white or darker tinted transparent glass in response to a weak electric current which may be activated, for example, by sensors that react to light intensity. The electrochromic layer consists of a cathode, an anode and an electrolyte. The anode responsible for colour change is often made of tungsten trioxide. The electrolyte is usually made of hydrogen or lithium. A metal oxide which changes in colour along with the anode is often used for the cathode. The colour shift depends on the choice of metal oxides.

Phototropic glass becomes darker as the solar load increases; this is a result of a reverse photochemical conversion triggered by variations in ultraviolet radiation.

Liquid crystal glazing consists of two layers of glass with 'liquid crystal molecules' laminated between them. When exposed to an electric current, all the molecules are aligned allowing light to pass freely through the glass. When the current is turned off, the molecular orientation becomes random, resulting in light diffusion, and the glass changes from clear to milky white.

Applications

Smart Glass is used mainly for solar control purposes, but it is relatively expensive compared with other solar glazing. Liquid crystal glass is used primarily for interior walls as an aid to privacy.

Colour	**variable**
Glossiness	**glossy, satin, matt**
Translucence (%)	0 – **20** – **40** – **60** – **80** – 100
Texture	sharp, medium, **dull**
Hardness	**hard**, soft, depressible
Temperature	warm, **medium**, cool
Odour	strong, moderate, **none**
Acoustic opacity	good, moderate, **poor**

Dichroic Glass

Changeantglas | Verre dichroïque | Cristal dicroico | Vetro dicroico | Dichroïtisch glas

Project Dichroic Light Field in Scottsdale Museum of Contemporary Art, Scottsdale (1999)
Designer/Architect James Carpenter | Will Bruder Architects
Photographer Bill Timmerman

More than 200 laminated glass fins protrude from a 30m x 18m glass façade above a busy Manhattan street. For this project, architect–artist James Carpenter used dichroic glass: a type of glass that changes colour during the course of the day and as one walks past it. Despite the façade's opacity, the glass creates an illusion of depth that serves to dematerialize its solidity.

Technical Aspects

Dichroic glass consists of a sheet of glass which has been given coatings of various metal oxides. These coatings split light into its spectral colours. Depending on the angle of incidence, and thus on the time of day and the observer's viewpoint, some light rays are transmitted while others are reflected, resulting in a range of colours. Using cathode atomization, 10 to 40 layers of the coating can be applied to sheets of glass measuring one square metre. The process is repeated until the desired optical effect has been attained.

Application

Dichroic glass can be used in façade openings. The constantly changing colours it generates can significantly liven up an otherwise neutral interior.

Colour	**variable**
Glossiness	**glossy**, **satin**, **matt**
Translucence (%)	**0 – 20 – 40 – 60 – 80 – 100**
Texture	sharp, medium, **dull**
Hardness	**hard**, soft, depressible
Temperature	warm, **medium**, cool
Odour	strong, moderate, **none**
Acoustic opacity	good, moderate, **poor**

Holographic Glass

Glas mit holographisch-optischen Elementen | Verre holographique | Cristal holográfico | Vetro olografico | Holografisch glas

Project Centre Euralille, Lille (1995)
Architect Jean Nouvel
Photographer Philippe Ruault

Holograms can bundle, diffract and diffuse light, enabling it to be projected further into an interior than is possible with conventional glass. Its advantage compared with other light regulating elements, such as prisms, is that it causes hardly any reduction in radiation intensity. Holographic glass can also be used decoratively for images that change as one walks past them. In addition to the wide range of standard patterns available, it is also possible to reproduce holographs of company logos or pictures.

Technical Aspects

Holographic glass consists of two sheets of glass laminated together with a transparent film interlayer bearing the holographic image. A hologram is a two-dimensional grid which produces a three-dimensional image. Holograms influence the refraction index of light such that a portion of the light falling on them can be directed in a desired direction.

Applications

Holographic glass can be treated in the same manner as other laminated glass products. It can be used in façade openings, but also in glass façades and internal glass partition walls.

Colour	**variable**
Glossiness	**glossy, satin, matt**
Translucence (%)	**0 – 20 – 40 – 60 – 80 – 100**
Texture	sharp, medium, **dull**
Hardness	**hard**, soft, depressible
Temperature	warm, **medium**, cool
Odour	strong, moderate, **none**
Acoustic opacity	good, moderate, **poor**

Methods of Working Glass

Glasbearbeitung | Méthode d'ouvrage de vitrages | Métodos para trabajar el vidrio | Tecniche di lavorazione del vetro | Bewerkingen van glas

Although its high silicon content makes glass a very strong material, it does not lend itself to plastic deformation. The slightest overstepping of its low elastic deformation limit immediately results in breakage. This is due to the absence of a crystalline structure, a deficiency to which glass owes its transparency but which also results in a lack of strong internal cohesion. When a crack develops, the material is consequently unable to compensate for it.

These properties of glass limit the number of ways in which solid glass can be worked. An extremely sharp instrument is needed to cut a sheet of glass, as any irregularities in the cut surface can lead to

Project French National Library, Paris (1995)
Architect Dominique Perrault
Photographer Georges Fessy, ADAGP

breakage. Cutting is often carried out at a precisely calculated angle using oil-filled cutters fitted with a small wheel of hardened steel. Diamond cutters are used mainly for straight lines. In the Middle Ages, this was done with die cutters which were heated before being drawn across the glass.

Engraving and Grinding

Engraving and grinding are the oldest methods for working glass, and date back to well before the Christian era. With both these techniques, a glass plate is worked by means of scratching. Today, this is done using a steel needle tipped with diamond grid. For grinding, the needle revolves; for engraving, it vibrates. Both crafts are still practised, but due to their labour-intensive character are not suited to industrial production and are only rarely used in the construction industry. Another very labour-intensive technique is that used in the production of stained glass, in which designs are painted on panes of glass and then fired in an oven so that they fuse with the glass. Stained glass has been used since the 13th century, chiefly in church building. The practise of mounting the glass panes in a lead frame derived from the fact that the maximum possible size of the panes was only a fraction of the size of the huge Gothic windows designed by mediaeval architects. Leaded stained glass continued to be regularly used in this way until the early 20th century when it experienced its last large-scale revival in the architecture of Art Nouveau, the Wiener Werkstätte and the Arts and Crafts movement. Victor

Horta, Josef Hoffman and Charles Rennie Mackintosh are only a few of the many designers who regarded stained glass as an essential component of architecture. However, this kind of glass has since priced itself out of the market because of its labour-intensive production method.

Etching

Another rarely used glass-working technique is etching, whereby a decorative design is applied in several stages to a sheet of glass with the help of hydrofluoric acid. In the construction industry, glass etching was especially popular in the nineteenth century and the first half of the twentieth century. Today the technique has all but died out and etched glass has been effectively supplanted by sandblasted glass. The result is comparable, but the process less time-consuming. In this method, a glass plate is selectively coated with adhesive oil after which the uncoated areas are pressure sprayed with a fine abrasive material. Originally sand was used, but nowadays finer aluminium oxide is often used instead. As with etched glass, sandblasting results in a matt surface.

Deformations

Because of its innate brittleness, almost any deformation of glass requires it to be first heated in a furnace until the deformation point of approximately 630 °C is attained. At this temperature it is plastic and can be moulded into any shape at all. Many deformations, both those limited to the material's surface (patterned glass) and those of a three-dimensional nature (glass profiles), are today carried out immediately after the basic glass manufacturing process and before the glass has cooled. As such, they are as much standard products as sheet glass. In thermally bent glass, however, the starting point is a fully cooled sheet of glass and this is reflected in the cost. When only slight deformations are required, a glass plate can be bent or twisted in the cold state. Erick van Egeraat's Town Hall at Alphen aan de Rijn in the Netherlands demonstrates the impressive results that can be attained in this manner with large glass surfaces.

Project KPN Telecom Office Tower, Rotterdam (2000)
Architect Renzo Piano Building Workshop
Photographer Sjaak Henselmans

Project City hall, Alphen aan de Rijn (2002)
Architect Erick van Egeraat Associated Architects
Photographer Christiaan Richters

Foam Glass

Schaumglas I Verre cellulaire : 'foamglas' I Espuma de vidrio I Vetro multicellulare I Geschuimd glas

Project Zaaneiland apartments, Zaandam (1997)
Architect Rudy Uytenhaak Architects
Photographer Rudy Uytenhaak Architects

Foam (or cellular) glass has been used as a thermal insulation material in the building industry for more than 50 years, but until recently it led a largely invisible existence, hidden behind the façade or beneath the roofing. Faced with a glass screen, however, the material can be exposed to excellent effect, a fine example being the apartment complex in Zaandam designed by Rudy Uytenhaak.

Technical Aspects

Foam glass is black or grey in colour and contains innumerable airtight cells. It is composed of a mixture of pulverized glass and carbon which is heated to a temperature exceeding 1000 °C. When the carbon oxidizes, foam is produced. The carbon molecules contain a very small quantity of sulphide contamination. Sulphide has a low olfactory threshold, giving foam glass a slight (but innocuous) sulphurous odour. Foam glass contains 66% recycled glass, obtained, amongst other things, from old car windshields and the greenhouse construction industry. Foam glass panels are completely impervious to water and vapour.

Application

Foam glass is used primarily as a thermal insulation material. It has a very high compressive strength, making it suitable for applications subject to high loads. For this reason, it is often used as a thermal break in a structural façade element or as an insulation material on flat roofs. Although completely waterproof, the glass cannot be used unprotected in façades, as the open cells on its surface are not frostproof. Foam glass is significantly more costly than other types of insulating panels.

Colour	**black**, **grey**
Glossiness	glossy, satin, **matt**
Translucence (%)	**0** – 20 – 40 – 60 – 80 – 100
Texture	**sharp**, **medium**, dull
Hardness	**hard**, soft, depressible
Temperature	**warm**, medium, cool
Odour	**strong**, moderate, none
Acoustic opacity	**good**, moderate, poor

Glass Wool | Glass Fibre

Glaswolle (Glasfaser) | Fibre de verre | Lana de vidrio (fibra de vidrio) | Lana di vetro (Fibra di vetro) | Glaswol

Project Minerva housing project, Arnhem (2001)
Architect Meyer en Van Schooten Architecten bv
Photographer Luuk Kramer

In the vast majority of cases, insulation materials like glass wool are no longer visible once a building has been completed. An exception to this is the Vaktechnisch Lyceum in Utrecht, the Netherlands, the façade of which was designed by Erick van Egeraat Architects.
A glass screen over the entire building leaves visible the façade insulation material, in this case rock wool. A splendid idea, but not without problems, since it turns out that the insulation material is prone to soiling.

Technical Aspects

Glass wool is yellow in colour. It is made by melting (sometimes recycled) glass granules, sand, limestone and soda ash into molten glass which is then fed into a rapidly rotating steel dish pierced with fine holes. Centrifugal force pushes the molten glass out through the holes, producing long glass fibres. Using synthetic resins as a binding agent, the fibres are then formed into mats. Aluminium laminate applied to one side of the mat gives the glass wool its vapour-resistant qualities.

Application

Glass wool is used as an insulation material for façades. Although its softness means that it can also be used for curved façades, the same quality normally prevents it from being used in situations where it is required to absorb pressure. For such purposes there is a special variant in which the slab is cut into strips and turned through 90 degrees so that the fibres lie at right angles to the insulation surface, making the resulting slab rigid and stable. This material is suitable for flat roofs. Another glass wool variant, intended for façades, consists of both hard and soft material. The soft side provides optimal coverage, while the hard side presents a taut surface for finishing.

Colour	**yellow**
Glossiness	glossy, satin, **matt**
Translucence (%)	**0** – 20 – 40 – 60 – 80 – 100
Texture	**sharp**, medium, dull
Hardness	hard, **soft, depressible**
Temperature	**warm**, medium, cool
Odour	strong, moderate, **none**
Acoustic opacity	**good**, moderate, poor

Enamelled and Screen-printed Glass

Email- und Siebdruckglas | *Verre emmaillé et imprimé* | *Cristal esmaltado y serigrafiado* | *Vetro smaltato e serigrafato* | *Geëmailleerd en gezeefdrukt glas*

Project In Holland university, Rotterdam (2000)
Architect Erick van Egeraat Associated Architects
Photographer Christiaan Richters

Enamel is a vitreous material which can be applied to standard float glass. The technique of enamelling, which predates the Christian era, was originally applied to precious metals in the making of jewellery.

Technical Aspects

Enamel is composed of feldspar (alkali aluminium silicate), quartz, borax, soda and various compounds containing fluorine. These substances are fused at 1300 °C. The resulting molten mass is cooled rapidly, causing granules or 'frit', to form. After the addition of water, the frit is ground to form a liquid enamel sludge that is applied to one side of a glass plate. The glass is heated in a furnace and cooled rapidly. The result is toughened glass with enamel fused to its surface. The enamel can also be sprayed on or applied by means of screen printing. The latter process makes it possible to apply screen patterns and a variety of decorative designs to the surface of the glass in addition to areas of colour. Most enamels have poor weather resistance and, for this reason, are applied to the inner side of the glass. However, if the enamel layer is given a transparent pyrolitic coating it can also be applied to the outer side.

Applications

Enamelled glass is mostly used for the spandrel panels in glass façades in order to hide the underlying construction. Because of its decorative effect, screen-printed glass is often used as heat-absorbing glass, even though other glass materials are better suited for this purpose. Of course, it is also used in façades for purely decorative reasons.

Project Stockley Park Offices, Uxbridge (1989)
Architect Foster and Partners
Photographer Richard Davies

Colour	variable
Glossiness	**glossy**, **satin**, **matt**
Translucence (%)	0 – 20 – 40 – 60 – 80 – 100
Texture	sharp, medium, **dull**
Hardness	**hard**, soft, depressible
Temperature	warm, **medium**, cool
Odour	strong, moderate, **none**
Acoustic opacity	good, moderate, **poor**

Mirror Glass

Spiegelglas | Verre de miroir | Luna de espejo | Vetro argentato | Spiegelglas

Project Fine Arts Museum, Lille (1997)
Architect Jean-Marc Ibos & Myrto Vitart
Photographer Ludwig Abache

Project Metamorphose, Deventer (1996)
Architect I'M Architects
Photographer Dick Bouwmeester

Mirror glass is not much used for façades. The mirror effect of some glass façades is often a side effect of a coating with a quite different purpose, such as solar control. However, spectacular effects can be achieved with reflective façades, an excellent example being the Musée des Beaux-Arts in Lille, by Jean-Marc Ibos and Myrto Vitart. Here, the existing, half-finished museum building in Beaux-Arts style is mirrored in the rectangular modern extension, whose huge glass façade is made up of innumerable tiny mirrors, thereby permitting a belated realization of the symmetry designed by the original architects but never implemented.

Technical Aspects

The origins of mirror glass are to be found in Venice, where small mirrors were already being made in 1317. In the 16th century, it became possible to make mirrors from flat glass, using a backing of mercury and tin. Today, mirror glass is made by coating a sheet of glass with stannous chloride solution. This coating serves as a base for the reflective layer which consists of a mixture of silver nitrate, ammonia, caustic soda and distilled water and is only 0.01mm thick. Once this layer is dry, an extra coating can be added as protection for the reflective layer.

Applications

Mirror glass can be used for façades and for interior walls. It can also be used in glass mosaics, optionally in combination with coloured glass. The English artist, Rebecca Newnham, creates a range of mirrors suitable for architectural applications, such as small mirror mosaic tiles for bathroom and kitchen walls.

Colour	variable
Glossiness	**glossy**, satin, matt
Translucence (%)	0 – **20** – **40** – **60** – **80** – 100
Texture	sharp, medium, **dull**
Hardness	**hard**, soft, depressible
Temperature	warm, **medium**, cool
Odour	strong, moderate, **none**
Acoustic opacity	good, moderate, **poor**

Toughened Glass

Sicherheitsglas | Verre trempé | Cristal reforzado | Vetro di sicurezza temprato | Gehard glas

Project ING Group Headquarters, Amsterdam (2002)
Architect Meyer en Van Schooten Architecten bv
Photographer Georges Fessy, ADAGP

Glass is a very hard material but its low deformation limit also makes it exceedingly brittle. Its mechanical properties can be improved, however, by a process known as toughening or tempering.

Technical Aspects
Glass can be toughened by either thermal or chemical means. With the thermal method, glass is heated in a furnace to about 650 °C, and then cooled rapidly with cold air so that its surface and edges shrink, giving rise to permanent compressive stress there. The allowable tensile stress of such toughened (or tempered) glass, is approximately four times as great as that of normal float glass. If glass only needs to be pre-stressed to enable it to absorb thermal stress, it is heat-strengthened rather than toughened. With this method, cooling takes place at a slower rate, yielding a tensile strength approximately twice that of normal float glass. The disadvantage of thermal toughening is that it results in a slightly wavy surface.

With chemical toughening, the glass is immersed in a salt solution containing potassium ions. Although the surface remains very smooth and flat with this method, it is more expensive than thermally toughened glass. Moreover, since the chemical action does not penetrate as deeply into the glass, irregularities in the glass's structure are more likely to lead to cracks. Chemical toughening does however result in greater dimensional accuracy, allowing it to be used for laminated curved surfaces.

Applications
Toughened glass is used in situations where the mechanical load is greater than normal, as in frameless façades or in applications in which glass plays a structural role. In the latter case, the glass is usually also laminated.

Project Schermerweg, Alkmaar (1999)
Architect Min2 bouw-kunst
Photographer Min2 bouw-kunst

Colour	**none**
Glossiness	**glossy, satin, matt**
Translucence (%)	**0 – 20 – 40 – 60 – 80 – 100**
Texture	sharp, medium, **dull**
Hardness	**hard**, soft, depressible
Temperature	warm, **medium**, cool
Odour	strong, moderate, **none**
Acoustic opacity	good, moderate, **poor**

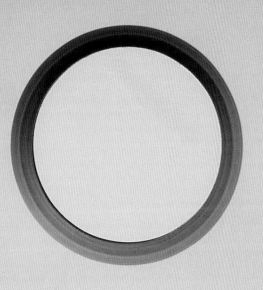

Curved Glass

Gewölbtes Glas | Verre bombé | Cristal curvado | Vetro curvato | Gebogen glas

Project Palais de Congres, Tours (1994)
Architect Jean Nouvel
Photographer Philippe Ruault

Project Tropenpunt Mauritskade, Amsterdam (2002)
Architect Erick van Egeraat Associated Architects
Photographer Christian Richters

Curved or bent glass offers a range of possibilities for the sculptural designing of glass façades and roofs. With relatively few distortions, spectacular curves or even twists are realizable for large surfaces. A fine example of this is the town hall at Alphen aan de Rijn by Erick van Egeraat Architects.

Technical Aspects

A sheet of glass can be bent when it reaches its softening point around 600 °C. At this temperature, the glass automatically assumes the form of the mould on which it is lying; it is then cooled. Where a large bending radius is involved, the glass is pressed into the mould with a countermould. If required, the glass can be pre-stressed by cooling it rapidly but otherwise it is essential that it be cooled slowly in order to avoid the formation of internal stresses. If the glass is then to be laminated, the component sheets are bent together to ensure that the curves are perfectly uniform. An alternative to the costly thermal bending process is so-called cold bent glass, i.e., thin, usually chemically toughened flat glass sheets which are bent in situ in aluminium profiles. In this case, though, only a modest radius is attainable. When a double glazed version is used, an inner sheet of acrylic plastic or polycarbonate may be added out of safety considerations.

Applications

Curved glass can be used in windows, glass façades and roofs.

Colour	**variable**
Glossiness	glossy, **satin**, **matt**
Translucence (%)	0 – 20 – 40 – 60 – **80** – **100**
Texture	sharp, medium, **dull**
Hardness	**hard**, soft, depressible
Temperature	warm, **medium**, cool
Odour	strong, moderate, **none**
Acoustic opacity	good, moderate, **poor**

Broken Glass

Gebrochenes Glas | Verre cassé | Cristal decorado roto | Vetro frantumato | Gebroken glas

Project Collingwood, London (1999)
Designer Yorgos
Photographer Jeff Roper

British glass artist George Papadopoulos makes attractive and interesting glass panels for architectural applications by sandblasting broken glass of different colours. His method exploits the decorative possibilities of the different crack patterns of both ordinary and toughened glass. Mass-produced broken-glass panels are also available which exploit the regular crack pattern of toughened glass.

Technical Aspects
Commercial broken glass panels consist of three layers of laminated toughened glass, the middle layer of which is broken. This layer shatters into small, regularly formed glass granules, rather than large fragments. The outer glass panes hold the broken glass together. A single hit with a hammer on the panel's side is sufficient to produce extensive break patterns. If the middle layer is made of standard float glass, the result is isolated lines of fracture across the glass panel.

Applications
The crack pattern of toughened glass causes it to lose its transparency either partially or entirely, whilst its translucency remains undiminished. As with milk glass, this makes it suitable for situations where both light and privacy are required. Broken glass panels can also be used for purely decorative purposes.

Project Zwitserleven Building, Amsterdam (1997)
Architect Pi de Bruijn, de Architekten Cie.
Photographer Brakkee & Scagliola

Colour	**none**
Glossiness	**glossy**, **satin**, **matt**
Translucence (%)	0 – 20 – **40** – **60** – 80 – 100
Texture	sharp, medium, **dull**
Hardness	**hard**, soft, depressible
Temperature	warm, **medium**, cool
Odour	strong, moderate, **none**
Acoustic opacity	good, moderate, **poor**

Figured Glass

Ornamentglas | Verre imprimé | Cristal decorado figurado | Vetro olofano | Figuurglas

Project Météor or Bercy, Paris (1996)
Architect Kohn & Associés
Photographer Kees Hummel

Patterned or figured glass is glass with a deformed surface. Such deformations are often used for decorative purposes, but they also cause the light falling on the glass to be transmitted in a diffuse manner. The degree of diffusion depends on the pattern used. Patterned glass is available in many different standard patterns, but it is also possible to use texts, logos or pictures of one's own choosing. A special type of patterned glass known as wired patterned glass, is made by adding wire netting while the glass is still molten. Curved or coloured glass panels are also possible.

Technical Aspects

The manufacture of cast glass is, like that of float glass, a largely automated process. The glass is heated to about 1200 °C and then passed between two water-cooled rollers, one or both of which have a pattern which is imprinted in the glass. During this process, the temperature of the glass drops to around 600 °C. Further cooling takes place gradually in the cooling tunnel, to prevent the formation of internal stresses. In the past, patterned glass was made by placing a sheet of glass over a mould and heating it until it softened sufficiently to take on the form of the mould. This is why patterned glass is still sometimes known as cast glass. However, this production method is rarely used nowadays for architectural applications.

Applications

Figured glass is used primarily for partition walls in interiors and façade panels in exteriors.

Project Odeon Cinemas, London (1998)
Architect/Designer Wolf Ollins | Black Dog Films | Fusion Glass Designs Ltd.
Photographer Philip Vile

Project Fusion Glass figured glass in interior Exxon Mobil, London (2000)
Architect Hok International Ltd.
Photographer Philip Vile

Colour	**variable**
Glossiness	glossy, **satin**, **matt**
Translucence (%)	0 – **20** – **40** – **60** – 80 – 100
Texture	sharp, **medium**, dull
Hardness	**hard**, soft, depressible
Temperature	warm, **medium**, cool
Odour	strong, moderate, **none**
Acoustic opacity	good, moderate, **poor**

Glass Blocks

Glasbausteine | Bloc de verre | Hormigón traslúcido o pavés | Blocchi di vetro | Glazen bouwstenen

Project Maison de Verre, Paris (1932)
Architect Pierre Chareau & Bernard Bijvoet
Photographer Kees Hummel

Glass blocks have been in use since the early 20th century. A particularly well-known and rigorous application is the Maison de Verre (1932) in Paris, by Pierre Chareau and Bernard Bijvoet, where the façades are constructed entirely of glass blocks.

Technical Aspects

To produce glass blocks, molten glass is cooled to around 1200 °C. The doughy mass is then pressed into half-block moulds. A glass block is formed by pressing two halves against each other; the connecting surfaces are heated so that they fuse. Further cooling causes a partial vacuum in the hollow interior space, resulting in a very robust unit. Condensation in the hollow space is impossible. Glass blocks are available in various sizes, shapes and colours and in a range of surface finishes. The blocks transmit around 75 per cent of the light falling on them. They can be joined using cement mortar, lightweight concrete or sealant in combination with a special frame. Glass blocks can also be delivered to the construction site in prefabricated panels.

Applications

Glass blocks can be used for interior and exterior walls, both flat and curved. The most widely used surface finishes yield blocks with minimal transparency, making them extremely suitable for applications where both light penetration and privacy are important. Glass block floors are typically used in situations where daylight must be delivered to the rooms below without compromising the floor's load bearing capacity.

Project Expansion Academy of Maastricht (1993)
Architect Wiel Arets
Photographer Kim Zwarts

Colour	**variable**
Glossiness	glossy, **satin**, **matt**
Translucence (%)	0 – 20 – 40 – **60** – **80** – 100
Texture	sharp, medium, **dull**
Hardness	**hard**, soft, depressible
Temperature	warm, **medium**, cool
Odour	strong, moderate, **none**
Acoustic opacity	good, **moderate**, poor

Sandblasted and Etched Glass

Sandgestrahltes und geätztes Glas I Verre décapé par jet de sable et gravé à l'acide I Cristal esmerilado y grabado I Vetro sabbiato e vetro trattato con incisione chimica I Gezandstraald en geëtst glas

Project Sporenburg, Amsterdam (2001)
Architect Rapp & Rapp
Photographer Kees Hummel

Project Town Hall, Innsbruck (2002)
Architect Dominique Perrault (in cooperation with Peter Kogler)
Photographer Roland Halbe

Glass surfaces can be given a matt finish by means of sandblasting or etching. With the help of stencils, the same techniques can also be used to decorate glass with all sorts of patterns. With sandblasting, not only smooth surfaces, but also recesses and depressions are possible.

Technical Aspects

Etching is done by bringing a glass surface into contact with an acid. The degree of mattness corresponds to the duration of the treatment. The longer the treatment, the coarser the surface becomes. Transparency decreases as the coarseness increases, causing light passing through the glass to be refracted. The contours of an object located directly behind the glass are clearly recognizable, but the further the object is moved from it, the more indistinct its contours become. In the case of sandblasting, sand and air are blown against glass, resulting in tiny scratches. Today, such surfaces are coated in order to protect them from greasy fingers. As a result, etched glass has become a substitute for sandblasted glass because its maintenance is much easier.

Applications

Sandblasted and etched glass are employed primarily for purposes of privacy or decoration, especially in the windows of private rooms that adjoin public areas.

Colour	**variable**
Glossiness	**glossy, satin, matt**
Translucence (%)	0 – **20** – **40** – **60** – **80** – 100
Texture	sharp, **medium**, dull
Hardness	**hard**, soft, depressible
Temperature	warm, **medium**, cool
Odour	strong, moderate, **none**
Acoustic opacity	good, **moderate**, poor

Madras® by Vitreal Specchi is chemically etched glass, compatible with all the mechanical and heat processes such as tempering, bending, laminating etc.

Channel Shaped Glass

U-Profilglas | Verre cannelé | Cristal acanalado | Vetro scanalato | Glazen bouwprofielen

Project Museum of Art, Winterthur (1995)
Architect Gigon & Guyer
Photographer Heinrich Helfenstein

U-shaped glass sections were originally used primarily in industrial buildings, but ever since Rem Koolhaas began using them on a large scale in the early 1990s, for example in the Kunsthal in Rotterdam and the Grand Palais in Lille, they have been increasingly used in public buildings, offices and even apartments. The advantages of this kind of glass are indeed considerable: large expanses of external glazing can be achieved with them at a far lower cost than with conventional glazing of the same dimensions. Spans in excess of five metres are possible without additional support.

Technical Aspects

As the ribbon of molten glass emerges from the oven it is pressed into a mould, so that its edges are bent at an angle of 90 degrees. Channel shaped glass is normally green in colour and translucent, with a coarse surface texture, although smooth and transparent surfaces are also possible. Wire may be added to the molten glass, resulting in wired channel shaped glass. The glass channels are fitted into an aluminium frame and fixed with a silicone sealant. Where the double glazed version is used, additional materials can be inserted into the cavity in order to improve its thermal, acoustic or solar control properties. Because the cavity between two glass channels does not have a completely dry and air-tight seal (unlike conventional double glazing), openings for letting in dryer outside air must be included in order to prevent condensation.

Applications

Channel shaped glass is used for façade openings and in large external walls. In its normal non-transparent form it is very suitable for private rooms adjoining public areas.

Project Kunsthal, Rotterdam (1992)
Architect Rem Koolhaas, OMA
Photographer Kees Hummel

Colour	**green**
Glossiness	glossy, **satin**, **matt**
Translucence (%)	0 – **20** – **40** – **60** – 80 – 100
Texture	sharp, **medium**, dull
Hardness	**hard**, soft, depressible
Temperature	warm, **medium**, cool
Odour	strong, moderate, **none**
Acoustic opacity	good, **moderate**, poor

Crystallized Glass

Kristallglas| Verre de cristal | Cristal adornado en cuarzos | Cristallo | Gekristalliseerd glas

Project Concert Hall extension, Amsterdam (1988)
Architect Pi de Bruijn, de Architekten Cie.
Photographer Kees Hummel

Crystallized glass is a Japanese invention which came on the market in 1974. Although made of glass, it is opaque. It is reminiscent of natural stone, but is glossier and smoother and has a more consistent texture. It is also stronger and more resistant to weathering than marble or granite.

Technical Aspects

Raw materials, including silica, feldspar, calcium carbonate, zinc oxide and barium carbonate, are mixed and then melted at a temperature of approximately 1500 °C. The molten glass is immersed in water, resulting in granulated glass with particles one to seven millimetres in diameter. The material is then placed in refractory forms and heated in a furnace to approximately 1100 °C. As soon as the heated glass particles have fused, numerous needle-shaped crystals begin to form around the particle boundaries. The panels are ground prior to being cut to standard dimensions. The panels can be reheated to facilitate bending.

Applications

Crystallized glass comes in the standard colours of white, grey, beige, brown, pink and blue. The maximum panel size is 900 x 1200 x 15mm. In addition to being used as cladding for façades and interior walls, it can also be used as a floor covering or worktop surface. It can also be bent, making it highly suitable as a facing for columns.

Project Nationale Nederlanden, Rotterdam (1992)
Architect Abe Bonnema
Photographer Charles Vermeulen

Colour	**variable**
Glossiness	**glossy**, **satin**, **matt**
Translucence (%)	**0** – 20 – 40 – 60 – 80 – 100
Texture	sharp, medium, **dull**
Hardness	**hard**, soft, depressible
Temperature	warm, **medium**, cool
Odour	strong, moderate, **none**
Acoustic opacity	good, moderate, **poor**

Mosaic Glass

Mosaikglas I Verre mosaïque I Mosaico de cristal I Vetro mosaico I Glasmozaïek

Project Commercial College, Shiba (1995)
Architect Teresa Reklewska & Witraze SC
Photographer Takashi Inoguchi

Project Glass mosaic in bedroom Juna Mahal Palace, Dungapur (13th century)
Photographer Thomas Dix

Mosaics are an extremely ancient form of wall and floor decoration. The oldest known example dates from around 1600 BC and was found in a Chaldean palace in the Sumerian city of Uruk, now Warka, Iraq. The art of mosaic making came to Europe around 325 BC as a result of the conquests of Alexander the Great. The Roman and Byzantine mosaic traditions were further refined by the Moors who made mosaics by pouring a gypsiferous binding agent between stone strips. Pieces of coloured glass, small stones or even precious metals were then pressed into the 'cement'. Today, figurative or geometric glass mosaics are still a very popular type of wall decoration, although their labour-intensive production makes them fairly expensive. A far less costly alternative is the factory-made product in which small glass tiles are glued to mats, giving an exceptionally regular result.

Technical Aspects

Glass mosaics are generally made using small pieces of coloured, barrel-polished glass with a grooved underside. An alternative is the Italian *smalti*: small, handmade pebbles of glass with a lead additive for softness and workability. The pebbles are kept in place with a glue-like cement.

There are two techniques for making figurative mosaic patterns by hand. In the first, a mirror image of the design is drawn on paper. The correspondingly coloured pebbles are glued to the drawing and then pressed into a bed of mortar. Afterwards the paper is soaked off. In the other technique, the pebbles are laid directly on a concrete or wood surface or a special glass-fibre mat.

Applications

Glass mosaic tiles are typically used for the walls and floors of bathrooms and other rooms with a moist atmosphere. They can also be used externally as a façade cladding, though ceramic mosaic tiles are better suited for this application as they are less susceptible to the effects of freezing. The frost resistance of the binder and the possibility of algae growth on the joints are other factors that should be taken into account when using glass mosaics outdoors.

Colour	variable
Glossiness	**glossy**, **satin**, **matt**
Translucence (%)	0 – **20** – 40 – 60 – 80 – 100
Texture	sharp, **medium**, dull
Hardness	**hard**, soft, depressible
Temperature	warm, **medium**, cool
Odour	strong, moderate, **none**
Acoustic opacity	good, moderate, **poor**

Metals

Metalle | Métaux | Metales | Metalli | Metaal

History

Stone, clay, bone, animal skins, wood and plant fibres were the first materials used by human beings to cover their structures with a skin. Then they discovered metals, first gold, then copper and silver, which they used to decorate their creations. The discovery of metals opened the door to new methods of processing: metal can be melted, it is malleable and it can be poured into moulds. Shimmering metals in particular inspired human creativity and were soon used to fashion luxury items and status symbols. In ancient times, many cultures made abundant use of local deposits of gold and silver to decorate people, implements and buildings. Scarcity played a minor role in the elitist status of these materials which they owed mainly to the level of skill and amount of labour required to process them. It was only much later that the sources of precious metals proved to be finite and gold fever in particular became an international epidemic. The number of large-scale applications decreased dramatically as the centuries went by and especially as the export of gold and silver across the globe increased.

Today's most frequently used metal element, iron, which only occurs in pure form in meteorites (with a small percentage of nickel), was originally used for jewellery and the occasional tool or utensil. Not until the nineteenth century, when the technology and furnaces necessary to produce iron from iron ore on a large scale were developed, did iron become a construction material for general use. Smelting furnaces turned out crude or 'pig' iron which was then converted into wrought iron in refining forges and puddling furnaces.

What is Metal?

'Metal' is the collective name for the largest set of chemical elements which are quite distinct from gases and non-metals. Metals are characterized by their lustre ('metallic lustre') and their good thermal and electrical conductivity. Metals can be combined to form alloys with significantly different properties from those of the individual. Add to this the fact that metals can be cold and hot formed, cast and welded, and the extensive use of metals in tools and utensils, technical applications and architecture is easy to understand. In addition, metals are fully recyclable, a factor of increasing importance in the choice of construction materials. The biggest enemy of metals is corrosion, or 'rust' as it is more commonly known. Exposure to air oxidizes metals, and ferrous metals in particular, so much so that over the course of time the material gradually 'disappears'. For most applications, therefore, it is necessary to give these metals an anti-corrosion treatment. Several options are available, the most popular being the application of a coating. In some cases, however, coating has a negative effect on the recyclability of metals.

Metal in Architecture

Traditionally, metal has two areas of application in architecture: constructional and ornamental. At first, given the few processing methods available, architectural applications remained limited to fastening devices (wall anchors, spikes and nails) and a time-consuming form of façade and roof covering (relatively small pieces of hammered-out sheeting). The development of casting technology resulted in a modest increase in the ornamental use of metal which took the form of cast iron door and window grilles, railings and balconies.

The industrial revolution and the rapid development of new manufacturing techniques for metals resulted in a wider range of applications. Structural *tours de force* attracted most attention in the eighteenth century: the Iron Bridge at Coalbrookdale, England (1779), came to symbolize the dawn of iron construction. Interestingly, the bridge was assembled as if it were a wooden construction, with dovetail joints and wedges. This period can be seen as the constructional revolution of metals. Iron and steel constructions acquired pleasing forms and were often provided with ornamental features. Alongside the development of structures in iron and steel there was also some experimentation with roofing and façade elements made from this new construction material. The first result was corrugated iron: galvanized corrugated iron made its appearance as a self-supporting roofing material in the nineteenth century. Façade constructions (frameworks) were made in iron and steel, but often filled in

Project Intentional rusting steel cladding Chameleon, Istanbul (2001)
Architect GAD Architecture
Photographer GAD Architecture

with other materials. In a few rare instances, such as in the Iron Homes by the Belgian engineer Delaveleye (1844), wrought iron panels were used. The façade panels of these houses, which were made of sheet iron riveted to a framework of cast and wrought iron, were two metres wide and four metres high.

Iron and steel construction suffered substantial setbacks when several high-profile iron-framed buildings were destroyed by fire. London's Crystal Palace was perhaps the most famous example. In the Netherlands, the fire in the Palace for Industry in Amsterdam in 1929 was the straw that broke the camel's back as far as worries over fire safety were concerned: metal was a serious fire risk and needed to be insulated with another material. As a result, many iron and steel constructions – often richly decorated – disappeared behind wooden and even concrete casings. Many of these buildings were restored to their former glory in the late twentieth century thanks to the development of fire-resistant retardent coatings and more sophisticated computational techniques which led to a reassessment of their inflammability. The problems with fire-proofing in Europe had little influence on the runaway growth of steel construction in the United States. With the development of the lift towards the end of the nineteenth century, the way was opened for high-rise structures. Steel-frame buildings grew taller and taller until eventually the skyscraper was born. More often than not, the steel framework was completely enclosed by a façade cladding in a 'fireproof' material like stone or concrete.

During the two world wars, little attention was paid to the development of new applications of metal in architecture, except in the case of heavily armour-clad building parts. Most available metal was used in the war effort. It was not until the late 1960s that a new trend emerged for metal façade panels that evoked comparison with aircraft or trains. This 'industrial architecture' was mainly expressed, as its name suggests, in industrial buildings and warehouses. This period also saw the birth of the sandwich panel: a fully prefabricated façade section consisting of two thin metal sheets glued either side of a layer of insulating material.

At the end of the twentieth century, movements advocating the use of 'honest materials' (which is to say, materials used in their natural, untreated state) led to a more frequent use of metals like copper, zinc and lead as façade and roof coverings. At the same time, a debate arose about the dangers posed by the leaching of these materials into the atmosphere. Lead and zinc were singled out in particular. A decade later, the materials have been largely exonerated, although some government authorities still require these materials to be treated prior to use. Artificial ageing (see *Patination*) has been shown to be an effective method of halting the leaching process in copper. Other materials, with the exception of stainless and weathering steel, require a coating. A rusted appearance came to be considered attractive in its own right and weathering steel accordingly grew in popularity as a façade application. CorTen, the brand name of a weathering steel launched by a Finnish company, has since become synonymous with this material. The oxidation process of weathering steel either ceases after a number of years or progresses thereafter so slowly that it can be used without any treatment.

Advancing automation of the design and production processes and the interlinking of architecture with other industries have had a clear influence on the use of metals on façades and roofs. The construction industry is experimenting more and more with technologies from the automotive and aerospace industries. Forms and construction methods from the offshore and shipbuilding industries, for example, have found their way into buildings. This gives rise to new building typologies and building shapes that call for a flexible skin, something which metal, with its extensive forming possibilities, is exceptionally well placed to provide. Such innovative architecture also extends to residential construction where recent decades have seen several examples of comfortable villas of metal and glass.

Glass and Metal

Lead was the first metal to be intimately combined with glass, in the form of window units for both interior and exterior walls. The craft of leaded glass dates back to the Middle Ages and has never gone out of style. Even in this day and age, buildings are still frequently embellished with coloured glass, in which lead is used to connect the mosaic of glass pieces. Once the industrial revolution was under way, the marriage of glass and iron was not long in coming. Glass palaces arose in which the architect/engineer pursued the limits of what was techni-

cally possible. The glasshouses and exhibition halls that were built in the course of the nineteenth century are excellent examples of this. Unfortunately, the largest such structure, the Crystal Palace by Joseph Paxton in London (1851), was destroyed by fire in 1936. But another Paxton building, the Palm House at the Royal Botanic Gardens in Kew (1848) is a well-preserved example of this building type. At the start of the twentieth century, the role of metal as a façade material began to grow, thanks in part to the technological developments in the United States that had made skyscrapers possible. Higher buildings required lighter building materials than the traditional stone and brick. Moreover, metal was an ideal material for prefabrication. Rolling mills were developed to turn out huge quantities of sheet metal and industrial methods devised to process this sheet material into manageable façade elements with unique textures and colours.

Despite the fear of fire danger in the early twentieth century, the advantages of iron and steel were of course not completely overlooked. The Dutch functionalist movement (Nieuw Bouwen), with architect Dudok at the forefront, used steel as a material for façades because of its near invisibility. The steel door and window frames in buildings created by this movement are exceptionally slender, fragile even. The restoration of these buildings can sometimes pose a problem in that current building regulations for (insulated) frames, virtually preclude such slim lines. Metal frames have never disappeared, however, and a substantial share of this market now goes to aluminium. In recent decades, the flourishing marriage of glass and steel has seen metal's share in the alliance diminish in favour of that of glass.

Project Scheepvaarthuis, Amsterdam (1928)

Architect J.M. van der Mey

Photographer Jan Derwig

Nonetheless, structural glazing, especially in floor-to-ceiling applications, still needs metal connectors to hold the glass in place.

Production Methods

Metals such as gold, silver, copper and tin are mined from the earth's crust in almost pure form. The ores from which lead, zinc and iron are produced must be heated to high temperatures to release the metals. In ancient times, furnaces were fired with coal to turn iron ore into usable iron by means of oxygen reduction. Highly complex processes are needed to manufacture (virtually) pure aluminium and titanium. For this reason, it has only been in the last half-century that these materials have experienced a surge in their use. Metals can also be used to make alloys: mixtures of different metals designed to combine certain properties or, conversely, to 'neutralize' them. Heating metals to extremely high temperatures render them fluid and thus suitable for casting in moulds. Cast metal's significance for façade architecture was limited to a short period in the late nineteenth and early twentieth centuries when iron and steel structural elements were made by means of casting. Columns complete with intricate ornamentation were cast in one piece. This application fell into disuse when the commotion surrounding the fire safety of iron and steel constructions came to a head. Thereafter, casting was used only on a small scale to produce architectural elements, such as lampposts, the previously mentioned door grilles and fences. In the 1970s, there was a brief revival when trendy architects like Norman Foster and Renzo Piano used cast steel for striking structural elements and connectors. The most eye-catching example of the use of façade-defining cast metal elements is the Centre Pompidou. A more recent example is the use of cast steel shields on the platforms of London Underground's Jubilee Line, where sophisticated design has imparted clear aesthetic value to a constructional element.

Processing Methods

There are a number of processes for turning metals into usable finished or semi-finished products. Forging and rolling are the traditional methods for processing metals. For metals that occur in pure form, a mechanical treatment is sufficient: the coppersmith's trade is a historical example of such 'cold forming' techniques. Forging, the earliest method of hot forming, demands force and high temperatures. Hot rolling, which developed from this process, produces sheets and profiles by feeding the hot metal with force through turning rollers. The extrusion process is similar, but here the metal is pulled through a stationary die. More die forms, including closed dies, are possible with extruding. There are many techniques available for applying relief, patterns and texture to sheet materials. The most frequently used ones are mentioned in the section on *Treatments*.

Joining Techniques

The first metal façades and roofs consisted to a large extent of other materials. The layer of metal was kept as thin as possible, which made fastening the material easier. Gold and silver leaf were bonded with an adhesive to a stone or wooden substrate. Copper and tin slates were fastened at the edges with small cleats to strips of wood called battens. These techniques have since demonstrated their timelessness: the basics of fixing metal are still the same, even if the materials used (glue, nails) have been improved over time.

Project Leaded claddings in De Hoep, Castricum (2003)
Architect Min2 bouw-kunst
Photographer Min2 bouw-kunst

Once it became possible to roll metal into larger sheets, the folded-seam technique made its appearance. In this method, (vertical) strips or bays of metal are attached at the sides to a timber framework. The edges of the metal strips are folded over one another to create a watertight and sturdy surface with concealed fixings. The other method is a combination of this fastening technique and that used for diagonally laid slates: overlapping sections are mechanically and invisibly fastened to the substrate and to one other using a folded seam. Structural connections underwent a different development. The dovetail joints and wedges of the Iron Bridge quickly fell from favour when the bolted connection made its appearance. Although the screw thread had been known since ancient times, it was some time before someone thought of using this principle in a large-scale structural application. Leonardo da Vinci (1452-1519) designed the first lathe for making screw threads but it was not until the middle of the nineteenth century that this principle was used for iron.Rivets became popular during the same period for attaching or joining metal sheeting and sections. With the rise of the aircraft industry, the use of blind riveting spread. There are also examples of twentieth-century buildings with metal façades fixed to the substrate with even rows of rivets.

Welding and forge welding are based on the same principle: localized heating of construction elements, bringing them into contact and allowing them to fuse as they cool. Modern welding methods – autogenous and electrical welding – were developed towards the end of the nineteenth century. Autogenous welding uses a tapered flame to heat the parts to be united to melting point. Separate welding material is then applied to the spot to be welded. This method is mostly used in welding thin sheet material. Arc welding makes use of metal rods that melt as the welding progresses, making it a less laborious process. This method is therefore by far the most popular.

With the introduction of sandwich panels, gluing (thin) sheets of metal to other types of materials has become a much-used technique. Glues are set to play an ever greater role in the fixing of metals and the development of new types of glues and gluing techniques is proceeding apace. Glued metal constructions may be rare now, but their time will definitely come.

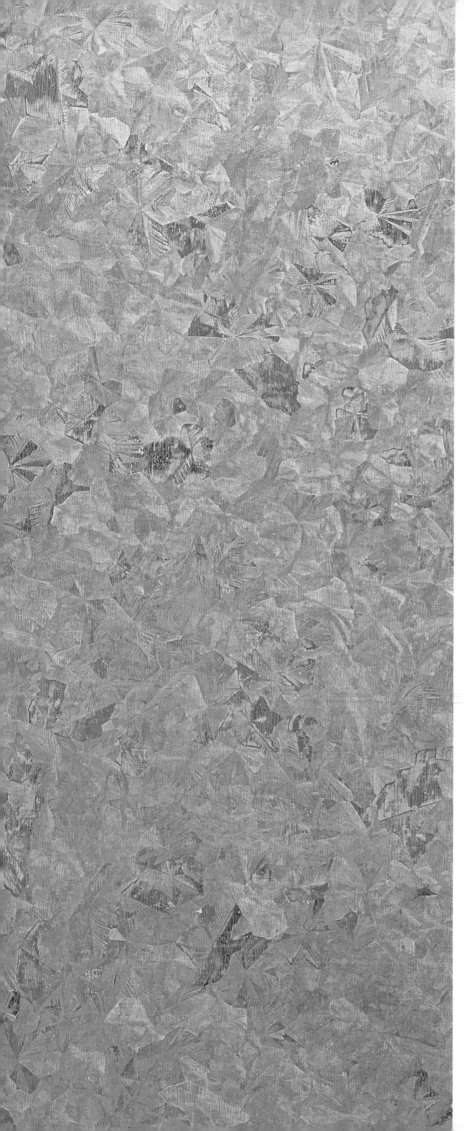

Ferrous Metals

*Eisenmetalle | Métaux ferreux | Metales ferrosos | Metalli ferrosi |
IJzerhoudende metalen*

Of all the metals used in the construction industry, ferrous metals
have by far the largest share. This is in no small part due to the many
constructional applications of steel. However, as a façade and roof
covering, other metals, in particular aluminium, are starting to give it
serious competition.

History

The importance of iron and steel in the construction process was
established in the nineteenth century during the industrial revolution.
The 'new' building material iron made possible structural forms and
building types that could not have been made with conventional
materials like stone, brick and wood. At first, iron was employed
using conventional building techniques (often derived from timber
construction), but before long, boosted by the material's popularity,
processing and joining methods were developed especially for iron.
The nineteenth-century fashion for exuberant ornamentation, which
also extended to structural elements, made early industrial iron structures a feast for the eye. Corrugated iron quickly appeared on the
scene, primarily in the form of a roofing material for uninsulated iron
structures. The first zinc-plated (i.e. galvanized) corrugated iron
sheeting appeared as early as 1850 because it had already become
apparent that iron required maintenance.

Two major threats to iron building components rapidly reared their
ugly heads: corrosion (rust) and fire. To avert the first danger, a pact
was sealed with the paint industry: proper conservation requires
regular maintenance. The second threat had bigger consequences for
exposed iron and steel in that many constructions were henceforth
encased in fire-resistant materials. Large iron canopies that were part
of public buildings, such as the winter garden at Hotel Krasnapolsky
in Amsterdam and the administration building of the National
Archives in The Hague, disappeared behind woodwork. Only with
the arrival, towards the end of the twentieth century, of fire-resistant
coatings and more accurate methods for calculating the strength of
a construction, could these magnificent spaces be restored to their
former glory.

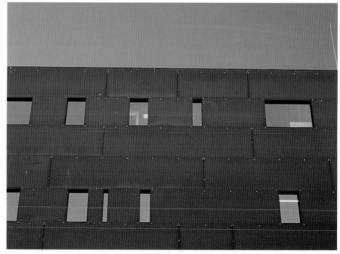

Project Paard van Troje venue, The Hague (2003)
Architect Rem Koolhaas, OMA
Photographer Jeroen van Amelsvoort

As production processes developed, a new and stronger material appeared towards the end of the nineteenth century. Steel, which has since completely ousted iron from the market, was produced in standard series of profile sections and sheet material. In the United States the tradition of all-steel buildings goes back to the nineteenth century. In Europe, it took longer for steel to win acceptance as an excellent 'all-round' construction material, suitable for both bearing structure and cladding.

Two major movements in art played a considerable role in steel's use in the façades of buildings: Art Nouveau (late nineteenth to early twentieth century) and Art Deco (the inter-war years of the 1920s and 1930s). In the United States, this was compounded by the rise of the skyscraper which fuelled the popularity of lighter steel façades. The rich ornamentation favoured by the two art movements, in which metals figured prominently, was integrated into the façade elements. The Chrysler Building in New York (Willem van Allen, 1930) is still a gleaming example of this architecture in steel, up to and including the huge stainless-steel-plated eagle heads on the top floor. The double advantage of cheap and rapid construction was a great stimulus for the material's use in a number of sectors. The mass-produced industrial building (often clad in profiled sheet steel), for example, has become a fixture of the European landscape. That such a mundane building type need not be dull and tasteless is demonstrated by the Renault Parts Distribution Centre by Foster Associates in Swindon, England (1982).

Steel has also garnered a substantial share of the office construction sector, both in the supporting structure and as façade material. The 'marriage' of steel and glass is expressed in steel frames and window walls that sometimes extend the full height of a building. But sheet steel is also much in use for solid outer walls. Moreover, architects are always on the lookout for new ways of presenting the material: flat sheet metal with a smooth coating is seldom used anymore. Stainless steel and weathering steel have also earned themselves a place in the façade, riding the wave of fashion trends. The fact that the material lends itself well to prefabrication in the form of large, insulated elements and sandwich panels, contributes to the wide range of applications: strictly controlled manufacturing and short construction times are major advantages in today's construction industry.

Materials and Properties

Iron is never used in its pure form: a small quantity of other elements (alloys) is always needed to give the material favourable processing properties. Iron is produced from iron ore, a compound of iron with primarily oxygen. This iron is called crude iron. Steel is the collective name for iron-carbon alloys that have good malleability and a limited carbon content. The variety of alloy combinations, each with different properties, has given rise to a great many different types of steel and a corresponding diversity of applications. Steel can be classified according to properties such as rust-resistance, heat-resistance and wear-resistance. Steel's full and relatively cheap recyclability is a major environmental advantage although some treatments (coatings, in particular) can have a negative effect on the material's reusability.

Manufacturing Methods

During the manufacturing process, molten pig iron leaves the blast furnace and is turned into steel by alloying the pig iron and removing unwanted elements. The molten steel is then cast in thick slabs which are subsequently hot-rolled into thinner steel sheeting or sections. During this hot-rolling process, oxidation causes a film of iron oxide to form. This 'mill scale' must first be removed by a process called pickling before any further processing can take place. Whereas iron was forged as well as rolled, steel is normally rolled or cast.

The Future

While the use of iron stagnated during the course of the twentieth century, steel captured a solid market position as a façade material. However, it now faces a serious challenge from aluminium which is

Project Renault Distribution Centre, Swindon (1982)
Architect Foster and Partners
Photographer Richard Davies

at least as ductile and also lighter. But because the price of the most common construction steel is so low, steel will remain the material of choice for certain types of buildings.

Stainless and weathering steel are the somewhat more exclusive steel types for the façade and their use is subject to the prevailing architectural fashion. This factor is also the reason for experimentation with possible treatments for sheet steel. Steel façades already have numerous manifestations and these will only increase with the development of new treatments and coatings.

Iron

Eisen | Fer | Hierro | Ferro | IJzer

Project Eiffel Tower, Paris (1889)
Architect Gustave Eiffel
Photographer Kees Hummel

Despite the fact that the production of iron more or less came to a halt at the beginning of the twentieth century in favour of steel, the material is still part of the modern street scene. It is impossible to imagine the European architectural heritage without the iron balcony railings, window gratings, fences and cast iron façade constructions, often hidden under several thick layers of paint. And the window grilles that once served a purely decorative purpose now double as anti-burglar grilles which is why a number of companies still manufacture this type of façade decoration.

Technical Aspects

Iron is a magnetic material which occurs in the earth's crust mainly in oxidized form. Even in its most pure form, iron is often naturally alloyed with nickel. Iron ores are found in iron formations, rocks with alternating layers of quartz and iron minerals. Pure iron is a very soft, silvery-white metal.

The production of iron begins with heating and reducing iron ore in a blast furnace until pig iron results. Iron is almost never used in pure form – a small amount of carbon will always be present. Exposure to moist air causes a thin layer of iron oxide, or rust, to form on the material. When used in applications where it is exposed to the outside air, iron always needs to be protected against corrosion.

Applications

Very few new types of iron façade elements have been manufactured since the early twentieth century. The iron that graces buildings today requires preservation above all. When this is no longer possible, such iron elements are often replaced by steel.

Project Former forge Beekman, The Hague (1898)
Architect J. Bosboom
Photographer Kees Hummel

Colour	**bluish grey**
Glossiness	glossy, **satin**, **matt**
Translucence (%)	**0** – 20 – 40 – 60 – 80 – 100
Texture	sharp, medium, **dull**
Hardness	**hard**, soft, depressible
Temperature	warm, medium, **cool**
Odour	strong, moderate, **none**
Acoustic opacity	good, moderate, **poor**

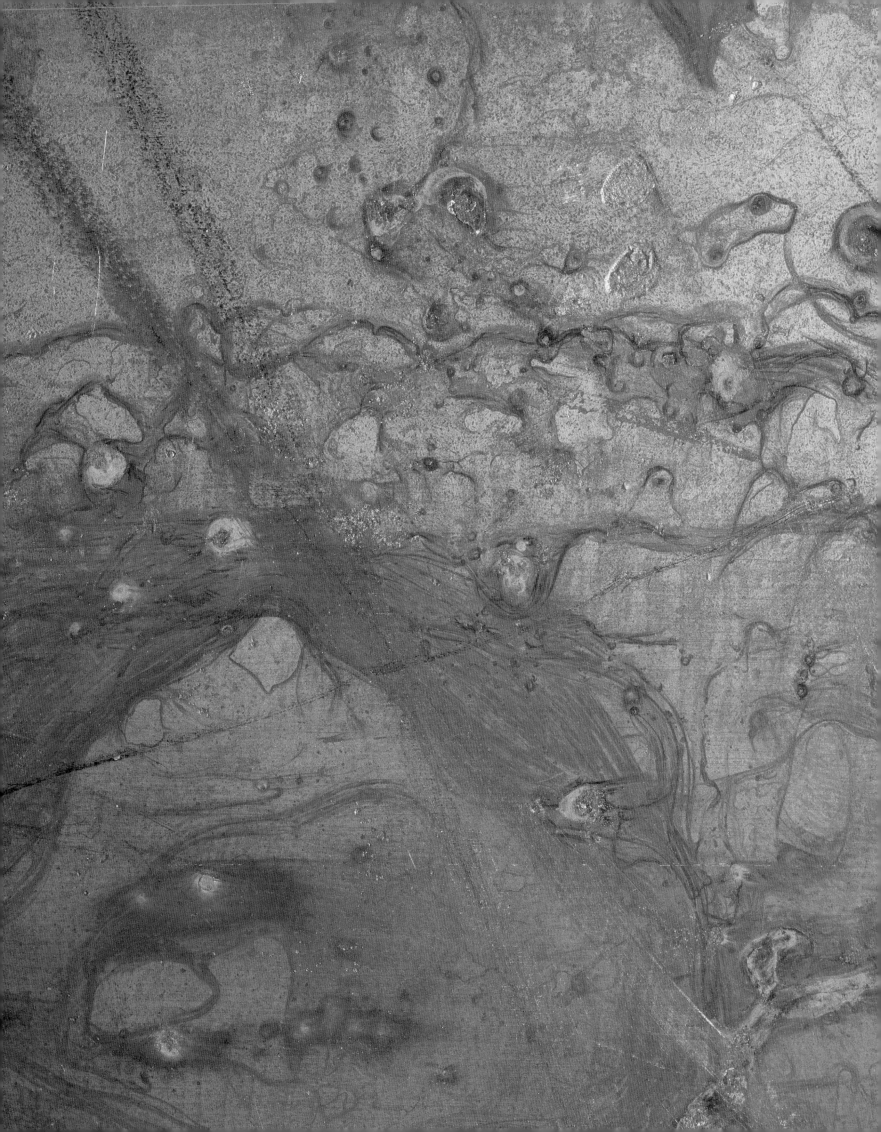

Steel

Stahl | Acier | Acero | Acciaio | Staal

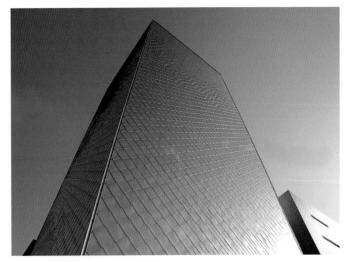

Project Naturalis, Leiden (1997)
Architect Verheyen, Verkoren, De Haan Architects
Photographer Jan Derwig

Steel appears in the façade in many different guises. The most familiar are steel frames, and window walls and façade elements of sheet steel. As the number of possible treatments multiply, so the material's versatility increases. Steel's suitability for prefabrication often plays a role in the decision to use this material since it means that a building can quickly be rendered wind and waterproof.

Technical Aspects

Steel is the collective term for iron-carbon alloys that demonstrate good malleability and contain little carbon. Steel also contains other elements, sometimes in the form of impurities, sometimes intentionally added. When these substances exceed a specified percentage, the material is classified as alloy steel. Alloys contribute to the exceptionally large number of steel types.

Unalloyed steel, also termed carbon steel, has good malleability and a carbon content up to 1.5%. Above this percentage, its malleability diminishes while its castability improves. Structural steel (the most common type) is low alloyed or unalloyed.

Applications

Rolled sheet steel, often in the form of an insulated façade element or sandwich panel, is the most common façade application of steel. Conventional steel is almost never used without some form of surface treatment, unless wear and tear as a consequence of corrosion has been factored in and a heavier sheet employed.

It is possible to apply texture or relief to the steel sheet before applying a coating. Creating bent or curved forms is becoming ever easier now that both the design and manufacturing processes are extensively computerized. This also applies to other façade applications using steel, such as frames and window walls.

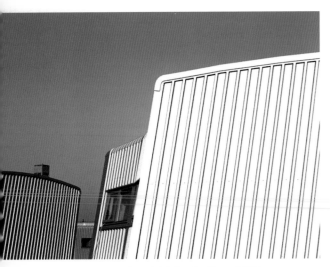

Project 't Schaartje, Hoorn (1996)
Architect Min2 bouw-kunst
Photographer Elly Valkering

Colour	**bluish grey**
Glossiness	glossy, **satin**, **matt**
Translucence (%)	**0** – 20 – 40 – 60 – 80 – 100
Texture	sharp, medium, **dull**
Hardness	**hard**, soft, depressible
Temperature	warm, medium, **cool**
Odour	strong, moderate, **none**
Acoustic opacity	good, moderate, **poor**

Weathering Steel

Witterungsbeständiger Stahl I Acier résistant à l'usure I Acero resistente a la intemperie I Acciaio resistente alle intemperie I Weervast staal

Project Borneo, Amsterdam (1998)

Architect Heren 5

Photographer Kees Hummel

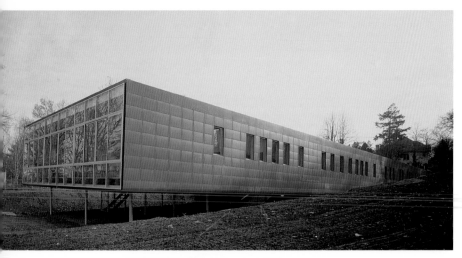

Project RVU Building, Hilversum (1997)

Architect MVRDV

Photographer Christian Richters

Weathering steel, often erroneously referred to by the brand name Cor-Ten, is a 'living' material: the rough, grainy surface in a warm, rust-brown colour changes with the incidence of light and the humidity. The material, which came into widespread use in the second half of the twentieth century, was particularly popular in industrial environments and difficult-to-reach locations, owing to its low maintenance requirements. Only towards the end of the century did the distinctive rough skin acquire aesthetic value and weathering steel start to appear in exciting architectural designs.

Technical Aspects

Weathering steel is characterized by a corrosion process that eventually results in an impermeable and tenacious oxide film (patina). Weathering steel can therefore be used without a surface treatment and is virtually maintenance-free. This characteristic is achieved by alloying steel with copper, chromium and nickel. Left to itself, the corrosion process takes approximately three years, but manufacturers can artificially reduce this process to a little over six months. The reduction in the thickness of the material from corrosion means that weathering steel must always be at least 3 mm thick. Careful detailing is necessary to prevent (non-toxic) rainwater run-off from staining adjacent materials.

The addition of alloy elements makes weathering steel more expensive than conventional carbon steel. The strength properties and manufacturing methods are the same, however. Although weathering steel lends itself well to recycling, the low volume of scrap does not warrant separate recycling.

Applications

Despite its suitability for external loadbearing constructions, weathering steel is nowadays used mostly in the form of sheet material. For insulated façade applications, architects can opt for sandwich panels or for a wind and watertight inner box construction to which the steel sheets can be fixed. Weathering steel is suitable for virtually every treatment that can be applied to carbon steel. Where rust-water runoff is a problem, a transparent coating can be applied.

Colour	**brown**
Glossiness	glossy, satin, **matt**
Translucence (%)	**0** – 20 – 40 – 60 – 80 – 100
Texture	**sharp**, **medium**, **dull**
Hardness	**hard**, soft, depressible
Temperature	warm, medium, **cool**
Odour	strong, **moderate**, **none**
Acoustic opacity	good, moderate, **poor**

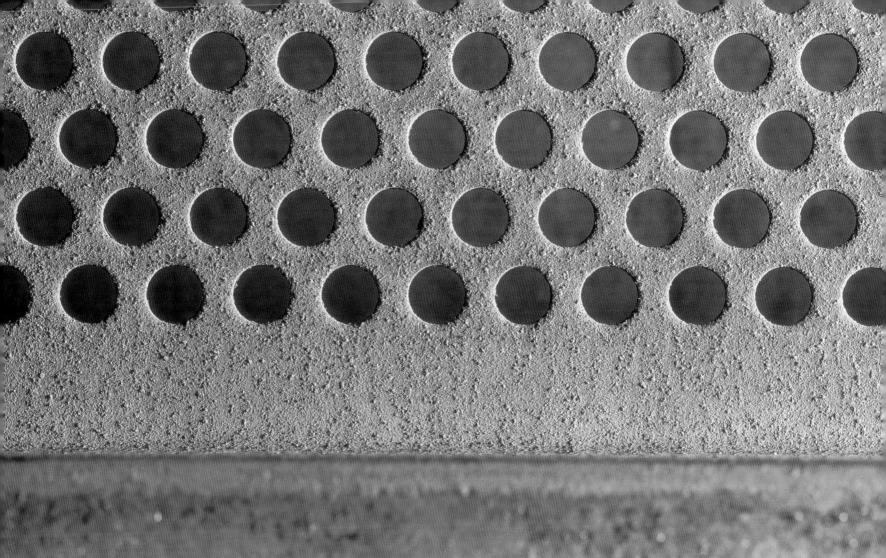
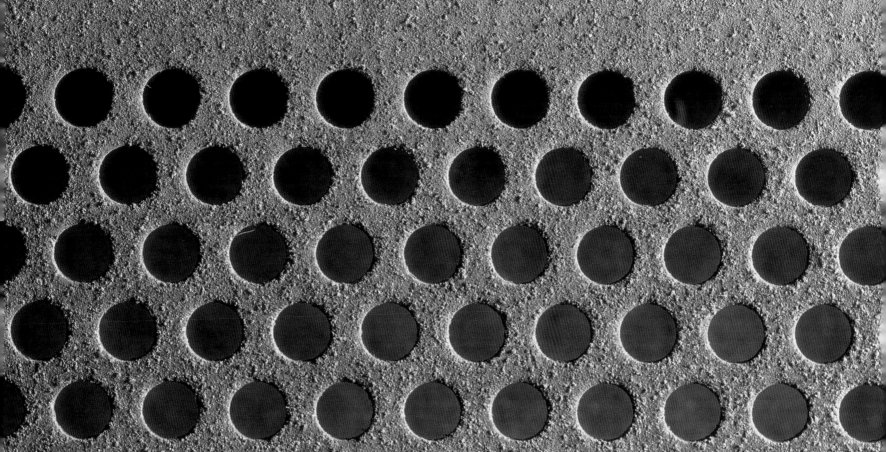

Stainless Steel

Nichtrostender Stahl | Inox | Acero inoxidable | Acciaio inossidabile | Roestvast staal

Project Bercy 2 Shopping Centre, Paris (1990)
Architect Renzo Piano Building Workshop
Photographer Kees Hummel

Project Pathé Arena, Amsterdam (2000)
Architect Frits van Dongen, de Architekten Cie.
Photographer Brakkee & Scagliola

Stainless steel is the elegant branch of the ferrous metals family: when polished, its shine rivals that of a precious metal. Thanks to its low-maintenance and the variety of finishes produced by different treatments, stainless steel is a popular material for both the façade and the interior.

Technical Aspects

Stainless steel is the name for several types of steel that do not corrode in the open air and are resistant to various chemicals. The material is also highly heat-resistant. The various types of stainless steel are alloys containing at least 11% chromium. The material owes its name to a thin, but extremely tenacious, chromium oxide film that forms in the presence of oxygen. Because the film is self-healing, corrosion is virtually eliminated, except at welded joints where the film is less corrosion-resistant.

Stainless steel grades with a low carbon content or alloyed with titanium are suitable for welding. Alloying with small quantities of nickel and manganese improves the material's cold ductility. There are EU standards for the composition of a large number of grades of stainless steel.

Applications

Since 'stainless steel' is a collective term, it is important to select the correct type of stainless steel for each application. For example, as several indoor swimming pool damage claims have demonstrated, many types of stainless steel are not proof against the combination of humidity, heat and the presence of chlorine.

Stainless steel is used in the form of façade panels, for structural connectors in glass curtain walls and in countless interior applications, such as handrails, balusters and door and window hardware. Nowadays, stainless steel is available in a number of rolled L-sections. Stainless steel wire is also used in metal cloth and mesh.

Colour	**bluish grey**
Glossiness	**glossy**, **satin**, matt
Translucence (%)	**0** – 20 – 40 – 60 – 80 – 100
Texture	sharp, medium, **dull**
Hardness	**hard**, soft, depressible
Temperature	warm, medium, **cool**
Odour	strong, moderate, **none**
Acoustic opacity	good, moderate, **poor**

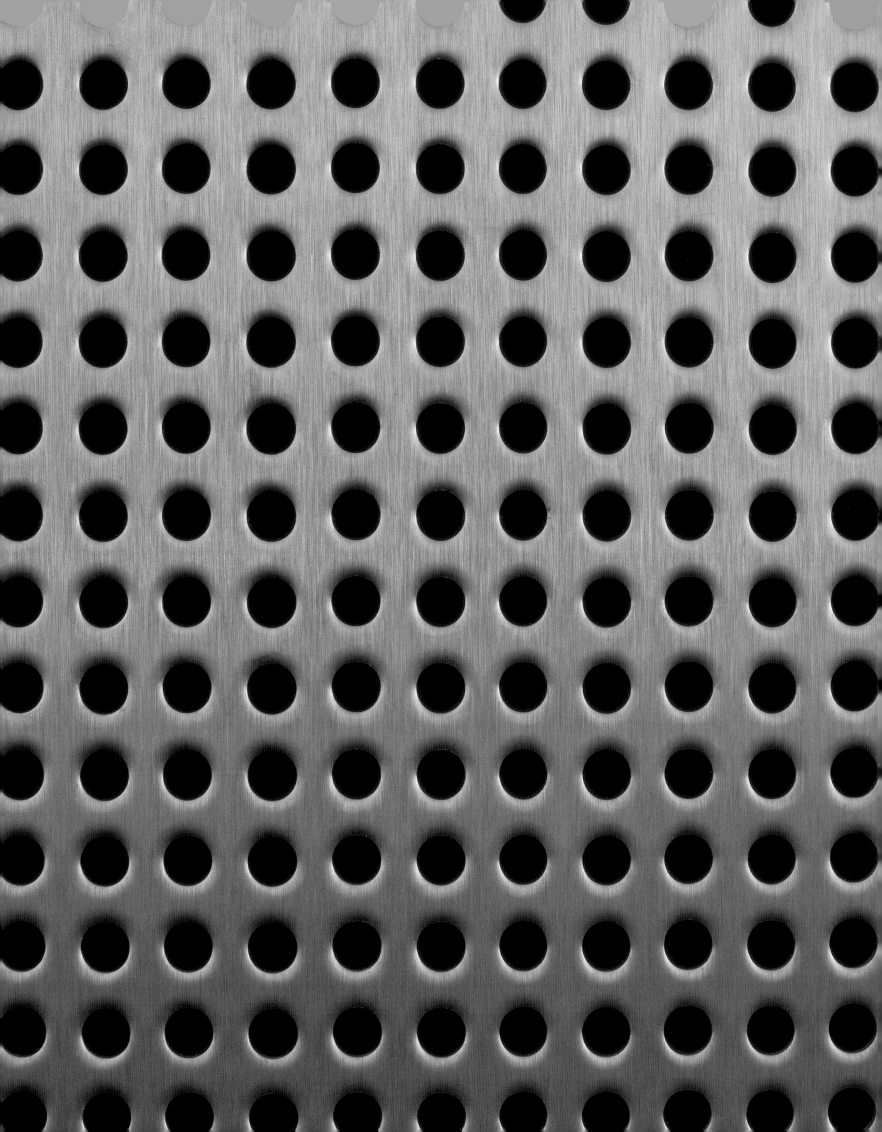

Non-ferrous Metals

Nichteisenmetalle | Métaux non ferreux | Metales no ferrosos | Metalli non ferrosi | Niet-ijzerhoudende metalen

The term non-ferrous metals, as its Latin root suggests, covers all metals with the exception of iron. The original reason for this distinction lies in the fact that the production of iron and steel is many times greater than the combined production of non-ferrous metals.

Bronze, silver, gold, tin, copper and lead have been used by human beings since antiquity because they occur in nature either in pure form or in easily reduced compounds. Silver and gold are discussed separately under *Precious Metals*.

Metals such as zinc, aluminium and titanium have been in production for little more than a century. Zinc was initially used solely in alloys with copper to create brass. Aluminium and titanium, the production of which began around the start of the twentieth century, are officially labelled as light metals (up to 4500 kg/m²). Lead, zinc, copper and the precious metals gold and silver are classified as heavy metals.

What makes the metal family so large, is the possibility of creating alloys: composites of different metals, whether ferrous or non-ferrous. Because properties such as corrosion resistance, tensile strength, castability and ductility differ between metals, alloys offer the opportunity of improving a metal's intrinsic properties. Some combinations, such as brass (a combination of copper and zinc), have become so commonplace that they can be classified as a separate metal.

Non-ferrous Metals in Architecture

Lead was the first metal to be categorized as a construction material. Lead was also the first metal to establish a liaison with glass: leaded glass is still used today for decorative, semi-transparent façades. But the most common use of lead was as flashing, a transition material used to make awkward junctions between different building materials watertight.

For a long time, the role of metals in building construction was confined to connecting elements or finishing work. Copper and lead were beaten or rolled into thin strips suitable for small-scale use. These strips were used primarily to cover roofs and dormers. Not until the industrial revolution in the second half of the nineteenth century were there significant developments in metal extraction, production and processing that allowed metal to become a full-fledged alternative in the range of available construction materials.

Until well into the twentieth century, the non-ferrous metals lead, copper and (occasionally) tin occurred mainly on the roofs of buildings, in sheet form. Interestingly, the methods used for attaching metals were virtually identical to and derived from those used for wood, stone and ceramic roofing materials. Small areas of lathing are spanned with the metal either by overlapping (as with roof slates and tiles) or by means of mechanical fastenings (as used for wooden elements). Only much later was a fastening system developed especially for metal. Known as the folded seam, this technique is not only less labour-intensive, but also makes it possible to cover much larger areas at a time.

Copper and lead have long been important raw materials for the paint industry. Copper or copper alloys form the basis for what is

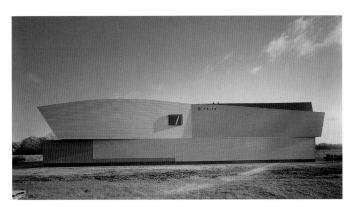

Project Karbouw, Amersfoort (1991)

Architect Ben van Berkel, UN Studio

Photographer Jan Derwig

known as ormolu, a gold-coloured metal powder used to make bronze gilding. Copper bronze is pure copper powder, an ingredient of the 'bronze bottom paint' used to protect wooden boats against fouling. Lead as a constituent of lead cyanamide is used in anti-corrosive paints and many pigments.

Without a doubt, the non-ferrous metal most frequently used in the construction industry is aluminium. In the last half-century, aluminium has become immensely popular as a loadbearing outer wall material (window and door casings and spandrel panels) and as a sheet material for façades. Aluminium is also a popular choice for fixed awnings where slender, extruded aluminium sections impart a striped motif to the façade. The use of other metals like copper, lead and titanium is subject to fashion. For example, the architectural movement generally referred to as Organic Architecture, displays a penchant for untreated metals such as copper and zinc.

Non-ferrous metals are also occasionally used to imitate other metals or building materials. Aluminium can be treated in such a way that it can pass for silver, while in certain situations brass can bear comparison with gold. But there are odder types of imitation, as when aluminium sheet is used to imitate roof tiles.

The Environment

The rise of the environmental movement and the concept of 'sustainable construction' during the last decades of the twentieth century, has cast a shadow over non-ferrous metals like lead and zinc. Both these metals are potentially toxic to humans. However, production methods for zinc have been improved to such an extent during this same period that it is now possible to remove the most toxic components from the material. The use of highly toxic lead has been almost completely eliminated in building elements that humans might come in contact with, such as pipes and paint. The use of untreated lead is strictly limited. Nevertheless, a number of municipal building codes still list both metals as 'prohibited building materials'.

However, other non-ferrous metals have gained in popularity as a result of environmental considerations. Non-ferrous metals that can be used in an untreated state, such as lead, copper and zinc, score very highly in terms of sustainability and recyclability.

Composites

New types of material combinations are gradually being introduced into architecture from other industries. One example is a wafer-thin layer of polypropylene between two very thin (≥ 2 mm) panels of aluminium sheeting. Developed in the aircraft industry, these sandwich panels can be easily cold formed and serve only as an aesthetic outer skin.

Another new type of panel, this time with an insulating function, is the curved sandwich panel, which has crossed over from the automotive industry. Combinations of aluminium and an insulating layer are placed in moulds and hot-pressed (see also *Thermoforming*). As soon as there are moulds that can be reused several times, these techniques will be financially feasible for the construction industry.

The glass industry is also actively exploring new combinations of metals with glass. This research focuses not only on structural aspects, but also on the performance of the building envelope. Glass sheeting with a core of sun-reflecting aluminium honeycomb is one example that has already been noticed.

The Future

Aluminium and titanium in particular look set to play an increasingly important role in architecture, not only in the aesthetic sense, but also in terms of construction. The source of this development lies in other industries. The aerospace and automotive industries have spent decades researching ways of exploiting the excellent properties of these materials in every possible form and application. The transition to the construction industry has yet to be made. One obstacle is that mass production is often limited in the construction industry, making the development and production costs for new applications very high, often prohibitively so. The quest continues for new alloys and metal combinations. Corus, a manufacturer of numerous metal products, is currently developing titalium sheet material consisting of an aluminium core with a layer of titanium on one or both sides. This sheet material could end up being less than a millimetre thick and up to 70% cheaper than pure titanium, giving it the potential to become an outstanding alternative for the construction industry.

Project Mezz Pop Centre, Breda (2002)

Architect Erick van Egeraat Associated Architects

Photographer Christian Richters

Aluminium

Aluminium | Aluminium | Aluminio | Alluminio | Aluminium

Project Aluminium Centre, Houten (2001)
Architect Micha de Haas
Photographer Kees Hummel

Project Möbel Egger, Eschenbach (2002)
Architect König Architektur
Photographer Michael Reinhard Photography

Few metals are as diverse as aluminium: it is light, easy to process and strong (although less rigid than steel). In architecture, aluminium is used in sheet form, extrusions or sections, where the usually non-transparent finish makes it almost impossible to distinguish it from steel. Yet aluminium constructions are potentially much lighter and more slender, while the pure material is far more corrosion-resistant than steel. The Aluminium Centre in the Dutch town of Houten (2001), a building in which both the construction and finishing were entirely of aluminium, is a fine example of architecture using this material, but it is only the tip of the iceberg as far as aluminium's possibilities are concerned.

Technical Aspects

Aluminium is a silvery white, naturally soft material that is easily cast, rolled into thin foil or drawn out to a fine thread. Although aluminium is very much a base metal, it remains almost untainted by air, since a thin layer of oxide on the surface protects the underlying metal.

Pure aluminium does not occur naturally, but is found in mineral ores, in particular bauxite. The aluminium is separated out by means of an electrolytic process. The preparation of aluminium is an intensive and energy-consuming process but it makes up for this 'environmentally-unfriendly' aspect by being eminently recyclable.

Aluminium is non-magnetic and non-toxic. It has a relatively low density, holds up well in aggressive outdoor environments, is ductile and possesses good thermal and electrical conductivity. By adding relatively small quantities of other metals it is possible to create alloys that are significantly stronger than regular construction steel.

Applications

Aluminium façade elements are often prefabricated in the form of sandwich panels in which a core of insulation material is sandwiched between thin sheets of aluminium which have already been worked and/or coated. Loadbearing sandwich elements are also available.

New composite forms are gradually being introduced into architecture from other industries. One example is an extremely thin sandwich panel ($\geq$ 2 mm) of aluminium sheets with an ultra-thin core of polypropylene. These panels, which originated in the aviation industry, can be cold-formed and serve only as an aesthetic outer skin. By contrast, curved sandwich panels are insulated. They derive from the automotive industry where combinations of aluminium and an insulating layer are hot-pressed with the help of moulds (see also Thermal Shapes).

Colour	**silver grey**
Glossiness	**glossy**, **satin**, **matt**
Translucence (%)	**0** – 20 – 40 – 60 – 80 – 100
Texture	sharp, medium, **dull**
Hardness	**hard**, soft, depressible
Temperature	warm, medium, **cool**
Odour	strong, moderate, **none**
Acoustic opacity	good, moderate, **poor**

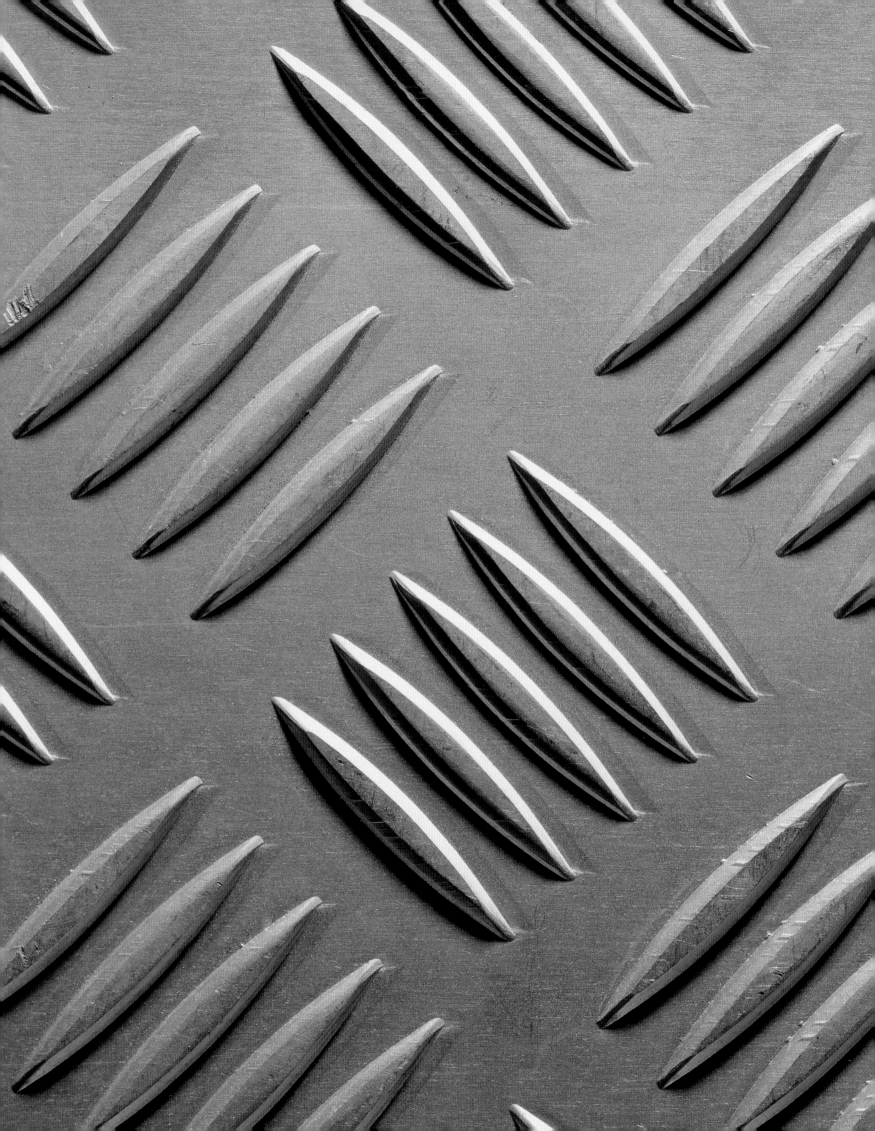

Titanium

Titan | Titane | Titanio | Titanio | Titanium

Project Scheepvaartmuseum depot, Amsterdam (2001)
Architect Zeinstra Van der Pol
Photographer Jan Derwig

Project Town Hall, Schouwen-Duiveland (2001)
Architect Rau & Partners
Photographer Herman van Doorn

Titanium played an important role in the manifestation of the architecture of the most recent *fin de siècle*. A number of epoch-making projects, such as the Frank Gehry's Guggenheim Museum in Bilbao, Spain, propelled this material, which is generally thought of as prohibitively expensive, into the international limelight. When at the end of the 1990s Russia started exporting unexpectedly large quantities, titanium became an affordable façade material for less prestigious projects as well.

Technical Aspects

Titanium is lighter than steel, stronger than aluminium and is almost as corrosion-resistant as platinum; it also holds up very well in chemically aggressive environments. Pure titanium is a silvery-white material that is easily processed. The preparation of metallic titanium is a laborious process because the readily obtainable titanium oxide is extremely difficult to reduce to pure metal. Processing this crude material into sheets must be carefully controlled to prevent contamination by oxygen or nitrogen. Titanium's strength can be increased by means of alloying. Although titanium does not lend itself very well to cold-forming, its ductility increases with temperature. Casting titanium is complicated by its high melting point and the high risk of contamination.

Applications

In architecture, titanium is used mainly as a sheet material for small surface areas. It is available in a range of colours, from silver to soft beige. The polished material has a permanent lustre, and although unpolished titanium acquires a dull film, it retains its reflective qualities.

Titanium cladding is usually installed on site where the strips are fixed to wooden lathing and joined together using the folded seam or diagonal slate-laying technique, both of which make it possible to cover curved or vaulted forms. Prefabricated façade elements (titanium sheeting folded around a wooden mould) are costly, especially in the case of curved forms which require a sophisticated calculation method coupled with very precise craftsmanship on location. Such elements do, however, generally result in a tauter appearance because titanium is smoother when shaped at the higher temperatures possible with prefabrication.

Colour	**silver grey to soft beige**
Glossiness	**glossy**, **satin**, **matt**
Translucence (%)	**0** – 20 – 40 – 60 – 80 – 100
Texture	sharp, medium, **dull**
Hardness	**hard**, soft, depressible
Temperature	warm, medium, **cool**
Odour	strong, moderate, **none**
Acoustic opacity	good, moderate, **poor**

Lead

Blei | Plomb | Acero | Piombo | Lood

Project Lavatory at Lunch Lounge, Co van der Horst store, Amstelveen (1999)
Architect Marcel Wanders Studio
Photographer René Gonkel

The strip of flexible metal that provides a sturdy and especially watertight seal around chimneys and frames, is the oldest roofing detail known to traditional construction. However, lead is not a popular metal for covering large surfaces where its weight and high ductility are more of a disadvantage (wrinkles and dents) than an advantage. The fact that lead is extremely toxic further complicates its use: only when all risk of leaching has been blocked (by some form of coating), may it be used in proximity to human beings.

Technical Aspects

Lead is a heavy, soft, highly malleable metal which, in its pure form, exhibits a bright blue sheen. When lead is exposed to the atmosphere, however, this sheen soon disappears beneath a greyish film of oxide which in turn gives the material a high resistance to corrosion. Lead is found in the earth's crust in low concentrations. Lead can be separated from other metals and purified by heating the ores and minerals in which it occurs. The metal's high sound damping capacity makes it suitable for use as a sound and vibration insulation in homes and factories. Lead has a high absorptive capacity for X-rays and gamma rays.

Applications

Lead is rolled out into thin sheets which are marketed in rolls. Because it has traditionally been used only for finishing work, lead is available in rolls of a limited width. Nonetheless, owing to the current popularity of untreated materials, lead has turned up in some unexpected places in recent decades. For example, Dutch designer Marcel Wanders used lead sheeting to cover the walls of a trendy furniture store lavatory in Amstelveen. Lead also crops up in modern garden designs as a finishing material for ornaments, follies or the occasional raised border.

Project Mining Archive Building, Clausthal-Zellerfeld (2000)
Architect Von Gerkan, Marg und Partners
Photographer Jürgen Schmidt

Colour	**bluish grey**
Glossiness	glossy, **satin**, **matt**
Translucence (%)	**0** – 20 – 40 – 60 – 80 – 100
Texture	sharp, medium, **dull**
Hardness	**hard**, soft, depressible
Temperature	warm, medium, **cool**
Odour	strong, moderate, **none**
Acoustic opacity	good, moderate, **poor**

Copper

Kupfer | Cuivre | Cobre | Rame | Koper

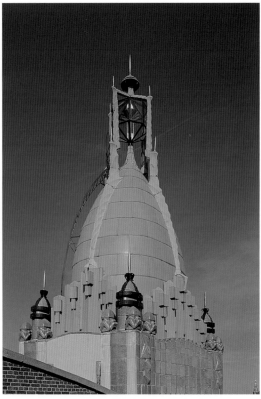

Project Tuschinsky theatre, Amsterdam (1921 | Restoration 2002)
Architect H.L. de Jong (Rappange)
Photographer Jan Derwig

Copper domes and roof finishes have been part of the urban land-scape for many centuries. After gold, copper seemed to be the best material for imparting an air of nobility to important architectural structures. And although copper starts out reddish-gold in colour, over time the slow-forming green patina gives it an increasingly dis-tinguished character. The past few decades have seen the material gain both in popularity and in the number of applications. The fash-ion for allowing roofs to flow over into the outside walls of a build-ing has suddenly given us the copper façade. The 'copper egg' of the HollandRama exhibition centre at the Netherlands Open Air Museum in Arnhem is a particularly striking example of this style.

Technical Aspects

Copper is a soft, malleable material whose strength and rigidity is increased by cold rolling. Pure copper is reddish in colour. The metal is non-magnetic, has the highest thermal and electrical conductivity of any metal with the exception of silver and is also extremely resist-ant to wear.

Exposure to air affects only the surface of copper, which over time acquires a greenish film (the patina) of basic carbonate and sulphate. This film can also be applied artificially (see *Patination*).

Copper occurs naturally in many different minerals, ores and carbon-ates from which it can be extracted by reduction and electrolysis. Copper forms the basis for several important alloys (see *Brass*).

Applications

Copper is usually rolled into thin sheets and applied in small strips, which makes it ideal for covering curved or vaulted architectural ele-ments. The strips are usually fastened to a wooden substrate in an overlapping or diamond tile pattern. Bays of copper sheeting the height or width of a façade can be fixed to a wooden framework using the folded seam method. In France copper is also seen as a cladding for timber frames, usually in historical buildings.

Project Baron Vert, Osaka (1992)
Architect Philippe Starck
Photographer Jan Derwig

Colour	**yellow red to green**
Glossiness	**glossy**, satin, matt
Translucence (%)	**0** – 20 – 40 – 60 – 80 – 100
Texture	sharp, medium, **dull**
Hardness	**hard**, soft, depressible
Temperature	warm, medium, **cool**
Odour	strong, moderate, **none**
Acoustic opacity	good, moderate, **poor**

Zinc

Zink | Zinc | Zinc | Zinco | Zink

Project Panopticon, Haarlem (1901 | Restoration 2002)
Architect Rijksgebouwendienst
Photographer Jan Derwig

Project The Whale, Amsterdam (2000)
Architect Frits van Dongen, de Architekten Cie.
Photographer Keith Collie

It would appear that in the love-hate relationship that architects and builders have with zinc, the pendulum is definitely swinging to the positive side. The material's propensity to leach gave it a bad reputation at the beginning of the 'sustainable building' hype in the early 1990s. But now that research has revealed that zinc is no more harmful than other frequently used metals, the robust material is being seen more often in architectural applications.

Technical Aspects

In untreated form, zinc is a bluish-white metal of limited strength. The metal's hexagonal crystalline structure makes it brittle when cold, but the application of relatively little heat (40 to 80 °C) renders it malleable. Natural corrosion in a neutral atmosphere results in the formation of a patchy film of zinc oxide and zinc carbonate which slows down the process of corrosion. This makes zinc a sustainable material, although conditions in coastal and industrial districts are significantly less favourable. Nonetheless, zinc is frequently used to preserve other metals (see *Coatings* and *Galvanization*) and in alloys with copper, aluminium, magnesium and other metals.

Applications

Zinc, the soft metal with a rugged look, is generally used in architectural applications in the form of sheet material produced by a hot-rolling process. Traditionally used as a roofing material and for rainwater pipes, in recent decades zinc has been used more prominently in the façades and even the interiors of buildings.

Fixing methods for zinc roofs do not differ much from traditional roofing techniques: strips of zinc sheeting are attached in situ using the folded seam or diagonal slate-laying technique, to a substrate of wooden laths. Thanks to its inherent flexibility, zinc can also be used to clad curved surfaces.

Colour	bluish grey
Glossiness	glossy, **satin**, **matt**
Translucence (%)	**0** – 20 – 40 – 60 – 80 – 100
Texture	sharp, medium, **dull**
Hardness	**hard**, soft, depressible
Temperature	warm, medium, **cool**
Odour	strong, moderate, **none**
Acoustic opacity	good, moderate, **poor**

Brass

Messing | Laiton | Latón | Ottone | Messing

Project Trump Tower entrance, New York (1983)
Architect Swanke, Hayden & Connell
Photographer © Gail Mooney | Corbis

Although brass is most closely associated with the nautical world, where the soft, shiny metal is widely used for equipment and trim on sea-going vessels, it can also be found in architecture, albeit rarely in façade-spanning applications. A lot of window and door hardware is made of brass (the best alternative to gold) and indoors the yellow metal also appears in the form of sheet material on walls and balustrades.

Technical Aspects

Brass, which has a yellowish sheen when polished, is an alloy of copper and zinc. The zinc component must be at least 5% and higher percentages result in a proportionally stronger material. The technical properties of brass can be enhanced by adding other elements to the copper-zinc alloy. The addition of lead creates an alloy known as leaded or free-cutting brass, which is a softer material with exceptionally high machinability. Naval brass contains tin which makes it more corrosion-resistant in seawater. Admiralty brass, which also contains tin, is more resistant to cavitation corrosion in seawater, a property it has in common with aluminium-brass alloys. Stamping, hot and cold rolling and numerous forms of casting are just some of the many ways brass can be processed. Only brass with a minimum copper content of 60% is suitable for casting.

Applications

One advantage of brass is that it can be used untreated, making this shiny compound suitable for exterior as well as interior applications. For hardware applications, brass is cast and polished. Sheet brass, with or without relief, perforations or other texture treatments, is found mostly in indoor applications.

Colour	yellow gold
Glossiness	**glossy**, satin, matt
Translucence (%)	**0** – 20 – 40 – 60 – 80 – 100
Texture	sharp, medium, **dull**
Hardness	**hard**, soft, depressible
Temperature	warm, medium, **cool**
Odour	strong, moderate, **none**
Acoustic opacity	good, moderate, **poor**

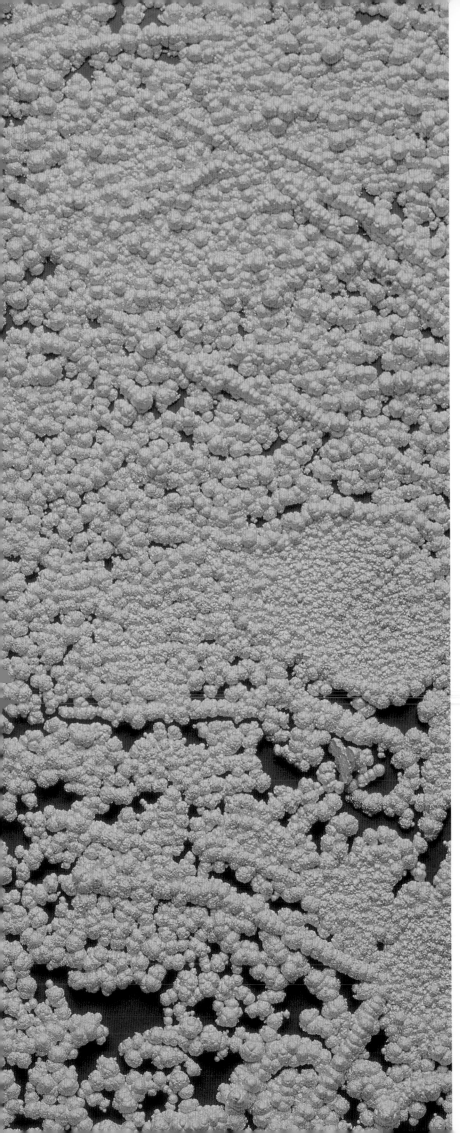

Precious Metals

Edelmetalle | Métaux précieux | Metales preciosos | Metalli preziosi | Edelmetalen

A precious metal is a metal that in its pure form is highly unreactive to agents that attack other metals, such as humidity or acids. One exception to this rule is 'aqua regia', a mixture of three parts hydrochloric acid and one part nitric acid, in which even gold, the king of precious metals, will dissolve. The following elements fall into the category of precious metals: ruthenium, rhodium, osmium, iridium, palladium, platinum and gold. Although silver is generally considered a precious metal, it falls outside the definition given because it is susceptible to corrosion by diluted nitric acid.

History

The most alluring precious metals are without doubt gold and silver, used since ancient times for personal adornment and for devotional purposes. Gold and silver were found in almost pure form, which greatly simplified their processing.

Throughout history, these precious metals were reserved for the social and/or religious elite. In the oldest human cultures, such as that of the ancient Egyptians and the pre-Columbian societies of Central and South America, gold in particular was used to decorate the buildings that served these elites. According to tradition, there were golden temples, silver places of worship and gleaming palaces for the wealthy. Unfortunately, not a single example or unambiguous illustration has withstood the ravages of time.

Description Temple of Emerald Buddha, Thailand
Photographer Fotosearch Stock Photography

Project De Kerkkroon stone tablet, Amsterdam (1725 | 2000)
Restorer Thobias Snoep
Photographer Kees Hummel

But more recent projects can give us some idea of the effect of using precious metals for buildings. Several centuries ago, before the price of gold skyrocketed, towers, ornaments and ceilings were covered with gold leaf or gold powder: always very small quantities of the pure material, ingeniously and skilfully utilized to achieve maximum effect and (literally) out of reach of 'the common man'. Much of this antique gold has disappeared over the course of time, however, through either wear or theft.

Precious Metals in Architecture
'All that glitters is not gold'. This proverbial saying is certainly true of most applications of precious metals in modern architecture where appearances do indeed deceive. Since the scarcity and resulting costliness of the pure materials preclude large-scale applications, it is only logical that people should have tried to find ways of mimicking the effect of precious metals. The last century in particular produced many examples of such imitation that owed much to advances in material technology. Gold and silver effects can be found elsewhere

in this book in the sections on *Non-ferrous Metals* and *Metal Treatments* and in the chapters *Glass* and *Fired Man-made Stone*.

The application of precious metals, or verisimilar substitutes, is subject to fashion. In the early twentieth century, the Art Nouveau and Art Deco movements gave a new impetus to the use of polished, highly reflective ornamentation. More recently, the 'new kitsch' or 'camp' trend in interior decoration sparked renewed interest in shiny elements, while the turn of the century saw the advent of the 'vintage' style, in which old was combined with new and antique mirrors – glass with a layer of genuine silver – were brought down from the attic once again.

Gold leaf is still used in building restoration by a dwindling number of craftsmen still versed in the technique. Very occasionally, an architect takes pleasure in incorporating an element of gold into a modern structure. Not infrequently, this gold decoration is a none-too-subtle allusion to the material's elitist status.

Materials and Properties
Gold is a mineral that occurs in pure form in nature. Gold also occurs in natural alloys, usually with silver (electrum), and in a few compounds (with the element tellurium, among others). There are many artificial alloys of precious metals, such as gold-silver, gold-copper, gold-platinum, and so on. Gold leaf and gold powder, however, are made from virtually pure gold which is hammered out to a minimal thickness or crushed to a very fine powder. Gilding is another method for applying a thin layer of gold, usually to a base metal (see also *Gold*).

In its pure form, silver too can be processed into thin sheets. The best-known application of silver in buildings, however, is the mirror, a sheet of glass coated on one side with a thin layer of silver (see also *Silver*).

There are no known architectural applications of any other precious metals in pure form.

Project La Defense, Almere (2004)
Architect UN Studio
Photographer Christian Richters

Gold

Gold | Or | Oro | Oro | Goud

Gold embodies luxury and prestige. Yet it is seldom real gold that glitters on façades, ornaments or spires. The golden gleam that finds its way into architecture is rarely that of the precious metal. Applications involving gold metal are expensive and generally require a high standard of craftsmanship. Gold accents, whether they be the metal itself or merely the colour, serve to enhance the building's image.

Technical Aspects

Gold is used in only very small quantities in architecture, the trick being to use a minimum amount of the material to maximum effect.

Gold leaf is virtually pure gold that is rolled into sheets a mere 0.001 mm thick. It can be glued to a variety of surfaces, flat or curved and generally wood, both indoors and out. In ancient times, egg white was used as an adhesive for gold leaf or gold powder. The layer of gold is smoothed onto the base material with a brush and the whole finished with a transparent varnish.

Gold-plating, which involves covering a material with a thin layer of gold, is nowadays done using chemical and electrolytic techniques. The old technique of fire gilding, in which a paste of gold powder and mercury was applied to objects, after which the mercury was evaporated, has completely disappeared. Chemical gilding takes place in baths containing gold salts. A layer of gold of the desired thickness is formed on the surface of a less precious metal through metal exchange (usually at high temperatures). Gentle polishing will impart an intense sheen to the material.

Applications

As a result of the persistently high gold prices, applications using this material, whether indoors or out, are destined to be confined to single ornaments. Applications are mainly to be found in prestigious restoration projects, where decorative gold leaf is used. Very occasionally gold leaf will be used in a new project, when the (usually historical) setting justifies such an investment or when the architect wants to strike a special note with a particular part of a building.

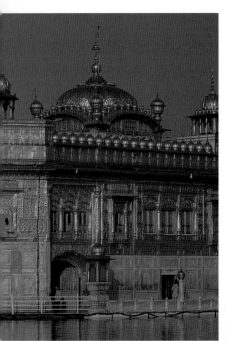

Project Golden Temple, Amritsar (1601)
Builder Shah Jehan
Photographer Thomas Dix

Project Lifting bridge Merwedekanaal, Nieuwegein (1999)
Architect Zwarts and Jansma
Photographer Herman van Doorn

Colour	**gold**
Glossiness	**glossy**, **satin**, matt
Translucence (%)	**0** – 20 – 40 – 60 – 80 – 100
Texture	sharp, medium, **dull**
Hardness	**hard**, soft, depressible
Temperature	warm, medium, **cool**
Odour	strong, moderate, **none**
Acoustic opacity	good, moderate, **poor**

Silver

Silber | Argent | Plata | Argento | Zilver

Project Hippodrome Theathre, Birmingham (2003)
Architect Buro Happold
Photographer HBG Constructions

Project Gilt leather, City Hall, Den Bosch (1670)
Photographer Gerard Monté

The mirror is the symbol of vanity, and without silver, there would be no mirrors. In the United States, shimmering 'silver' skyscrapers were built as early as the 1930s (the Art Deco era) and Europe was not far behind in embracing the trend for reflective façade surfaces. Although the extremely bright, shiny colour of the material still connotes prestige and a stylish image, the element silver has been a rare feature of façades in recent decades. Given the importance now attached to the transparency of the façade, one is more likely to see a treated glass surface (see *Glass*) with a silvery look.

Technical Aspects

Like gold, silver is only used as a (very thin) finishing coat. Silver leaf is made of pounded pure silver and can be affixed to nearly any surface. When used outdoors, a transparent protective coating is required.

Silver plating involves applying a layer of silver to a surface by chemical or electrolytic means. The basis for chemical silver-plating is a silver/ammonia solution. In the manufacture of mirrors, this solution is sprayed onto a glass surface that has been treated with tin chloride.

Galvanic or electrolytic silver-plating is one of the oldest applications of electroplating. The addition of brightening agents to the silver baths enhances the shine of the silver precipitate. The characteristics of silver, such as its bright colour and excellent electrical and heat conduction, remain intact with these techniques. To obtain a high sheen, the material is polished gently.

Applications

Plated silver is rarely used in outdoor applications, since from a distance the silver colour seldom matches the magical shine of gold. In interiors, on the other hand, walls and surfaces with a silver content are more common. Mirror walls or a single wall covered with silver leaf can create extraordinary spatial effects. Since the rise of the recent trend for 'vintage' interiors, antique mirrors (with or without peeling silver backing) have enjoyed considerable popularity.

Colour	silver
Glossiness	**glossy**, **satin**, matt
Translucence (%)	**0** – 20 – 40 – 60 – 80 – 100
Texture	sharp, medium, **dull**
Hardness	**hard**, soft, depressible
Temperature	warm, medium, **cool**
Odour	strong, moderate, **none**
Acoustic opacity	good, moderate, **poor**

Metal Treatments and Finishes

*Bearbeitung von Metallen | Traitements de métaux | Tratamiento de metales |
Trattamenti dei metalli | Bewerkingen van metaal*

Metals lend themselves to many different treatments, but can themselves be used in treatments and finishes applied to other materials. Some metals are even suitable for finishing other metals. When it comes to obtaining specific material properties or an aesthetic effect, the metals family demonstrates great flexibility and compatibility: certain treatments are universal to most metals (profiling and perforating, for example), in others one metal complements another (as in zinc and chrome plating). Metal treatments can be roughly divided into mechanical treatments and surface finishes. Mechanical treatments modify the relief, texture and/or form of the base product. In the case of surface finishes, the product is coated with another material in order to add colour or texture.

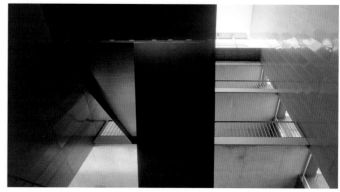

Project Headquarter Barcelona Activa (2003)
Architect Roldán + Berengué
Photographer Eva Serrats

This section confines itself to the most common treatments and finishes applied to metals. The focus is on the appearance of the material rather than the shape of the building element. Techniques such as welding, folding and thermal or laser cutting are therefore not dealt with here. Rather, the emphasis is on the treatment of sheet material, as this product is usually the starting point for a metal façade or skin. Exceptions to this are treatments involving metal wire.

Sheet Metal Treatments

Nowadays, architects wanting to impart a unique relief or pattern to a façade surface have a wide range of techniques to choose from. Patterns (perforations or surface relief, for example) can be applied with rollers, special presses can punch or stamp out figures in the materials and now there is even 'explosive forming', a technique for shaping sheet metal by means of explosions. Whereas in the past patterns were designed for individual façade elements, the present trend is for patterns that extend across the entire façade. This requires highly accurate preparation and production, something that can only be achieved by linking the computer programs used by the architect and the steel processing industry. Whereas only a decade ago, perforated panels were cut out of one large perforated sheet, nowadays it is possible to order individually perforated panels. Customized work is on the increase and is proving sufficiently affordable to make the use of slightly more expensive metals, like stainless steel, copper and brass, an interesting prospect. Processing techniques borrowed from other industries are also changing the face of architecture. Thermoforming, for example, was developed for

Project Acanthus, Amsterdam (2003)

Architect Branimir Medic and Pero Puljiz, de Architekten Cie.

Photographer Jeroen Musch

plastics, but the principle can also be applied to metals. The resulting curved elements are a further enrichment of the façade.

The Dutch applied research organization, TNO, was commissioned by SCOM (Foundation for Collective Metals Research) to develop a flexible bending technique using 'rubber presses'. This technique, which is economical even for short runs, makes it possible to bend profiles of different cross-sections into a variety of contours using a universal set of tools. Most applications to date have been in shipbuilding and vehicle engineering.

The Addition of Metal

Using metal to protect or beautify another metal is a simple concept with endless possibilities. The immersion bath technique for coating base metals with a more noble metal was driven by economics. It enabled a cheap base material to be turned into an elegant ornament (see also gold and silver-plating in the *Precious Metals* section). But the same process can equally well be used for plating steel with zinc in order to protect the steel from corrosion. Copper and lead have long been important ingredients in the production of paint. Copper or copper alloys form the base material for what is called ormolu. This is a gold-coloured metal powder used for making

Project French National Library, Paris (1995)

Architect Dominique Perrault, Paris

Photographer Georges Fessy, ADAGP

painter's gold, a substitute for genuine gold. Pure copper powder is the key component in 'bronze bottom paint', used for protecting wooden boats against fouling. Lead as a component of lead cyanamide is used in anti-corrosive paints and many pigments, although the use of such paints is nowadays subject to strict regulations owing to lead's high toxicity. Aluminizing, in which an aluminium coating is applied by thermal spraying, is a fairly recent technique designed to protect steel against corrosion. Although more expensive than zinc plating or non-metal coatings, aluminizing is extremely durable with a lifespan of some thirty to fifty years.

Additions to Metals

Surface treatments were originally developed to slow down or halt corrosion or leaching of metals. But protection is not the only reason for using surface treatments: beautification is at least as important a reason. Hence the close cooperation in this area between the steel and paint industries which work together to develop exciting new coatings, the most recent being fire-resistant intumescent paints and

Project Technical Pavilion, Hellevoetsluis (2003)

Architect Syb van Breda, Royal Haskoning

Photographer Syb van Breda

a special mother-of-pearl coating. The latter, which originated in the automotive industry, causes surfaces to change colour in response to changes in light intensity and viewing angle.

Metal Wire

The use of knitted and woven metal wire is relatively new in the field of architecture. The discovery of this material, in which French architect Dominique Perrault played a major role, has launched an entirely new industry. Until about ten years ago, the use of metal fabrics was almost completely confined to conveyor belts for the glass, meat and food processing industries. Since then, there has been a veritable explosion of architectural applications for woven metal mesh, due in no small part to the reflective qualities of these materials and the wide variety of textures, colours and visual densities available. This is an excellent example of how certain branches of industry, which on first sight have little or nothing to do with architecture, can nevertheless be a source of inspiration.

Profiling

Profilieren | Profilage | Perfilado | Profilatura | Profileren

Project CMC Building, Delft (1999)

Architect Syb van Breda, Royal Haskoning

Photographer Herman van Doorn

Profiling, which together with punching is one of the oldest metal-working techniques, is used for two reasons. Altering the cross-section of a sheet of metal can serve to give the construction element concerned greater strength and/or rigidity. But there may also be aesthetic reasons for changing the surface appearance of metal sheeting and it is this type of profiling that is dealt with here.

Corrugated metal sheeting, a common building material since the early nineteenth century, is the most familiar example of profiling. Applying a profile to a sheet of metal has since become an extremely versatile industrial technique. Nowadays, rather than being restricted to a single construction element, the profiling pattern tends to be applied across the entire length and height of the structure, creating the effect of a seamlessly profiled skin.

Technical Aspects

Most profiles are produced by roll forming, whereby a thin sheet of metal is passed over or between one or more rollers. In addition to the wide range of standardized profiles, project-specific profiles can now be produced at a reasonable price, provided a minimum purchase is guaranteed. Sheet thicknesses vary from 0.5 mm to 10 mm and widths up to 5 metres wide can be processed.

A pattern can also be applied by pressing a sheet against a mould. The high level of automation of these processes makes it possible, in a subsequent stage, to produce complex forms or perforations in sheets using advanced cutting and punching machines. Most metals of a given hardness are suitable for the application of a pattern or relief, the best known patterns being tear plate and button plate. After the relief is applied the sheet undergoes a surface treatment, which in most cases consists of a coating.

Applications

Profiled sheet metal is typically used in exterior applications. Once intended for industrial buildings and manufacturing plants, it is now a universal façade material. The most commonly used metals are steel and aluminium, which are coated before use. Profiles can also be made in brass, copper and stainless steel sheet. These metals can be used untreated in both interior and exterior applications.

Project Akerveld 4, Badhoevedorp (1997)

Architect Paul De Ley

Photographer Ger van der Vlugt

Colour	**variable**
Glossiness	glossy, **satin**, matt
Translucence (%)	**0** – 20 – 40 – 60 – 80 – 100
Texture	sharp, medium, **dull**
Hardness	**hard**, soft, depressible
Temperature	warm, medium, **cool**
Odour	strong, moderate, **none**
Acoustic opacity	good, moderate, **poor**

Profiled design metals come in all shapes and forms.
Kabel-Zaandam *helps to make the right choice for all design purposes,*
and produces a ready-for-use end product as well.

Expanding

Strecken | Expansion | Expansión | Mandrinatura | Strekken

Project Expanded metal by Kabel-Zaandam bv in Philips High
Tech Campus parking place, Eindhoven (2001)
Architect JHK Architects
Photographer Darius Lankhorst

Project Design expanded metal from Kabel-Zaandam bv in
Vrijthof parking place, Maastricht (2003)
Architect HS1 Architects
Photographer Riesjard Schropp Fotografie

Expanded metal is a relatively inexpensive product that can be used both horizontally and vertically. Industry, which is the biggest customer for expanded metal, generally uses it for horizontal applications such as floors, ceilings and stair treads. Expanded metal façades, in which the ruggedly industrial character of the material is used to make a statement, are a fairly recent phenomenon.

Technical Aspects

Expanded metal is produced by an expanding machine, which uses a pressured slitting and stretching process to transform solid metal sheets into expanded mesh. A variety of patterns, including the traditional diamond-shaped openings, can be produced, although the variations are limited to adjusting the length of the slit or the intensity of the stretch. After stretching, the sheet can be rolled to produce flattened expanded metal.

Steel is generally used for this process and finishes include galvanizing, anodizing, enamelling and painting. Alongside a standard range of expanded metal sheeting, most manufacturers supply standard building elements such as stair treads and floor units.

Applications

Zinc-plated steel elements made from expanded metal are increasingly finding their way into architecture. Not only is it a sturdy material (and consequently impact- and burglar-resistant), but its open structure can be exploited to modulate views through and insolation. For indoor applications, standard expanded metal ceiling 'tiles' are available in a range of metals. The open structure of expanded metal is a factor in the acoustics of any space in which it is used.

Colour	**variable**
Glossiness	glossy, **satin, matt**
Translucence (%)	**0** – 20 – 40 – 60 – 80 – 100
Texture	**sharp, medium, dull**
Hardness	**hard,** soft, depressible
Temperature	warm, medium, **cool**
Odour	strong, moderate, **none**
Acoustic opacity	good, moderate, **poor**

Ambasciata is an excellent example of a 'design expanded-metal'.
Kabel-Zaandam *supplies this and other designs for any project, from basic material off stock to a ready-for-use end product.*

Perforation

Perforieren | Perçage | Perforado | Perforazione | Perforeren

Project Centre for Human Drug Research, Leiden (1996)
Architect Cepezed
Photographer Bouwen met Staal

Project Media Library, Venissieux (2001)
Architect Dominique Perrault
Photographer ADAGP

'Personally I prefer to use circles. They stamp out more cleanly than squares.' Architect Herman Hertzberger clearly prefers circles, but had he so wanted he could have had flowers, diamonds or his own initials, for the sky is the limit when it comes to perforation. Hertzberger mainly uses perforated steel for railings or balustrades. However, façade-height applications have been spotted as well. One example in which perforated screens function as light and wind-breaks is the Centre for Human Drug Research in Leiden, the Netherlands, designed by the Delft architectural firm Cepezed. Here the perforations have been so designed to give employees a good view of the outside world, while at the same time creating a comfortable micro-climate in the zone between the screens and the building.

Technical Aspects

Perforating is nothing more than punching holes in a sheet of metal. It is done by placing the sheet over a matrix with holes and bringing a punch press down onto it with great force and velocity. An all-across perforating press can process sheets up to 1.5 m wide in a single pass. Most metals are suitable for perforation, although in practice only a few are used. The thickness of the metal sheet can vary from a few tenths of a millimetre (foil) to more than 10 mm.

Applications

The widespread use of perforated panels is not solely due to their decorative properties. Because they let through light, air and sound, the functional applications for such panels are infinite.

Perforated panels intended for exterior use are generally made of steel or aluminium. For interior use, perforated sheets of brass, copper and stainless steel are also available. In interior modular construction, standard wall and ceiling panels with a perforated metal skin and insulated core are available. These panels also serve an acoustic function.

Colour	variable
Glossiness	glossy, **satin, matt**
Translucence (%)	**0 – 20 – 40 – 60 – 80** – 100
Texture	**sharp, medium**, dull
Hardness	**hard**, soft, depressible
Temperature	warm, medium, **cool**
Odour	strong, moderate, **none**
Acoustic opacity	good, **moderate**, poor

There exists a wide range of perforated-metals.
*With **Kabel-Zaandam** there's lots of choice for all projects, from*
basic material off stock to a ready-for-use end product.

Thermoforming

Wärmebehandeln | Thermoformation | Moldeado por calor | Termoformatura | Thermovormen

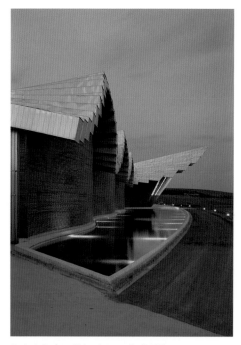

Project Bodega Ysios, Laguardia (2003)

Architect Santiago Calatrava

Photographer Bodegas & Bebidas Iverus San Sebastián

Michelangelo once said, 'Every work of art has at least twelve façades'. Nowadays, too, the idea that a building has only four walls and a roof seems quite outdated. However, the introduction of curved shapes in the façade surface has completely blurred the boundaries of the single external wall. Curved forms in the façade are easily achieved with metal, even when prefabricated insulated façade panels are used.

Technical Aspects

It is well-known that a sheet of metal is easier to shape when it is heated. If this heated sheet is then pressed into a mould, the result, after cooling, is a highly precise form. In this way, single or multiple two and three-dimensional forms with extremely low tolerances can be produced. Aluminium is the most common metal used in this method.

Thermoforming is an extremely popular process in the plastics industry. In the construction industry, working with moulds and short production runs always entails additional costs and a longer production time. The moulds themselves are made with the aid of 3D design programs. After the material has been shaped it often undergoes a final surface treatment.

Applications

Thermoforming is only economically feasible for large buildings where a large section of the façade is designed in a certain form. There is (as yet) no profit incentive for manufacturers to produce standard curved panels, although the possibility of reusing the moulds would certainly help.

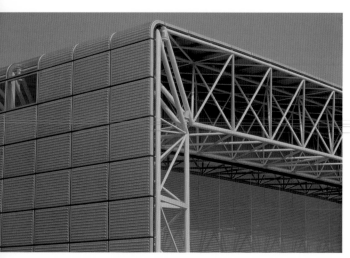

Project Sainsbury Centre for Visual Arts, Norwich (1978)

Architect Foster and Partners

Photographer John Donat

Colour	variable
Glossiness	**glossy**, satin, matt
Translucence (%)	**0** – 20 – 40 – 60 – 80 – 100
Texture	sharp, **medium**, dull
Hardness	**hard**, soft, depressible
Temperature	warm, medium, **cool**
Odour	strong, moderate, **none**
Acoustic opacity	good, moderate, **poor**

Explosive Forming

Exploforming | Exploformer | Exploforma | Formatura ad esplosione | Exploformeren

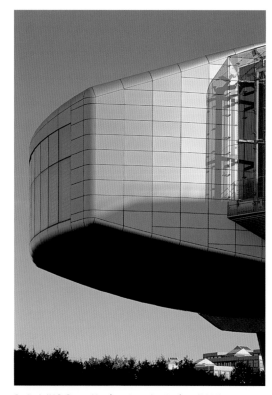

Project ING Group Headquarters, Amsterdam (2002)
Architect Meyer en Van Schooten Architecten bv
Photographer Georges Fessy, ADAGP

Project Haarlemmermeer Pavilion, Floriade 2002, Haarlemmermeer (2002)
Architect Asymptote Architects
Photographer Kees Hummel

What do you do if you want a wavy façade surface but no standard profiled sheet gives the desired effect? The solution, as Dutch architect Dirk Jan Postel discovered when he was looking for a special façade cladding for a theatre in Alphen aan den Rijn, is 'explosive forming', a technique that makes it possible to create panels with a unique relief that is also attractively asymmetrical. The aluminium panels that will eventually grace the theatre have been dubbed Desert Storm, an allusion to the rippling sand that inspired the undulating pattern.

Technical Aspects

Explosive forming, begins with the construction of a die, the form of which is determined with the aid of a 3D AutoCad program. The design is first tested in a number of sample dies in a different material, after which the actual die is milled from solid steel. After the aluminium sheet has been placed over the steel die, die and panel are placed in a vacuum chamber and submitted to the blast of controlled explosions that press the panel against the die.

This technology enables highly complex forms to be made. Although aluminium is the ideal material, harder metals such as steel are also suitable. However, the process is labour-intensive and the time it takes to design and manufacture the moulds makes for a relatively long preparation phase. Once formed, the panel can undergo conventional surface treatments.

Applications

Because it allows great freedom of design and is also suited to short production runs, this technique is mostly used for works of art and lettering on façades. The technique is also particularly suitable for façades with an unusual pattern in which case the shaped panels can be attached to an insulated substrate using mechanical fastenings or glue.

Colour	**variable**
Glossiness	**glossy, satin, matt**
Translucence (%)	**0 – 20 – 40 – 60 – 80 – 100**
Texture	sharp, **medium**, **dull**
Hardness	**hard**, soft, depressible
Temperature	warm, medium, **cool**
Odour	strong, moderate, **none**
Acoustic opacity	good, moderate, **poor**

Coating

Beschichten\ Enrobage | Imprimación | Coating | Coaten

Project Odyssey, Belfast (2000)
Architect MHB Design, London (in cooperation with Consarc, Belfast)
Photographer TBC

The discovery that the application of a layer of paint or some other coating provides excellent protection from corrosion was made at the time of the earliest iron structures. It is hardly surprising, therefore, that the paint industry has come to play an important role in the use of metals in architecture. The development of new types of paint or application methods goes hand in hand with the increasing use of metals in façades. The latest innovation is one that crossed over from the automotive industry: a mother-of-pearl coating that changes colour in response to changes in light intensity and viewing angle.

Technical Aspects
Painting, varnishing or coating are different names for the principle of applying an airtight and waterproof layer to metal with a view to preventing corrosion. Basically the treatment consists of three stages: preparation of the surface, the application of the paint and the final inspection. Surface preparation often entails abrasive blasting and smoothing of the metal.

Most types of paints consist of a mixture of binding agents, fillers, pigments and solvents and thinners. There are various ways of applying the paint: with brush or roller, by spraying, immersion, mechanical roller or drum or by way of casting. A much-used method for façade panels is powder coating, a process whereby paint is sprayed onto the metal in the form of an electrostatically charged powder which adheres to the grounded part. The part is then placed in a curing oven where the particles melt and fuse to provide a continuous smooth coating. With duplex systems, the surface is first hot-dip galvanized and then coated.

Applications
Nearly all steel and aluminium elements used on the exterior of buildings are finished with a coating. Coatings are available in the full range of RAL colours. If possible, façade elements should be wholly prefabricated so that the protective layer of paint can be applied under optimal conditions. The detailing of joints between elements requires special attention as damage to the coating (during on-site assembly, for example) can result in corrosion.

Project Water villa, Middelburg (2000)
Architect Hertzberger Architectuurstudio
Photographer Gerrit Min

Colour	**variable**
Glossiness	**glossy**, **satin**, **matt**
Translucence (%)	**0** – 20 – 40 – 60 – 80 – 100
Texture	sharp, medium, **dull**
Hardness	**hard**, soft, depressible
Temperature	warm, medium, **cool**
Odour	strong, moderate, **none**
Acoustic opacity	good, moderate, **poor**

HPS200® by Corus. Colour selected with Repertoire™.
Website: www.colorcoat-online.com

Anodizing

Anodisieren | Anodisation | Anodización | Anodizzazione | Anodiseren

Project Center for Book Treatment, Bussy Saint Georges (1995)
Architect Dominique Perrault
Photographer Georges Fessy, ADAGP

Before sophisticated coatings and enamels appeared on the scene, anodizing was the method for protecting aluminium from corrosion. This process gives aluminium a hard, glassy and corrosion-resistant layer, making it possible to use the metal 'au naturel' in architectural applications. The addition of pigments during the process adds colour to the otherwise transparent coat.

Technical Aspects

Anodizing is a surface treatment for metals. It is an electrolytic process, where the metal to be treated is introduced anodically (attached to the positive pole) into an electrolyte. Oxygen, which is produced on the metal by the electrical current, generates a strong oxide layer that increases the metal's resistance to corrosion. This is an especially popular method of protecting aluminium, which is usually anodized in sulphuric acid, a procedure that makes it possible to add colour to the protective layer. The pigments are added after rinsing and before sealing. It is also possible to apply colour directly when anodizing, either with a special bath solution or by using a particular aluminium alloy.

Other examples of metals that can be anodized are zinc and titanium. The chromic acid method used for zinc imparts a green protective layer to the material. Anodizing titanium gives the metal a dull grey surface.

Applications

Anodized aluminium is used on the outside of buildings in the form of façade panels, shop fronts, frames and doors. This protective process is also used to treat stairway components and window and door hardware. In detailing anodized elements, designers should allow for slight dimensional changes: the anodized layer thickens the material somewhat.

Project ING Group Headquarters, Amsterdam (2002)
Architect Meyer en Van Schooten Architecten bv
Photographer Georges Fessy, ADAGP

Colour	**variable**
Glossiness	**glossy, satin, matt**
Translucence (%)	**0** – 20 – 40 – 60 – 80 – 100
Texture	sharp, medium, **dull**
Hardness	**hard**, soft, depressible
Temperature	warm, medium, **cool**
Odour	strong, moderate, **none**
Acoustic opacity	good, moderate, **poor**

Enamelling

Emaillieren | Emaillage | Esmaltado | Smaltatura | Emailleren

Project Amstel Poort, Amsterdam (1983)
Architect Ben Loerakker
Photographer Kees Hummel

Project Exxon headquarters, Southampton (1995)
Architect Swanke | Hayden | Connell
Photographer David Bartok for Polyvision nv

Although enamel forms only a thin layer on metal, it is a layer with visual depth. This characteristic helps to make enamel perhaps the most decorative method of protecting metal, as does the fact that enamelling is the perfect technique for applying multiple colours to a metallic surface.

Technical Aspects

As a coating for metal, enamel is midway between glass and ceramic and bears comparison with a glaze. It starts as a mixture of glass powder, clay, water, pigments and fillers. This slurry can be applied to the (primed) metal in several ways: by immersion, spraying or a turn and coat technique. Newer methods are electrostatic spraying and electrophoretic enamelling. After the coating has dried, the object is fired in an oven where the temperature can reach as much as 800 °C for steel. The result is a hard, non-transparent layer that protects the metal well against corrosion. Enamel also comes as a dry powder which can be sprinkled on a preheated metal object.

In the past, enamel had the reputation of chipping easily. Modern enamelling techniques produce a highly impact resistant and resilient coat.

Applications

Because of the superior strength characteristics of enamel, this method of protecting surfaces is perfect for exterior applications or where the object will be subjected to extreme conditions (high temperatures or chemical fumes and spills). But the decorative aspects of this surface treatment also offer many possibilities: advertising signs, signposts, et cetera. The use of enamel has decreased with the development of coatings, because the preparation time and the enamelling process are labour-intensive and consequently more expensive.

Colour	**variable**
Glossiness	**glossy**, **satin**, matt
Translucence (%)	**0** – 20 – 40 – 60 – 80 – 100
Texture	sharp, medium, **dull**
Hardness	**hard**, soft, depressible
Temperature	warm, medium, **cool**
Odour	strong, moderate, **none**
Acoustic opacity	good, moderate, **poor**

Galvanization

Galvanisieren | Galvanisation | Galvanizado | Zincatura | Verzinken

Project Business Circuit, New Vennep (2002)
Architect GroupA Architects
Photographer Brakkee & Scagliola

The motorway crash barrier, a metal product most people whizz past without a second glance, has metamorphosed as a façade material in the hands of GroupA Architects who used metre after metre of zinc-coated steel crash barrier for the façade of a multiple occupancy office building in New Vennep, in the Netherlands. This is but one example of a trend that has seen galvanized steel being increasingly used as a façade material and in other high visibility applications.

Technical Aspects

Hot-dip galvanization coats steel with an impermeable, self-healing oxide film. Immediately after galvanizing, the treated metal is a shiny grey, which gradually dulls and turns slightly darker.

Before being galvanized, steel must first be thoroughly cleaned by means of abrasive blasting and pickling. The steel element can then be dipped into a bath of molten zinc. It is essential that vent holes are made in the element to avoid the formation of potentially explosive air bubbles. Zinc baths can be as much as 3 metres deep, 2 metres wide and 15 metres in length. Several measures are necessary to prevent steel from warping during the process. Elements should be constructed as symmetrically as possible, large differences in material thickness in a single object should be avoided and thin sheet steel should be supported with cross stays.

Applications

Galvanized steel, in the form of gratings, stairs or structural components, is primarily used in locations with a corrosive environment and where maintenance is difficult. Galvanized steel façade elements are becoming increasingly popular, however, as the material can be used without any further treatment.

Project Borneo Sporenburg, Amsterdam (2003)
Architect M3H Architects
Photographer Michel Claus

Colour	**grey**
Glossiness	glossy, **satin**, **matt**
Translucence (%)	**0** – 20 – 40 – 60 – 80 – 100
Texture	sharp, medium, **dull**
Hardness	**hard**, soft, depressible
Temperature	warm, medium, **cool**
Odour	strong, moderate, **none**
Acoustic opacity	good, moderate, **poor**

Patination

Patinieren | Patinage | Pátina | Patinatura | Patineren

Project New Metropolis, Amsterdam (1997)
Architect Renzo Piano Building Workshop
Photographer Kees Hummel

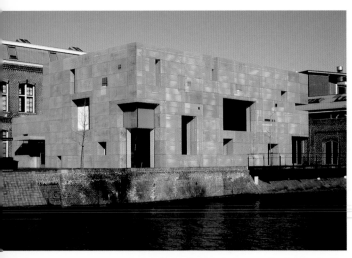

Project Manually patinated copper, Sarphatistraat offices, Amsterdam (2000)
Architect Steven Holl
Photographer Jan Derwig

Hand in hand with the late 20th-century desire to use 'natural' metals in façades and roofs came an environmentally inspired concern with the 'leaching' of metal oxides from such claddings. Architects were keen to find some way of sparing the environment while continuing to use untreated metals. They found it in 'patination', the artificial ageing of metal that all but halts the leaching process. This artificial application of a patina that usually takes many decades to evolve naturally, has become extremely popular, especially for copper. Copper's fairly even discoloration under this process is greatly appreciated by architects. Renzo Piano clad his NEMO science centre in Amsterdam with an almost evenly green patinated copper.

Technical Aspects

Patination, or the artificial ageing of metals, is a chemical procedure that is carried out at high temperatures. The oxide layer ('patina') that is artificially applied to copper consists of a basic copper sulphate. This protective layer is stable and self-healing and therefore highly resistant to corrosion. Patinated copper is available in the familiar yellow-green to blue-green colour range and in a dark-brown version that turns almost dark grey over time.

After an artificial patina has been applied, losses in material thickness are insignificant, a maximum of 0.3 mm per year. Although leaching is negligible, rainwater pathways must be taken into account in detailing to prevent local discoloration by dirt or oxides.

All the usual ways of working metal, such as lockforming and bending, are possible with patinated copper as are soft solder joints.

Applications

Patinated copper is used for both roofs and façades. Often the material is applied in bays and attached using traditional folded seam techniques. Because the material can be easily cold-formed in the direction of the bay, curved shapes are easily formed.

Colour	variable
Glossiness	glossy, **satin**, **matt**
Translucence (%)	**0** – 20 – 40 – 60 – 80 – 100
Texture	sharp, medium, **dull**
Hardness	**hard**, soft, depressible
Temperature	warm, medium, **cool**
Odour	strong, moderate, **none**
Acoustic opacity	good, moderate, **poor**

Chrome Plating

Verchromen I Chromage I Cromado I Cromatura I Verchromen

Project Chrysler Building, New York (1930)

Architect William van Alen

Photographer © Peter Mauss I Esto

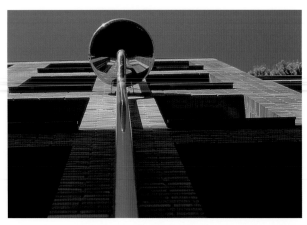

Project Rainwaterdrain Vrolikstraat, Amsterdam (1997)

Architect M3H Architects

Photographer Kees Hummel

Chrome-plated objects shine like silver. And therein lies the market for this treatment: wherever the shine of silver is required, but not its price tag. It is therefore not surprising that chrome plating is a treatment that is subject to the vagaries of fashion.

In present-day architecture and interior design its use is mainly confined to door and window hardware.

Technical Aspects

Decorative chrome plating uses electroplating techniques to apply a layer of chromium to a metal substrate (usually nickel) in thicknesses ranging from 0.25 to 0.3 μm. The thin layer of chrome contributes greatly to corrosion resistance as well as being hard-wearing and scratch proof. With hard chrome plating (entailing a thicker layer of 15 to 300 μm), the chromium layer acquires the function of a wear-resistant layer. Applications include shock absorbers and landing gear in the aircraft industry. This form of chrome plating may be followed by a finishing process, such as grinding or polishing.

Modern high-lustre nickel baths make it possible to carry out the entire process of pre-treatment and chrome plating in a single sequence. However, because chrome baths generally provide inadequate coverage, auxiliary anodes should be attached in order to allow the current to penetrate the depths and ensure that chrome as well as nickel is deposited in the deeper parts of profiled objects.

Applications

In architecture, chrome-plated elements are chiefly used in interiors, in elements such as handrails, fittings and door and window hardware. Outdoor applications are few, despite the fact that the finished products lend themselves superbly to exterior applications, due to the excellent wear-resistant and corrosion-resistant qualities of the chrome layer.

Colour	**silver**
Glossiness	**glossy**, satin, matt
Translucence (%)	**0** – 20 – 40 – 60 – 80 – 100
Texture	sharp, medium, **dull**
Hardness	**hard**, soft, depressible
Temperature	warm, medium, **cool**
Odour	strong, moderate, **none**
Acoustic opacity	good, moderate, **poor**

Blasting and Shot-Peening

Sandstrahlen | Décapage au jet de sable | Acabado al chorro de arena | Sabbiatura | Stralen

Project Extension Rembrandthuis, Amsterdam (1998)
Architect Zwarts & Jansma
Photographer Jan Derwig

Textural differences or even contrasts are a favourite instrument of architects and designers. By using the same material, but blasting or shot-peening only certain sections, the designer can use the façade to play with daylight by creating differences in how light is reflected. This is especially true where the selected metal is one that does not require a surface treatment, such as stainless steel.

Technical Aspects

Blasting is often still erroneously referred to as 'sandblasting', even though the use of sand (or grit containing quartz) has been prohibited by law since 1956,* due to the unacceptably high risk of black lung (silicosis). Hazardous substances may also be released during the use of other, legal, blasting agents. Blasting and shot-peening are therefore always subject to strict health and safety regulations. The process is used for cleaning, polishing or decorating surfaces. Particles are sprayed with immense force against the surface of the sheet metal or other material in a carrier of water or air. The difference in medium – sharp-edged grit in the case of blasting and spherical beads in the case of peening – is reflected in a difference in appearance after treatment.

Blasting for decorative purposes is completely computer-controlled nowadays: digitally-fed patterns can be transferred to large surfaces (in sections) where they are manifested through the contrast between matt/rough and shiny surface areas.

Applications

Because blasting must take place under properly ventilated conditions, façade elements that incorporate blasted sheet metal are always prefabricated. Decorative patterns are usually found in advertising (lettering, signs) or in interior applications. The most frequently used metals are stainless steel, aluminium, copper and brass.

* in the Netherlands; now prohibited throughout the European Union.

Colour	**variable**
Glossiness	glossy, **satin, matt**
Translucence (%)	**0** – 20 – 40 – 60 – 80 – 100
Texture	**sharp, medium,** dull
Hardness	**hard,** soft, depressible
Temperature	warm, medium, **cool**
Odour	strong, moderate, **none**
Acoustic opacity	good, moderate, **poor**

Weaving and Knitting

Stricken und Weben | Tricotage et Tissage | Soldado y Forjado | Lavorazione in maglie e tessitura | Breien en weven

Project Watchtower Documentation Centre Berlin Wall
Architect Zerr Hapke Nieländer Architekten
Photographer Grohe Lichtbogen, Berlin

Project French National Library, Paris (1995)
Architect Dominique Perrault, Paris
Photographer Georges Fessy, ADAGP

Woven or knitted metal fabric, also called wire mesh, is a popular material in the glass and meat processing industries, where it is used for conveyor belts. It is said that while French architect Dominique Perrault was researching materials for his Bibliothèque National in Paris, he happened to visit a family friend who ran a slaughterhouse and that it was here that he 'discovered' wire mesh for architecture. In Perrault's National Library, frames with metal mesh stretched across them like canvases are positioned behind the building's glass façades in order to screen out or modulate daylight.

Knitting or interlacing of metal wire is a centuries-old technique: knights wore a medieval version of the bullet-proof vest known as chain mail. Whereas the historical garment was composed of small steel rings, modern knitted metal is a mesh of interlocking loops and is available in a variety of patterns. The material is generally used as a free-hanging curtain behind a transparent façade.

Technical Aspects

Machine-woven wire mesh is available in many different patterns, dimensions and weave densities. Steel, stainless steel or aluminium wire are the most commonly used metals, although rare instances of brass and copper have been noted in interior applications. The common wire diameters for knitting and weaving vary from 0.2 mm to 3.0 mm, which produce meshes with translucencies of 35% and 80%. Woven metal mesh is mounted on frames and some pre- and/or post-tensioning is usually necessary to compensate for some stretching or sagging due to the weight of the material.

Most metals are suitable for knitting although in architectural applications the most commonly used are steel, stainless steel and aluminium. Manufacturers can supply a range of structures or patterns in which the wire diameter and wire count of the fabric are variable. The translucency of the material can be anywhere between 30% and 80%. Because knitting is 'cast off' (the edges are finished) the material can be top-hung like conventional draperies, although it is necessary to allow for the fact that the fabric will stretch slightly due to its own weight.

Applications

In the past decade, metal mesh has outgrown its industrial image and acquired a wide range of new applications. It is still most frequently encountered as a daylight-filtering curtain directly behind transparent outer walls, often mounted on movable panels. Woven and knitted metal mesh can also be used as an area divider or to hide certain parts of a building (such as wiring or ducting at ceiling level). Depending on the material used, metal mesh can also be used in exterior applications, for example as a sun control element or as façade cladding, as in another building by Dominique Perrault, the Berlin velodrome (1997).

Colour	variable
Glossiness	**glossy**, **satin**, **matt**
Translucence (%)	0 – 20 – 40 – 60 – 80 – 100
Texture	sharp, **medium**, **dull**
Hardness	hard, soft, **depressible**
Temperature	warm, medium, **cool**
Odour	strong, moderate, **none**
Acoustic opacity	good, **moderate**, poor

The ARTOS® stainless steel woven screen is produced by Andreas Kufferath & Co. in Düren, German. Andreas Kufferath & Co. is one of the world's leading metal weavers.

Plastics

Plastik | Plastiques | Plásticos | Materie plastiche | Plastic

In 1961, you could buy a plastic house in the Detroit suburbs.
They came on two trucks, and crews bolted them to cement bases,
so they wouldn't blow over...
The ads said: 'Live in the Future!' and 'Science Comes Home!'...
Our kitchen table was plastic. Our radio was plastic.
Our couch was not leather or fabric, but somewhere in between.
My mom bought some plastic fruit for decoration.
We were like Eskimos, living in a suburban igloo,
and we loved it.

From 'Plastic House' by Alan Mitchell

Plastic is the newest family of building materials. Initially, it was used for purely utilitarian purposes in the form of plastic sheeting, insulating foam, rainwater pipes and coatings. However, in the 1960s and '70s, manufacturers began exploring the aesthetic potential of plastics. As with all experimentation, it was a long time before the technical properties of plastic had been developed to the point where it became a full-fledged building material – durable, UV-resistant and weatherproof.

The search for an inexpensive and technically superior substitute for natural materials began early in the 19th century. The era of synthetics commenced in 1860 with Adolf von Bayer's discovery of a chemical phenol bond. The Belgian scientist, Leo Baekeland, later developed this finding into phenolic resins, which were to become well-known under the brand name Bakelite. Powdered Bakelite was placed in moulds and deformed under high temperatures and pressures, so becoming the first material to shape itself, as it were; it was used primarily for making household items. It was followed by the urea and melamine resins, best know from their use in kitchen tables and cupboards. Between 1910 and 1940 one plastic after another was developed in rapid succession: polyvinyl chloride (PVC), acrylic plastic (including PMMA), polystyrene (PS), polyester, melamine and epoxy resins, polyamides, et cetera.

In the years leading up to the Second World War, defence departments actively encouraged further development in the plastics field. In the United States, silicones, polytetrafluoroethylene (PTFE or Teflon) and ABS plastics were introduced in the 1940s. The production of polyurethane (PU), polycarbonate (PC) and polypropylene (PP) began in the 1950s. During the energy crisis of the 1970s, the plastics industry experienced a downturn due to the high production costs and environmental concerns. Despite investment in safer and environmentally friendlier production techniques and recycling systems, there has been no real development of plastics for the building industry since that time.

Thermoplastics, Thermosets and Elastomers

Plastic is a collective name for a huge variety of materials, each with its own specific properties. The most general classification of plastics relates to their thermal deformability, the three main categories being thermoplastics, thermosets and elastomers.

Thermoplastics become soft above a certain temperature – the so-called glass transition temperature – and as it cools, it re-vitrifies. The process is endlessly reversible so that having been deformed, a thermoplastic can be 'remelted' and given a different shape. This is impossible with a thermoset: once heated above its glass transition temperature, unbreakable bonds are formed, making reshaping impossible. Bakelite is a typical thermoset: hard, brittle and breakable and not thermally deformable. Elastomers are thermosets that are lightly cross-linked making possible an elasticity exceeding 100%. Some 61% of elastomers are synthetic in origin or a by-product of the oil industry; the rest are latex derivatives.

Most of today's plastics consist of synthetic polymers, in particular synthetic resins, plastics and synthetic rubbers. The rest are biopolymers occurring in living organisms, such as cellulose, celluloid, casein, cellophane, ebonite, rubber and starch.

Architectural Applications

The word *plastic* is derived from the ancient Greek word *plastikos*, meaning 'suitable for forming'. Plastic's flexible properties make it highly suitable for making free, round or undulating forms. In the construction industry, where plastic was initially used as a substitute for more expensive materials, ease of maintenance and durability were emphasized alongside the low cost. In the 1950s, while American and Scandinavian designers such as Charles and Ray Eames, Verner Panton, Eero Saarinen and Arne Jacobsen were busy pioneering the use of plastic in furniture, the material was still something of an outsider in the construction industry where even today the use of plastic remains controversial. Early versions in particular,

Project Futuro House (1968)

Architect Matti Suuronen

Photographer Corbis

429

Project Kunsthal, Rotterdam (1992)
Architect Rem Koolhaas, OMA
Photographer Kees Hummel

The first house to be constructed entirely of plastic was designed by an American engineer, Albert G.H. Dietz. The first structure made entirely of composites was the Maison des Arts Ménagers by French architect, Ionel Schein in collaboration with R.A. Coulon and Yves Magnant. Disneyland's House of the Future, opened in 1957, was a project of the American firm, Monsanto and the architects Hamilton and Goody, in collaboration with M.I.T.

The floors, walls and ceiling of this house were all made of plastic. In addition, it contained not a single piece of furniture made of a natural material: everything was 'ultra modern' and almost entirely synthetic. The furnishings, which reflected a period dominated by futuristic technical developments (inspired by the recent moon landing), featured amongst other things a high-tech kitchen equipped with a then revolutionary microwave oven. Ironically, when the house came to be demolished in 1967, the scheduled one day stretched to two weeks because the wrecking ball kept bouncing off the walls. In the end the house had to be sawn into pieces.

Finnish architect Matti Suuronen designed this UFO-shaped dwelling in 1968 for use as a ski cabin or holiday home. The design concept was a reflection of the optimistic belief prevailing in the 1960s, that technology was the answer to all of mankind's problems. People looked forward to a new era, the Space Age, in which everyone would have more leisure time for holidays away from home.

Completely furnished and able to accommodate eight people, the Futuro House was constructed entirely of a new, light and inexpensive material, reinforced plastic. The plan was to mass-produce the house so that it would be cheap enough to house people all around the world. Its light weight made it easy to transport and brought mobile living – the trend of the future – within reach. People would be able take their movable home with them wherever they went and live like 'modern nomads'. Unfortunately, the 1973 oil crisis put paid

such as melamine and the first HPL panels, had the disadvantage of discolouring and soiling easily.

Natural materials like wood, stone and metals become more attractive and valuable with age. Plastic, in contrast, is not a 'living' material and as it ages it often does so ungracefully. Moreover, architects interested in working with plastics have to contend with a dearth of useful information on plastics. Aside from a confusing list of abbreviations, such as PMMA, PP, PC, PVC, ETFE, et cetera, which does not make the subject any more accessible or easy to understand, most architectural courses pay precious little attention to plastics.

However, plastic is slowly shedding the negative image it once had because of its use as an imitator of other materials, and, thanks to improved quality, as well as the positive effects of so-called blob architecture and free design, plastic is now getting a new lease of life. It is extremely suitable for making complex shapes, something that might even be done on an industrialized scale in future, rather than being restricted to high-budget projects. At present, the development of plastics for the construction industry is pretty well confined to the improvement of existing claddings and products.

Project Olympic Velodrome, Berlin (1999)
Architect Dominique Perrault
Photographer Georges Fessy and Werner Huthmacher, ADAGP

to all these fine plans. Soaring plastic prices made production unprofitable. In the end, only twenty Futuro Houses were ever built.

Olivetti's training centre in Haslemere, England, designed by James Stirling and built between 1969 and 1973, is a magnificent example of how the use of plastic as a construction material can result in industrial architecture with a new and striking look. The building's steel frame is clad with glossy, brightly coloured, prefabricated glass fibre reinforced

Project Schaulager Museum, Basel (2003)
Architect Herzog & De Meuron
Photographer Thomas Dix

plastic panels. With its rounded corners, a roof that carries over into the façade, small integrated windows and use of colour, this building exploited the design potential of plastic to the full.

Gunter Behnisch is another architect who has worked a lot with plastic, including in his spectacular Olympic Stadium in Munich (1972) where the entire ingenious roof construction of cables and guys is clad with lightweight, transparent acrylic panels.

Another popular application of plastic is as a substitute for glass. Transparent acrylics and polycarbonates are impact resistant, lightweight and available in insulating, multi-wall versions. These products are best known as a cladding for skylights and light domes, but they can also be used as façade panelling, as in 'The Plastic Lantern', a dance centre in Deptford, London, designed by Herzog & De

Meuron. It admits daylight, insulates and, at night, illuminates the building with a mysterious, multi-coloured glow.

Koen van Velsen's Pathé Cinema in Rotterdam is another building that lights up at night, in this case like a warm, festively glowing, just landed UFO. The entire façade is clad in corrugated single-wall polycarbonate panels, normally a quite prosaic product available from any building supplies shop but in this case made fire resistant with a special additive. Unfortunately, it is just as prone to soiling as its poorer do-it-yourself relative.

Textile architecture, for the most part tent and pneumatic constructions, can be made from a variety of plastics such as polyester textile, with or without a PVC coating, or the much more durable glass fibre fabrics with a Teflon coating. These textiles have undergone vast improvement and are produced in a range of qualities. They are available in virtually any colour, printed or perforated, self-extinguishing, from opaque to almost transparent, from foldable to rigid.

Although an extruded film rather than a textile, ETFE is nevertheless an extremely strong and durable addition to this field and one with spectacular applications, ranging from a simple party tent to the Millennium Dome. ETFE's greatest advantages are its light weight, mobility, large surfaces and, thanks to technical improvements, its increasing durability.

Coatings are in the vast majority of cases plastic products. Initially developed as a protective coat, they are now employed by architects as a seamless, lustrous, encompassing skin. Italian-born architect Gaetano Pesce is especially fascinated by plastics because of their contemporary quality. For his TBWA offices in New York (1994), he coated the entire interior, with the objective of giving the offices, which feature optimal contact with the outside world via integrated telecommunications and computers, a more domestic atmosphere.

In 1992 Pesce developed polyurethane blocks with a view to stacking them to create a façade, a plan he put into practice in 1998 in his Bahia guest house. Pesce's choice of plastic is quite deliberate: 'As an architect, you use the materials of your time and of the future – if I had wanted to use natural stone, my name would have been Brunelleschi.'

Since their earliest beginnings, plastics have appealed to the imagination: new forms, colours and techniques inspired many designers to adopt a new style. Plastic has never lost its futuristic character, and even though the development of new plastics for the construction industry is presently on the back burner, blob architecture, innovative composites and knowledge exchange between different branches of industry, augur well for the future of plastics in building – no longer as a cheap substitute for conventional materials, but one with its own identity, performance qualities, design and image.

Thermosets, Thermoplastics and Elastomers

Duroplaste, thermoplastische Kunststoffe und Elastomere | Thermosets, thermoplastiques et élastomères | Termosets, termoplásticos y elastómeros | Termoindurenti, termoplastici ed elastomeri | Thermoplastics, thermoharders en elastomeren

The world of plastics is a complex and extraordinarily multifaceted one. Plastics are so versatile that it can confidently be stated that they are now poised to replace the entire spectrum of traditional materials, such as wood, ceramics, metal and glass.

Every material has its own life cycle. For the last one hundred years, the primary material employed in the construction industry has been steel. However, the possibilities for technological development in metals have been exhausted to such an extent that very few improvements or innovations in respect of these materials or their exploitation can be expected in the foreseeable future; and yet this is precisely what a material needs in order to 'survive'. Plastics, on the other hand, are still in their infancy as a construction material. Of particular interest are the seemingly limitless possibilities of composites and custom made products designed to fulfil precisely a given project's requirements for strength, impact resistance, scratch resistance, ultraviolet resistance, transparency and reflection, insulating properties, et cetera.

For pioneering architects interested in taking full advantage of the possibilities offered by plastics, it is essential to develop a familiarity with their basic properties and typology. To begin with, plastics can be divided into three main groups: thermoplastics, thermosets and elastomers. The difference between the first two lies in their reaction to heat.

Thermoplastics and Thermosets

At ambient temperatures, thermoplastics are brittle or plastic-elastic (a high volume percentage of plasticisers present); however, at high-

Project 'Light Building' Museum pavilion, Rotterdam (2001)
Architect Atelier Kempe Thill, Rotterdam
Photographer Bastiaan IngenHousz

er temperatures (80 to 120 °C) they become deformable because the crosslinks between the polymer chains are thermally activated, enabling the chains to shift in relation to one another. Unlike thermoplastics, thermosets cannot be returned to a plastic, deformable state following deformation and hardening. The cause lies in the chemical composition and structure of the various plastics.

The main properties of thermoplastics compared with thermosets are:
• Thermoplastics are temperature-sensitive
• They dissolve or soften in solvents
• Thermoplastics are generally softer
• They can melt or burn
Some examples of thermoplastics are PMMA (Plexiglas) PC (Makrolon and Lexaan), PVC, polystyrene, polypropylene and polyethylene.

The main properties of thermosets compared with thermoplastics:
• Less temperature-sensitive than thermoplastics
• They do not dissolve (at most they swell)
• They are harder, less elastic
• Thermoplastics do not melt or burn, or do so poorly.
Some examples of thermosets are Bakelite, epoxy, polyester.

Elastomers
Elastomers are characterized by a coarse-meshed, three-dimensionally crosslinked structure brought about by a process of vulcanization. This makes them very elastic (i.e. the material returns to its original form) under moderate stress at ambient temperatures. The vulcanized crosslinks between the chains, also referred to as network structures, are not liable to thermal activation. Thus elastomers continue to behave elastically and have neither a plastic nor a liquid state. At very high temperatures (+300 °C), they ignite. Natural rubber, silicone rubbers and some elastic polyurethanes, as well as the roofing material EPDM, are elastomers.

The above applies to plastics in their pure form. However, in practice, including in the construction industry, much use is made of various fillers and reinforcing fibres which compensate the negative properties of pure plastics. For example, glass fibre reinforced plastic has a higher fire and UV resistance, and coatings and co-extrusion substances can render a material scratch-resistant, UV resistant and dirt repellent.

A plastic's hardness is indicated by means of the Shore Scale. There are two hardness scales, Shore A and Shore D, each having a range from 10 to 90. A is for soft plastics, D for harder ones. For example: Shore A 20 is as soft as putty, Shore A 40 is like a rubber eraser and Shore A 90 is roughly equivalent to Shore D 30

The technology and use of plastics originated in the aerospace and automobile industries. Now the possibilities offered by the malleability, lightness and performance qualities of plastics are leading to them being increasingly chosen over glass. For example, the complex side window of the Smart car is made of polycarbonate. Similarly, for the windows of Werner Sobek's R129 housing project, acrylic glass (PMMA) was laminated to 1 mm-thick chemically prestressed glass, in order to make the windows scratch- and chemical-resistant.

Project The Reality, Almere (1990)
Architect Teun Koolhaas Associates
Photographer Jan Derwig

A low-E coating guarantees temperature regulation throughout the year, while an electrochromic layer makes it possible to adjust the amount of light admitted. The PMMA sheets and the glass were glued together without any auxiliary construction and are self-supporting. Extruded sheets are, in contrast to moulded sheets, less resistant to chemical agents because of their shorter molecular chains. Careful detailing is required to allow for expansion.

Forms
Plastics are subject to 'creep', a material's tendency to deform under its own weight. With the addition of glass, carbon or aramide fibre, plastics become an excellent structural material in the form of binding agents, although up to now they have only been used in relatively small structures or bridges. Tent structures are another matter. Here the vastly improved technical performance of textile laminates and coatings have led to the increasing use of textiles as a full-fledged building material rather than just for temporary party or circus tents. Architectural textiles are undergoing an evolution, from non-breathing, polluting polyester fabric, heavily coated with PVCs, to Teflon-coated glass fibre fabric and the even more durable silicone-coated glass fibre fabric, all the way to state-of-the-art transparent, self-cleaning, strong and durable ETFE foil.

As a result of the marked improvement in durability and technical performance which plastics have undergone in the last 70 years, they are rapidly becoming the dominant material across the entire construction industry. As stated above, composites, with their seemingly limitless possibilities, are the leading category. And not just fibre-reinforced plastics but also plastics with other additives, in particular waste products from other industries, are now possible. Techwood, for example, is a product consisting of a mixture of pinewood fibre and recyclable PE, extruded into a range of profiles, round, square, star-shaped and flat. Deck planks and façade panels with an integrated extruded weatherboard profile are made of wood, but have the durability of a modern plastic. In addition, loam, natural stone granules and waste glass can – when combined with a synthetic resin – be transformed into a completely different material with vastly improved properties.

Polyvinyl Chloride (PVC)

Polyvinylchlorid | Polyvinyle Chloride | Cloruro de Polivinilo | Cloruro di Polivinile | Polyvinylchloride

Description Bee Bo PVC profiles by Deceuninck, (2003)

Polyvinyl chloride (PVC) is the construction industry's most diligent 'pragmatist'. It is familiar to us in the form of building plastic, rainwater pipes and drains, various trims and seals and, naturally, as window and door frames. Together with PE and PS, it accounts for 55% of the world's turnover in plastics. It has a somewhat downmarket image, but with a bit of imagination can be given a surprising image upgrade, as long as it does not try to imitate traditional materials.

Technical Aspects

Hard PVC is free of plasticisers, rigid and very strong. It has a low sensitivity to light and heat and good weather resistance. It has a high cold resistance in closed cell form and can be deformed in the heated state. PVC is also available as hard foam or structural foam. The addition of plasticisers makes it soft, in which state it is flexible and rubber-like but not elastic. Plastic frames are made from extruded PVC. However, the moulds used for PVC extrusion are much more costly than moulds for, say, aluminium extrusion, making it more expensive to develop profiles for a single project. To make PVC more resistant to sunlight, water and other influences, so-called stabilizers are added to it. These are often compounds containing zinc or tin, while PVC building materials may also contain lead. The industry is currently trying to replace these lead compounds with environmentally friendlier alternatives. With the exception of a few special applications where long durability is required, cadmium is no longer used. PVC's dangerous component, vinyl chloride, can be captured and neutralized during the production process.

Applications

In the construction industry, PVC is used primarily in the form of films, such as roofing membranes, soil protection sheeting and transparent draught doors and as a floor covering, such as vinyl. Hard PVC foam is used as a core material in sandwich panels. Structural foam is available in the form of panels and profiles (including for façades); these have high flexural stiffness, surface hardness, impact resistance and corrosion resistance.

Project Laboratory Rijksgebouwendienst, Eindhoven (2004)
Architect Vera Yanovshtchinsky
Photographer Sjaak Henselmans

Colour	**variable**
Glossiness	glossy, **satin**, matt
Translucence (%)	**0** – **20** – 40 – 60 – 80 – 100
Texture	sharp, **medium**, **dull**
Hardness	**hard**, **soft**, depressible
Temperature	**warm**, medium, cool
Odour	strong, moderate, **none**
Acoustic opacity	good, **moderate**, poor

Polypropylene (PP)

Polypropylen | Polypropylène | Polipropileno | Polipropilene | Polypropeen

Project Vario-Line® treehouse by Vario-Line Systems, Dresden (2003)
Distributor Vink Kunststoffen
Photographer R. Konsulke

First produced in 1958, polypropylene is manufactured in large quantities, with production increasing by 10% per annum. Philippe Starck called attention to the material in his own inimitable way when he used it in chairs bearing such fascinating names as Miss Balu, Soft Egg and Lord Yo. These affordable designer chairs are suited for both interior and exterior use and available in a range of pastel colours. Starck chose the material because of its excellent workability, designer friendliness, lightness, affordability and recyclability.

Technical Aspects

Polypropylene is inert and easily recycled, and is a major PVC substitute. With the appropriate additives, it can be made fireproof and UV resistant. It makes an inexpensive, lightweight, low-strength plastic. As a fibre, though, its strength rating is high, which is why it is often used in ropes and as a modern fibre reinforcement in concrete. In the construction industry it is also often used in the form of a film. Because of its relative weakness in pure form, it is often reinforced with glass fibre or talc. It is available in a range of colours and transparencies.

Applications

Polypropylene is not widely used in façades. However, it is used as a binder for wood fibre, which can in turn be extruded to make façade panels, tubes, profiles, deck planks, et cetera. Gritblasting the surface exposes the wood fibres, resulting in a panel that looks like wood and will eventually turn grey. Left as it is, the transparent coating will turn white and the panel will have the look of plastic. The material can be worked in the same way as wood.

Colour	**variable**
Glossiness	glossy, **satin**, **matt**
Translucence (%)	**0** – 20 – 40 – 60 – 80 – 100
Texture	sharp, **medium**, **dull**
Hardness	**hard**, **soft**, depressible
Temperature	**warm**, medium, cool
Odour	strong, moderate, **none**
Acoustic opacity	good, **moderate**, poor

Expanded Polystyrene (EPS)

Polystyrolschaum | Polystyrène Expansé | Poliestireno Expandido | Polistirolo Espanso | Polystyreen

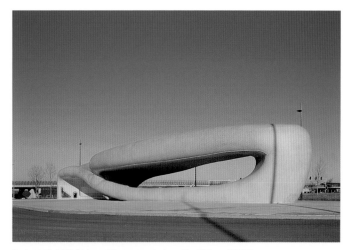

Project Fluid Vehicle public transport stop, Hoofddorp (2001)
Architect Maurice Nio, VHP Architects
Photographer Kees Hummel

In the construction industry, expanded polystyrene, or EPS, is known primarily as an insulation material, used in sheet form on façades and flat roofs. However, since the advent of techniques like computer-controlled laser cutting and milling which allow EPS to be processed three-dimensionally, it has gained increasing use as a building material suitable for creating three-dimensional forms.

Technical Aspects

EPS consists of millions of beads, each of which forms an extremely fine, closed cell structure. Only two to six per cent of its volume is polystyrene, the remaining 94 to 98 per cent is air, trapped in the cells. Despite its very light weight, EPS is relatively speaking very strong, fairly elastic and yet extremely stable, all of which makes it an excellent shock absorber. It is also a fine insulator, absorbs very little moisture, is fungus-resistant and impervious to most salts, acids and fats. EPS is also extremely hygienic and may come into direct contact with food products. In addition to the standard quality, a self-extinguishing version is also available. Both types come in a wide range of hardnesses, making it possible to match the material to the demands of a given application. EPS is an ecologically friendly material: it is completely free of CFKs, is produced in an energy-efficient way and is fully recyclable.

Applications

EPS was originally used as invisible insulation for roofs and façades. It owes its recent application as a visible façade material to computer-controlled milling techniques borrowed from model-making. Maurice Nio's Hoofddorp bus station is an example of a structure made from elements fashioned in this way. They were glued together on site and then given a polyester coating. Because of polyester's sensitivity to moisture, the structure was built under a tent construction.

Colour	**variable**
Glossiness	**glossy**, **satin**, **matt**
Translucence (%)	**0** – 20 – 40 – 60 – 80 – 100
Texture	sharp, **medium**, **dull**
Hardness	**hard**, **soft**, **depressible**
Temperature	**warm**, medium, cool
Odour	strong, moderate, **none**
Acoustic opacity	**good**, **moderate**, poor

Polycarbonate

Polycarbonat | Polycarbonate | Policarbonato | Policarbonato | Polycarbonaat

Project Fixed panels of translucent polycarbonate, Newton House, Australia (1998)
Architect Lahz Nimmo Architects
Photographer Brett Boardman Photography

The screen-printed polycarbonate panels of Herzog & De Meuron's Mulhouse project demonstrate effectively that polycarbonate (PC) is more than just a transparent glass substitute. With the exception of acrylic plastic, PC is the clearest plastic, distinguishing itself from other plastics by its combination of optical purity and high impact resistance. PC panels are 250 times stronger than glass of the same thickness. In addition, PC is hard, weather resistant and transparent.

Technical Aspects

Polycarbonate is deformable in a cold state which means it can be bent to the required shape on site. It is available in solid or extruded sheets. The latter can be joined with tongue and groove joints, enabling them to be used to span skylights and façades unaided. Polycarbonate can withstand great fluctuations in temperature and is self-extinguishing. To make PC scratch and graffiti resistant (it is by nature less scratch resistant than acrylic plastic), it is given a polysiloxane coating. As with all plastics, the fixing of PC sheets should be stress-free to allow for expansion. Extruded polycarbonate sheets are available in lengths up to 11 metres but for special projects 18 metres is also possible. Polycarbonate without glass fibre reinforcement can be recycled after being granulated.

Applications

Polycarbonate is frequently used to make translucent sheeting for façades and roofs, ranging from corrugated roofing for garden sheds and multi-wall extrusion sheeting for industrial buildings, to decidedly upmarket translucent, internally illuminated cladding for façades and internal walls. It is impact resistant, dirt repellent, clear and lightweight, screen printable and UV resistant and, being a thermoplastic, recyclable as well. PC: a new competitor for glass.

Project Nicolaas Maesschool, Amsterdam (1999)
Architect Meyer en Van Schooten Architecten bv
Photographer Jan Derwig

Colour	**variable**
Glossiness	**glossy**, **satin**, **matt**
Translucence (%)	**0 – 20 – 40 – 60 – 80 – 100**
Texture	sharp, **medium**, **dull**
Hardness	**hard**, soft, depressible
Temperature	**warm**, medium, cool
Odour	strong, moderate, **none**
Acoustic opacity	good, **moderate**, poor

Acrylics – PMMA

Acryl | Polyméthylméthacrylate | Acrílicos | Acrilici | Acrylaten

Description LENZ acrylic glass in simulation by LENZ (2004)

Project Brederode College, Amsterdam (2000)
Architect Dick van Gameren and Bjarne Mastenbroek, de Architectengroep
Photographer Christian Richters

Best known by the brand names Perspex and Plexiglas, acrylic (PMMA or polymethyl methacrylate) has the highest transparency of all plastics. Bernd van der Stouw printed a prismatically profiled acrylic sheet in such a way that its colour and pattern change depending on the angle at which it is viewed. Without additives, acrylic is extremely transparent – more so than even glass. Due to its strength – approximately 25 times that of glass – it is used extensively for roof lights and transparent roof coverings.

Technical Aspects

Transparent acrylic sheeting is available in both a standard and a UV-permeable version. The sheets can be moulded or extruded. They are available in white opal or smoky tints, or in solid colours with both glossy and matt surface finishes. A range of surface textures can be applied during the moulding process. Acrylic is thermoformable and can be fashioned into a variety of three-dimensional objects, such as light domes. It also comes in multi-walled extruded sheets that are much less breakable than glass. Lightweight and yet extremely rigid, multi-walled sheeting can be used to make large spans with a minimum of support. The lower total weight of roof constructions in this material results in a lighter, less massive construction. Acrylic is durable, very lightweight and weather resistant and does not yellow through exposure to ultraviolet light. Multi-walled sheeting, which can attain insulation values up to 1.67 W/m², is easy to work by mechanical means but less impact resistant than polycarbonate. PMMA expands in response to temperature change and for this reason must be firmly fixed in order to prevent bulging.

Applications

Acrylic is used for roof coverings, conservatories, rooflights and façades. Sheets with a textured or mat finish can be used both indoors and outdoors as a wall cladding, for illuminated signs or as a translucent building element.

Colour	variable
Glossiness	**glossy**, **satin**, **matt**
Translucence (%)	**0** – **20** – **40** – **60** – **80** – **100**
Texture	sharp, **medium**, **dull**
Hardness	**hard**, soft, depressible
Temperature	**warm**, medium, cool
Odour	strong, moderate, **none**
Acoustic opacity	good, moderate, **poor**

Polyester Resins

Polyesterharz I Résines polyester I Resinas de poliéster I Resine poliestere I Polyesterharsen

Project Mathenesserlaan, Rotterdam (2003)
Architect Marco Henssen, M3H Architects
Photographer Marco Henssen

Project Chill Out Bijenkorf, Amsterdam (2004)
Architect Kees Rijnboutt, de Architectengroep
Photographer Kees Hummel

Polyester resins are two-component products frequently used in combination with glass fibre for casting moulded components, mounting wall panelling and carrying out repairs. Glass fibre reinforced polyester moulded components are made by placing several layers of glass fibre matting in a mould and saturating them with polyester resin. The smooth outer surface of the moulded part consists of a protective layer of gel coat. Existing products made of wood, PUR foam, plaster or concrete can also be covered with one or more layers of glass fibre for increased strength, rigidity and resistance to wear, or in order to make their surface impervious to liquids. The resulting laminate is finished with a topcoat.

Technical Aspects

Unsaturated polyester is a reaction resin and will harden only after the addition of a hardening agent. Without the addition of fillers, its colour ranges from almost completely transparent to yellowish. It can be pigmented in a range of colours, including transparent ones. The addition of a reinforcement (e.g. glass fibre matting) can, depending on the reinforcement used, greatly improve the strength, elasticity and impact resistance of the polyester. It does not become brittle at low temperatures (unlike epoxy), it can be made extremely fire-resistant with the appropriate additive, and weather-resistant if given an impervious resin surface. Any desired shape can be realized by placing glass matting on a mould and rubbing each layer with polyester resin. The surface of the finished article can be polished smooth.

Applications

Reinforced polyester resin is used to make a variety of products used in the construction industry. They include corrugated sheeting, skylights, partition walls, bathroom tiles, greenhouse siding, billboards, balcony profiles and façade cladding.

Colour	**variable**
Glossiness	**glossy, satin, matt**
Translucence (%)	**0** – **20** – 40 – 60 – 80 – 100
Texture	sharp, **medium**, **dull**
Hardness	**hard**, soft, depressible
Temperature	**warm**, medium, cool
Odour	**strong**, moderate, none
Acoustic opacity	good, **moderate**, **poor**

Epoxy Resin

Epoxidharz | *Résine époxy* | *Resina Epoxy* | *Resine poliestere* | *Epoxyharsen*

Project Epoxy resin and printed polyester in Freeze coffee table (2001)
Artist David Heldt
Photographer David Heldt

The chief advantage of fibre reinforced synthetic resins is that they make it possible to realize strong and rigid constructions with a relatively light weight, which is good news for mobile, prefab and temporary constructions.

Technical Aspects

Epoxy resin is a high-quality, transparent, strong and hardwearing material. Like polyester resin, it is often used for 'freezing' all manner of objects, from screws to insects. In construction and especially in boat-building it is used mainly in fibre-reinforced constructions. It will adhere to virtually any substrate (e.g. polyester foam), but unlike polyester resin it does so without attacking the substrate. As epoxy resin does not shrink when it hardens, it is often used to make moulds. Owing to differences in viscosity, epoxy resins can be used as a coating, adhesive, filler or laminating resin. Below 10 °C, it has a tendency to crystallize. This can range from slight clouding to a completely hard and 'sugared' material, and is one of the reasons why it is primarily used for indoor applications. Another reason is that hardened epoxy resin has fairly poor UV resistance; it yellows somewhat and its surface will become dull. For this reason, it advisable always to give epoxy elements a coat of varnish; if a transparent varnish is used, it should preferably be one with an ultraviolet filter. Reinforcement usually takes the form of woven mats of glass, Kevlar or carbon fibre. Ordinary chopped strand mats are not recommended because the binding agent in these mats does not dissolve (as it does in polyester), thus preventing the matting from becoming properly wet and pliable. Like polyester, epoxy can be coloured with pigments or, mixed with fillers, used as moulding material.

Applications

Solvent-free epoxy resins are eminently suitable for preserving, gluing or restoring wood, or for laminating it to glass fabric. The absence of solvents also means that epoxy resins can safely be used on all types of foam.

Colour	variable
Glossiness	**glossy**, **satin**, **matt**
Translucence (%)	0 – **20** – 40 – 60 – 80 – 100
Texture	sharp, **medium**, **dull**
Hardness	**hard**, soft, depressible
Temperature	**warm**, medium, cool
Odour	strong, moderate, **none**
Acoustic opacity	good, **moderate**, poor

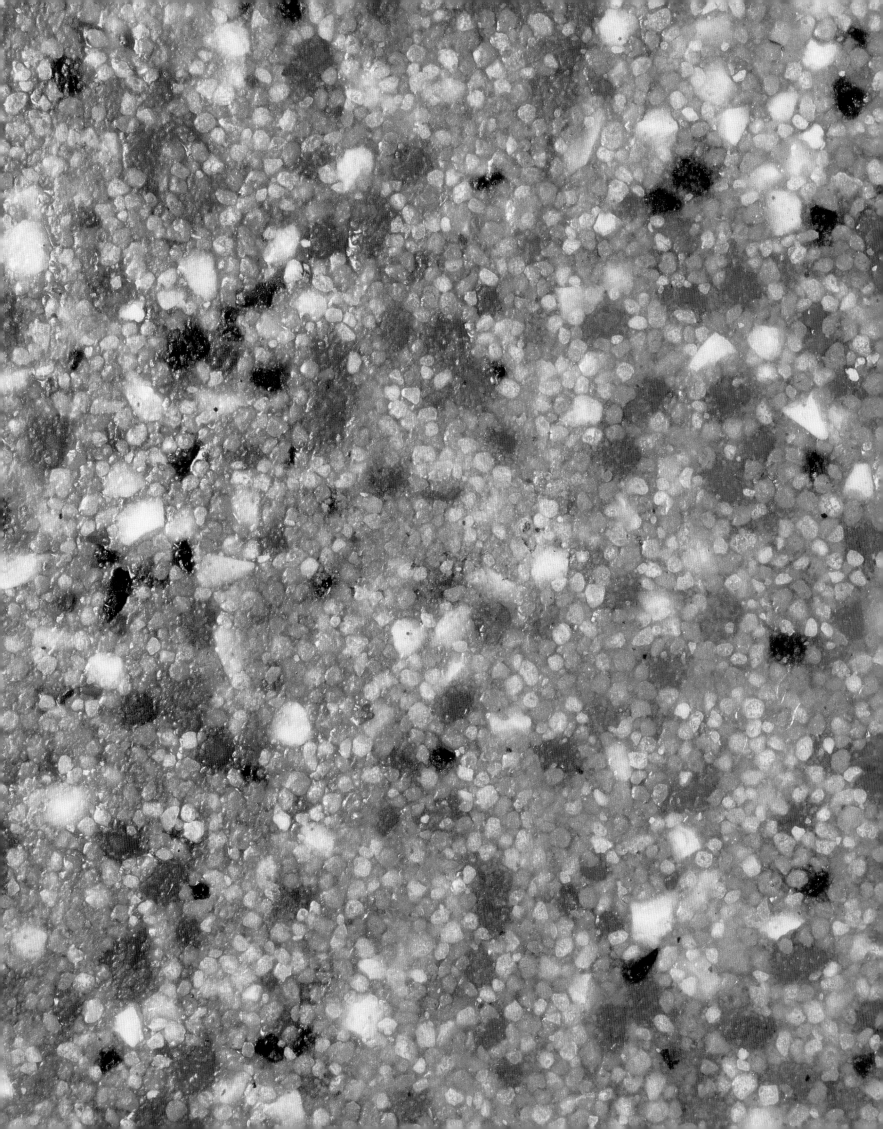

Polyurethane

Polyurethan | Polyuréthane | Poliuretano | Poliuretano | Polyurethanen

Project WOS 8 (Heat Transfer Station 8), Utrecht (1998)
Architect NL Architects
Photographer NL Architects

Project Thonik Artists' Apartment, Amsterdam (2001)
Architect MVRDV
Photographer Kees Hummel

Polyurethane is one of the most versatile polymers in the world of plastics. It is made into resins, foams, elastomers, putties, adhesives and varnishes, amongst other materials. Combined with the appropriate substances, it can be either a thermoset or a thermoplastic, but since the former predominate it is usually classified as a thermoset. Polyurethane paint, a slightly elastic, skin-like and durable coating can also be used as a seamless façade finishing, as it was used by NL Architects in the WOS 8 heat transfer station, and by MVRDV in their Amsterdam studio dwellings.

Technical Aspects

In the construction industry, polyurethane is most often used as insulating foam in façades and roofs and in sandwich façade panels. It is also known as a crack filler. As a coating, it is frequently employed as a finishing for concrete floors or cast to make parking deck systems. Polyurethane is available as a one or two component product, with or without solvents. In contrast to polyester and epoxy, it is rarely used in combination with fibre reinforcement. It can be cast, pressed, injection-moulded or foamed and is, in each of its forms, available in several hardnesses and qualities; as a coating it is available in the full spectrum of colours. Polyurethane is an excellent mould material; in the concrete industry it is often used to make casts from natural stone, wood and prints, in order to add a texture to concrete. The two-component product is extremely sensitive to moisture and temperature and should be used in an air-conditioned environment. In the unpredictable Dutch climate, NL Architects enveloped WOS 8 in a tent construction before spraying its façade with a polyurethane coating.

Applications

The Italian architect, Geatano Pesce, used a colourful, viscous polyurethane coating to create a seamless interior with smooth transitions between floor, walls and ceiling. Due to its durable and hygienic character, polyurethane is frequently used as a floor coating in gyms, laboratories and hospitals.

Colour	variable
Glossiness	**glossy**, **satin**, **matt**
Translucence (%)	0 – **20** – 40 – 60 – 80 – 100
Texture	sharp, **medium**, **dull**
Hardness	hard, soft, **depressible**
Temperature	**warm**, medium, cool
Odour	strong, moderate, **none**
Acoustic opacity	good, **moderate**, poor

EPDM (Ethylene Propylene Diene Monomer)

EPDM (Ethylen-Propylen-Dien-Monomer) | EPDM (Ethylène Propylène Diène Monomère) | EPDM (Etileno propileno monómero) | EPDM (Terpolimero-etilene-propilene-diene) | EPDM elastomeer

Project 013 | Popcluster, Tilburg (1998)
Architect Benthem Crouwel Architects
Photographer Kees Hummel

A roof covering as façade cladding? It seems logical enough. After all, the roof is often referred to as a fifth façade, so why shouldn't its cladding be used on the fourth façade? The firm of Benthem & Crouwel did precisely that: they used EPDM, better known as a roof covering and pool liner, to create an exciting padded acoustic façade for Tilburg's Pop Centre.

Technical Aspects

EPDM is strong and permanently elastic, contains no plasticizers, can be worked in a wide range of temperatures (-40 to +100 °C) and is highly resistant to ultraviolet radiation. In addition, it is impervious to root penetration (except some species of reed and bamboo) and resistant to acid rain and other common chemical and biological influences. EPDM is not proof against petrol, methyl benzene, white spirit, oil and the like. It is fabricated in a standard width of 1.5 metres and these sheets can be hot-bonded to one another to form any kind of prefab component, including 3D shapes. The material has a lifespan of 30 to 50 years.

Applications

EPDM is widely used as a durable roof covering. It is also used in environmentally friendly, energy-efficient building and in the construction of green and recreational roofs (in part because of its resistance to root penetration). Up to now it has been recycled by means of pulverization, the resulting powder being used as a raw material for rubber products, such as buffers, resilient tiles and street furniture. New technological developments now make it possible to reduce EPDM rubber to its original ingredients which can in turn be re-used to make new products of a comparable quality.

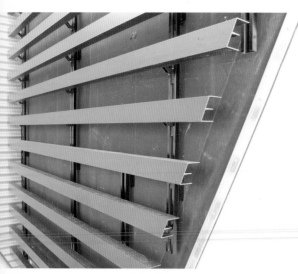

Project Leon Mode, New Vennep (2003)
Architect ONX Architects
Photographer ONX Architects

Colour	black
Glossiness	glossy, satin, **matt**
Translucence (%)	**0** – 20 – 40 – 60 – 80 – 100
Texture	sharp, **medium, dull**
Hardness	hard, soft, **depressible**
Temperature	**warm**, medium, cool
Odour	strong, moderate, **none**
Acoustic opacity	good, **moderate**, poor

Additives for Plastics

Zuschlagstoffe für Plastik | Additifs pour Plastiques | Aditivos para plásticos |
Additivi per materie plastiche | Toevoegingen aan plastic

Additives for plastics fall into a number of categories. Plastics themselves nearly always consist of a combination of ingredients, but
other materials can be added to improve their performance. This
produces what is known as a composite, such as fibre reinforced
plastic. Another type of additive is applied to the surface of the
plastic, purely in order to enhance the material's appearance or to
protect its surface. Finally, plastic can itself can be added to construction components, yielding composite components, such as a plastic-
filled air cavity.

Composites

In creating composites, the unique properties of individual materials
are combined to yield a 'tailor-made' product with the required characteristics. In itself, plastic is not a particularly strong material and

Project Mandarina Duck, Paris (2000)
Architect NL Architects
Photographer NL Architects

needs fibre reinforcement in order to attain a good tensile strength.
Fibres, moreover, can absorb tensile stress in all directions. Basically,
a rigid composite product consists of fibre which has been placed in
a mould and then 'frozen' with the help of a polymer resin. Fibres
are often very strong, rigid and light in comparison with steel or
aluminium. Widely used fibres include glass, carbon and aramides
with a thermoset as matrix material. A laminate's properties can be
adjusted by changing the direction of the fibres.

Vacuum Injection

The fibre material can be impregnated manually using a paint brush
or pressure spray, or by vacuum injection. In the latter process, the
product is placed in a vacuum where it sucks up the resin. This
requires some preparation, technical knowledge and special equipment, but ultimately vacuum injection makes for higher-quality and
lighter laminates and produces them faster and more cleanly.

The leading architectural composite material, high pressure laminate
(HPL), consists of layers of paper saturated and pressed in a resin.
Another example is Alucobond, a sandwich panel of aluminium with
a polyethylene core. Hylite is another such laminate, only thinner.

The advantage of Hylite panels is that they are deformable in the cold state. However, as their visible side consists of aluminium, they fall outside the scope of this chapter.

Coatings

Plastic in exposed work is of course amply represented in the field of coatings. Originally, coatings were applied to wood, steel and aluminium as protection against the elements; wood is protected against moisture and ultraviolet rays, metal against moisture and acids. These traditional coatings consisted of organic substances like linseed oil, ox blood, egg yolk and starch. Contemporary coatings are composed of a chemical mix that satisfies specific requirements with regard to elasticity, degree of adhesion, acidification and method of application. Choosing a coating today is not simply a matter of looking for the right colour: as well as covering the entire colour spectrum, coatings range from matt to high gloss, from rock hard to soft as skin. They can be plain or metallic, with mother-of-pearl or iridescent effect, can change colour in response to light or heat (from intense black to bright fluorescent yellow), or even function like solar panels. In addition to their extensive aesthetic possibilities, the technical performance of coatings (durability, resistance to climatic extremes) is continually being improved. Other examples of ongoing technical innovation are the low-emissivity coating on HR++ glass, waterproofing of brick structures, anti-graffiti coatings, water- and dirt-repellent coatings. Coatings can be applied with a paintbrush, roller, spray can, electrostatic spray gun or by means of a film which acts as carrier. In this last method, plastic film is printed with a pattern or picture and placed face up on the surface of a water bath. It is then sprayed with a substance that separates the film from the coating, causing the film to sink to the bottom. The element to be printed is now laid on the surface of the water whereupon the image affixes itself to it. Using the same technique, it is possible to apply an image over all sides of three-dimensional elements and to the sides of panels.

Façade elements (e.g. aluminium frames, wooden façade frames, metal façade panels) are usually coated in the factory, in some cases electrostatically. However, monolithic, seamless coatings that wrap around the façade like a skin, are applied in situ and can be completely tailored to the requirements of a given project. In this context, the plastic floor covering industry offers a variety of special surfaces that are increasingly being used for façades. For example, the sidewalk portion of Rotterdam's Erasmus Bridge consists of a cast in situ plastic floor with carborundum particles added to the surface. On a sunny day, this glittering, black, stone-like material gleams and sparkles as it reflects the sunlight. These floor systems, which are available in epoxy, polyester or polyurethane depending on the application, are thicker than normal coatings and consequently suitable for the addition of a variety of additives. Transparent plastics with glitter, multi-coloured confetti, glass cullet or stone chippings are all possible, as are panels with colourful pictures.

On, under and between

Plastic is becoming ever stronger, more scratch resistant, UV-resistant, durable and environmentally friendly and its enormous diversity makes it a welcome material for use in roofs, façades and interiors.

Project To celebrate the Nike and Nationale-Nederlanden sponsorship of the Dutch National football team. European Champion's League celebration, Rotterdam (2000)
Designer Wieden & Kennedy
Photographer 3M

Just as double glazing's performance is continually being improved through the addition of acoustic and heat-insulating gases in air cavities, so the same gases can be used to fill the hollow core of extrusion panels. Plastic can be inserted between glass sheets for increased rigidity (laminated glass), or for aesthetic reasons (iridescent 3M-film). A recent development is 3M Optical Light Film which can be placed behind glass and photo reproductions on façades (during the 2000 Football Championships, two façades of the 150 metre-high Nationale Nederlanden insurance building in Rotterdam were covered with a photo of footballer Edgar Davids).

HPL Sheets

HPL-Platten (Hochdruckschichtstoff) | *Feuilles stratifiées HPL (en haute pression)* | *Láminas HPL* | *Laminati HPL* | *HPL platen*

Project Laboratory Rijksgebouwendienst, Eindhoven (2004)
Architect Vera Yanovshtchinsky
Photographer Sjaak Henselmans

Project Abet building, IJsselstein (2001)
Architect Abet
Photographer Kees Hummel

HPL (high pressure laminate) façade cladding, which is produced by impregnating plastic hardboard with resin, is a product of the 1960s. Trespa HPL panels were used as façade cladding in 1967. The original product discoloured, became easily soiled and could be recognized by its visible plastic covering caps. Choice was restricted to a narrow palette of light colours. The present generation of HPL panelling offers an extremely wide range of textures and colours and can now be fixed invisibly, for example by gluing. The quality and durability of both the outer coating and core are so much improved that it is now possible to give 10-year colour guarantees in even the most polluted environments.

Technical Aspects

There are several varieties of HPL panelling in which the basis if formed by layers of paper or by wood fibre. Trespa Meteon, for example, is a flat panel based on thermosetting resins, homogeneously reinforced with wood fibre, and manufactured under high pressure and at high temperatures. Its integrated decorative surface is based on pigmented resins cured by electron beams. HPL panelling is a good substitute for painted wood panels. It is very weather resistant, exhibits low thermal movement, is easy to work and is available in a range of surface textures and colours. Colourfastness is vastly improved compared with the earliest versions, and the surface and core are unaffected by polluted or corrosive environments, such as industrial or coastal areas. The dark core is visible on the sawn edges. Infill elements can be made to measure, for which purpose the sheets can be bent or have pieces cut out of them and then given a three-dimensional shape. Complex corner and infill pieces can be made in this way. A variety of surface textures are available, from matt to high gloss, as well as a range of 3D structures, enabling a façade to produce varying effects through light reflection. If desired, the surface may be colour printed with illustrations or photographic material.

Applications

HPL sheets can be used to good effect as a finishing panel, fascia, edging strip and, naturally, façade cladding. Its invisible fixing ensures a smooth result, and the joint often contributes to the overall effect of the façade. HPL panels are suitable for soffits and façade finishings. Special top coatings also render them suitable as worktops and for facing sanitary units and interior walls.

Colour	**variable**
Glossiness	**glossy**, **satin**, **matt**
Translucence (%)	**0** – 20 – 40 – 60 – 80 – 100
Texture	sharp, medium, **dull**
Hardness	**hard**, soft, depressible
Temperature	**warm**, medium, cool
Odour	strong, moderate, **none**
Acoustic opacity	good, **moderate**, poor

Granulate

Granulat | Granulats | Granulado | Granulato | Granulaat

Project De Hoep, Castricum (1995 | 2003)
Architect Min2 bouw-kunst
Photographer Tom Croes

Industrial floors in warehouses, gymnasiums and laboratories must all meet high standards with regards to strength, resistance to chemical substances, elasticity, seamlessness and low maintenance. Such floors are always poured in situ, but the material can also be used for façades and precast elements. That material is often polyurethane, which is tricky to apply to exterior surfaces as it is sensitive to temperature and moisture. The great advantage of this highly viscous coating is that a wide range of additives can be added to its surface, as the plastic carrier behaves like an enormous layer of glue.

Technical Aspects

Façade elements made of polyester concrete (see *Unfired man-made stone*) can be given a variety of surface treatments. Such elements are cast in a horizontal position and while they are still soft stone chippings, glass cullet or slivers of mirror glass are tapped into the surface. The colours, textures and effects that can be obtained in this manner are well nigh endless. The overall effect is due to a property of polyester, which shrinks as it dries, firmly fixing the aggregates in place. When the mixture for cast polyurethane floors is used on a façade it has to be sprayed on, thus precluding the use of such additions. However, if the façade cladding is precast, the same aggregates used for cast floors can be added: glitter, stone chippings, carborundum, small light-reflecting balls of glass, coloured glass chips, coins in a transparent coating, et cetera. A disadvantage of precasting is that it is not possible to make the vertical wall entirely seamless.

Applications

Polyurethane systems originally developed for floors can – if properly executed – also be used for façades (sprayed on or precast), interiors, trade fair stands and bridge deck elements.

Colour	**variable**
Glossiness	glossy, **satin**, **matt**
Translucence (%)	**0** – 20 – 40 – 60 – 80 – 100
Texture	sharp, **medium**, **dull**
Hardness	**hard**, soft, depressible
Temperature	**warm**, medium, cool
Odour	strong, moderate, **none**
Acoustic opacity	good, **moderate**, poor

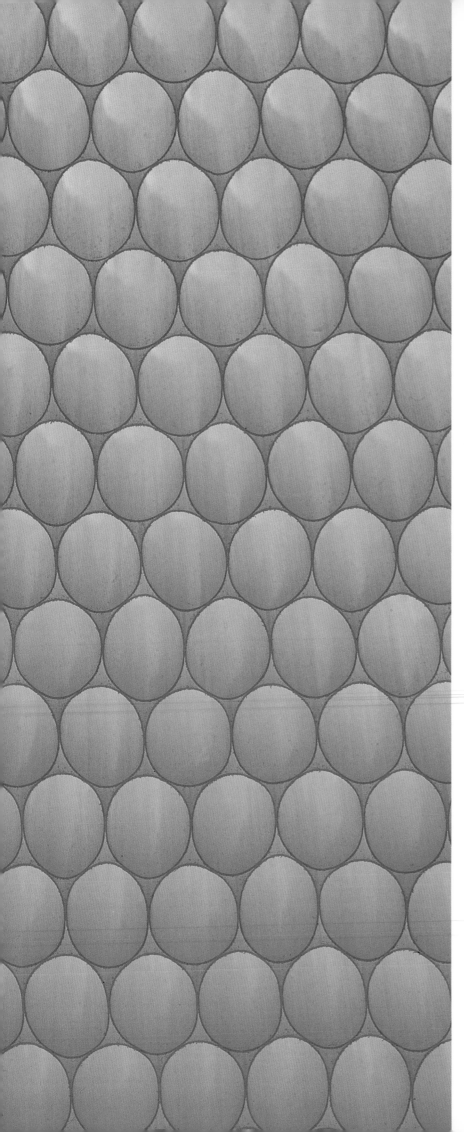

Plastics
Treatments

Bearbeitung | Traitements | Tratamientos | Trattamenti | Bewerkingen plastics

The invention of plastics opened up a new world of voluptuous, three-dimensional forms, smooth, soft, shiny surfaces and any number of new surface textures. Indeed, the design freedom they afford has long been considered one of their prime features, along with their low cost, ease of maintenance and durability.

Plastics also win hands down when it comes to variety in design possibilities: from granulate to linear products, from film to panels to three-dimensional elements or various combinations of these and with other materials. Plastic is a highly versatile material. It can be worked using the entire range of traditional tools, but it can also be moulded, extruded, injection moulded, immersed, laminated, laser sintered, sprayed and, with the addition of reinforcement, undergo even more forms of processing or changes in appearance.

Project Ricola Europe Factory, Mulhouse (1994)
Architect Herzog & De Meuron
Photographer © Thomas Dix | Architekturphoto

The construction industry is geared to the use of standardized elements that can be deployed with a high degree of flexibility in assembling larger building components which may or may not require further finishing. Thus, for façade and wall cladding, plastic has until now been offered primarily in the form of sheeting material, whereas its great strength compared with other materials is its ability to take on three-dimensional shapes. The plastics industry is therefore now following the example of the concrete industry and increasingly dealing directly with designers and architects so as to be able take advantage of project-related developments.

In its 'raw' form, plastic is available as a granulate. If it is thermoplastic, this basic material can be extruded, injection moulded, thermoformed, moulded, blown, drawn and foamed. Designer Saar Oosterhof has produced some colourful injection-moulded interior floor and wall tiles with a surface that creates a holographic illusion. Extruded profiles are found mainly in the form of frames and copings, but tongue-and-groove siding can also consist of extruded plastic panels with hollow cores for extra strength. In addition, multi-wall polycarbonate and hollow-core acrylic sheets are often extruded.

The Extrusion Process

A production line for the extrusion of profiles consists of a number of machines connected in series. Compound coming out of a silo enters the heated cylindrical chamber of the extruder via a hopper. In the chamber, it is heated to a temperature of 150-200 °C. The rise in temperature thickens the compound which is simultaneously moved forward by two rotating feed screws. The plastic mass is continuously pressed – extruded – through a profiled slit (die), after which the resulting plastic profile is guided through a calibration box. The profile is then cooled to fix its shape. Further cooling occurs in a water bath. Polyvinyl chloride (PVC) is a popular extrusion material. Unfortunately, PVC is not colourfast when used as a façade cladding so frames and façade sections are now made by means of co-extrusion in which the basic form of the profile – the PVC melt – is thermally fused with a coloured acrylic melt. The latter is placed very precisely on the profile surface that will subsequently be exposed to the environmental effects of light, rain, snow and temperature fluctuations. The profile emerges already two-toned from the co-extrusion nozzle.

Extrusion is an efficient one-step method of producing panels of the desired profiling and thickness. Since extrusion moulds for plastic are approximately ten times as costly as those for aluminium, there must be a guaranteed market for the products. This allows little opportunity for innovation and experimentation for project-specific products.

Sandwich Panels

One way of making a rigid but lightweight panel is by combining a lightweight core with thin outer layers. An example of this is PepCore[a], which consists of a core and covering layers on either side. The core is made by heating a sheet of thermoplastic material (polystyrene, PMMA, PETG or PC) in a special machine and then stretching it until the desired thickness is obtained. Covering layers of various materials can then be glued to the core, although the latter's irregular structure and transparency also make use of the core without covering layers an interesting proposition.

In view of the material's many excellent qualities – high rigidity, light weight, good thermal and acoustic insulation, impact resistance, temperature range, glueability – and its relatively low price, it can be used for making entire buildings, bridges, walls, façades and floors. HPL panels, aluminium, steel, natural stone, other plastics or wood can all be glued to the PEP core.

Sandwich panels are primarily used in situations where lightness is a priority, such as in boat, ship and aircraft building, caravan interiors and all things mobile. A special form of sandwich panel is made by saturating a 3D textile with resin by means of a vacuum technique that causes it to harden into a panel. The capillary action causes the threads at right angles to the fabric to stand on end, resulting in a two-layered panel. Examples of this technique are Parabeam and Paraglass which have a core of 3D glass textile and are available in several thicknesses. This 3D weaving technique originated in the velvet weaving industry where the woven fabric is cut lengthways to produce the characteristic piled surface.

Sandwich panels can also be made by combining different elements. For instance, Butzbach makes panels whose core consists of plastic profiles to which thin, glass fibre reinforced sheets are fastened. Length, width and thickness are variable. Originally, these were used to make industrial doors, but due to their transparent, attractively austere appearance they were adapted for use as an insulating rapid-construction façade system.

Moulded Panels

Plastic gets its surface structure from its mould, which raises the possibility of an endless variety of textures, transparencies, profilings and degrees of lustre. If transparent plastic is used, all kinds of materials can be added to the mix, such as coloured plastic remnants or any material that is compatible with the plastic concerned. Liquid plastic is particularly suited to vacuum moulding techniques. One method of producing laminated glass entails interspersing layers of glass with PVB film (polyvinyl butyral) and combining them in a compression tank to produce a strong, transparent sheet. However, it is also possible to layer the glass sheets with some other thin material and to fuse the layers by pouring liquid resin between them from above and drawing off any remaining air via an opening between the glass sheets at the bottom. It is important to ensure that no air is trapped inside as this would result in an uneven distribution of stress.

Foaming

Due to its low weight and high strength, foamed plastic is a popular choice of material for façade panels. These cladding profiles consist of a core of hard PVC foam (with an insulation value far exceeding that of wood and concrete) and an outer face of smooth, impact-resistant hard PVC. Fused to one another by means of co-extrusion, the top and core layers form a unified whole.

Printing

Plastic can also be printed using screen-printing techniques, as Herzog & De Meuron did with the transparent polycarbonate façade of their Ricola Europe factory in Mulhouse. Some HPL façade panels, such as those from Trespa and Abet, are marketed with natural or abstract patterns. However, it is also possible to decorate a façade by having a pattern, photograph or illustration of one's own choice screen printed on a HPL façade panel.

Bending and Three-dimensional Shaping

Plastic is perfect for making three-dimensional shapes on a small or large scale. As long ago as the 1960s, the material opened the way to futuristic-looking buildings that could never have been realized without plastic. Now, developments in computer-aided free design are fuelling intensive experimentation with techniques. For example, using a CNC (computer numerical controlled) milling technique, three-dimensional models made of polystyrene foam are milled and then coated with polyurethane.

Bencore | CompoSied

Bencore | Bencore | Bencore | Bencore | Bencore

Description Bencore | CompoSied partitioning by Bencore | Pyrasied

Project Floating bridge with five layers of Birdwing® panels, Brugge (2002)
Architect Toyo Ito and Associates
Photographer Bencore

In the States a honeycomb panel made from a thermoplastic has been on the market quite some time under brand names Pepcore and Norcore. The European producer uses the brand name Bencore (distributed in the Benelux as CompoSied). All names refer to the same kind of material. The core forms the basis of many strong, lightweight sheet materials with a variety of finishes. These light-weight materials are especially important for mobile structures like aircraft and boats, but even in fixed structures they can contribute significantly to the speed and ease of the construction process.

Technical Aspects

The manufacture of Bencore panels begins with a polymer sheet made from a thermoplastic such as transparent polycarbonate, SAN, polystyrene, PETG or recycled PC. The sheet is placed between two heated vacuum-moulds. The moulds are closed and the sheet is heated to a temperature of 200 ºC, after which the moulds are drawn apart to a distance equal to the thickness of the finished core. Following partial cooling, the panel is removed from the moulds for further processing. Due to its structure, Bencore is strong and rigid, has good sound and thermal insulation and is light in weight. It can be used as is in inner walls and ceiling panels, but it can also be given a facing of metal, wood, plastic or natural stone, yielding a lightweight, strong panel. The core itself can also be shaped three-dimensionally. This can be done by means of the 'drape forming' process: the panel is heated and placed over a mould. Counterpressure is then exerted by another mould until the panel has assumed the desired shape. This technique is only suited to modest deformations. For more extensive ones, the material is shaped using a vacuum process. Here the panel is placed over the mould and heated, after which the mould is pressed into the panel and a vacuum applied to the space between the panel and the mould.

Applications

Bencore can be used for automotive body work, boat building, con-structions, (shop)interiors, façades, walls and ceilings. Its transparent, open structure is especially suitable for indoor applications where acoustics play a role. As the core of a laminated panel, it can be used in any situation where a strong, lightweight finishing panel is need-ed. Bencladding consists of a core panel faced by a thin layer of nat-ural stone, with an aluminium backing, especially suited for facades.

Colour	**variable**
Glossiness	**glossy**, satin, matt
Translucence (%)	0 – 20 – 40 – **60** – **80** – **100**
Texture	sharp, medium, **dull**
Hardness	**hard**, soft, depressible
Temperature	**warm**, medium, cool
Odour	strong, moderate, **none**
Acoustic opacity	good, **moderate**, poor

Parabeam® 3D Glass Fabric

Parabeam® 3D Glasfasergewebe | Parabeam® 3D tissue de Verre | Tejido de vidrio Parabeam® 3D | Parabeam® 3D tessuto in fibra di vetro | Parabeam® 3D glasvezel

Description Covering Radardome with Parabeam® 3D Glass Fabric
Photographer Parabeam

Parabeam Inc., was established in 1989 with the object of developing new applications in the technical textiles market. The existing concept of velvet weaving, in which two layers of fabric are woven simultaneously with connecting piles that are subsequently cut over the length of the fabric to yield velvet cloth, served as the basis for what are now known as Parabeam® 3D Glass Fabrics.

Technical Aspects

When woven using a 100% E-glass yarn (instead of the mohair yarn originally used in velvet) and impregnated with a thermoset resin, the unique capillary forces of the (glass) piles in the fabric absorb the resin and ensure that the fabric bounces back to its pre-set original height, resulting in a rigid and extremely lightweight sandwich. The piles are woven into the facings, thus forming an integral sandwich structure. Fire resistance can be built in by using phenol or polyester resin. The finished panels, which are available in thicknesses from 3 to 22 mm, are lightweight, strong, resistant to micro-organisms, not prone to delamination, thermally insulating and translucent. One disadvantage is that they are available only in a translucent colour that is subject to slight yellowing.

Applications

Because of its high strength and light weight, ParaGlass is particularly suitable for aircraft and boat building and demountable interiors, especially in the fire resistant version. In addition, its transparency and rapid assembly make it a popular choice for partition walls and display units in museum, domestic and shop interiors.

Colour	white, **beige**
Glossiness	glossy, **satin**, **matt**
Translucence (%)	0 – **20** – **40** – **60** – 80 – 100
Texture	sharp, **medium**, **dull**
Hardness	**hard**, soft, depressible
Temperature	**warm**, medium, cool
Odour	strong, moderate, **none**
Acoustic opacity	good, **moderate**, poor

Foam

Schaum | Mousse | Espuma | Espanso | Schuim

Project Beeftink, Doetinchem (1992)
Distributor Vink Kunststoffen
Photographer Studio Layahe

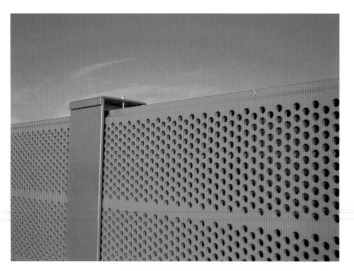

Description Foam panels by Deceuninck, Asten (2003)

Plastic foams are lightweight and very useful as a filling material. There are two categories of foam plastics: soft and hard. Hard foam plastics, which usually have a base of PVC and polystyrene, are primarily used in sandwich constructions in situations where they will be exposed to low compressive loads. Soft foam plastics usually have a polyurethane base and are used to fill hollow objects, giving them rigidity with a minimum of additional weight.

Technical Aspects
Foam can be produced in two different ways. In both cases the cell structure is generated by gas expansion. In the physical foaming process, the raw material, plastic, is liquefied, a liquid with a low boiling point is pumped into the molten material after which the mixture is allowed to cool under controlled conditions. When water is added, for example, hydrolysis takes place and the polyurethane foams.

In chemical foaming, a chemical foaming agent (CFA) is placed in a plastic matrix and the temperature of the matrix raised until the foaming agent decomposes and releases a gas which causes the plastic, the viscosity of which is now low enough to allow air bubbles to form, to foam. A foam's density and thermal insulation properties depend on the size and structure of the cells and the quantity of vapour these contain per volume. Additives can be used to give the foam a colour or to improve properties such as conductivity or fire retardation. PVC foam façade elements are available which consist of a core of hard PVC foam with an insulation value far exceeding that of wood or concrete. They are faced with a smooth, impact-resistant layer of hard PVC. The top and core layers are fused into a single unit by means of co-extrusion.

Applications
PVC elements can be used in façades, fascias, roof edge and balcony finishings, et cetera.

Colour	**variable**
Glossiness	glossy, satin, **matt**
Translucence (%)	**0** – 20 – 40 – 60 – 80 – 100
Texture	sharp, medium, **dull**
Hardness	hard, **soft**, **depressible**
Temperature	**warm**, medium, cool
Odour	strong, moderate, **none**
Acoustic opacity	good, **moderate**, poor

Textiles

Textilgewebe | Textiles | Textiles | Tessile | Textielen

The oldest form of shelter – after the cave, of course – is the tent. From North Africa to the eastern border of Tibet, nomadic peoples have utilized this mobile, flexible, lightweight construction on their treks since time immemorial. The original tent may seem a quite primitive affair, but in fact it is a very sophisticated, useful and adaptable form of housing. For example, the black goat's hair tent traditional in the Sahara insulates its occupants from the intense cold at night, whilst during the day its black colour absorbs the infrared rays of the sun rather than letting it penetrate the interior. Incredible as it may seem, these black tents are capable of maintaining a temperature difference of 30 °C between inside and outside in the sweltering desert heat. The tent used by the Tuareg people of the Sahara and Sahel Deserts is made of goat leather rubbed with butter to make it water repellent during the rainy season. The Inuits (Eskimos) used a tent made from sealskins in the summer months. The *yurt*, or *ger*, is a traditional Nepalese tent consisting of a collapsible wooden framework covered with felt blankets made from a mixture of sheep's wool and horsehair.

In 1917, the English engineer, F.W. Lanchester, patented 'an improved construction of tent for field hospitals, depots and like purposes'. The design, based on a difference in air pressure between inside and outside, was never realized. The development of tent construction did not really take off until 1950 when new materials started to become available. Tent construction was first discussed as a fully fledged technology in 1980, in the American architecture magazine, *Progressive Architecture*.

Types of Textile

Nearly all textiles used for tensile tent constructions and air-supported structures are based on polyester or glass fibre fabrics. These are then given one of several coatings as protection against dirt and damage. PTFE (short for polytetrafluoroethylene), which was developed in 1970 by DuPont under the name Teflon, consists of microscopic glass particles which can be applied to a glass fibre fabric by sintering. The fabric supplies the strength of the finished product while the coating provides durability. Teflon-coated fabrics are water repellent, chemically inert and noncombustible. A disadvantage of Teflon-coated glass fibre fabric is that its brittle surface means that it cannot be folded, making it unsuitable for structures that must be assembled and disassembled. PVC-coated polyester fabrics are more pliable and as such more suitable for demountable structures. They are not very durable, however, owing to softeners in the PVC coating, which gradually rise to the surface. This not only makes the coating sticky and thus prone to attract dirt, but also makes it brittle and liable to crack. PVC-coated polyester, which is available in a variety of colours, is the least expensive coating and has a design life of 15 to 20 years, depending on the effects of ultraviolet light and the quality of the chosen coating.

The newest development in the coatings field involves silicones. Silicone-coated fabrics are extremely flexible within a temperature range of -50 to +200 °C. The combination of virtually non-degradable glass fibre fabric and the hydrophobic property of silicones is a guarantee for prolonged outdoor life. In addition, glass and silicone are not affected by exposure to ultraviolet radiation. An extra surface coating promotes greater handling ease during manufacture, improved dirt resistance and easier cleaning. There is no emission of toxic fumes at high temperatures.

Tent Shapes

Architect Frei Otto, a pioneer in the field of tensile tent construction, draws inspiration from nature when devising the shapes of his structures. While computer technology enables architects like Otto to create complex designs, the sheer complexity of the construction, tensile stresses, connections and material mean that architects must work closely with tent membrane specialists. Tensile tent constructions can be divided into four basic shapes: simple saddle, wave, arch and highpoint. All other shapes are derivatives of these.

Another type of tent construction are the inflatables whose membrane fabric can be inflated to yield enormous structures. The newest variant in this field are ETFE air cushions, the best-known example of which is Nicholas Grimshaw's Eden Project.

Tent constructions are typically light, flexible, easy to transport and translucent. Two notable disadvantages are their relatively limited lifespan (although that also depends on the chosen quality), and lack of insulating capacity. The latter can be solved by using several layers of fabric; research into better solutions is ongoing.

The use of textiles is not confined to tent constructions or sun awnings. Owing to their flexibility and lightness, they are also increasingly being used for billboards, advertising banners and trade fair installations, in both printed and unprinted form. Buildings undergoing renovation are ideal candidates for a printed 'wrapping'

Project NBC Today Show Pavilion, Sydney (2000)
Architect Lahz Nimmo Architects
Photographer Brett Boardman Photography

Project Buckminster-Fuller Dome, Weil am Rhein (1950)
Architect Buckminster Fuller
Photographer Thomas Dix

which protects passers-by from falling debris while at the same time leaving its mark on the streetscape. The textile can be printed with any manner of images from life-size photos of the (original) building to advertising material.

The canvas and cotton tents used by the military are heavy and slow to dry, making them even heavier after rain. Unlike nylon, however, they can breathe and are moisture regulating. All modern textiles are

essentially composites in which the combination of fibres is responsible for the performance and quality of the final product. Cotton tents, for example, contain polyvinyl alcohol, a substance which swells when exposed to moisture. The fabric closes up when it rains and opens up again once it has stopped raining, enabling vapour exchange to take place.

The French manufacturer, Groupe Ferrari, produces special sunscreen fabrics made from polyester with an anti-fungal agent, PVC coating and a dirt-repellent polymer. Textiles for daylight regulation are becoming more and more sophisticated in particular with respect to their cooling and breathing capacity. Hostaflon FEP, produced by Hoechst, is a fluoroplastic film that can be applied to glass fibre fabric; the application of several layers of film causes small, thermally insulating air cushions to form. An important advantage of Hostaflon is its transparency.

Attempts are currently being made to improve the insulating capacity of textiles by developing a layered fabric incorporating a phase change material (PCM). The PCM used here is a paraffin that starts to store energy when it reaches its boiling point and releases it in the form of heat as it cools. PCMs have the potential to give any lightweight material a warmth-accumulating capability. This and other innovations in material technology will continue to improve the performance of architectural textiles.

ETFE

Ethylen Tetrafluoroethylen | *Copolymère Ethylène / Tétrafluoroéthylène* | *Etileno Tetrafluoretileno* | *Etilene Tetrafluoroetile* | *Ethyleen Tetrafluorethyleen*

Project Eden Project Visitors Centre, Cornwall (2000)
Architect Nicholas Grimshaw
Photographer Peter Cook, VIEW Pictures

Project Pinas, Den Helder (2003)
Architect Cepezed
Engineering D3BN | Tentech
Photographer Tentech

The architectural application of the relatively new material, ETFE foil, became well-known through Nicholas Grimshaw's Eden Project in Cornwall. This immense greenhouse is constructed of transparent 'cushions' mounted in a hexagonal aluminium frame. Each cushion consists of three sheets of ETFE foil welded together at the edges and separated from one another by a layer of air. ETFE admits ultra-violet radiation and, because the cushions are inflatable, extra air can be pumped in for added insulation in winter, while in summer the pressure can be reduced. ETFE foil is a perfect covering for greenhouses because of its strength, transparency and lightness. A piece of ETFE weighs less than 1 per cent of a piece of glass with the same volume. It is also a better insulator than glass, and much more resistant to the weathering effects of sunlight.

Technical Aspects

ETFE® (Ethyl tetra fluoro ethylene) is a thermoplastic copolymer derived from the polymerization of Ethylene and Tetrafluoroethylene (TEFLON®) monomers. This resin is extremely tough and abrasion resistant, and has excellent chemical resistance, dielectric strength, and a low coefficient of friction. Initially it was used chiefly in the chemical and petrochemical industries, but because of its strength, transparency, durability, insulating properties and light weight, the cushion form is starting to become an important building material. It is typically installed within special aluminium boundary profiles, which are in turn supported by steel, timber or bi-directional cable nets. Foil thicknesses between 50 and 250 microns are usually employed in 2 or 3 layer cushion constructions with a constantly maintained air pressure between 200 and 750 Pa. This pressure can be automatically increased to support higher snow loads.

Applications

Apart from its use in air cushion roofs for swimming pools, zoos, greenhouses, roof and dome lights, the foil is also suitable for many other applications. It is extremely elastic and available in large formats. It can also be printed for purposes of solar control and if two of the three layers are printed, it is even possible to adjust the degree of solar control by varying the air pressure in the two air chambers between the layers. The foil is easy to cut, trim and weld. It is available in a transparent and a white translucent version.

Colour	**white**
Glossiness	**glossy**, **satin**, matt
Translucence (%)	0 – 20 – 40 – 60 – 80 – 100
Texture	sharp, medium, **dull**
Hardness	hard, soft, **depressible**
Temperature	**warm**, medium, cool
Odour	strong, moderate, **none**
Acoustic opacity	good, **moderate**, poor

PVC-coated Polyester Textile

PVC-beschichtetes Polyester-Gewebe | Textile de Polyester enrobé de PVC | Tejido de poliéster recubierto de PVC |
Tessuto poliestere con rivestimento di PVC | PVC gecoate polyester

Project Carton Dome, IJburg, Amsterdam (2003)
Architect Shigeru Ban
Engineering Octatube | Tentech
Photographer Tentech

Project The Butterfly, Floriade 2001, Haarlemmermeer (2001)
Architect / Engineering OK5 | Tentech
Photographer Tentech

For situations where a portable, sturdy, collapsible, relatively durable tent construction is required, polyester textile with a coating of PVC (polyvinyl chloride) is probably the best choice. It is affordable, folds well and is available in a wide range of colours. It crops up all over the place and in all shapes and sizes, from circus tents to party tents, from emergency housing to roofs.

Technical Aspects

Although the PVC coating is applied to both sides of a polyester fabric, the resulting product is neither as strong nor as durable as glass fibre fabric with a PTFE coating, as the softening agents in the PVC are liable, over the course of time, to rise to the surface, making it sticky and easily soiled. Because the coating is applied to the fabric rather than the unwoven fibres, the textile retains its shape even when subjected to great tensile strains and the tensile strength of the entire piece of fabric is the same in all directions. Coatings are available in a wide range of colours. Detailing must allow for the fact that the material does not breathe. Various recycling methods are possible.

Applications

PVC-coated polyester textile is eminently suitable for temporary tent constructions, such as party tents, emergency housing, restaurant tents, roofs and façades.

Colour	variable
Glossiness	glossy, **satin**, **matt**
Translucence (%)	**0** – **20** – **40** – **60** – **80** – 100
Texture	sharp, medium, **dull**
Hardness	hard, soft, **depressible**
Temperature	**warm**, medium, cool
Odour	strong, moderate, **none**
Acoustic opacity	good, **moderate**, poor

Polytetrafluoroethylene (PTFE) or Teflon

Polytetrafluoroethylen (PTFE) oder Teflon | Polytétrafluoroéthylène (PTFE) ou Téflon | Politetrafluoroetileno (PTFE) o teflón |
Politetrafluoroetilene (PTFE) o Teflon | Teflon glasvezel

Project The Millennium Dome, Greenwich (1999)
Architect Richard Rogers
Photographer QA Photos

Project Air cushioned awning Apenheul, Apeldoorn (2002)
Architect Guido Bakker
Photographer Buitink Technology

PTFE, or Teflon as it came to be called, was discovered accidentally in a DuPont laboratory in 1938 and was initially disregarded. Today, its inventor, Dr Roy Plunkett, is included in America's National Inventors' Hall of Fame, alongside such figures as Thomas Edison, Louis Pasteur and the Wright Brothers. The 1938 discovery turned out to be of inestimable importance for modern society and has made a major contribution to the development of aerospace technology, communications, electronics, industrial processes and architecture.

Technical Aspects

A waxy substance resistant to virtually all chemical substances, PTFE is considered the most slippery material in existence. PTFE is almost completely chemically inert, is resistant to moisture and micro-organisms and has good self-cleaning properties (better than those of a comparable and less expensive coating, silicone). In architecture, PTFE is most frequently used as a coating for glass fibre fabrics where its expense is compensated by glass's long design life (30 years or more). A disadvantage of PTFE-coated glass fibre is that it is difficult to handle and to transport in large pieces because the PTFE coating visibly 'bruises' when sharply folded. PTFE glass fibre textile is available only in white. PTFE itself is available as a transparent film under the brand name Nowofol, and as a weather-resistant textile (Gore Tenara).

Applications

Teflon-coated textiles are used in permanent tent constructions with a long lifespan, such as roofs for gyms, sports centres, stadiums and airports.

Colour	**white**, **beige**
Glossiness	glossy, **satin**, **matt**
Translucence (%)	0 – **20** – **40** – **60** – **80** – 100
Texture	sharp, medium, **dull**
Hardness	hard, soft, **depressible**
Temperature	**warm**, medium, cool
Odour	strong, moderate, **none**
Acoustic opacity	good, **moderate**, poor

Pneumatic Membrane / Inflatables

Pneumatische Hüllen | Membrane pneumatique | Lámina neumática | Membrane gonfiabili | Pneumatische folie

Project DREAMSPACE III (2000-2001)
Artist Maurice Agis
Photographer Paloma Brotons

Project Tennis Hall, De Lier (2002)
Architect / Engineer Tentech
Photographer Tentech

Inflatables are transparent, lightweight and transient: so totally at odds with everything one associates with building, that they offer an excellent opportunity for breaking all the established laws of construction. Inflatable constructions are familiar to us from toys, from hot air balloons and Zeppelins, from film props, as well as many artworks. The first architectural structures were intended mainly for military purposes, such as inflatable shelters or inflatable space stations.

Inflatables were extremely popular – and politically charged – in the 1960s, reaching the height of their popularity during the French student revolt of 1968. At the École des Beaux Arts in Paris, for example, the *Utopie* group used inflatable structures to symbolize their desire to break away from the established order and its architecture.

Technical Aspects

Designing inflatable structures calls for an extensive knowledge of construction, for if the whole thing is not cut and stitched properly, the entire structure will collapse. In a way, the architect of inflatables is more of a tailor than a builder: it is not gravity which must be conquered, but compressive forces and tensile stresses. A double layer of gas-tight fabric is inflated, and the air pressure maintained by means of a system that replaces any air lost. Three-dimensional inflatable structures are based on the same principle, but use a lighter membrane such as polyester with a polyurethane coating. The most spectacular structures to date are by architect Mark Fisher who has designed gigantic pigs for Pink Floyd and Indian priestesses for the Rolling Stones. Thin fabrics are stitched, thicker ones welded. The simplest form of inflatable construction consists of a single-layer inflatable hall with a special air-locked entry. The air pressure is low, around 200 to 600 Pascal. The shape of double-walled inflatable structures is sometimes maintained by textile partitions.

Applications

Aside from countless inflatable toys and gadgets, inflatables are used for entire sport complexes, such as tennis halls and swimming pools. Other applications include interior walls, trade fair stands, lightweight roof constructions (like that of the Villa Arena shopping mall in Amsterdam), and temporary outdoor structures.

Colour	**variable**
Glossiness	glossy, **satin**, **matt**
Translucence (%)	**0** – 20 – 40 – 60 – 80 – 100
Texture	sharp, medium, **dull**
Hardness	hard, soft, **depressible**
Temperature	**warm**, medium, cool
Odour	strong, moderate, **none**
Acoustic opacity	good, **moderate**, poor

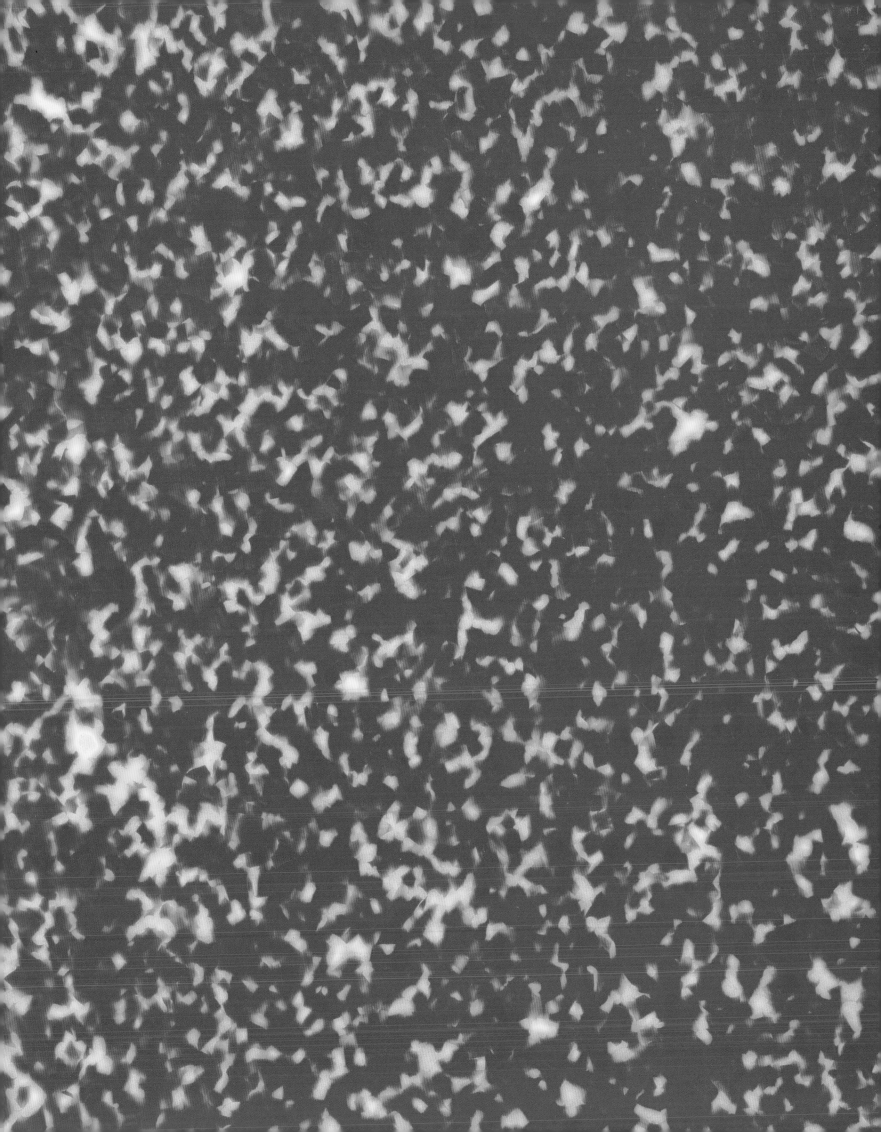

Future Materials

Werkstoffe der Zukunft | Futur | Futuro | Futuro | Toekomstige materialen

From Prehistoric Times to the Present

Human prehistory is divided into several successive 'ages', the Stone Age, the Bronze Age and the Iron Age, named after the material that reflected the prevailing stage of technological development. Each of these materials was at one period the most innovative material of its time and it was the ability to mine, process and use that material which gave some people an advantage over others. Thus history is to a degree determined by the materials available for making things and by the development of techniques for working and improving on those materials.

Each family of materials included in this book has undergone an evolution wrought by human hands. Wood has been transformed from the simple tree trunk used in log cabins, into a highly versatile material whose use today ranges from loadbearing construction panels to wood meal, a component of three-dimensionally extrudable materials. Metal has gone through just about every imaginable development up to and including foam metal. Glass, a major constant in architecture, continues to evolve with innovations in this material rapidly becoming standard products. In no time at all, HR+ glass – a window system with a high thermal insulation rating achieved by means of special coatings and a gas-filled cavity – went from being a novelty to a standard material in public housing, and if the construction glass industry has its way, the same will happen with self-cleaning glass. Natural stone itself may not be very receptive to innovation, but the same cannot be said of the techniques for working it, examples being the production of super-thin translucent slices of stone or the use of granulated stone in a wide range of composites. Clay can be made into innumerable types and colours of brick, and, in the hands of Renzo Piano, is entering a whole new phase of refinement as a façade material. Concrete continues to evolve in terms of workability (think of self-compacting concrete) and improved structural performance (through the addition of different reinforcement fibres). The newest family of construction materials, plastics, has hardly begun to tap its developmental potential.

Most of the research carried out into these material families over the last fifty years has been directed towards the development of composites, which is to say customized materials. The combination of project-specific structural, physical and aesthetic requirements and new processing techniques has proven very fruitful, resulting in an enormous freedom of choice. Instead of being limited by what the market offers, we are moving ever closer to a situation in which materials are produced to order to meet a whole range of performance requirements in the fields of energy consumption, cost, comfort, health, efficiency, aesthetics, individuality, flexibility, environmental friendliness, recyclability and safety.

Manipulation

Composites are the result of manipulation at the material level. Since the final years of the 20th century, it has been possible to understand and manipulate materials at the molecular level (nanotechnology). For this reason, the present century has been called 'the century of materials'. We are now able to create materials embodying the features we desire, as well as to use less raw material and energy for the same level of performance. Obviously, such tech-

nological developments concern only part of the world, the industrialized West. As such, 'development' is a relative term, given that half the world's population still live in homes made from one of the most primitive of building materials, adobe, or sun-dried clay.

Nanotechnology

What is nanotechnology and what does it have to offer architecture? Nanotechnology is the study and design of systems at the nanoscale, the scale of the atom. Chemical compositions built from nano particles (i.e. particles measured on a nanometric scale, a nanometre being equal to one billionth of a metre) are multifunctional elements which react to changing conditions. They are found in such everyday substances as clay, metal and glass, but their own properties differ significantly from those of their bulk counterparts. Metals become pigments, ceramics function as electrical conductors and glass can become glue. With manipulation, nano particles are capable of physical feats unthinkable in their normal material manifestation. These new materials are intended for use in architecture, electronics and energetic materials technology, the medical industry and environmental technology. Some ten years of research have yielded a number of applications, such as fireproof natural fibres for fire-safe wood panelling, electrochromatic glass for self-cleaning windows, graffiti-resistant coatings, easy-to-clean coatings for sanitary fittings, corrosion-resistant coatings for metal, heat-resistant and scratch-resistant

Project 'Clubbie Max' structures, Sydney (2000)
Architect Lahz Nimmo Architects
Photographer Brett Boardman Photography

paints and UV-resistant pigments. Fire-resistant glass, an innovation made possible by nanotechnology, is 35% lighter than normal fire-resistant glass.

It is worth noting that nano-applications are generally more expensive than traditional applications and take about ten years to research and develop. For the foreseeable future, therefore, the application of nanotechnology in architecture will be mainly directed towards coatings and surface treatments.

Smart Materials

A development of particular interest is the 'smart façade' which is able to react to changing weather conditions. It is made possible through the use of photochromatic glass, which becomes darker, and thus heat absorbing, when exposed to ultraviolet rays. The same glass can be used for heat regulation: an insulated façade panel can be fitted with glass with a transparent electrochromatic coating. As it reacts to temperature fluctuations, this thermochromatic element automatically regulates the transmission of heat through the wall in both directions.

Other examples are heat-excluding, environmentally-friendly glass-fibre insulation and a self-cleaning coating for glass that makes it possible to rinse away dirt with water. The latter works as follows: ultraviolet rays activate the coating, which degrades and loosens the dirt by means of oxidation. After the next shower of rain, the glass is clean. The glass industry sees great potential for this in industrial and public-utility buildings because of savings in maintenance costs.

Materials that react actively to changing conditions are also known as 'smart materials'. Such materials are equipped with a processor, an

Project Dual pigmented coating in Acanthus, Amsterdam (2003)
Architect Branimir Medic and Pero Puljiz, de Architekten Cie.
Photographer Jeroen Musch

acceptor and a reactor. The acceptor registers change – in temperature, pressure, light, humidity, or whatever – and sends a signal to the processor. This activates the reactor which in turn brings about a change – colour, volume, rigidity, transparency, et cetera – in the material itself.

Another phenomenon likely to fuel future materials development is cross-fertilization between different fields of knowledge. One example is aerogel, a material originally developed by NASA as an insula-

Project Living Tomorrow pavilion, Amsterdam (2003)
Architect UN Studio
Photographer Christian Richters

tor for the Pathfinder spacecraft. Consisting of silicon and 98% air, aerogel is the lightest solid known. As it is transparent and insulates twenty times better than insulating glass, it is presently being studied with a view to possible construction applications. Outlast, a paraffin phase-change material originally used in sportswear, is now also being used for ceiling panels and plastering. Outlast stores latent energy during the phase change at around 23°C, and releases it in the form of heat as it cools.

Biomimetics is a science devoted to the study of materials and processes in nature for the purpose of applying them in technology. For example, the insulating properties of a penguin's plumage are vastly superior to those of the rock and glass wool blankets currently used in buildings. Instead of a haphazard pad of fibres, a penguin's coat consists of a carefully graduated structure of down layers. In Japan, scientists are studying a component of the skin of the sea cucumber that enables this invertebrate to vary its stiffness in response to the pressure exerted upon it, a principle with important implications for building foundations in earthquake-prone areas.

Although such applications appear to be mainly concerned with technical performance, they will also inevitably lead to new designs. The possibilities include reactive façades capable of changing their colour or degree of transparency, and which may or may not be luminous and/or dynamic as well (for example, solar shading in the form of slivers of mica that swirl upwards in an air cavity under the influence of sunlight); lighter and more slender constructions; façades which are transparent yet insulating; interiors fitted out with wall and floor coverings and furniture whose sensory qualities can be adjusted according to the desired mood or atmosphere (with obvious workplace and entertainment centre applications).

Domotics

Intelligente Häuser | Matériaux Intelligents | Materiales inteligentes |
Materiali intelligenti | Intelligente materialen

It is human nature to want to create an environment that is as pleasant, comfortable and convenient as possible. One way to do this is to delegate the less pleasant tasks to someone else, and to ensure that everyone is happy, we much prefer that 'someone else' to be a mechanized assistant. The supreme mechanized assistant is the 'intelligent building', an age-old dream that finally became feasible during the electronic age by means of a form of applied intelligence known as 'domotics'.

The term domotics derives from *domus-robotica* meaning 'home automation', and is a collective term for products and technologies created for the purpose of automating building functions. It involves devices that can make the home environment safer and more comfortable as well as saving on electricity, gas and water. With domotics, heating, lighting, ventilation, electrical appliances, solar shading, warm water and access control are all regulated by a single central system that also ensures that everything works as efficiently and economically as possible. The system, which can be operated by remote control, voice recognition, verbal commands or even clapping, can perform any number of necessary, useful and soothing functions: it can automatically open and close the curtains, refill the refrigerator, switch lights on and off when you enter or leave a room, adjust temperature and humidity levels in individual rooms, brew a cup of coffee to greet you upon waking, and so on.

Smart Materials
Building materials, too, can behave intelligently. Smart materials differ from traditional ones in that they have a 'memory' and the capacity to react to changing circumstances, such as fluctuations in ultraviolet radiation, temperature, pressure, potential difference, moisture and chemical composition. Like all smart devices, they are equipped with an acceptor, a processor and a reactor. Here, the acceptor is the sensor while the processor is the central 'brain' which regulates changes via the reactor. Although many smart materials are initially developed for the aerospace and defence industries, they eventually find their way to the consumer. Although this often begins with fairly banal gimmicks, like colour-changing Barbie hair, increasingly the functional aspects and possibilities of smart materials are being recognized.

Material with a Memory
'Shape memory materials' also fall within the category of smart materials. One such material is nitinol, a nickel-titanium alloy used as a sound-absorbing material for submarines in the 1960s. Nitinol exhibits both high plastic deformability and 'pure elastic deformability' or superelasticity. When exposed to temperature changes it displays a spectacular thermal shape memory effect, such that above or below a certain temperature, the metal will reassume its original shape. This property is exploited, for example, in the automatic switches of electric kettles which shut off as soon as the water boils. Memory foam is another material that regains its shape after being depressed, thus offering interesting possibilities for furniture.

Phase Change Materials
Yet another smart material is phase change material (PCM). During the phase change from solid to liquid to gas, an energy exchange (in turn based on the molecular structural organization) takes place. That energy is stored temporarily and later released again. For example, paraffin stores energy when it reaches its melting point (approx. 24°C) and releases it again in the form of heat as it cools and solidifies. This property has obvious applications for sports clothing. However, in view of its excellent heat-accumulation capacity, the Fraunhofer Institute has also tested paraffin in plaster for interior walls and in ceiling panels.

From Gadget to Function
The best-known smart materials are photochromatic, thermochromatic and electrochromatic inks. Margareth Orth and Joanna Berzowska recently designed an electric blanket using a material that in fact consists of one long flexible electrical circuit. This was printed with thermochromatic ink which continually changes colour while the blanket is turned on. The same technology can be used to create an interior whose colour can be adjusted to fit the mood or style of the moment.

GloCar
Henry Ford famously quipped that customers could buy one of his Model T motorcars in any colour they wanted 'as long as it's black'. Designer Laurens van den Acker is aiming at quite the opposite effect with his GloCar: a car that can assume any colour, as long as it *isn't* black. With the GloCar, it is possible to take the children to school in the morning in a bright orange car and then drive on to work in a glowing blue one. 'With the GloCar's range of colours and intensities, you can choose whether to stand out from, or blend in with the traffic,' van den Acker explains. 'The GloCar is constructed of an aluminium space frame with a body of injection-moulded translucent plastic panels. The chromatically variable illumination

Project GloCar (2003)
Designer Laurens van den Acker, Ford Motor Company

consists of red, green and blue LEDs controlled by a microprocessor. The motor runs on fuel cells. The design dispenses with separate lights; the vehicle's sides simply blink to signal turning, and the entire rear portion lights up when you brake. This saves quite a lot on parts by making use of smart materials capable of fulfilling more than one function.'

More functional applications concern façades. On the principle that dark façades become warmer than light-coloured ones, a coating capable of changing colour can be deployed as a means of thermal

Nanotechnology

Nanotechnologie | Nanotechnologie | Nanotecnología | Nanotecnologia | Nanotechnologie

insulation. In this way, an increase in temperature of up to 4°C can be achieved in winter and a decrease of 8°C in the summer.

Liquid Drapes

Liquid crystals are a substance we associate with digital watches, calculators and other consumer electronics products with display screens. LCDs (liquid crystal displays) can now be found almost everywhere. This is because they fulfil a simple but extremely useful function: reacting visibly to magnetic and electrical fields. LCDs have an 'on' colour and an 'off' colour.

Some five years ago, 3M (the inventor of the ubiquitous Post-It notes) developed Privacy Film, a paper-thin, electrically sensitive film, based on patents held by Kent State University and Raychem Corporation. Today, Viracon, an architectural glass company, manufactures a product consisting of a layer of liquid crystals sandwiched between two sheets of privacy film, which in turn are held between panes of glass. When electricity is applied to the film, the liquid crystals line up and the previously foggy material becomes clear. When the current is withdrawn, it becomes foggy again. The result: Privacy Glass. Now you see through it – now you don't.

Electrochromatic material which changes colour can also be used as a heat absorbing film for windows. In this case, the current is triggered by the strength of ultraviolet radiation reaching the film. This system can be switched off at will, unlike direct photochromatic film on glass (film with a photochromatic coating which reacts to fluctuations in ultraviolet radiation).

Biomimicry

Biomimicry is a science concerned with translating biological processes and structures into human design. The highly successful swimsuit based on the self-repairing skin of the shark is an example of biomimicry. The principle of self-repair was applied in a modified epoxy resin, a 'healing' agent (dicyclopentadiene) and a catalyst. The resulting autonomous healing system has as its basis microcapsules 100 microns in diameter which were incorporated into the polyester fabric together with the catalyst. When damage occurs, the microcapsules release the healing agent which, together with the catalyst, forms a new layer at the site of the damage. This happens within a few minutes, before water can have a deleterious effect. At present, the product is used in aerospace applications and complex industrial processes, where tear formation or surface damage can have dangerous consequences. As far as architecture is concerned, one can imagine it might be extremely useful in vandalism-prone areas.

Whether 'intelligence' is obtained through mechanical, biological or chemical means, cross-fertilization between scientific fields is essential if it is also to be applied intelligently. Obviously, materials play a central role in such applications, whether as a visible 'skin' or hidden away in other materials like concrete and composites. In that respect, the construction industry has a lot to look forward to.

In the 20th century, the shift in emphasis from mechanization to microelectronics caused an explosion in technological development. Now, in the 21st century, increasing globalization and competition together with scientific cross-fertilization, are expected to have a similarly enriching effect. Seventy per cent of all western industrial products are material-based, so that, given the global nature of technology today, any innovation in the field of materials could potentially be of global importance. Industrial innovation demands superior knowledge of technology and industrial processes and there will be an increasing need for specialized knowledge of material development within specific fields. Nanotechnology in particular is expected to play a particularly important role in material development. Not only does it open up the prospect of totally new materials, but it can also be expected to deliver qualitative and quantitative improvements in performance, as well as cost savings in the production process.

The prefix nano- comes from the Greek word *nanos*, meaning 'dwarf'. Nanotechnology, or molecular nanotechnology, as it is sometimes referred to, involves the study and development of structures on a nano-scale, (i.e. in the range of 0.1 nanometre to 100 nanometres). A nanometre (nm) is equal to one billionth of a metre. A central aim of nanotechnology is to manipulate and reposition atoms in such a way as to form a new structure. Broadly speaking, the process of creating nano-materials involves three steps:

1. Scientists must be able to manipulate individual atoms. This means that they must first develop a technique for grabbing single atoms and moving them into the desired positions.
2. The next step is to develop nanoscopic machines, called assemblers, which can be programmed to manipulate atoms and molecules at will. It would take thousands of years for a single assembler to produce any kind of material one atom at a time. Trillions of assemblers are needed to develop products within a viable time frame. In order to create enough assemblers to build consumer goods, some nanomachines, called replicators, will be programmed to build more assemblers.
3. Trillions of assemblers and replicators fill an area smaller than a cubic millimetre, too small to be seen with the naked eye. The theory is that assemblers and replicators working together like hands will construct products automatically, eventually replacing traditional labour methods. This will vastly decrease manufacturing costs, thereby making consumer goods plentiful, cheaper and stronger.

The Development of Nanotechnology

This new science can already look back on a number of historic moments. In 1959, Richard P. Feynman gave a lecture at California Institute of Technology (Caltech) entitled 'There's plenty of room at the bottom', in which he discussed the challenges and opportunities already existing at that time for manipulating and multiplying processes and structures at the atomic level. In 1981, the Scanning Tunneling Microscope (STM) was invented by Heinrich Rohrer and Gerd Karl Binnig, who five years later received the Nobel prize for physics for their achievement. The STM enabled scientists for the first time to see individual molecules. The year 1986 saw the publication of *Engines of Creation, the Coming Era of Nanotechnology*, in which

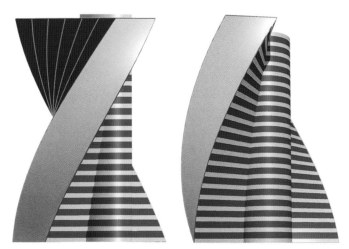

Project Tordeergevel – all 20 floors of this 60 metres high, twisting tower are equal; repetition of the components reduces the production costs considerably (1998)
Designer Karel Vollers
Drawing Globel Hellevoort

K. Eric Drexler sketched the potential of molecular nanotechnology and the special products it would make possible. Four years later, in 1990, IBM researchers succeeded, with the help of the STM, in moving and positioning 35 xenon atoms on a nickel crystal surface to spell out *IBM*.

These discoveries and developments spawned a utopian conviction that, armed with nanotechnology, there will be no limits to what mankind will be able to build in future. Nanotechnology promises to bring important changes to virtually every field. The first major breakthroughs are expected to be in the medical, computer and automobile industries, after which they will gradually be adopted and adapted by other sectors, such as the construction industry.

The first products of nanotechnology will consist of reinforced fibres, but in the long run it will be possible to reproduce everything, including diamonds, water and food. Food synthesis would make it possible to combat hunger in areas suffering from drought or poor soil fertility. In the computer industry, where transistors on silicon microprocessors are just about as small as they can get with present technology, nanotechnology will usher in a new generation of still smaller computer components capable of storing billions of bytes on structures the size of a sugar cube. Nanotechnology's greatest impact, though, will be in the medical industry, where utopian scenarios are already being sketched of patients swallowing tiny nano-robots which then proceed to attack and eliminate cancer cells or viruses. Other wishful predictions include an increase in average life expectancy, the elimination of wrinkles and other symptoms of age, small operations carried out internally by nano-robots and cosmetic operations without scars. Even more enthusiastic proponents are predicting that nano-robots will enable us to improve the earth's environment by repairing the ozone layer.

Nanotechnology in the Construction Industry

As far as the construction industry is concerned, nanotechnology is for the time being focused on the development of coatings –

scratch-proof paints, ultraviolet-resistant coatings, water-repellent surfaces, fire-resistant and high-insulation glass constructions. Improving the performance of a building's 'skin' can have several advantages. For example, self-cleaning glass will yield significant maintenance savings; with fire-resistant coatings, glass constructions will be cheaper, lighter and use less material; the durability of façades will be extended; and solar control will be possible without the need for electronics.

In addition to coatings, there are plenty of other examples of how nano-materials might be applied in the construction field, such as monitoring changes in the strength or composition of concrete from the inside. Besides improvements to technical performance, nano-technology is also expected to bring aesthetic improvements. In par-ticular, manipulated smart materials, which change under the influ-ence of their surroundings, will be able to alter the lighting, texture, structure and translucency of a façade and in this way affect the streetscape. At the same time, materials that are rarely used at pres-ent due to poor durability, will suddenly have a much wider range of application. Textiles that are water and dirt-repellent and at the same insulating and vandal proof, offer exciting possibilities for tent and pneumatic constructions. All in all, a plethora of material for future development.

Materials and the Environment

*Materialien und Umwelt | Matériaux et Environnement | Materiales
y medio ambiente | Materiali ed ambiente | Materialen en milieu*

Among architects, as well as between governments and industry,
there are a number of conflicting views as to what 'environmentally
friendly construction' really means. While some argue for a return to
building with straw, clay and thatch, others think there is more to be
gained by deploying high-tech industrial solutions. The disagree-
ments and conflicts surrounding the concept of *life cycle analysis*
(LCA) serves as an excellent illustration of this.

The LCA of a building material is based on a number of factors,
starting with the raw material itself, the energy required to extract
or manufacture it, its durability and workability, preservation treatments, waste processing, recyclability and, finally, the energy cost of
demolition and any combustion emission following demolition.
Everyone is agreed that the amount of construction and demolition
waste needs to be reduced. The most effective method of reducing
such waste is re-use, or 'integrated chain management'. Three types
of re-use can be distinguished:
1. At the building level: the building is assigned a new use, with the
   shell being preserved as far as possible.
2. At the component level: components of a building are removed
   and re-used elsewhere. This is especially common with historic
   elements like ornaments and cast-iron railings. This 'second-hand
   market' in window sills, doors, roof tiles, ceilings and the like may
   also prove useful for former East Bloc countries or developing
   countries.
3. At the material level: re-use of natural stone and characteristic
   old bricks.

The ideal situation occurs when the raw material of a particular
building material can be re-used at the end of the building's life
cycle, with its original usage value intact. In such cases, the material
can be considered *recyclable*. However, the reuse of materials is not
restricted to such rational considerations, for materials also embody
emotions, tradition, history and ambience. Nowhere is this more evident than in the restoration sector, where the watchword is

'reversibility'. Impregnating powdery natural stone with plastic, for
example, is taboo, even though it is invisible and often the only way
of maintaining a monument.

Steel

Steel is recycled into steel. In Europe, this fluctuates between 30%
and 50%, whilst in North America almost 70% of steel recovered
from cars, consumer products, construction steel and packaging is
recycled. That even recycled materials are not without emotional
associations, became clear with the recycling of the steel from the
World Trade Center in New York, which is being sold to be melted
down and recycled all over the world. Part of this scrap metal will be
used for a battle ship to be deployed 'in the fight against terrorism
and the pursuit of world peace'. Some 70,000 metric tons have been
shipped to Asia where India is one of the world's greatest waste
processors. Each year, millions of metric tons of plastic, steel and old
computers are dismantled there for re-use, often by workers drawn
from the poorest strata of society. They carry out this heavy work for
low pay and under questionable health and safety conditions.
Normally they are prepared to accept these risks, but many labourers
will not have anything to do with World Trade Center waste, as it is
believed to be under a curse.

Fired and Unfired Man-made Stone and Natural Stone

Brick and unfired man-made stone such as concrete, are ground into
rubble granulate and used as a substitute for gravel, especially for
street and road construction. Natural stone is often re-used because of
its unique character and durability. An ironic fact in this connection is
that the stone wall cladding of Berlin's subway stations came
from Adolf Hitler's Chancellery, a building deliberately destroyed by
Soviet forces in 1945 in their attempt to wipe out all traces of the period. Understandably enough, this fact was never publicized, but it was
clearly considered too great a waste of material not to use the stone.

Glass

Glass, too, can be fully recycled. Waste glass is used in the manufacture of window glass, for example, but in this case it is 'waste' from
the manufacturing process itself: when the raw ingredients are
switched in order to change to a different colour, production does
not stop and the glass produced between the two production runs is
treated as 'waste' and reused. Glass from demolition tends to be
incorporated into the recycling circuit for bottle glass and as such is
reused over and over again. Research is currently being carried out
into the feasibility of returning this glass to the construction industry
in the form of an additive for concrete, for example. Verrazzo,
a scaled-up version of terrazzo consisting of large pieces of glass
embedded in concrete, which may or may not be polished, has
promising visual and structural properties.

Wood

Owing to its renewability and extremely low environmental impact
when burned, wood is an extremely environmentally friendly material. A material is considered renewable if it is sustained through
growth, such that its use will not lead to a reduction of existing
stocks. On the other hand, wood's quality and durability is inversely
proportional to its growth rate. The best approach to wood (and

Project Homeless houses, Parade 2003

Artist Karolien Helweg, Ruben La Cruz

Photographer Kees Hummel

Project Star and Arts, Bareveld (2002)
Architect Onix
Photographer SAPh, Rob de Jong

grass) as a material is consequently to use quick-growing varieties
and to make them more durable using more environmentally friendly
methods like the Plato method, whereby the structure of the wood
is altered by 'cooking' or acetylating it. The principle of acetylation is
very simple: micro-organisms eat the wood, especially the hydrophilic
compound in its cellulose. When the hydrophilic compound is replaced by an acetyl compound by immersing the wood in a bath of
acetic acid, the wood can be upgraded from Durability Class 5 to 1.

Plastic

DDT, PCBs, PVC, PAK, CFCs, 'damage to the ozone layer' and 'the
Seveso disaster': all inooke notorious environmental issues and all
have been the subject of heated debates. The release of dioxins into
the environment by waste incineration plants, the plasticizers used in
toys, diminishing human (and sea-snail) fertility as a result of increasing amounts of pseudo-oestrogens in the environment which disturb
the hormonal balance, are other well-known examples of contamination of the environment and ourselves. While the environmental
lobby cries foul, industry retorts that there is still no convincing scientific proof of the adverse effects of their activities.

Plastic, long considered the black sheep of materials in the environmental context, is highly suitable for recycling, and the number of
initiatives for developing the logistical and organizational structure to
facilitate its re-use are on the increase. For example, manufacturers
of plastic frames already have a good collection and recycling system
in place. Other manufacturers of plastic products such as roof
cladding and façade panels, have the option of joining this system or
setting up their own. The most-used plastic façade material, high
pressure laminate (HPL), contains 80% paper and 20% resin and can
be treated as a normal household waste product, since no dangerous
substances are released when it is burned.

The Environment

The impact of the industrialized world on the environment will undoubtedly continue to be a source of concern. We and future gener-
ations are a part of that environment. Government and industry
need to recognize their responsibilities and come up with appropriate
legislation on both the national and the global level. As long as this
does not happen, the problem will simply shift to poorer countries,
which are understandably inclined to view both production and
waste processing in terms of economics rather than the environment.

Sensory Table

Property	Douglas | Oregon Pine	European Redwood | Scots Pine	Larch	Spruce | Whitewood	Western Red Cedar	Azobé	Bankirai	Beech	Iroko	Karri	Mahogany	Maple	Meranti	Merbau	Oak	Robinia	Sapupira	Teak	Vitex	Walnut	Bamboo	Sedum, Green Façades and Green Roofs	Cardboard	Coconut Fibre	Cork	Paper	Reed and Cane	Willow Rods	Linoleum	Cement-bonded Particle Board	Woodwool Slabs	Laminates
Colour																																
beige																																
black																																
blue																																
bluish grey																																
brown							●								●									●	●			●				
brown grey														●																		
caramel																					●											
dark blue																																
gold																																
green																						●										
grey																														●		
grey blue																																
none																																
pink																																
reddish brown										●			●	●																		
rusty																																
silver																																
silver grey																																
variable	●	●	●	●	●	●		●	●		●						●	●	●	●					●	●	●		●	●	●	
white												●																				
woody																																●
yellow												●			●																	
yellow brown															●						●										●	
yellow gold																																
yellow red																																
Glossiness																																
glossy																																
satin								●				●		●		●		●		●												
matt	●	●	●	●	●	●	●		●	●	●		●		●		●		●		●	●	●	●	●	●	●	●	●	●	●	●
Translucence (%)																																
0	●	●	●	●	●	●	●	●	●	●	●	●	●	●	●	●		●	●	●	●	●	●		●	●			●	●	●	●
20																											●	●				
40																								●								
60																	●															
80																																
100																																
Texture																																
sharp								●									●					●					●	●		●		
medium	●	●	●	●	●	●	●		●	●	●	●	●	●	●	●		●	●	●	●					●			●			●
dull																								●	●							●
Hardness																																
hard																					●									●		
soft	●	●	●	●	●	●	●	●	●	●	●	●	●	●	●	●	●	●	●	●			●	●					●		●	●
depressible																	●					●			●	●	●	●				
Temperature																																
warm	●	●	●	●	●	●	●	●	●	●	●	●	●	●	●	●		●	●	●			●	●	●	●	●	●	●		●	●
medium																	●				●									●		
cool																																
Odour																																
strong		●			●						●											●		●								
moderate	●		●	●		●	●	●	●	●		●	●	●	●	●	●	●	●	●					●	●	●	●	●	●	●	●
none																					●		●									
Acoustic opacity																																
good																								●	●						●	
moderate	●	●	●	●	●	●	●	●	●	●	●	●	●	●	●	●	●	●	●	●	●	●				●	●	●	●			●
poor																							●							●		

484

Material / property matrix (Natural Stone section)

Property	Plywood	Timber Composites	Coating, Preserving and Modifying	Veneering	Milling	Perforating and Punching	Bending	**Natural Stone**	Black Granite	Gray-Shulman	Multicolour Red – Migmatite	Basalt	Basalt Lava	Blue Limestone	Saint Maximin	Comblanchien	Travertine	Trani	Boulders	Sandstone	Shell Limestone	Danube Limestone	Tuff	Quartzite	Azul Macaubus Bahia	Gneiss	Slate	Serpentine	Greek Marble	High-tech Stone	Stone-glass Laminate	Sandwich Façade Panels
Colour																																
beige															•	•		•														
black														•					•						•							
blue														•											•							
bluish grey																					•											
brown																			•													
brown grey																					•	•										
caramel																																
dark blue																																
gold																																
green																																
grey										•				•					•													
grey blue													•																			
none																																
pink															•	•									•							
reddish brown																																
rusty																																
silver																																
silver grey																																
variable			•						•		•	•					•		•	•				•	•	•	•	•		•	•	•
white																									•				•			
woody	•	•		•	•	•	•																									
yellow																																
yellow brown																																
yellow gold																																
yellow red																																
Glossiness																																
glossy			•						•	•	•			•										•	•			•		•	•	•
satin			•	•			•		•	•	•		•	•		•	•	•	•						•			•	•	•	•	
matt	•	•	•	•	•	•	•		•	•	•	•	•		•	•	•		•	•	•	•	•	•	•	•	•	•	•	•	•	•
Translucence (%)																																
0	•	•	•	•	•	•	•		•	•	•	•	•					•	•	•	•	•	•	•	•	•	•	•	•	•	•	•
20			•			•									•	•	•															
40			•			•																								•		
60			•			•																										
80			•			•																										
100			•																													
Texture																																
sharp			•	•	•	•						•					•		•					•	•	•		•				•
medium	•	•	•	•			•		•		•	•	•	•	•	•	•	•	•	•	•	•	•	•	•	•	•	•	•	•	•	•
dull			•	•					•	•	•		•	•	•	•	•	•	•	•	•	•	•	•	•	•	•	•	•	•	•	•
Hardness																																
hard			•		•				•	•	•	•	•	•	•	•	•		•			•		•	•	•	•	•	•	•	•	•
soft	•	•			•	•	•																									
depressible																																
Temperature																																
warm	•	•			•																											
medium			•				•		•	•	•	•	•	•	•	•	•		•	•	•	•	•	•	•	•	•	•	•	•	•	•
cool																	•															
Odour																																
strong			•																													
moderate	•	•	•																													
none			•						•	•	•	•	•	•	•	•	•	•	•	•	•	•	•	•	•	•	•	•	•	•	•	•
Acoustic opacity																																
good					•	•																										
moderate	•	•	•	•	•	•	•																									
poor									•	•	•	•	•	•	•	•	•	•	•	•	•	•	•	•	•	•	•	•	•	•	•	•

Fired Man-made Stone spans: Hand-moulded Bricks, Press-moulded Bricks, Extruded Bricks, Pantiles, Plain Roofing Tiles, Ceramic Slates, Ceramic Tiles, Glazed Stoneware Tiles, Extrusion Panels, Colour, Porosity, Printing, Sanding, Combustible Additives, Slip, Glazing, Reducing

Unfired Man-made Stone spans: Concrete, Sand-Lime Bricks, Polyester Concrete, Gypsum Plaster

	Natural Stone Granulate	Rough Hewing / Splitting	Sanding and Honing	Flaming	Bush Hammering	Polishing	Milling	Chipping and Tooling	Hand-moulded Bricks	Press-moulded Bricks	Extruded Bricks	Pantiles	Plain Roofing Tiles	Ceramic Slates	Ceramic Tiles	Glazed Stoneware Tiles	Extrusion Panels	Colour	Porosity	Printing	Sanding	Combustible Additives	Slip	Glazing	Reducing	Concrete	Sand-Lime Bricks	Polyester Concrete	Gypsum Plaster
Colour																													
beige																													
black																													
blue																													
bluish grey																													
brown																													
brown grey																													
caramel																													
dark blue																													
gold																													
green																													
grey																										•			
grey blue																													
none																													
pink																													
reddish brown																													
rusty																													
silver																													
silver grey																													
variable	•	•	•	•	•	•	•	•	•	•	•	•	•	•	•	•	•	•	•	•	•	•	•	•	•				
white																											•	•	•
woody																													
yellow																													
yellow brown																													
yellow gold																													
yellow red																													
Glossiness																													
glossy	•					•	•									•							•	•					
satin	•		•								•	•	•	•	•	•	•	•	•					•	•				
matt	•	•		•	•		•	•	•	•	•	•	•	•	•	•	•	•	•	•	•	•				•	•	•	•
Translucence (%)																													
0	•	•	•	•	•	•	•	•	•	•	•	•	•	•	•	•	•	•	•	•	•	•	•	•	•	•	•	•	•
20																													
40																													
60																													
80																													
100																													
Texture																													
sharp	•	•																										•	
medium	•				•																	•		•		•	•		•
dull	•		•	•		•		•	•	•	•	•	•	•	•	•	•	•	•	•	•	•	•						
Hardness																													
hard	•	•	•	•	•	•	•	•	•	•	•	•	•	•	•	•	•	•	•	•	•	•	•	•	•	•	•		•
soft																													
depressible																													
Temperature																													
warm									•	•	•	•	•	•	•	•	•	•	•	•	•	•	•	•	•				•
medium	•	•	•	•	•	•	•	•																•		•	•	•	
cool																													
Odour																													
strong																													
moderate																												•	
none	•	•	•	•	•	•	•	•	•	•	•	•	•	•	•	•	•	•	•	•	•	•	•	•	•	•	•		•
Acoustic opacity																													
good																													
moderate									•	•	•	•	•	•	•	•	•	•	•	•	•	•	•	•	•				
poor	•	•	•	•	•	•	•	•																		•	•	•	•

	Clay Plaster	Spraying	Formwork	Concrete Block	Washing	Acid Etching	Abrasive Blasting	Grinding	Splitting	Bush Hammering	Printing	Colour Coatings and Lazure	Rust	Plasterwork	Perforated Texture	Moroccan Plasterwork	Italian Stucco	Rendering	Texturing in Wet Plaster	Split-Faced Sand-Lime Bricks	Superplasticizers	Natural Stone Granules	Pebbles, Crushed Demolition Waste, Glass	Pigments	Aluminium Powder	Organic and Mineral Fibres	Shells	**Glass** Float Glass	Coloured Glass	Wired Glass	Laminated Glass
Colour																															
beige																															
black																															
blue																															
bluish grey																															
brown																															
brown grey																															
caramel																															
dark blue																															
gold																															
green																															
grey																															
grey blue																															
none																												•			
pink																															
reddish brown																															
rusty													•																		
silver																															
silver grey																															
variable	•	•	•	•	•	•	•	•	•	•	•	•		•		•	•			•	•	•	•	•		•	•		•	•	•
white															•			•	•						•						
woody																															
yellow																															
yellow brown																															
yellow gold																															
yellow red																															
Glossiness																															
glossy								•								•	•							•	•			•	•	•	•
satin								•									•					•	•	•		•				•	•
matt	•	•	•	•		•	•	•		•	•	•	•	•	•	•	•	•	•	•	•	•	•	•	•	•	•			•	•
Translucence (%)																															
0	•	•	•	•	•	•	•	•	•	•	•	•	•	•	•	•	•	•	•	•	•	•	•	•	•	•	•				
20																															
40																													•		
60																													•		
80																														•	
100																												•	•	•	•
Texture																															
sharp		•			•					•					•							•	•	•	•						
medium	•		•	•		•	•	•		•	•	•	•	•	•						•	•	•	•			•			•	•
dull			•													•		•	•	•						•	•	•	•	•	•
Hardness																															
hard	•	•	•	•	•	•	•	•	•	•	•	•	•	•	•	•	•	•	•	•	•	•	•	•	•	•	•	•	•	•	•
soft																															
depressible																															
Temperature																															
warm	•													•	•	•	•		•						•	•					
medium		•	•	•	•	•	•	•	•	•	•		•									•	•	•				•	•	•	•
cool																															
Odour																															
strong																															
moderate																															
none	•	•	•	•	•	•	•	•	•	•	•	•	•	•	•	•	•	•	•	•	•	•	•	•	•	•	•	•	•	•	•
Acoustic opacity																															
good																															
moderate																															
poor	•	•	•	•	•	•	•	•	•	•	•	•	•	•	•	•	•	•	•	•	•	•	•	•	•	•	•	•	•	•	•

487

	Insulating Glass	Photovoltaic Glass	Smart glass	Dichroic Glass	Holographic Glass	Foam Glass	Glass Wool	Enamelled and Screen-printed Glass	Mirror Glass	Toughened Glass	Curved Glass	Broken Glass	Figured Glass	Glass Blocks	Sandblasted and Etched Glass	Channel Shaped Glass	Crystallized Glass	Mosaic Glass	**Metals** Iron	Steel	Weathering Steel	Stainless Steel	Aluminium	Titanium	Lead	Copper	Zinc	Brass	Gold	Silver	Profiling
Colour																															
beige																								•							
black						•																									
blue																															
bluish grey																			•	•		•			•		•				
brown																					•										
brown grey																															
caramel																															
dark blue																															
gold																													•		
green																•										•					
grey						•																									
grey blue																															
none	•									•		•																			
pink																															
reddish brown																															
rusty																															
silver																															
silver grey																														•	
variable		•	•		•			•	•		•	•				•	•														•
white																															
woody																															
yellow							•																								
yellow brown																															
yellow gold																												•			
yellow red																										•					
Glossiness																															
glossy	•	•		•	•	•		•		•		•			•		•		•	•	•	•	•	•	•	•	•	•	•	•	
satin	•	•	•	•	•	•		•	•	•	•	•	•	•	•	•	•	•	•	•	•	•	•	•	•	•	•	•	•	•	•
matt	•	•	•	•	•	•		•		•	•	•	•	•	•	•	•	•	•	•		•	•		•	•		•	•	•	•
Translucence (%)																															
0				•	•	•			•							•			•	•	•	•	•	•	•	•	•	•	•	•	•
20	•		•	•	•	•			•			•			•	•															
40	•		•	•	•	•			•		•		•	•	•																
60	•		•	•	•	•			•		•	•	•	•	•																
80	•	•	•		•	•			•		•	•			•																
100	•	•	•		•	•						•		•																	
Texture																															
sharp						•	•														•										
medium						•						•									•										
dull	•	•	•	•	•				•	•		•			•		•	•	•	•	•	•	•	•	•	•	•	•	•	•	•
Hardness																															
hard	•	•	•	•	•			•	•	•	•	•	•		•	•	•		•	•	•	•	•	•	•	•	•	•	•	•	•
soft							•																								
depressible							•																								
Temperature																															
warm						•	•																								
medium	•	•	•	•	•			•	•	•		•	•	•		•	•														
cool																			•	•	•	•	•	•	•	•	•	•	•	•	•
Odour																															
strong						•																									
moderate																					•										
none	•	•		•	•			•		•		•		•	•	•	•		•	•		•	•	•	•	•	•	•	•	•	•
Acoustic opacity																															
good						•	•																								
moderate										•						•															
poor	•	•	•	•	•			•		•		•		•	•	•	•		•	•	•	•	•	•	•	•	•	•	•	•	•

488

	Expanding	Perforating	Thermoforming	Explosive Forming	Coating	Anodizing	Enamelling	Galvanizing	Patination	Chrome Plating	Blasting and Shot-Peening	Knitting and Weaving	**Plastics**	Polyvinyl Chloride (PVC)	Polypropylene (PP)	Expanded Polystyrene (EPS)	Polycarbonate (PC)	Acrylics (PMMA)	Polyester Resins	Epoxy Resin (EP)	Polyurethane (PUR)	EPDM (Ethylene Propylene Diene Monomer)	HPL Sheets	Granulate	Bencore	Parabeam® 3D Glass Fabric	Foam	ETFE	PVC-coated Polyester Textile	Polytetrafluoroethylene (PTFE) or Teflon	Pneumatic Membrane | Inflatables
Colour																															
beige																										•				•	
black																						•									
blue																															
bluish grey																															
brown																															
brown grey																															
caramel																															
dark blue																															
gold																															
green																															
grey								•																							
grey blue																															
none																															
pink																															
reddish brown																															
rusty																															
silver										•																					
silver grey																															
variable	•	•	•	•	•	•	•			•	•	•		•	•	•	•	•	•	•	•	•	•	•	•		•	•		•	•
white																										•		•		•	
woody																															
yellow																															
yellow brown																															
yellow gold																															
yellow red																															
Glossiness																															
glossy			•	•	•	•	•			•		•		•	•	•	•	•	•	•				•				•			
satin	•	•	•	•	•	•	•			•	•	•		•	•	•	•	•	•	•	•	•	•	•		•		•	•	•	•
matt	•	•	•	•				•	•		•	•		•	•	•	•	•	•	•						•	•		•	•	•
Translucence (%)																															
0	•	•	•	•	•	•	•	•	•	•	•	•		•	•	•	•	•	•	•	•	•	•	•		•					•
20		•										•		•	•		•	•	•					•			•	•		•	•
40		•										•		•	•		•	•	•					•			•	•	•	•	•
60		•										•		•	•		•	•	•					•	•	•	•	•	•	•	•
80		•										•		•	•		•	•	•						•	•	•	•		•	•
100														•	•		•	•							•	•					
Texture																															
sharp	•	•	•	•							•	•													•						
medium	•	•	•	•					•			•		•	•	•	•	•	•	•				•		•					
dull	•		•	•	•	•	•	•	•	•		•		•	•	•	•	•	•	•	•	•	•	•	•	•	•	•	•	•	•
Hardness																															
hard	•	•	•	•	•	•	•	•	•	•	•	•		•	•	•	•	•	•	•	•			•	•	•		•			
soft														•	•	•											•				
depressible											•			•								•	•	•			•	•	•	•	•
Temperature																															
warm														•	•	•	•	•	•	•	•		•	•	•	•	•	•	•	•	•
medium																															
cool	•	•	•	•	•	•	•	•	•	•	•	•																			
Odour																															
strong																			•												
moderate																															
none	•	•	•	•	•	•	•	•	•	•	•	•		•	•	•	•	•		•	•	•	•	•	•	•	•	•	•	•	•
Acoustic opacity																															
good																•															
moderate	•	•										•		•	•	•	•		•	•	•	•	•	•	•	•	•	•	•	•	•
poor			•	•	•	•	•	•	•	•	•	•						•	•												

489

Index - English

Index - German

Index - French

Index - Spanish

Index - Italian

Index - Dutch

Sponsors

Wood

Bruynzeel Multipanel

Bruynzeel Multipanel International BV
P.O. Box 59
NL-1500 EB Zaandam
T +31 (0)75 655 42 00
bouw@bruynzeelmultipanel.com
www.bruynzeelmultipanel.com

Unfired Man-made Stone

Eternit NV
European Building Materials
Division
Tervurenlaan 361
B-1150 Brussels
T +32 2 778 13 79
www.eternit.com

Traditional timber weatherboard-ing is great for enhancing the appearance of a building, but it needs continual maintenance to prevent its disadvantages. Eternit's weatherboard is a man-made and attractive product to timber cladding designed to replicate the visual appeal of the original, with a lot of advantages (easy to install, no rotting, stands up the harshest weather conditions…) and avoid-ing the disadvantage of the tradi-tional product. Therefore, Eternit's weatherboard is not only your ideal alternative but it also adds interest and value to your home.

Glass

Solutia SA|NV
Parc Scientifique Flemming
Rue Laid Burniat 3
B-1348 Louvain-la-Neuve
films-archi@solutia.com
www.vanceva.com/design

Solutia is the leading world-wide manufacturer of PVB, used in lam-inated architectural glass applica-tions. Solutia provides PVB (poly vinyl butyral) to the largest glass manufacturers throughout the world. The new generation of Vanceva™ Design interlayers extends the technical and aesthet-ic benefits of specifying laminated glazing by offering many new solutions for designers and archi-tectural specifiers. Click on www.vanceva.com/design to find the glass manufacturer partner who best meets the needs of your specific project.

Solutia ….
Solutions For A Better Life

Vitreal Specchi S.r.l.
Via 4 Novembre, 95
I-22066 Mariano Comense (Co)
T +39 (0)31 74 50 62
F +39 (0)31 74 31 66
info@vitrealspecchi.it
www.vitrealspecchi.it

Metals

Ten Berge Coating
A. van Leeuwenhoekweg 56
NL-2408 AN Alphen aan de Rijn
T +31 (0)172 47 88 88
F +31 (0)172 47 81 81
info@tenbergecoating.nl
www.tenbergecoating.nl

Corus Colors
P.O. Box 10000
NL-1970 CA IJmuiden
T +31 (0)251 49 22 06
F +31 (0)251 47 04 90
corus-colors-ijmuiden@
corusgroup.com
www.colorcoat-online.com

Kabel-Zaandam BV
Noorder IJ- en Zeeweg 15
NL-1505 HG Zaandam
P.O. Box 130
NL-1500 EC Zaandam
T +31 (0)75 681 82 00
F +31 (0)75 681 82 03
info@kabelzaandam.nl
www.kabelzaandam.nl

Kabel-Zaandam BV, the number 1 supplier of 'metals for architectural and design purposes' helps you in your engineering of metal prod-ucts for all kinds of projects. From infrastructural and façade claddings to interior design pieces. With the widest range of design metals on stock and our experi-enced inn-house manufacturing division we help you to bring the end product you develop on a high quality level.

To look at and 'feel' a selection of the design metals of today, come and visit our showroom!

KUFFERATH

Andreas KUFFERATH GmbH & Co KG
P.O. Box 101130
D-52311 Düren
T +49 +24 21 | 80 13 21
F +49 +24 21 | 80 13 07

KUFFERATH is one of the world's leading metal weavers. Thanks to their high corrosion and weather resistance, the stainless steel woven screens developed here by ARTOS® can be used inside or outside. Many types of materi-al, which according to require-ment, can form other designs within the products through vary-ing material strength or types of weave and can be delivered stan-dard. Together with the stylist, KUFFERATH will develop the required weaves and fastening methods suitable for the task. The charm of the upper surface and its many variations of shade and light produced depend on the mesh strength and design.

Contributors

Wood

Amsterdamse Fijnhouthandel
Minervahavenweg 14
NL-1013 AR Amsterdam
T +31 (0)20 682 80 79
www.fijnhout.nl

Centrum Hout
(Information Centre Wood)
P.O. Box 1350
NL-1300 BJ Almere
T +31 (0)36 532 98 21
houtblad@centrum-hout.nl

Van Drenth Groep
Houtbuigerij Doetinchem bv
(Solid Bended Wood)
Fabriekstraat 10
NL-7005 AR Doetinchem
T +31 (0)314 32 60 20

Forbo B.V.
P.O. Box 13
NL-1560 AA Krommenie
T +31 (0)75 647 74 77
www.forbo.nl

Plyboo®
Ronde Tocht 2
NL-1507 CC Zaandam
T + 31 (0)75 614 51 50
www.plyboo.nl

 DURA VERMEER

Prinsen Waterbouw bv
Dura Vermeer Infra
P.O. Box 30110
NL-1303 AC Almere
T +31 (0)36 549 53 50
www.duravermeer.nl

Riet ABC bv
(Dutch Federation of Thatchers)
P.O. Box 1003
NL-3860 BA Nijkerk
T +31 (0)33 246 44 50
vakfederatie@riet.com
www.riet.com

Van Schaik
(Willow Rods)
Vossenpassenweg 5
NL-4031 KR Ingen
T +31 (0)344 60 25 48

Natural Stone

Ariostea S.p.A.
Via Cimabue, 20
I-42014 Castellarano
T +39 0536 81 68 11
www.ariostea.it

Beisterveld Natural Stone
P.O. Box 40208
NL 3504 AA Utrecht
T + 31 (0)30 241 40 21
www.beisterveld.nl

Boucher Natural Stone
Van der Madeweg 29
NL-1099 BS Amsterdam
T +31 (0)20 692 71 50
www.xs4all.nl/boucher

Jorna Natural Stone
Schenkenschans 4a
NL-8912 AL Leeuwarden
T +31 (0)58 212 64 53
www.jorna-natuursteen.nl

Scheuermann GmbH & Co.
Natural Stone Works
Malsenbacher Strasse 3
D-97271 Kleinrinderfeld
T +49 (0)93 66 I 907 00
www.scheuermann-naturstein.de

**Voorlichtingscentrum
Natuursteen**
(Information Centre Natural
Stone)
P.O. Box 40295
NL-3504 AB Utrecht
T +31 (0)214 24 85
www.natuursteensector.nl

Fired Man-made Stone

Hillegom Building Materials
P.O. Box 199
NL-2180 AD Hillegom
T +31 (0)252 53 59 19
www.bmhillegom.nl

**Koninklijk Verbond
van Nederlandse
Baksteenfabrikanten**
(Royal Union of Dutch Bricks
Manufacturers)
P.O. Box 51
NL-6994 ZH De Steeg
T +31 (0)26 495 91 10
knb@knb-baksteen.nl

**St. Joris Keramische
Industrie bv**
(Ceramic Industries)
P.O. Box 4805
NL-5953 ZL Reuver
T +31 (0)77 474 01 00
verkoop@stjoris.nl

Kooy Baksteencentrum bv
(Bricks Centre)
Rembrandtlaan 38
NL-3723 BJ Bilthoven
T +31 (0)30 228 61 41
www.kooy.nl

LAFARGE DAKPRODUCTEN

Lafarge Dakproducten bv
(Roofing Products)
P.O. Box 1108
NL-6040 KC Roermond
T +31(0)475 34 92 00
F +31(0)475 32 42 32
info@lafarge.nl
www.lafarge.nl

Royal Tichelaar Makkum
P.O. Box 1
NL-8754 ZN Makkum
T +31 (0)515 23 13 41
info@tichelaar.nl

Wienerberger Bricks B.V.
P.O. Box 144
NL-5300 AC Zaltbommel
info.nl@wienerberger.com

Wienerberger I Terca Briques
Parc du Moulin de Massy
P.O. Box 215
F-91882 Massy Cedex
T +33 1 60 11 11 60

**Wienerberger Ziegelindustrie
GmbH**
Oldenburger Allee 26
D-30659 Hannover
T +49 (0)511 61 07 00
info@wzi.de

Unfired Man-made Stone

Art Ferro®
Walls of Art
's Gravendamseweg 28
NL-2215 TA Voorhout
T +31 (0)252 22 16 77
www.artferro.nl

Decomo NV-SA
Bd. Industriel 96
B-7700 Mouscron
T +32 (0)56 I 85 07 11
www.decomo.be

ENCI B.V.
Heidelberg Cement Group
Sint Teunislaan 1
NL-5231 BS 's-Hertogenbosch
T +31 (0)73 640 11 70
www.enci.nl

FeBe
Federation of Concrete Industries
Fédération de l'Industrie du Béton
Rue Volta 12
B-1050 Brussels
T +32 (0)2 735 80 15
www.febe.be

Gyproc I BPB
P.O. Box 73
NL-4130 EB Vianen
T +31 (0)347 32 51 00
www.gyproc.com

Jora Vision
Floralaan 2H10
NL-2231 ZV Rijnsburg
T +31 (0)71 40 26 747
www.joravision.com

Keim Nederland bv
P.O. Box 1062
NL-1300 AB Almere
T +31 (0)36 532 06 20
www.keim.nl

Knauf bv
Mesonweg 8-12
NL-3542 AL Utrecht
T +31 (0)30 247 33 11
www.knauf.com

MBI
P.O. Box 259
NL-5460 AG Veghel
T +31 (0)413 349 400

Mebin bv
P.O. Box 3232
NL-5203 DE 's Hertogenbosch
T +31 (0)73 640 11 60
www.mebin.nl

Prepoton Panelcraft Group BV
Hogeveldseweg 5
NL-4041CP Kesteren
T +31 (0)488 481457

Tierrafino ®
Tweede Helmerstraat 51
NL-1054 CD Amsterdam
T +31 (0)20 689 25 15
www.tierrafino.nl

Xella Cellenbeton Nederland bv
P.O. Box 23
NL-4200 AA Gorinchem
T +31(0)183 67 12 34
www.xella.nl

Glass

Fusion Glass Designs Ltd
365 Clapham Road
London SW9 9BT
T +44 (0)171 738 5888
www.fusionglass.co.uk

Saint-Gobain Glass Nederland
P.O.Box 507
NL-3900 AM Veenendaal
T +31 (0)318 53 13 11
www.saint-gobain-glass.com

Visual Impact Technology
352 W. Bedford #107
Fresno, California 93711
T 559 432 1323
www.vitglass.com

Witraze SC
Architectural & Stained Glass
ul. Kakolowa 24a
Po-04-848 Warszawa
T +48 22 872 04 17
www.witraz.com

Yorgos Studio
31, Tower Gardens Road
London N17 7PS
T +44 (0)20 88 85 20 29
info@yorgosglass.com
www.yorgosglass.com

Metals

HBG Construction
Holly Grange - Holly Lane
Balsall Common
UK-CV7 7EB Coventry
T +44 (0)1676 536 300
www.hbg.co.uk

KM Europa Metal
P.O.Box 146
NL-3300 AC Dordrecht
T + 31 78 621 29 91
www.thecopperlink.com
www.tecu.com

POLYVISION A Steelcase Company

Polyvision
East Street
Wimborne, Dorset
UK-BH21 IDX England
T 0800 587 33 74
www.polyvision.com

 RIDDER

**Ridder Ridder Metalen Dak-
en Wandsystemen bv**
(Metal Roofing and Wall Systems)
P.O.Box 4149
NL-1620 HC Hoorn
T +31 (0)229 215025
www.riddersystems.com

Schöne Edelmetaal B.V.
Meeuwenlaan 88
NL-1021 JK Amsterdam
T +31 (0)20 435 02 22

Tulleners Amsterdam
Stoombootweg 31
NL-1035 TT Amsterdam
T +31 20 633 20 08
www.tulleners.com

Plastics

3M

3M Nederland B.V.
Commercial Graphics
P.O. Box 193
NL-2300 AD Leiden,
T +31 71 5 450 444
www.scotchprintgraphics.nl

ABET BV
Lagedijk 4
NL-3401 RG IJsselstein
T +31 30 686 84 50
www.abet.nl

Buitink Technology
Nieuwgraaf 210
NL-6921 RR Duiven
T +31 (0)26 319 41 81
www.buitink-technology.com

Deceuninck N.V
Benelux Division
Bruggesteenweg 164
B-8830 HOOGLEDE-GITS
T +32 51 239 272
www.deceuninck.com

Hardick bv
P.O.Box 281
NL 7500 AG Enschede
T +31 53 425 32 35
www.hardick.nl

Parabeam ® **3D Glass Fabrics**
P.O. Box 134
NL-5700 AC Helmond
T +31 (0)492 591 222
www.parabeam3d.com

Phelps Engineered Plastics
36, Kenosia Avenue
Danbury, CT 06810
T 001 203 792 5110
www.pepcore.com

Pyrasied
Apolloweg 26
NL-8938 AT Leeuwareden
T +31(0)58 21 506 51
www.pyrasied.nl

Tentech bv
P.O.Box 619
NL-2600 AP Delft
T +31 (0)278 42 80
www.tentech.nl

Vink Holding bv
Runetoften 14
DK-8210 Aarhus
T +45 89 11 02 71
www.vink.com

Sources and References

Wood

Houtvademecum, S.I. Wiselius, Ten Hagen Stam, isbn 90-4400-2711 (NL)

Bouwstoffen HTO, L. Ploos van Amstel, Leiden, Nijgh & Van Ditmar 1973 (NL)

Trees of the world, Scott Leathart, The Hamlyn Publishing Group Limited 1977 (GB)

The love of trees, Kenneth A. Beckett, Octopus Books Limited 1975 (UK)

The New Wood Architecture, Naomi Stungo, Gingko Press 1998, isbn 3-9272-5888-1 (USA)

Houtdocumentatie, J.A.M. Kickken, Ten Hagen Stam, isbn 90-5404-6449 (NL)

Detail in Architectuur, Ten Hagen Stam (NL)

Het Houtblad, Het Houtblad BV (NL)

Hout in de Bouw, Nijgh Periodieken BV (NL)

PUU, Puuinformaatio ry (FIN)

Houtnieuws, Houtvoorlichtingscentrum vzw (B)

Séquences Bois, Comité National pour le Développement du Bois (FR)

SHR info, Stichting Hout Research (NL)

Natural Stone

Detail Magazine, Institut für internationale Architektur-Dokumentationen (D)

Naturstein und Architektur, Margret und Horst Wanetschek, Callway Verlag München 2000, isbn 3-7667-1438-4 (D)

Naturstein, Ebner Verlag (D)

PCI Journal, Architectural Precast Concrete Services (USA)

STEIN, Das Magazin für den Natursteinmarkt, Callway Verlag München (D)

www.stone-panels.com

Stone Work: Designing With Stone, Malcolm Holzman, Images 2002, isbn 1-8647-0083-1 (UK)

Fired Man-made Stone

Bouwkunde. Deel 2. Hand- en studieboek voor den bouwkundige en den metselaar, G. Arendzen I J.J. Vriend, Amsterdam (NL)

Nederland onder dak, F. Goos, (ed.) (NL)

Bouwkundige termen. Verklarend woordenboek van de westerse architectuur-en bouwhistorie, E.J. Haslinghuis I H. Janse, Utrecht I Antwerpen, 1997, isbn 90-7431-077x (NL)

Baksteenfabricage in Nederland 1850-1920, G.B. Janssen, Arnhem, Walburgpers 1987, isbn 90-6011-5449

Noorderhof – 170 x het mooiste huis, K. Peterse, Amsterdam, 1999 (NL)

Bouwstoffen HTO, L. Ploos van Amstel, Leiden, Nijgh & Van Ditmar 1973 (NL)

Baksteen in Nederland. De taal van het metselwerk, C.J.M. Schiebroek e.a., Den Haag I De Steeg, 1991 (NL)

Bouwkunde. De voornaamste materialen der bouwambachten. Eerste deel: Steen, D. de Vries I P.A. Schroot, Groningen, 1925 (NL)

Dynamisch Keramisch, Detail In Architectuur, E. Zijlstra, Rotterdam, 2000 (NL)

Unfired Man-made Stone

Bouwstoffen HTO, L. Ploos van Amstel, Nijgh & Van Ditmar (NL)

Bouwen met beton, Editing Atelier Kinold, München, edition i.c.w. cement industries in Switzerland, Belgium, Netherlands, United Kingdom, issn 0930-0252 (EU)

Betonpocket 2003, ENCI Media, 's-Hertogenbosch, isbn 90-71806-50-2 (NL)

Cement, Stichting ENCI Media, 's-Hertogenbosch (NL)

Concrete Architecture, Tone Texture, Form, David Bennett, Birkhäuser Publishers 2001, isbn 3-7643-6271-5 (D)

Concrete Construction Manual, Kind-Barkauskas e.a., Birkhäuser Publishers 2002, isbn 3-7643-6724-5 (D)

Deutsche Bauzeitschrift, Beton, Bertelsmann 2002 (D)

Deutsche Bauzeitung, Deutsche Verlags-Anstalt, Stuttgart (D)

ENCI Betoniek, 2003 (NL)

Handboek Cellenbeton, J.M.J.M. Bijen et al, NCV, Brouwershaven, 1995 (NL)

Schoon beton, Vereniging Nederlandse Cementindustrie 1990, isbn 90-71806-11-1 (NL)

www.cvk.nl

www.mbi.nl

www.schoonbeton.nl

Glass

Glass in Structures, Elements, Concepts, Designs, Rob Nijsse, Birkhaüser Publishers 2003, isbn 3-7643-6439-4 (D)

Glas, Glasherstellung und Glasveredlung, Prozesse und Technologien, Walter Brockmann u.a., VDMA I Messe Düsseldorf, 2002 (D)

Glas, Material, Herstellung, Produkte, Chris Lefteri, Avedition Verlag 2002, isbn 3-9296-3861-4 (D)

Glas, Konstruction and Technologie in der Architektur, Sophia Behling I Stefan Behling, Prestel Verlag 1999, isbn 3-7913-2155-2 (D)

Glass Construction Manual, Christian Schittich I Gerald Staib I Dieter Balkow I Matthias Schuler I Werner Sobeck, Birkhaüser Publishers 1999, isbn 3-7643-6077-1 (D)

Glass Buildings, Material, Structure and Detail, Heinz Krewinkel, Birkhaüser Publishers 1998, isbn 3-7643-5650-2 (D)

Gevels & Architectuur, Façades in glas en aluminium, Just Renckens, TU Delft I VMRG I VAS 1996, isbn 90-9009-2668 (NL)

Friedrich Grimm, Energieeffizientes Bauen mit Glas, Callwey Verlag München 2004, isbn 3766715771

Metals

Bouwen met Staal magazine, Stichting Bouwen met Staal

De Architect, Ten Hagen & Stam Publishers
Detail in Architectuur, Ten Hagen & Stam Publishers

Bouwtechniek in Nederland, J. Oosterhof I G.J. Arends I C.H. van Eldik I G.G. Nieuwmeijer, Delft University Press I Rijksdienst voor de Monumentenzorg 1988, isbn 9062754597 (NL)

Titaanzink in de bouw, L.J. de Klerk I P.A. Schut-Baak, Billiton Zink BV 1986, isbn 90-71596-01-X (NL)

Overspannend Staal, W.H. Verburg I W.L.M. Adriaansen et.al., Staalbouwkundig Genootschap 1996, isbn 90-72830-18-0 (NL)

Een halve eeuw Kwaliteit en Duurzaamheid, Martin Franken, Stichting Doelmatig Verzinken 2002, isbn 90-807387-1-9 (NL)

Aluminium in de gevel, J. Wieland, Kosmos (NL)

Aluminium by Design: Jewelry to Jets, Sarah C. Nichols, Harry N. Abrams for Carnegie Museum of Art, 2000, isbn 0-88039-5 (USA)

Mutant Materials in Contemporary Design, Paola Antonelli, Harry N. Abrams for The Museum of Modern Art 1995, isbn 0-8109-6145-8 (USA)

Plastics and Future

Van Bakeliet tot composiet, design met nieuwe materialen, desk editor M.E. Buckquoye, Stichting Kunstboek 2002, isbn 90-5856-086-4
Dictaat kunststoffen, part 5, TU Delft Industrial Design 1992
www.deceuninck.be
www.trespa.nl

Credits

Concept and Editorial Board

Piet Vollaard – architect, architecture critic and teacher, author, and director and co-founder of Archined

Els Zijlstra – architect and founder/director of Materia

Authors

Wood – Tom de Vries – structural engineer, freelance construction journalist and founder/director of Contekst Tekstbureau Tom de Vries

Natural Stone – Ed Melet – author of *Sustainable Architecture: Towards a Diverse Built Environment* and *The Architectural Detail*, founder/director of Xploring, teacher at the Hogeschool van Amsterdam and the Amsterdam and Tilburg Academies of Architecture

Fired Man-made Stone – Dr. Kees Peterse – founder/principal of PANSA bv

Unfired Man-made Stone – Ine ter Borch – journalist and PR consultant, founder/director of Archispecials.com.

Glass – David Keuning – editor in chief of *Detail in Architectuur*

Metals – Caroline Kruit – structural engineer and journalist, founder/director of CCK Publicaties and editor in chief of *Bouwen met Staal*

Plastics and Future – Els Zijlstra - architect and founder/director of Materia

Technical Advisers

Wood – W.J. Homan

Natural Stone – A.J. van Luijk

Fired Man-made Stone – E.L.J. van Hal, KNB | T. Eyck, Royal Tichelaar | Lafarge Roofing | Molenaar & Van Winden Architects | Dr. J.A. Kamermans, Nederlands Tegelmuseum | Soeters Van Eldonk Ponec Architects | Stichting Dakmeester | drs. J.C. Maks, TCKI | St. Joris Keramische Industrie bv | Wienerberger Bricks bv

Unfired Man-made Stone – Hans Köhne, ENCI BV | Hans van den Heuvel, MBI

Glass – Prof. Rob Nijsse

Metals – Cor van Eldik

Plastics and Future – Prof. Helmut Schmidt, Institut für Neue Materialen, Prof. Julian Vincent, Biomemetics, University of Bath

Translators

James Andrick (Metals)

John Kirkpatrick (Wood)

Nicholas Lakides (Natural Stone, Glass, Plastics, Future)

Mari Shields (Wood)

Trador (Fired and Unfired Man-made Stone)

Antoinette Aichele (German)

Isabel Núñez (Spanish)

Gammon Sharpley (French)

Tom Verrillo (Italian)

Editor

Robyn de Jong-Dalziel

Photography

Jeroen van Amelsvoort (pages 12, 16, 23, 28, 35, 43, 49, 51, 53, 55, 81, 104, 108, 111, 115, 116, 119, 121, 122, 125, 129, 131, 133, 136, 139, 141, 145, 146, 149, 151, 153, 155, 157, 159, 169, 172, 175, 177, 181, 183, 185, 187, 188, 199, 202, 209, 218, 221, 227, 229, 233, 235, 236, 238, 242, 255, 256, 259, 287, 296, 309, 321, 407, 466, 473, 496)

Edwin Blum, Drost (page 291)

Jan Derwig (page 249)

Corus (page 413)

ENCI Media (pages 171, 245, 265, 269, 303)

Heinrich Helfenstein | Harald F. Müller (page 281)

Kees Hummel (pages cover, 19, 21, 25, 27, 31, 33, 37, 39, 41, 45, 47, 57, 59, 60, 63, 65, 67, 69, 71, 73, 75, 77, 78, 83, 85, 87, 89, 91, 92 95, 97, 99, 101, 103, 127, 135, 143, 160, 163, 166, 179, 192, 194, 205, 207, 213, 217, 225, 246, 251, 253, 261, 263, 267, 271, 273, 275, 279, 283, 285, 289, 293, 295, 299, 301, 305, 311, 312, 317, 318, 322, 325, 327, 329, 331, 335, 337, 338, 341, 343, 345, 347, 349, 351, 353, 355, 357, 359, 361, 363, 365, 366, 370, 373, 375, 377, 379, 380, 383, 385, 387, 389, 391, 393, 394, 397, 399, 400, 403, 405, 409, 411, 415, 417, 419, 421, 423, 425, 427, 435, 437, 439, 441, 443, 445, 447, 451, 452, 455, 457, 461, 463, 465, 469, 471, 475, 480, 488, 492, 494, 498)

Materia (pages 277, 428, 432, 449, 458, 476)

Ingeborg Nefkens (page 215)

Nederlands Tegelmuseum (page 210)

Ogilvy & Mather (page 490)

Kees Peterse, Pansa (pages 197, 201, 223, 231)

Christian Richters (pages 165, 333)

Wim Tholenaars, Xella (page 307)

Gerald Zugmann (page 113)

Photo Editor

Sylvia van de Poel

Lithographer

Rob Geukes, Electronic Publishing Services

Designer

Onno de Haan, b-up.

Project Coordinator

Sylvia van de Poel

Printer

A&P Printing / D2Print

Publisher

Rudolf van Wezel
BIS Publishers
Herengracht 370-372
1016 CH Amsterdam
www.bispublishers.nl

ISBN 90 6369 042 8